The Magnificent Mrs Tennant

The Magnificent MRS TENNANT

The Adventurous Life of
Gertrude Tennant, Victorian *Grande Dame*

DAVID WALLER

YALE UNIVERSITY PRESS
NEW HAVEN AND LONDON

For information about this and other Yale University Press publications, please contact:
U.S. Office: sales.press@yale.edu   www.yalebooks.com
Europe Office: sales@yaleup.co.uk   www.yalebooks.co.uk

Set in Baskerville by J&L Composition Ltd, Scarborough, North Yorkshire
Printed in Great Britain by the MPG Books Group, Bodmin and Kings Lynn

Library of Congress Cataloging-in-Publication Data

Waller, David, 1962-
   The magnificent Mrs. Tennant : the adventurous life of Gertrude Tennant, Victorian grande-dame / David Waller.
      p. cm.
   Includes bibliographical references and index.
   ISBN 978-0-300-13935-8 (alk. paper)
   1. Tennant, Gertrude, 1819-1918. 2. Socialites—Great Britain—Biography. 3. Gentry—Great Britain—Biography. 4. Salons—Great Britain—History—19th century. 5. Salons—France—History—19th century. 6. Great Britain—Social life and customs—19th century. 7. Great Britain—Intellectual life—19th century. 8. Tennant, Gertrude, 1819–1918—Diaries. 9. Tennant, Gertrude, 1819–1918—Correspondence. I. Tennant, Gertrude, 1819–1918. II. Title.
   DA565.T46W35 2009
   942.081092—dc22
   [B]

                                                                    2008051692

A catalogue record for this book is available from the British Library.

10 9 8 7 6 5 4 3 2

CONTENTS

LIST OF ILLUSTRATIONS

A Long Line of Collier Heroes

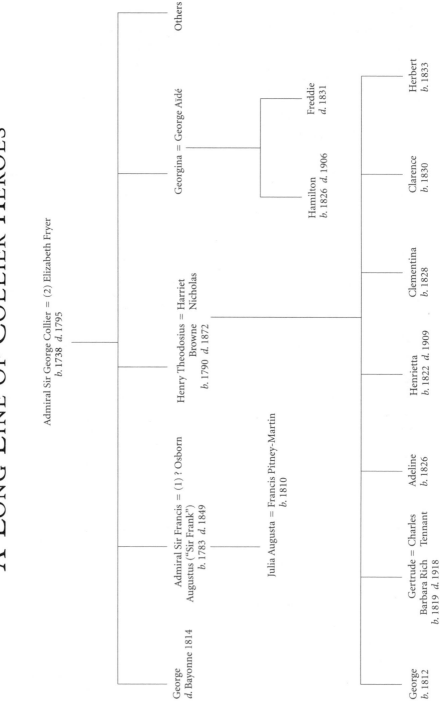

Admiral Sir George Collier = (2) Elizabeth Fryer
b. 1738 *d.* 1795

George
d. Bayonne 1814

Admiral Sir Francis = (1) ? Osborn
Augustus ("Sir Frank")
b. 1783 *d.* 1849

Julia Augusta = Francis Pitney-Martin
b. 1810

Henry Theodosius = Harriet
Browne Nicholas
b. 1790 *d.* 1872

Georgina = George Aïdé

Others

Hamilton
b. 1826 *d.* 1906

Freddie
d. 1831

Gertrude = Charles
Barbara Rich Tennant
b. 1819 *d.* 1918

George
b. 1812

Adeline
b. 1826

Henrietta
b. 1822 *d.* 1909

Clementina
b. 1828

Clarence
b. 1830

Herbert
b. 1833

The Tennant Dynasty

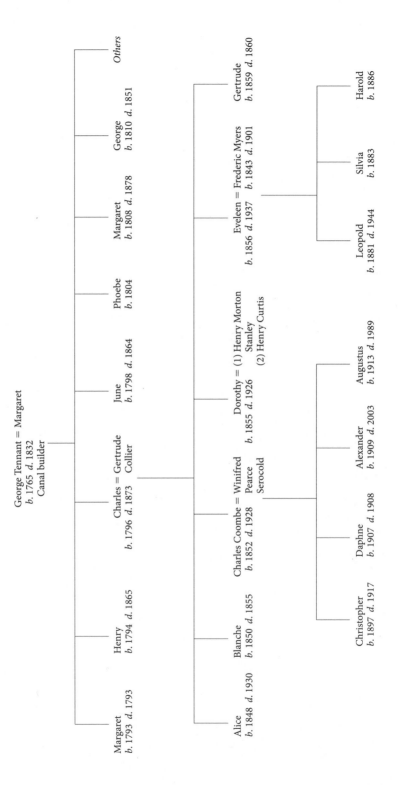

George Tennant = Margaret
b. 1765 d. 1832
Canal builder

Margaret
b. 1793 d. 1793

Henry
b. 1794 d. 1865

Charles = Gertrude
b. 1796 d. 1873   Collier

June
b. 1798 d. 1864

Phoebe
b. 1804

Margaret
b. 1808 d. 1878

George
b. 1810 d. 1851

Others

Alice
b. 1848 d. 1930

Blanche
b. 1850 d. 1855

Charles Coombe = Winifred
b. 1852 d. 1928   Pearce
Serocold

Dorothy = (1) Henry Morton
b. 1855 d. 1926   Stanley
            (2) Henry Curtis

Eveleen = Frederic Myers
b. 1856 d. 1937   b. 1843 d. 1901

Gertrude
b. 1859 d. 1860

Christopher
b. 1897 d. 1917

Daphne
b. 1907 d. 1908

Alexander
b. 1909 d. 2003

Augustus
b. 1913 d. 1989

Leopold
b. 1881 d. 1944

Silvia
b. 1883

Harold
b. 1886

CHAPTER 1

How I Found Gertrude Tennant

Mrs C-T, who married the grandson of the heroine of this book, knew that I had long been interested in the Victorian books sitting on the shelves of her farmhouse. One day early in 2005, she called me and invited me to come and explore the attic. We climbed the steep wooden stairs, unlocked the door of a room the size of a child's bedroom, pushed aside broken tennis racquets, ancient loudspeakers and other bric-à-brac to make our way to a pair of oak chests. 'One belongs to Gertrude and the other to her daughter Dolly,' explained Mrs C-T. The last time anyone had taken a look at the contents was half a century ago. She suggested that we start with Gertrude's chest; and we opened the lid, propping it up with a volume picked at random from the floor of the room.

Inside, we found layer upon layer of books, bags, envelopes of different shapes and sizes, bundles of letters tied in red cord, old newspapers, diaries of parchment and leather, yellowing manuscripts covered in spidery and fading handwriting. We gave way to the irresistible temptation to rummage. Someone had tied a blue ribbon around one particular bundle of letters, and in an antique hand labelled them: *Correspondence From Various Distinguished Persons, Do Not Throw Away.* Mrs C-T and I sat on either side of a small Formica-topped table and impatiently untied the bundle. It took a while to get used to the handwriting. The letters, about one hundred in total, were scribbled in haste, it appeared, written as casually and with as little regard for posterity as you or I dashing off an e-mail today. The signatures were immediately legible, however. As we passed the letters to one another across the table, stopping every now and again to decipher the script, it was as though the guests at Gertrude's glittering dinner parties were coming alive in front of our eyes. Here was Gladstone, accepting an invitation, there John Everett Millais, writing to compliment Dolly on her latest paintings. We found Robert Browning politely declining an invitation to tea, Oscar Wilde writing to discuss Dolly's illustrations for children's stories, and Henry James scrawling we knew not what at this stage (there were many letters from James and his thick handwriting became quickly recognisable, even if the content did not yield itself up). On this and subsequent visits, the archive revealed other treasures – dozens of letters from Gustave Flaubert and first editions of *Madame Bovary* and *Salammbô*, and the *Trois Contes*, all dedicated by the author to Gertrude; love letters from Henry Morton Stanley to Dolly; youthful memoirs; diaries galore; and thousands of family letters from the first half of the nineteenth century, neatly folded away into their minuscule envelopes, three inches by two, and tied into bundles.

At first, many of the papers were indecipherable – Gertrude's father wrote in a series of dashes and dots that looked more like semaphore than sentences – and the letters from her mother and sisters were 'cross-written', each sister writing a note, backwards and forwards across the same page, producing a result that looked more like the abstract art of Jackson Pollock than intelligible communication. Over time, I was able to make sense of the letters and diaries (see the Note on Primary Sources for the use I have made of them) and a remarkable story emerged – the tale of an acutely intelligent woman who, like many a heroine of a nineteenth century novel, was born with brains, good looks and a respectable social position to uphold, but next to no money. She sprung from vigorous, upper-middle-class stock, with uncles, cousins and grandfathers who were admirals and soldiers at a time when men had unlimited opportunities for a life of action, adventure and public service, thriving in a world in which the whole of the British Empire was a playground. Women, on the other hand, were deprived of everything but the most haphazard education and were expected to stay at home and raise children; they were excluded from the professions and from political activity; had few legal rights and were obliged to find fulfilment in the purely domestic arena as mothers and wives. With charm and intelligence, Gertrude Tennant was able to transcend the boundaries of her time and gender to establish an influential position at the heart of European cultural and social life.

* * *

Gertrude is now almost completely forgotten, remembered quite literally as a footnote to the lives of men such as Flaubert and Stanley. But this was not always the case and on Saturday, 10 July 1890 she and her daughter Dolly were the most talked about women in London. On that morning, the crowds started to gather around Westminster Abbey from eleven o'clock, sheltering under umbrellas and in the porch of St Margaret's church. Despite the heavy rain, the lady out collecting for the Hospital Saturday Fund had decorated her stall on the corner of Victoria Street with a special wedding bouquet, and street vendors were already hawking photographs and prints of the bride and groom. By one o'clock, an hour before the ceremony began, the rain had stopped. Parliament Square and Whitehall were thronged with thousands of well-wishers and by now there was a crowd outside Gertrude's residence on Richmond Terrace and traffic had ground to a halt throughout Westminster.

'It was the typical London sight-seeing crowd,' sniffed the *Pall Mall Gazette*, 'of the Lord Mayor's Show type, abounding with those sad-eyed specimens of semi-shabby gentility seen only at a public ceremonial in the metropolis.' Inside the Abbey, by contrast, the social pedigree of the guests was not open to question. Their names, the *Gazette* reassured its readers, would be familiar to everyone, and were indeed printed over extensive column inches in this and countless other publications around the world, allowing the curious to study the eclectic mix of statesmen, soldiers, artists and men of letters who attended one of the great celebrity weddings of the late nineteenth century. The guests were issued with entry tickets and instructed to arrive at half-past one, but anticipating the crush, many ordered their carriages to come earlier. Those who arrived punctually found they had lost their seats and were reduced to standing on chairs or on the bases of monuments or columns with the hope of securing an elevated view. At ten minutes to two, the choir and transepts of the ancient cathedral were packed. Dressed in the height of fashion and bathed in the refracted light of the stained-glass windows, the guests were dappled with all the colours of the rainbow. The organ thundered, the time for polite chatter and discreet glances at fellow guests' fashionable attire came to an end, as with the help of a stick the groom at last made his slow, unsteady way down the aisle to take his seat. Henry Morton Stanley, the explorer recently returned from his fourth and most controversial expedition to the heart of Africa, was about to make a journey into the uncharted territory of married life.

A few hundred yards to the east of the Abbey, Dolly was at home, putting the finishing touches to her toilette under the close supervision of her 70-year-old mother. The bride was wearing a dress fashioned out of white corded satin, 'with pearls meandering over its surface, with as many windings and as many tributaries as the Congo itself'. Around her neck she arranged a wedding present from Queen Victoria, a miniature of the monarch suspended from a necklace of diamonds, and around her wrist, a bracelet given by the King of the Belgians, her husband-to-be's dubious patron.

The wedding coincided with the high noon of British imperialism. Queen Victoria had ruled for fifty-three years, during which time Great Britain had emerged as the world's supreme economic and political power. Yet this domination was far from secure: the unbridled optimism of the mid-century had given way to *fin de siècle* decadence and fears of national decline. Other countries were emerging to challenge Britain's supremacy, and Africa was the battle-ground for these new superpower rivalries. Stanley's exploits were pivotal in opening up the 'Dark Continent' to the Western powers and at this precise moment in history his achievements had made him one of the most famous men on the planet. Later in the year, the Lion of the Season would be pilloried as the King of the Beasts, but this week there was little interest in the alleged brutalities of his latest expedition. The main concern in the days ahead of the wedding was the condition of the explorer's stomach.

Stanley was ill, and thanks to the exhaustive newspaper coverage of the wedding, everybody inside and outside the Abbey knew it. Forty-eight hours before, the groom had been stricken by an attack of gastritis, and confined to his bed. Perhaps he would not make it, and the wedding would be called off at the last minute? There was a collective sigh of relief when the crowd saw that, once again, the diminutive man with the grim face, determined mustachioed mouth, penetrating grey eyes and hair as white as the snows of Ruwenzori, had lived up to his reputation and seen off insuperable obstacles, this time the turmoil in his gut rather than the flesh-eating tribes of the Ituri forest. He was accompanied by the five surviving officers of his latest expedition and by his best man, Count Aarache, the personal representative of the King of the Belgians.

Stanley knelt down in prayer before the altar, the exact spot where the royalty of England had so often been married over the previous millennium. Plantagenets, Tudors, Stuarts had all come to receive the blessing of the Church. Now it was the turn of Henry Morton Stanley, born John Rowlands, the workhouse-raised, illegitimate son of a Welsh barmaid, to be married here. Truly, 'one of the most striking events in [Westminster Abbey's] story of a thousand years', the leader writer of the London *Daily News* had reflected on the eve of the marriage. 'The Thing is absolutely unique.' 'If Miss Tennant were a princess of the blood greater interest could not be taken in her marriage,' agreed the *St James's Gazette.* It was, indeed, the nearest thing to a royal wedding that the late Victorian press and public could imagine. 'If in point of public interest it comes . . . behind a coronation, it may be said of it that few social events can take precedence of it . . .'

As Stanley prayed, two closed carriages were fighting to make their way out of Richmond Terrace, a street of substantial Georgian residences directly across Whitehall from Downing Street, down to the Abbey through the mêlée of hansom cabs, carriages, heavily laden drays, omnibuses and advertising vehicles. 'All that could be seen by the "man and woman in the street" was the gleam of the occasional bouquet, and the stray tip of someone's nose,' observed one newspaper reporter. The bride in all her finery could not be seen behind the closed windows of the carriage, and the only evidence that this was the wedding party was the presence of the 'Zanzibar lad', one of Stanley's native servants, perched on the box-seat of a carriage. Still the crowds cheered as the vehicles made the short journey along Whitehall. Stanley remained seated as Dolly entered the Abbey through the Dean's Gate on the arm of her brother, Charles Coombe Tennant (her father, Gertrude's husband, had died long ago). She carried in her hand a white wreath which had in its centre a scarlet letter 'L'. After a few moments, she broke the line of the procession and walked slowly and sadly to the grey tablet beneath which lie to this day the mortal remains of David Livingstone. (Stanley's career was launched in 1871 with the discovery of the Scottish missionary by the shores of Lake Tanganyika, where he uttered the legendary greeting: 'Dr Livingstone, I presume.') Dorothy reverently set the tribute on the tomb, alongside other wreaths placed there by Stanley and his retinue, and was then guided to the altar by her brother. Her veil of tulle was fastened by a diamond crescent; she held a bouquet of white sweet peas and orange blossom, and her train was carried by a pageboy and two tiny maidens dressed in seventeenth-century costumes. Tall and fair-haired, with deeply set blue eyes, a straight nose and handsome teeth, Dolly was a head higher than the groom.

With the aid of his stick, Stanley found the strength to stand throughout the half-hour service, at the end of which he and Dolly were man and wife. Stanley was so ill by this point that after the signing of the register he was obliged to lie down in the back of the carriage as he, his wife and some close friends made their way back through the crowds to Gertrude's home. Sitting at Dolly's side was Sir John Millais, the society painter and long-standing friend of the family, whom many mistook for the groom. Mindful of Dolly's charms, Millais jokingly confided to friends that he wished it was so, and said that Stanley was a 'lucky dog' for carrying off so beautiful a bride.[1] This afternoon, however, Stanley was in no condition to enjoy his luck, and on arrival at Richmond Terrace was rushed upstairs to bed, without a chance to visit the three drawing-rooms in which tables had been erected to display the presents. These included: a silver inkstand (from the Prince of Wales); quantities of silver plate and jewellery; the stuffed head of a grizzly bear (from an American gentleman); a cabinet of 1,000 cigars (from a Havana cigar merchant); a mother-of-pearl fan (from the statesman Joseph Chamberlain); seven volumes of William Ewart Gladstone's philosophical *Gleanings*, from the author himself, and a scientific instrument called a Geochronoscope, from a certain Mr Kelt.

Sedated with a morphine injection, administered under the supervision of his new mother-in-law, Stanley lay in bed as the hundreds of guests gathered for the wedding party held in the gardens of Richmond Terrace. The lawns, leading down to the Thames, presented a brilliant sight in the unexpected afternoon sunshine: there were marquees, and tables glittering with glass and silver, covered with delicacies, laid out under the trees. 'Crimson-covered chairs were placed in abundance for the accommodation of guests,' noted *The Times*, 'and here and there the bright tints of Indian and Persian rugs added to the colour-brightness of the scene.' Beautiful children, flitting about in their white pageboy costumes, added to this kaleidoscope of colours; in the neighbouring garden, lent to Mrs Tennant for the occasion, played the full brass band of the Grenadier Guards, the bandsmen dressed in scarlet uniform. At four o'clock, the guests bid farewell to the bride and now recovered groom as they made their way to the first stage of the their honeymoon, at Melchet Court, an Elizabethan mansion belonging to Dolly's friend Lady Ashburton. Later that evening, police had to clear the crowds from the platform when they arrived at Romsey station.

Before the wedding, Gertrude had written sternly to newspaper editors:

As long as [Dolly's] name is Tennant, I will not consent to her face hanging up in shop windows and being made public property. I have had twenty letters from photographers in every part of England, *demanding* her photograph as a right; and one person threatened to take it and publish it, whether I liked it or not, by some process called instantaneous photography! All this publicity is very distasteful to us![2]

Now Dolly's name had changed, editors saw no reason to heed Gertrude's disingenuous instructions, and pictures of the new Mr and Mrs Stanley would soon appear on the front page of newspapers all around the world. For all the publicity accorded to the newly married couple, this was Gertrude's hour of triumph.

* * *

Born in 1819, at the end of the Regency period, a matter of weeks before the death of King George III, in the same year as such distinguished Victorians as Queen Victoria herself, Charles Kingsley, Arthur Clough and John Ruskin, and within days of George Eliot, Gertrude Tennant outlived them all. She died in 1918, in the modern age, in her ninety-ninth year, weeks before the guns of the First World War fell silent. She lived through an extraordinary period of history, and in later life she was on intimate terms with the men who made it so: the statesmen and soldiers who turned Britain into the most powerful nation on earth, and the poets, painters and novelists who created the nineteenth century's great works of literature and art. Thomas Carlyle had famously said that the history of the world is no more than the history of great men such as these. 'We cannot look, however imperfectly, upon a great man without gaining something by him,' he wrote in his essay *On Heroes, Hero-Worship and the Heroic in History.* 'He is the living light-fountain, which it is good and pleasant to be near.' Gertrude was fascinated by such men, and late in life made it her vocation to bring them together in her drawing-room or around her dining-table. Her life sheds light on many of the century's most enduringly celebrated personalities, from Gustave Flaubert to Henry Morton Stanley, but Gertrude Tennant is much more than the sum total of her interactions with distinguished people. Not a celebrity in her own right, Gertrude is a powerful personality, a woman whose connections and experiences open up a vast panorama of social and cultural history. She is the central character in a multi-generational, matriarchal family epic, that takes us from the age of Nelson to the Somme, from the last days of the

Regency to the reign of George V, from industrial South Wales to the decadence of *fin de siècle* London, and from the pious certainties of evangelical religion to the flummery of psychical research. Her life can be interpreted as a story of vitality and determination, but also as a morality tale showing the vanity of celebrity.

CHAPTER 2

BORN INTO A LONG LINE OF HEROES

[You are a] descendant from a long line of heroes whose names are honourably recorded in the history of their country; on both sides of [your] ancestral pedigree
Letter from Charles Tennant to Gertrude Collier, 26 March 1847

Gertrude Barbara Rich Collier was born on 9 November 1819 at Newcastle Lodge in County Galway, a small house overlooking the storm-tossed waters of Lough Corrib. She was delivered at nine in the morning by Dr McCew, an old man with a face scrunched up like an owl, who had journeyed through the snow from nearby Galway town to attend to her mother Mrs. Harriet Collier in the last stages of her confinement. The baby was sickly-looking with long brown hair hanging around her head and ears, as her mother recollected many years later.[1]

The Colliers found themselves in this wild and remote spot by accident, having been driven ashore on the treacherous Atlantic coast of Ireland some weeks before the birth. Gertrude's father, the euphoniously named Lieutenant Henry Theodosius Browne Collier, RN, was in command of HMS *Falmouth* when it ran aground. According to his wife, writing many years later, he took more interest in the fate of his ship than the security of his wife and newborn child. While he busied himself with repairs, they were left alone in the Lodge with a pretty Irish maid called Biddy, who among other eccentricities bathed every morning in the chilly waters of the lake directly in front of the house, danced around the kitchen with few clothes on, and sang lullabies in Gaelic. (George Baring Collier, Gertrude's elder brother, was two or three years old at the time but was not with them: he had been left with relatives in England.)

Storms raged and snow fell, but it was not merely the weather that was inhospitable: the local people were starving and hostile to the English, as Mrs Collier found out one day shortly after the birth when she received a visit from a gang of wreckers, desperate men seeking to profit from her husband's disabled ship. Through the drawing-room window, the men politely informed the young mother that they had unanimously resolved to murder the Captain at the first convenient opportunity. They withdrew after delivering this warning, but came back another evening and surrounded the house.

'You can see them pressing their faces against the window and they are beating against the doors,' Biddy cried out to her mistress. 'What am I to do?'

Harriet was wearing a white embroidered dressing gown, her naturally curly auburn hair roughly twisted on the top of her head, the picture of feminine defencelessness. With surprising sang-froid, she ordered Biddy to invite the wreckers into the house and hear their grievances. There was a solitary candle on the table as the men marched into the room, she recalled. Harriet instructed Biddy to bring more light.

'I am all alone here in this house, what do you want from me?' she asked.

Biddy translated the reply from the Gaelic: 'We want food and we want money.'

Harriet asked for more chairs to be brought into the room, bade the men sit down and cut them slices of cold salt beef. One of the men caught sight of a precious pocket watch lying on the table: it was a present from her father, ornamented on the outside with a Cupid and Venus.

'I have nothing in the house worth giving to you,' Harriet told the chief of the brigands, who was ogling the valuable timepiece. 'What I have got I will give you, apart from this watch which I cannot part with.'

Biddy translated and the leader of the brigands laughed at her spirited defence of her property.

'You had better go on your journey,' Harriet went on, offering the men a few silver pieces and some beer. 'You will find, as you know, in the town of Galway, people better able to help you than I am.'

Something in her tone impressed the outlaws, and as night descended, the men quietly took their leave, each one insisting on shaking her hand on the way out. When the Lieutenant did finally return, he congratulated his wife on a narrow escape and praised her for her presence of mind. With a panache that she inherited from her aristocratic forebears, she had managed to avert a robbery – or far worse.

There were no further visits from brigands, the only nuisance coming when an Englishman waylaid Biddy and offered her a piece of gold if she would cut off one of Mrs Collier's curls when she was asleep. Biddy said she would try, but her courage failed her and she confessed all to her mistress. Harriet later identified the man as a lovelorn young officer quartered at Galway, who would very often meet her when out walking and insisted on bowing and trying to enter into conversation. After Biddy's confession, the plot was abandoned, and Harriet escaped the fate of Belinda in Alexander Pope's *Rape of the Lock*. In later life, she would laugh uproariously whenever the story was mentioned.

* * *

With her bright hair and intensely blue eyes, Gertrude's mother was considered very beautiful. She had first met Henry Collier one summer's morning in 1816, walking down Wimpole Street in the West End of London with her sister, a footman walking behind them holding a tall stick, as was the fashion in those far-off days. Like Catherine Morland and Isabella Thorpe in Jane Austen's *Northanger Abbey*, the two sisters chattered away about the paucity of eligible men.

'How very seldom one meets a handsome man,' Harriet's younger sister is supposed to have remarked.

'Yes, we never meet any handsome young men, never,' Harriet sighed in agreement.

'But do look at that person coming towards us,' the sister said. 'Did you ever see anyone so good-looking?'

Harriet looked up and into the eyes of a handsome young man who was looking straight at her. The man, who was of course Lieutenant Collier, said nothing but watched the sisters enter a house in Wimpole Street. He found out later that the girls' father was Mr Robert Nicholas, a man of distinction in Regency England – a Member of Parliament and Chairman of the Board of Excise for more than thirty years. A few days later, Collier presented himself to this plenipotentiary at his home in Wimpole Street.

Collier was shown into the study and gave his name.

'May I ask you your reason for wanting to be introduced to me?' said Mr Nicholas, looking up from a mountain of papers. Nicholas was a busy, learned and accomplished man, full of his own affairs, and did not enjoy frivolous social engagements.

'I want to be introduced to a daughter of yours whose beauty attracted me.'

'Oh,' said Mr Nicholas. 'Is that all? Well, what is her name?'

'I do not know, Sir, I have never spoken to her.'

Mr Nicholas touched the bell and ordered three of his daughters to come down. (This gentleman was energetic in his private as well as his professional life: he had sired nine daughters and eight sons from two marriages.)

'You will then be so good as to point out the person you wish to know.'

They stood in a row, and Henry Collier walked up to the youngest of the three girls, who was standing at the end of the line. This was Harriet. She recognised him as the good-looking officer she had seen in Wimpole Street. They exchanged a few awkward words, before Mr Nicholas told him to return the next day.

Collier called the next morning and was obliged to submit to a perfunctory but decisive interrogation.

'Who are you?' he was asked.

Henry explained that he was fifth and youngest son of Admiral Sir George Collier, a hero of the American War who had died in 1795, when Henry had been just five years old. Mr Nicholas said he had known the Admiral and his wife. He commented on Lady Collier's beauty, and asked where she now lived. The Lieutenant replied that his widowed mother now lived in Manchester Square, a respectable West End address, not far from Wimpole Street.

Having established Collier's social standing, it was time to evaluate his finances.

'Who is your banker?' asked Mr Nicholas.

Collier said that he had independent means. He had inherited a small property of his own from his eldest brother Lieutenant-Colonel George Collier of the Coldstream Guards, who had died of his wounds after the sortie of Bayonne[2] in August 1814. Mr Nicholas's interest quickened: his own, favourite son William, of the Royal Engineers, had been killed leading the attack at the third siege of Badajos in April 1812. Another son had been killed in battle; yet another lost at sea.

'I always leave London at the end of June,' he said, 'and you must make up your mind to be married before then: I am very busy. Fix it up with my daughter, whose name is Harriet.'

He named a day when the Lieutenant was to come and dine. It was a difficult evening, as both Lieutenant Collier and Miss Nicholas, sitting next to one another at table, were stricken with shyness. But Collier asked if he could visit again, and the romance took its rapid course. They were married on 21 June 1816, a matter of weeks after the first meeting. Harriet was 23, Henry Collier 26 years old.

* * *

In the months that Gertrude's parents were conducting their speedy courtship, Jane Austen was hard at work in a cottage in Hampshire, completing the final chapters of *Persuasion*. Set in the immediate aftermath of Napoleon's defeat, Austen's last completed novel features a surplus of energetic, under-occupied naval officers who find themselves ashore with time to devote to finding a spouse. The book illuminates the circumstances in which young Henry Collier found himself on the outbreak of peace. Peace, for such young men, was a burden: it denied them the opportunity of active employment, let alone promotion and the chance of getting rich by taking prizes. They were obliged to stay at home on half-pay in the hope of a renewal of hostilities. There were some consolations: staid country drawing-rooms were enlivened by tales of naval derring-do, and many a young lady's heart was set aflutter by the arrival of a good-looking Captain Wentworth and his friends. Not all approved of this influx of vigorous young men just back from the wars, however. Sir Walter Elliot, the savagely caricatured embodiment of the enfeebled landed gentry, observes caustically that naval service was 'the means of bringing persons of obscure birth into undue distinction, and raising men to honours which their fathers and grandfathers never dreamt of'.

His comment, ironically intended as it might have been, could be applied to the Collier family. Delve back three or four generations to the beginning of the eighteenth century, and we find that the Colliers were City of London solicitors and merchants, their Christian names – Jabez, Theophilus, Ebenezer – suggesting socially dubious Nonconformist origins. It was Ebenezer's grandson Admiral Sir George Collier (1738–95) – Gertrude's grandfather – who brought the family to prominence. He rose from obscurity to become an authentic national hero; if not in the same league as Admiral Rodney or the Earl St Vincent, he was still one of those lesser Nelsons for whom England's naval wars of the second half of the eighteenth century created spectacular opportunities for heroism and self-advancement. Collier went to sea at 13 and served with distinction in the Seven Years War (1756–63), but the highlight of his career was the American War of Independence. In 1776, he conducted a series of attacks still remembered on the eastern seaboard for the scale of the destruction inflicted on the American forces. During the course of one especially incendiary fortnight, he led a raid on the Chesapeake where he destroyed or captured 137 revolutionary vessels with a value of one million pounds, and burned down the biggest shipyard in America.[3] The rampage continued with the sinking of a further forty-seven vessels at Penobscot Bay in Maine – the United States would not suffer so devastating a defeat on its own territory until Pearl Harbor. On his return to New York after these exploits, he discovered to his disgust that someone else had been appointed over his head as commander on the North American station. He resigned in a fit of pique and sailed back to England, where he told King George to his face that 'nothing but ruin and defeat were to be hoped from continuing the war'.[4] However prescient his remarks, his career went downhill thereafter. He spent a number of undistinguished years as Member of Parliament for Honiton in Devon, before returning to sea in 1790.

Of course, Gertrude never met her heroic grandfather, but later in her life she took enough interest in his personal history to edit and see through to publication his memoir of a visit to pre-Revolutionary France.[5] The Admiral's second wife will play a part in our story, as Gertrude's forbidding grandmother. She was a Miss Elizabeth Fryer, the daughter of a rich Exeter merchant. The Admiral met her at a county ball when he was already well advanced in years, and they married in 1781. The second Lady Collier bore the Admiral six children: two girls, and four boys, of whom Henry was the youngest. He was just five years old when his father died in 1795.

On her mother's side, Gertrude could trace her ancestors back to the reign of Edward I in the early fourteenth century when a forebear settled in north Wiltshire, in the vicinity of Devizes. There, or thereabouts, the family had stayed for more than six hundred years – for the first 450 years the family seat was at Roundway, and then in the mid-eighteenth century they moved to Ashton Keynes nearby. It was an ancient family, rooted in the affairs of the county, and from time to time a Nicholas achieved national prominence. The most notable forebear was Oliver Cromwell himself, the Lord Protector and regicide from whom Gertrude was directly descended. Only seven generations separated Gertrude from Cromwell, a fact of which she and her mother were inordinately proud. A family tree showing the descent from Cromwell's fourth daughter Frances was one of Gertrude's prized heirlooms.[6]

With these distinguished ancestors, the marriage of Henry Collier and Harriet Nicholas achieved the union of energetic new blood with the old landed gentry, the combination celebrated at the end of *Persuasion* when the well-born Anne Elliot marries Captain Wentworth. It locates Gertrude fairly and squarely in that somewhat indefinable but quintessentially English caste: the upper middle classes who formed the bedrock of social and professional life throughout the nineteenth century. She inherited a vast network of cousins and a tradition of independence and public service, but not much in the way of material assets. There were rich uncles and aunts, and more distant relatives with land and titles, but Henry Collier himself depended on his half-pay and the small legacy from his brother George.[7] It was pre-ordained that any Collier boys would be sent away to school as children and then into the services, where they would be expected to die for their country at the drop of a hat: indeed, no fewer than six of Gertrude's uncles fell while on active service during the French Revolutionary and Napoleonic Wars. But for the women there was no comparable path to glory or fulfilment, at least not in the world outside the home: the girls would have to grow up to marry and bear children, or face the ignominy of life as a governess or unmarried aunt. We can see Gertrude's adult life as an attempt to renegotiate the terms of her inheritance so that she could bring the energy and independence of her male forebears into the female sphere. For now, the peculiar conditions of the naval service in peacetime would have the greatest influence on her young life.

CHAPTER 3

EARLY ADVENTURES

The Admiralty punished Henry for the shipwreck by ordering him to sail the damaged vessel home from Ireland to Plymouth and then on to the West Indies. After some six months at sea, Henry 'invalided' from the *Falmouth* at the Leeward Islands – that is, was declared unfit for service; suffering from some unspecified tropical disease, he was sent back to England to rejoin his wife and children. For two years, the family enjoyed a period of unaccustomed stability. They lived in a village near Plymouth, in a thatched cottage surrounded by violets and primroses. Gertrude by now had rosy cheeks and her hair was neatly parted and smoothed down. Here she was baptised at the parish church of Stoke Damerel, taking the middle name Rich in honour of her father's lieutenant on the ill-fated Irish voyage. Henry had the inheritance from his brother George to administer, and presumably he was looking for another command. His petitions to the Admiralty eventually bore fruit and he was posted to the Cape of Good Hope. He came home to break the news to his wife, who was by now pregnant with her third child.

'You know the law is that no man can possibly be allowed to take his wife on board,' he told her. 'He may take his grandmother or his cousin, but he cannot take his wife.'

'Really, this is too ridiculous,' Harriet replied, angrily. She had shipped with her husband to the west coast of Ireland, and saw no reason why a longer voyage should be prohibited. 'Do you mean to say that I am to be left here by myself? That is quite impossible.'

So she hatched a plan.

'I will go up to London and I will go to the Admiralty, and I will tell them that I have no mother, that I have nobody in the world to take care of me but my husband and that I mean to go with him in his ship to his command.'

She travelled all the way from Devon to London to pay a visit to the Admiralty. The gentlemen were considering naval affairs when this young woman in a muslin frock was shown in. 'I am the wife of Captain Collier, and I am told I cannot go on board his ship,' she said. 'I come to tell you that I mean to go on board and I shall be turned out of the ship by force if those are your orders.'

'Impossible,' the admirals said, astonished and not a little impressed by her impertinence, 'impossible!'

'Gentlemen,' said Harriet. 'I wish to tell you the word "impossible" is not understood by me. I mean to go in my husband's ship.'

They laughed and looked at her admiringly. The spirited young woman who had faced down a band of Irish brigands had no trouble in finding the right tone with a committee of superannuated seadogs. She got up and bowed to them all round and left the room, and went home.

'They have agreed to my going,' she told her husband.

He looked very pleased, and so it was that Henry Collier embarked for the Cape in March 1823, in command of the 18-gun brig-sloop *Espiègle*, together with his wife, by now twenty weeks pregnant, and the three-year-old Gertrude. George was left behind in the care of a maiden aunt. It was the beginning of another adventurous, even dangerous, phase of Gertrude's short existence.

The voyage to the Cape was notoriously long and uncomfortable and exposed Gertrude to many perils and adventures, although at the time she was principally aware of the friendly attentions of the sailors. In the Bay of Biscay, she slept through a storm of such severity that no one on board expected to survive, and the ship was forced to put in for repairs at Corunna, where she heard the sound of Spanish guitars. From there, the *Espiègle* proceeded to Madeira, where Gertrude inhaled the island's flower-perfumed air, and then on to Tenerife, where she rode on a camel. Safely arrived at the Cape Colony, she was carried ashore through the surf in the arms of a sailor. From there, her father was promptly posted to the Île de France (modern-day Mauritius), more than 2,000 miles to the north-east. On arrival at Port Louis, Sir Francis Royer, Governor of the island, took a liking to the Collier family, and they were all invited to stay at his official residence.

Despite the constant threat of yellow flies, mosquitoes and the more mundane chickenpox, it was a happy time for the little girl. Fussed over by the government servants, she spent her days exploring the magnificent gardens that surrounded the house, delighting in the exotic flowers and birds. One day, Gertrude recalled many decades later, she was sitting under a bower of passion flowers, dressed in a blue gauze frock and white trousers, sorting through a selection of brightly hued morocco skins for a new pair of shoes. She picked up a grain of maize that had fallen from the cage of a golden king parrot above her head. This action provoked a peacock, which flew at the little girl and tore a strip of flesh from just below her right eye down the length of her cheek. 'It felt like a long piece of ribbon bleeding profusely,' Gertrude remembered. Her mother screamed; Gertrude was shocked into silence before breaking out in deep sobs; her father expressed his horror at the probable loss of beauty. The ship's doctor was called and Gertrude was undressed and put to bed, covered in plasters. She soon got better and the wound left no permanent scarring.

Some weeks later, Collier received orders to set sail on a journey of exploration, and the heavily pregnant Harriet insisted on going with him.

Gertrude, left in the care of Lady Royer, was told that her father and mother were gone. She was indifferent, as there was always some animal to play with or some servant to pet her, but unknown to her the lives of her mother and unborn sister were in danger. According to sailors' lore, Madagascar was a treasure island, a repository of untold quantities of gold. It also had the reputation of being exceedingly unhealthy, and Collier had been warned that no sailor should be allowed to sleep in the open on the island, as it meant certain death.

On arrival at Madagascar, Harriet went ashore with a few men. The island turned out to be a grave disappointment: the landscape was dreary and there was no gold. Harriet complained of feeling sick and was bundled back to the ship, while a party of sailors was left behind to complete a survey. The ship returned to Port Louis and it was here at Government House, on 8 July 1822, that Harriet gave birth to her third child, Henrietta Augusta Royer Collier – the middle name an expression of gratitude to the governor and his wife. Lady Royer became Henrietta's godmother. The sailors who remained on the island were not so lucky: they succumbed to Madagascar fever (presumably malaria) and later died.

* * *

Early in January 1823, a packet of letters arrived from England containing the momentous news that Henry had at last been promoted to the rank of post captain. 'For a short space,' Harriet recalled, 'all was joy.'

The significance of this promotion for any navy officer of the time cannot be overestimated: it meant a higher salary, automatic promotion and, at least in theory, the opening up of greater professional opportunities. In the Royal Navy, post captains commanded all ships above the size of sloops (whose masters – lieutenants or commanders – had only the courtesy title of 'Captain') and they automatically climbed up the 'post-list' of captains until they reached the bottom rung of the ladder of flag officers (admirals). The right to automatic promotion was important in peacetime, when there were few opportunities to distinguish oneself in active service. A man like Henry Collier could, and did, find himself professionally becalmed.

He had entered the Navy in April 1800 at the age of 10 or 11, and there is no reason to doubt that he would have risen quickly to the highest ranks had there been a decent chance to do so. Henry Collier was well-connected and pugnacious, just the qualities needed in an ambitious officer. From his very first posting as a volunteer on board the *Brilliant*, he was in the thick of the guerrilla-style raids and skirmishes that were the hallmark of everyday naval warfare at the time. Like the fictional Jack Aubrey, he sailed up and down and around the Mediterranean, and further afield, to Asia and the West Indies, in search of combat, glory and prize money. He was one of the party who captured and destroyed enemy ships off Belle-Ile in Brittany and at Ferrol on the north-west coast of Spain; he participated in the boarding and capture of the French Corvette *La Guepe* in Vigo Bay; he helped capture the *San Jago*, a Spanish 12-gun schooner, run down in the Bay of Biscay, and so on for a number of exciting and eventful years until his career suffered a reversal. According to an article in the *United Services Gazette*, Henry was 21 years old, senior lieutenant on the *Leda* at the conquest of the island of Java in 1811, when his patron Admiral Drury – Commander-in-Chief on the station – died an untimely death. The young lieutenant found himself 'passed over in favour of Commodore Broughton's followers, and lost that promotion to which his services and position so well entitled him. . . by this misfortune he lost ten years' rank as Post Captain'. Collier was instead posted to be Deputy-Governor of the Naval Hospital at Madras on the east coast of India, a role that cannot have suited his active disposition. He managed to get back to sea in the latter half of 1812, and there followed a series of uninspiring postings leading up to the Peace of 1814 and his subsequent marriage.

The contrast with the fortunes of his brother Francis is telling. Francis, always known as Frank, was the elder by seven active wartime years in which he was able to get ahead. According to family legend, Admiral Nelson was on leave in Bath in January 1798 when he caught sight of a young midshipman in naval uniform whose appearance pleased him. 'He entered into conversation with him, and finding that he was the son of Sir George Collier, he called upon Lady Collier, and was very urgent to have him under his wing.' Nelson summoned him to the *Vanguard*, and the young Frank participated as a midshipman in the long hunt for Napoleon's fleet, which led the *Vanguard* from northern Italy to Alexandria, and back again via Cyprus and Sicily, before returning to Egypt and surprising the French late in the afternoon at Aboukir Bay. Nelson decided to attack there and then, and as a result Frank witnessed at close quarters the drama of one of Nelson's greatest engagements.[1] Frank subsequently served with Nelson on the *Foudroyant*, and after a sequence of commands in the West Indies and elsewhere was appointed post captain in 1808, at the age of 25. Even after Napoleon's downfall, Frank was kept busy. While Henry was on his way to the Cape, his elder brother was in naval command of a joint naval–military expedition sent to the Persian Gulf to stamp out the piracy that was damaging trade with India.[2] He arrived home in October 1822 after the successful completion of this mission, and it is likely that Frank Collier had some influence on the Admiralty's decision to promote his brother Henry, which dated from Boxing Day of that year.

* * *

Under the byzantine rules of the Royal Navy the *Espiègle* was too inconsequential a ship to be commanded by a post captain, so Gertrude's father was immediately relieved of his command. By virtue of his promotion, he had to get himself and his family back to England at his own expense. He later calculated, no doubt with a touch of exaggeration, that the return journey cost him £1,000, a significant sum which dwarfed the benefits of his pay rise. The first stage of the return voyage was from Port Louis to the Cape of Good Hope. The Colliers were 'guests at their own board' while Captain Chapman was in command of the vessel. Chapman proved unequal to the task, the ship carried too much sail and was 'taken aback': the wind filled her sails from the wrong direction, threatening to capsize the vessel. 'The whole ship fills with water – a sailor holds the screaming child on the top of a bookcase,' recollected Harriet many years later in an understandably melodramatic account of the voyage. 'There is but one more such sea between us and eternity. The ship rights herself, and we are saved.'

At the Cape they transferred to the *Clydesdale*, a merchant vessel, where Gertrude and her infant sister were among a group of fifteen children on board fated to endure a particularly stormy passage home. On the night they left port, there was a cry of 'All hands on deck' – there were breakers directly in front of the vessel, signalling the presence of the Bellows Rock, a notorious reef. Collier took the helm and was able to put the ship about. Other skippers in the same convoy of merchantmen were not so capable or lucky, and Gertrude remembered her mother telling her that six out of the seven merchant ships that left the harbour went to the bottom of the sea that night. The victims included a friend of her mother's called Mrs Saunders, together with her seven children.

Amid the panic, the children were forgotten and Mrs Collier came on deck in her dressing gown. Suddenly she asked her husband: 'Oh, where is the child?'

'I don't know, I thought she was with you,' he replied.

An old sailor called Jacob said she must be in the cabin.

'She can't be in the cabin,' Harriet answered, panicking. 'Everything is floating about in there.'

However, in the cabin Jacob found Gertrude sitting complacently in a hammock watching the water rolling in. The water came up to the sailor's waist, but he waded to the little girl, told her to put her arms round his neck, then carried her up on deck and put her to bed in his own berth.

After these excitements, most of the rest of the journey was slow and uncomfortable – there were reduced rations of food and water – and Harriet occupied herself making shoes for Gertrude out of the borders of the flannels in which the infant Henrietta was wrapped. After three months at sea, the *Clydesdale* encountered another destructive storm, this time off the port of Holyhead on the island of Anglesey, in which the sails were split and at least one mast cracked and went overboard. When she reached Liverpool a few days later, the *Clydesdale* was a virtual wreck, and had long been given up for lost.

In the winter of 1823, some two years before the inauguration of George Stephenson's Stockton and Darlington Railway and seven before the Liverpool and Manchester Railway, this was still the age of the stage-coach. Captain Collier and his young family took a coach through the snow on the long and uncomfortable journey from Liverpool to Southampton. Collier had returned to England in the hope of advancing his career. In fact, he would never see active service again. When he finally went to see his mother, she had some terrible news. Stephenson, the banker to whom he had entrusted all the money inherited from his brother, had absconded earlier in the year, and the bank had failed.[3] Not a farthing was saved.

Henry must have tried to salvage something from the wreck of his finances, or at least seek another posting from the Admiralty, for the family stayed in Southampton for more than a year before deciding to leave the country for good. In the spring of 1825 they left England in the dead of night, in a fishing boat, bound for the French coast. Collier was 35 years old when he set out on this undignified sea voyage, with the best and most active years of his life behind him. The five-year-old child would not have known it, but she was to remain in France for more than twenty years, with only brief holidays spent in England, and her upbringing would be decidedly unconventional by the standards of her English contemporaries.

CHAPTER 4

ARRIVAL IN PARIS

Gertrude's parents were among those William Makepeace Thackeray called the 'hardy adventurers' who sought, in the aftermath of the Napoleonic Wars, to find a better life, or at least respite from creditors or the constraints of respectable English society, on the other side of the Channel. While English girls of her age grew up in a society shaped by the forces of industrialisation and urbanisation, of evangelicalism and gradual social reform, Gertrude lived a picaresque expatriate existence.

France, open again to British visitors after a blockade lasting nearly fifteen years, had rapidly become the preferred destination for disgraced or impoverished Englishmen or those fleeing creditors. Lady Hamilton, for example, Nelson's former lover, absconded to Calais in 1814 to escape the reach of the King's Bench, and died a few months later in drunken squalor, while the regency dandy Beau Brummell fled to the same seaside town in 1816 after losing once too often at cards, ending his days in the lunatic asylum at Caen. Later in the century, comte d'Orsay, Brummell's successor as arbiter of fashion in London society and a close friend of the young Benjamin Disraeli, experienced a similar tumble from grace and followed in Brummell's footsteps to France. Thousands of more or less respectable countrymen made the same journey in the decades following the end of the Napoleonic Wars, including Thackeray, who spent several years living in Paris (and whose first full-length book was *The Paris Sketch-Book*); his mother and stepfather lived round the corner from the Colliers in the Champs-Elysées. Many distinguished Victorians were brought up in France, including Ford Madox Brown, the painter, and George du Maurier, the artist and illustrator whose father was French, while others lived for a time in the English expatriate community, notably George Henry Lewes, the writer and consort to George Eliot; Edward Fitzgerald, the poet, and Fanny Trollope, mother of Anthony and a best-selling novelist and travel writer in her own right. (Her *Paris and the Parisians in 1835* was a popular account of the pleasures of Restoration Paris.) By the early 1820s, it is thought that more than 20,000 English had settled in Paris, a considerable reversal from earlier in the century when the English were banned from the continent. The cost of living was a great deal cheaper on the other side of the Channel and English bankruptcy law did not apply, but there were other good reasons for heading for France.

'The English were taught to hate the French as well as to observe the Ten Commandments,' noted Captain Gronow, an English officer, 'and a Frenchman, on the other hand, was educated with the idea that his only enemy on the face of the earth was an Englishman.'[1] However, at this juncture in history, the traditional animosities were in abeyance. Ever since the Duke of Wellington and the victorious Allies arrived in Paris after the Battle of Waterloo, the English had received a cautious welcome in France, at least from those who supported the restoration of the Bourbon monarchy. This was in contrast to the reception given to the Prussians, the co-victors at Waterloo, who arrived in Paris determined to avenge the insults and atrocities dealt to their own people during the French occupation of Berlin, or the Russians, who also sought revenge for the hard usage they had suffered at the hands of the *Grande Armée*.

When the Russians and the Germans entered Paris, they occupied themselves in anti-social behaviour such as cutting down the trees in the Bois de Boulogne, insulting women, smashing up shops and brutalising the citizenry. During the three-year occupation, the British soldiers in Paris were quiet and well-behaved by comparison, camping out among the trees of the Champs-Elysées, walking about the city in groups of a dozen and amusing themselves by watching the mountebanks, jugglers and rope-dancers on show at the Boulevard du Temple, buying cakes, gingerbread, fruit and lemonade for all the world as if they were at the fair. From time to time, one of their officers would fight a duel with a Frenchman, and Frenchwomen would affect to be terrified by the sight of Scottish soldiers in their kilts, but by and large they were peaceable, and they would inter-vene to stop the vandalism of the Prussians and Russians. As a result of this good behaviour, there was for a short time evidence of that rare phenomenon in international affairs: gratitude. The goodwill had abated by the mid-1820s, when George Canning's aggressive foreign policy led to a resurgence of tensions between the old enemies, but Collier must have calculated that the prestige of an English naval officer would still be high in Restoration France.

* * *

The morning after their arrival in France, Captain and Mrs Collier, together with their two daughters, boarded a rattletop carriage called a *coucou* and were driven to Honfleur, a quaint fishing village close to Le Havre. The Colliers spent six months there in a small house rented by the Captain as a stopgap measure as he pondered his next move. Oblivious to the family's straitened circumstances, Gertrude embraced the new country and its alien customs with enthusiasm. She horrified her mother by bolting her breakfast and going outside without her bonnet, a most unladylike way of behaving, and unhealthy, too, to be out without a hat in the heat of the July sun, but she was so curious to see a Catholic procession taking place in a neighbouring garden. She recalled being beaten across the shoulders with a slipper by a great brute of a nurse called Judd. A more significant legacy of her sojourn in Honfleur was that she learned to speak French like a native.

Her mother tried to instil in her the basics of arithmetic at home, but Gertrude could make neither head nor tail of the multiplication table, and in despair Harriet marched her daughter up a steep hill to a nearby convent that was known to take in pupils. Gertrude was understandably nervous as they reached an enormous iron gate. Perhaps, like her brother left behind in England to be educated, she was to be handed over to this institution for good? Her mother rang a bell and the door was opened by an ugly, ancient nun, dressed entirely in black. With copious references to a dictionary she had brought with her up the hill, Harriet managed to convey in execrable French that she would like to talk to the Abbess. Still clutching the dictionary, she asked this lady whether they would take in the little girl and teach her the basics of the French language. The Abbess looked at her tenderly, took her face in her hands and kissed it, and agreed to take her there and then. Harriet was instructed to pick her daughter up at seven o'clock that evening.

On her first day, Gertrude met two much older Irish girls, who became firm friends and helped her overcome the initial language barrier. Soon, though, she was reciting the Lord's Prayer in French, speaking and thinking in French, and although she later complained that she was not taught anything at all at this school, she found it much more stimulating than being at home with her mother, nurse and baby sister. She exchanged her prettily embroidered *pélisse* for the regulation white dress worn by all the other girls, and as there were a great number of festival days, she participated in numerous processions through the extensive grounds of the convent, marching alongside her Irish friends. By virtue of her facility with the language, she became an important personage in the Collier household, correcting her mother and speaking for her father, who never spoke anything but English in the many decades he remained in France, and indeed remained entirely contemptuous of the French. 'He swore by his blue jackets,' Gertrude recalled, 'and prided himself on not under-standing a word of French.' His daughter adopted the opposite approach and soon spoke the language fluently.

At the end of six months, Collier's affairs had improved: there was some money to be recovered from the bank, and his sister Georgina Aïdé had offered to help the family move to Paris. So they mounted a carriage called a diligence, and embarked on the bone-shaking, vomit-inducing 24-hour journey to the capital, amid (as Thackeray described the same journey) 'much jingling of harness-bells and screaming of postillions'[2]. They arrived in the Faubourg Saint-Denis very early on the morning of Gertrude's sixth birthday (9 November 1825). She remembered that the city was locked up behind large *barrières* that had to be opened to let them in. They were shown up a staircase to squalid lodgings on the sixth floor of a hotel. When Mrs Collier asked for a basin in order to wash she was told there was one in the room. It was a small pie dish, in which Gertrude was obliged to wash her face. There is no record of the delights in store for breakfast.

The next day, they took a small coach called a fiacre to look over Paris for somewhere to live. Henrietta and the nurse were left at home, while Gertrude accompanied her parents, as the only one of the party who could get by in French. She commanded the driver to take them to the Champs-Elysées, a long way to the west, and thus began a journey full of frights for the girl. As they drove through Saint-Denis, out of the gloom emerged a portrait of Madame Pompadour and then an enormous blood-red hand, bigger than any human hand, swinging terrifyingly outside a shop; shortly afterwards there was another, still more hideous hand. Gertrude began to scream, convinced that they were alive. She was pacified only when her mother explained these were hoardings advertising the wares of glove shops and mercers. For the next two days her services as interpreter were dispensed with and she was left in the rooms with the hated nurse and the screaming baby. At last, on the third day, the Captain delivered the news that they had found a new home: No. 4 rue de

Ponthieu, an apartment next to a wood-yard, on the corner of the Champs-Elysées. They took the fiacre to their new home that evening. Gertrude negotiated the payment for the hire of the carriage, before climbing the 112 stairs to the fourth-floor apartment and being sent to bed with a biscuit and a glass of water. Hanging outside her window was a solitary oil lantern, slung across the street on a cord attached to wooden poles. At the time of the Terror, the mob strangled their victims with these cords and strung them up, crying 'Les aristocrats à la lanterne', and Gertrude went to sleep terrified by the ghastly quivering light of the lantern dangling over the rue de Ponthieu.

The next day, Captain and Mrs Collier went out to buy provisions. At the neighbourhood *épicerie* they bought coffee, sugar, treacle, semolina, dried plums, salt and pepper and nothing else. When the shopkeeper asked to be paid, Collier held out his hand with some French money in it; the man helped himself to the appropriate coins and indicated that he would send the goods to the apartment. Collier wanted some tea but the grocer did not sell this staple of an English family's existence – had never even tasted the stuff, thought it was some kind of powder – and thus referred the English couple to an *apothécaire*, or chemist, further down the street. The chemist had a glass jar full of some old leaves. Collier bought half a pound of this unappetising substance, which turned out to be undrinkable pure green tea. Without a cup of tea to soothe their nerves, the first day in their new Parisian home ended miserably for Captain and Mrs Collier. Within a few years of their arrival, however, Parisian shops seemed to stock nothing but English food, or at least so discovered Lady Morgan, author of a number of best-selling accounts of Restoration France who visited Paris in 1829. Asking at a *pâtisserie* for *diabolitins en papillote*, *pastille de Nantes* and other French delicacies, the *demoiselle* replied to her in broken English: 'We sell no such a ting', offering instead shelves piled high with 'de cracker, de bun, de plom-cake, de spice gingerbread, de mutton and de mince-pye, de crumpet and de muffin, de gelée of calves foot, and de apple dumpling, as bespoke'. Close to the Tuileries Lady Morgan found a large blackboard advertising hot mutton pies, oyster patties, Devonshire cider, spruce beer and London porter. 'I thought I should never get out of the atmosphere of Cornhill or St. Paul's churchyard,' the author lamented.[3]

Gertrude made herself indispensable to her father. She became his interpreter, as he could never make it understood what he wanted to buy when he went shopping. 'Tell that damn fellow that I am an Englishman and that one Englishman is worth ten Frenchman,' he would say as he entered a shop, his daughter at his side. I shall tell him that I am saying that but I will not say a word of it, Gertrude thought. And so she began with great politeness, just as she had been taught by the nuns – always to curtsey, always to address people by their names and titles. The shopkeepers would remark on her wonderfully perfect French and her *belles manières*, such good manners. Her father would say: 'Now tell them that one Englishman could knock out four Frenchmen and they must send me what I am going to order.'

Gertrude would order the things they wanted: sugar, bread, butter, vegetables. Her father went in and out of shops ordering more things and the shopkeepers took down his name and address and then wrote on a piece of paper what he had to pay. The arithmetic was too much for the little girl, so her father took the paper and crumpled it up in his hand, saying, 'You call at my house tomorrow morning and I will pay you'. They did call the next morning, with a very long bill. Gertrude could not read the writing and her father could not understand it, but somehow or other the Captain managed to pay it and they went away.

Her mother, by now pregnant with her fourth child, contrived to furnish the apartment from local furniture shops where she found an old English carpet, an old-fashioned sofa, a few chairs and a bookcase for the drawing-room. This room was decorated with two very large mirrors, and looked out on to the trees of the Champs-Elysées; in one direction, it opened with folding doors into the dining-room, a large room with a floor of black and white stone; in the other, there was a tiny bedroom where Gertrude slept, and a large dark room, leading through to a better room for the nurse and baby Henrietta. Further still, was the kitchen. On the other side of the apartment, at the back of the building, were the best bedroom and her father's dressing room, which looked out on to a yard.

Within a week or two of his arrival in Paris, Captain Collier donned his naval uniform and paid a formal visit to the British Embassy on the rue du Faubourg Saint-Honoré – one of the great town houses of Paris, with a paved courtyard in front, and at the rear two long wings (one a ballroom, the other a state dining-room) and a leafy garden running down to the Champs-Elysées. Despite being hard up, he possessed his good looks and his rank, and he must have cut a dashing figure as he went to introduce himself to the ambassador. Lord Stuart de Rothesay granted him an interview and invited the new arrival to dinner in a week's time.[4] Lord Stuart Melville, his brother officer, the Knoxes and Lord and Lady Ranfurly would also be dinner guests.

Gertrude's father returned home and told his wife that they had received this splendid invitation, but Harriet was horrified. 'I have no clothes,' she protested. 'I cannot wear my morning things, and at my first appearance amongst these friends of yours they will not be terribly impressed if I go looking like a housemaid.'

Henry called Gertrude and asked her to go downstairs and ask a neighbour, General Delort, if he could help a fellow officer in this emergency. The six-year-old girl, dressed as a little English girl should be, in a short frock, long trousers, and her hair prettily curled, knocked on the door and explained her errand to the maid. 'Faites la entrer,' said the General; she was shown in.

'I am come to ask you from my father, who is an English officer, do you know of any dressmaker?' she asked.

The general burst out laughing, and called for his wife, who kissed Gertrude, took her hand, and said she was a dear little girl.

'My mother wants a dressmaker as she is going to a dinner party,' said Gertrude.

'I understand,' Madame Delort replied. 'I will certainly recommend a person to her who will provide everything that is necessary in due course.'

Gertrude went back upstairs, triumphant.

Her mother took her out to visit a bonnet-maker by the name of Monsieur Herbault, celebrated as the high priest at the temple of Parisian fashion. Gertrude was asked to explain what she wanted. The fabled milliner paid her a compliment: 'with such a pretty face I ought to make a very pretty bonnet'. He refused to accept a commission on any terms but his own, saying, 'As your eyes are so blue, you must have something blue in your bonnet and I do not care very much for your instructions. I shall make a bonnet that I think will suit you and you can take it or leave it just as you like.'

The order was given; the bonnet was divinely beautiful, and shockingly expensive.[5] Mrs Collier had no money to pay for this, let alone the dress that was being made for the dinner party. After much thought, she had ordered a plain black dress with large open-work net sleeves trimmed with embroidery and worked with pearls. The day came to try it on, and it fitted perfectly. She was afraid to ask the price. She looked perfectly à la mode, but there was one outstanding question: how should she arrange her hair? It was decided to put it up in what were called *coques*, an arrangement of loops and frizzes that gave her height and made her look beautiful and fashionable. 'I am glad you are decently dressed because I would not have taken you if you were not,' her husband said, ungallantly.

Harriet was still concerned about paying for the bonnet and the dress. She wrote to the bonnet-maker to ask for his bill, but Herbault told her that 'it did not press', and she could wait until the New Year to pay (this would be an extension of weeks rather than months, as by now it was late November or early December 1825). The dressmaker demanded immediate payment. Harriet did not know what to do, but that morning a letter arrived from her sister-in-law Georgina Aïdé in London:

> I am sorry, dear, you have had had so much trouble to escape. I hope the dear children are well. I should have liked to have given you a something as a souvenir before you left, but it is very difficult to send presents to Paris in these times so I enclose in this letter a cheque for a hundred pounds. You must take great care of it for it is part of my allowance, and on receiving this write and let me know that you have got the cheque safe, and the English banker settled in Paris will give you a hundred pounds in French money.

Harriet decided not to tell Henry about this gift – he was unable to live within their limited means, being 'excessively fond of buying pretty things' – and she wrote back to tell Georgina she had not said anything to her husband and would be using the money to pay for the dress.

* * *

As winter turned into spring, and the Champs-Elysées were filled with the sound of birdsong and the scent of wallflowers drifting down from numerous balconies, no one paid much attention to Gertrude or her schooling. Her mother was distracted by the arrival of a new baby – Gertrude's second sister, Adeline Louisa Letitia was born in the apartment in April 1826 – and in any case her father believed, in common with most Englishmen of his day perhaps, that girls did not need to be educated at all. There were no toys in the nursery apart from an ugly Dutch doll left behind by a visitor, and the only books were *Mrs Trimmer's History of Rome*, a small square volume in large print, and another short book entitled *A Visit to Malta*. Gertrude was a clever, inquisitive girl, and she somehow taught herself to read English by obliging Nurse Judd to sit down with her and read through these uninspiring tomes. She learned mostly by looking and listening, and by exploring the busy, fashionable neighbourhood. She made faces at an old woman who sat between the poles holding up the lanterns in the rue de Ponthieu, selling apples and pears, and eventually entered into conversation with her, persuading her to give her an apple for nothing. She ran along the road to the *épicerie*, where the shopkeeper gave her dried old prunes as a treat. She was allowed to run downstairs and buy cherries from a woman who sold her wares from two panniers strapped on either side of a donkey, calling out, 'A la douce cérise, à la douce.'

There were many processions – with the support of King Charles X, the Roman Catholic clergy were making an effort to revive religious observance – and Gertrude watched, fascinated, as long files of priests in their sacerdotal vestments glittering with gold embroidery, and their acolytes in white, made their way down the street.[6] They chanted the ancient liturgy as young girls and children strewed the ground with flowers and left offerings at shrines mounted in the walls of the houses. One of these *réposoires* was directly opposite the entrance to the apartment, built up with green branches, moss and flowers, decorated with tinsel, glass beads and wax figures of the Virgin and Child embedded in cornflowers.

Gertrude spent many an hour looking out of her bedroom window directly on to the heads of passers-by. It was a joy to wander down this thoroughfare in her new bonnet, accompanied by a French *bonne*, or maid. She would stare at the supremely elegant denizens of the Parisian *haut monde* as they promenaded up and down the Champs-Elysées and round the Rond-Point, now a traffic-snarled roundabout but then a place to see and be seen, to walk and to engage in conversation. Too poor to emulate these rich and glamorous Parisians in the way she dressed, Gertrude could at least ape the grown-ups by looking into the large plate-glass windows of the fashionable boutiques that lined both sides of the street, and do some shopping of her own. She stopped at the *bonbonnerie*, where the maid would treat to her to a bag of glistening sweets. She would be taken to the Tuileries Gardens, some twenty minutes' walk from the Rond-Point, where under the shade of enormous chestnut trees, hoops and skipping ropes were to be had from open booths, and on strings from tree to tree were hung caricatures of the royal family. (She remembered in particular a picture of Charles X as a donkey, surrounded by a family of donkeys of different shapes and sizes.) There, she encountered some memorable characters. One was the so-called Marchande de Plaisirs, a wizened old lady with snow white hair under a white cap, and dark eyes and eyebrows, who carried a fancy straw basket lined with linen under her arm, in which thin, wafer-like cakes were daintily arranged. In her other hand she carried a tall walking stick. Children would approach and deposit their small coins, *sous* or *liards*, in a saucer placed within the basket, and take a leaf of cake in return. It was said that she was a former great lady, her fortunes ruined by the French Revolution, and the children and their nannies treated her with a reverence that befitted her natural nobility. 'If she had been Marie Antoinette in person, she would not have been treated with more respect!'

A similar story was told about a celebrated character on the streets of Paris known as the marquis de Carabas. This good-looking young man was supposed to be a real marquis, formerly the possessor of great estates, whose father had been a victim of the Terror. He had lost everything except his manners, his violin and an old court suit, complete with hat, sword, red high-heeled shoes, sparkling buckles, embroidered silk stockings and lace ruffles: the clothes a *grand seigneur* might have worn at the court of Louis XIV. To the delight of the children, and many other citizens of Paris, he made witty speeches, played a *ritournelle* on his violin, and danced a few steps with elegant precision. He affected an aristocratic indifference to money, and handed out coins wrapped up in a leaf taken from a printed songbook. These were returned immediately, together with any addition people sought fit to make, and in this way he made a living. The title of marquis de Carabas was bestowed on him by the people of Paris in honour of the fairy-tale aristocrat in *Puss in Boots*: nobody knew his real name.

As a young girl, Gertrude was dandled on the knee of an incontrovertible marquis: Trophime-Gérard, marquis de Lally-Tollendal (1751–1830), a citizen aristocrat who had been elected deputy to the Estates-General in 1789 before becoming disillusioned with the course of the Revolution and emigrating, like so many others, to England.[7] She met him at the home of Sir James and Lady Wedderburn-Webster,[8] friends of her parents, where he gave her sugared plums out of a crystal and gold *bonbonnerie* he carried in the pocket of his puce-coloured silk coat. His face was pale and puckered with wrinkles and he had rolls of white muslin about his throat and lace ruffles around his wrists. Gertrude remembered that he stood on ceremony and insisted upon being addressed as Monsieur le marquis de Tollendal, rather than plain Monsieur de Lally. Immensely fat, he was described by a contemporary wit as: 'le plus gras, le plus gai, le plus gourmand des hommes sensibles' – 'the fattest, the gayest, the most greedy of sentient men'.

One day, Gertrude caught a glimpse of an old gentleman wearing a plum-coloured silk suit with lace ruffles – this was said to be the abbé Sièyes, the regicide of whom Gertrude's maid was most disapproving: 'c'est un méchant homme, il a voté la mort du Roi'.[9] She also saw Marie-Thérèse de Bourbon, the duchesse d'Angoulême, who was the plain and grumpy daughter of the executed Louis XVI and Marie Antoinette, and niece of King Charles X. (Many English visitors were struck by her lugubrious expression, but tended to be sympathetic. 'Her expression is a confirmed melancholy,' commented an English visitor at this time, 'with a redness in her eyes, as if she had been in tears.')[10] Given the fate of her parents, her aunt and her younger brother (who died at the age of 10 in a squalid Revolutionary prison) she of all people had good reason to be morose, but she was not the child's idea of a royal princess at all. Some time later, Captain and Mrs Collier were presented to this duchess and formed an equally unfavourable impression. They attended an evening function at the Château, as the Royal Palace at the Tuileries was known in those days. Gertrude stayed up late, under the mistaken impression that a meeting with royalty might mean a present for her when her parents returned. Her mother reported that the duchess was ill-tempered and shabby, despite being got up with a great many diamonds. The only words to have passed her lips when they met were: 'Madame, il y a beaucoup d'anglais ici ce soir'. Her father harrumphed when these words were translated, saying: 'I should like to know where they would all be but for "les anglais"'.[11] Gertrude was left with a clear understanding of the colossal ingratitude of the French royal family, and the immense superiority of the English.

Some years later, Captain Collier took his family to the Place de la Révolution (subsequently renamed the Place de la Concorde) to witness a great ceremony when a massive obelisk from Egypt was to be hauled into place. The obelisk, now marooned at the centre of possibly the most frightening traffic junction in Europe, was to be erected close to the spot where the duchess's parents and more than a thousand others were guillotined at the height of the Terror. Drums were beating, flags were flying, there was singing and a great roar from the crowd as the operation began. Gertrude's father was fascinated by the mechanics of the procedure, declaring that they would never achieve the task unless they were helped by Englishmen. And it seems that when it was almost up the cords began to give way and a great many English sailors in the crowd began shouting: 'Water, water!' Efforts to lift the mighty obelisk were stopped and the cords were soaked with water. Gertrude's father, with supreme contempt, said, 'Ho! They would never have done anything without Englishmen!'

* * *

Very early one morning, some years after the family settled in Paris, Gertrude was awakened by a tremendous ring on the doorbell. She jumped out of bed and looked out of the window, where she saw a beautiful yellow chariot with two magnificent horses, and servants in livery looking frightened. Gertrude was ordered to go back to bed, but as we might expect of this inquisitive and independent-minded little girl, she stood with her ear pressed to the door of her bedroom to hear what had happened. The carriage, she learned, belonged to Princess Bagration, a Russian aristocrat who had sent the vehicle to fetch Captain Collier.[12] Harriet went out into the street and found that nobody could speak English. Gertrude was summoned and the head footman, known as a chasseur, informed her that Mr Aïdé had fought a duel that night and was lying critically injured at a roadside inn on the way to Montmorency.

Gertrude had to ask whether her uncle, a man whom she knew and cared for, was still alive; the chasseur told her the doctors believed it unlikely he would see the sun rise. The Captain got dressed and was driven to a public house in Montmartre. On arrival at the squalid hostelry, Collier asked where to find the wounded man. 'Vous voyez,' they told him. He could not understand what they were telling him, but followed their gestures and made out George Aïdé lying on the brick floor with some tattered, heavily bloodstained towels and blankets around him. Immediately it was clear that Aïdé was fatally injured.

'Well, Aïdé, you will soon be better,' said the Captain, with as much conviction as he could muster.

'Oh,' he said, 'I shall never be better. But I want to tell you – I was wounded by the marquis de Bourbelle. I left your sister at the ball . . . I was valsing with Princess Bagration's niece and he pushed up against me. He ought to have stopped, but he did not, and this happened a second time, on which I turned round and struck him and I said: "I am an English gentleman – you have no right to insult me."

'He said: "I did not intend to insult you, it was a pure accident."

'I said: "Not at all; it was no accident, I must have reparation."'

They declared they would fight with swords, and Mr Aïdé was mortally wounded in the liver. That morning he passed away in a good deal of pain. 'You will find my will in the heel of my boot,' he told Gertrude's father.

The Captain returned to the Champs-Elysées to tell Harriet the sad news. Gertrude listened to every word, not understanding much of the conversation, but fathoming that her dear uncle had been killed and that she would never see him again.

* * *

By this time, the Collier family had emphatically settled in Paris. The peripatetic days were over, and whatever hopes Captain Collier may have had of returning to active service, or of finding employment of any kind, or indeed of returning to England, were abandoned: he contrived to live as a gentleman in France on his captain's half-pay and the remnants of his inheritance. For a long time, scholars investigating Gustave Flaubert's connection with the Collier family maintained erroneously that Henry had a job as naval attaché at the British Embassy; this, however, seems to be a late-Victorian fig leaf draped over the fact that he was never again gainfully employed. (The Foreign Office has no record of Collier working in this embassy or in any other consulate.) At the time, there was nothing to be ashamed about in being idle and on half-pay, but one is compelled to ask what Captain Collier did all day long apart from accompany his wife to balls at the embassy or occasionally even the royal palace, or take a cabriolet to the Galignani reading room in the rue Vivienne with his daughter at his side, where together they would read the English newspapers. 'For about three shillings a fortnight, one has access to all the principal London papers, besides everything of the kind published in Paris, damp from the press,' wrote one appreciative visitor of such daily visits to this elegant reading room.[13] 'Information of all public matters, sights, fetes etc etc, is to be obtained here; and hardly anything can occur to puzzle an Englishman, but he will have it here unravelled.'[14]

Galignani's Messenger, an English-language newspaper first published in 1814, became essential reading for English expatriates throughout the nineteenth century: 'the exile's best friend', Thackeray called it in *Vanity Fair*. Jos Sedley, Becky Sharp's buffoonish admirer, 'used to favour the ladies with extracts from this paper during their breakfast', taking especial delight in reading out the accounts of military movements ('The Arrival of ——th Regiment. – Gravesend, June 20. The Ramchunder, East Indiaman, came into the river this morning, having on board 14 officers and 132 rank and file of this gallant corps. They have been absent from England fourteen years . . ..') or announcements of promotions and deaths. Captain Collier would have relished such military gossip, but the newspaper also provided a guide to the respectable attractions of the metropolis for the English community. Like the English living in Hong Kong or the Gulf today, there was much that enabled them to recreate the pleasures and pastimes of home without having to fraternise overmuch with the natives. They had to endure living in apartments – a form of residence that would not become fashionable or usual in London for many decades – but otherwise they could live a comfortable and congenial life, at a fraction of the cost required to maintain a comparable existence in London. Concentrated in the fashionable north and north-western *arrondissements* of the city, they were insulated from the malodorous, overcrowded and frequently disease-ridden medieval heart of Paris.

'They had themselves proposed and seconded for the Cercle Anglais in the Rue Sainte-n'y Touche,' wrote George du Maurier in *Trilby*, a novel that both celebrated and poked fun at the gaiety of expatriate life in Paris, 'a circle of British Philistines of the very deepest dye, and went to hear divine service on Sunday mornings in Rue Marboeuf [the location of one of the three English Protestant churches in the city].' He was writing about the Paris of the mid-century, but the gentle jibe at the double standards of the English (Rue Sainte-n'y Touche translates roughly as Hypocrisy Street) would have found its mark in the 1820s and 1830s as well. As diaries and contemporary novels make clear, there were many less than salubrious temptations on offer for a gallant and good-looking naval officer. The heart of Parisian dissipation was the Palais Royal, the hereditary palace of the ducs d'Orléans. This is now an enchanting backwater for tourists, but at the time of the Restoration was a cornucopia of dissolution. In vastness and variety, it was said to exceed the Louvre itself. Here is a fascinated and horrified description from James Simpson, an Englishman who wrote an account of his visits to Paris in the aftermath of Waterloo:

> It is an oblong quadrangle, with piazzas completely around it, enclosing a garden planted with rows of trees, and laid with gravel, with flower and grass plots enclosed . . . It has long ceased to be a palace . . . and has, in short, become the great mart of Parisian luxury. It has been called a world in itself; it is at least a city. It encloses more ground than most of the London squares; and exhibits, under its piazzas, by far the most brilliant shops in Paris, in countless numbers. On the same ground floor are numbers of coffee-houses and restaurants, fitted up with great variety and taste, and at night brilliantly lighted. On the principal floor upstairs are superb coffee-houses, gaming-houses, exhibitions etc. etc. Higher up, all sorts of vice and profligacy abound; and the attics are inhabited by filth, misery and crime, in endless variety . . . Of such consequence is the Palais Royal to the Parisians, that Paris would be almost half-annihilated were this, its very heart, suddenly destroyed; while, on the other hand, should a powerful reforming process be put in

action with regards to Paris, half its work would be done at once by cauterising at once this immense gangrene.[15]

Men of all nationalities gathered of an evening to dine at famous restaurants, gamble in celebrated clubs and squander their winnings on costly baubles and beautiful women, thousands of whom milled about in the crowded piazzas, 'all in high dress, and apparently in high spirits'. Among the men, there were two topics of conversation: gambling and women. 'Men's thoughts, in this region, seemed to centre night and day upon the *tapis vert* . . . in one room was the *rouge et noir* table, which from the hour of twelve in the morning, was surrounded by men in every stage of the gambling malady,' wrote Captain Gronow, who arrived in Paris after Waterloo and liked it so much that he stayed there for forty years. The floor above the gambling-house was occupied by unmarried women, up-market prostitutes who benefited from the largesse of the winners at the table: a common practice was to spend one's winnings on jewellery and other trinkets so that the money could not be squandered at the roulette wheel. Gronow relates how one officer of the Grenadier Guards came to Paris on leave, took apartments there, and never once left the Palais until his time of absence had expired. Back in London, a friend asked whether this was true, to which he replied: 'Of course it is, for I found everything I wanted there, both for body and mind.'

Perhaps the Captain won some money at the gaming table, or one of the innumerable aunts and cousins left him another legacy, for as time went on, there was more money around. It paid for long summer holidays at seaside resorts like Dieppe, Le Havre and Boulogne, where Gertrude enjoyed meeting and playing with other English children as much as the holiday pleasures of bathing in the sea, strolling on the sands and riding out in open carriages. And in 1829, the Colliers were well enough off to move to a bigger, better apartment, on the Rond-Point of the Champs-Elysées itself. The extra space was needed to accommodate a growing family: Clementina Frances, the last of the four Collier girls, was born at rue de Ponthieu in December, 1828. Clarence Augustus was born while the family was on holiday at Le Havre, on 29 July, 1830. On 19 July, 1833, Herbert Cromwell, the last of the children, was born at St Germain-en-Laye outside Paris, when Gertrude was 13. With her brother George away at school in England, Gertrude grew up as the eldest of six children in Paris, as much a mother to her siblings as their big sister.[16] In her reminiscences, Gertrude barely mentions her brothers and sisters, a strange omission given that they shared her unorthodox upbringing. But she was nearly three years older than Henrietta, an eternity when one is a child, and she grew up with an acute sense of facing life's challenges very much on her own. Her childhood stories have a chiaroscuro tone. The light is the sheer gaiety and excitement of growing up in Paris; the dark is resentment of her parents' indifference to her own happiness, and their complete neglect of her education.

CHAPTER 5

UNSENTIMENTAL EDUCATION

Gertrude's grandmother Lady Collier (widow of the old Admiral Sir George) came to Paris to console her daughter Mrs Aïdé after she lost her husband in the duel. The old lady's arrival was a mixed blessing for Gertrude. Lady Collier now enjoyed spending time with her eldest granddaughter, taking her into her bedroom and playing games, but she was highly critical of the girl's educational attainments. She was passionate about poetry, and especially fond of James Thomson's *The Seasons*, and she used to read these poems to Gertrude. The heroine in Thomson's poem is called Lavinia, 'and Lavinia bored me to death,' remembered Gertrude.

'Ah you do not know what poetry means,' Lady Collier said. 'You had better read *John Gilpin*. That is more suited to your character.'

'Well,' said Gertrude, 'give me *John Gilpin*.'

'Oh,' she responded caustically, 'I do not travel about with trash such as that.'[1]

Her grandmother then said: 'I think you now ought to begin to write. Can you sign your name? Can you write 'Gertrude Barbara Rich Collier'?'

'I cannot write more than Gertrude,' said the poor child.

Lady Collier expressed her dissatisfaction with Gertrude's ignorance and stupidity, and sent her home. She suggested that a governess be hired to take care of the little girl's education. Gertrude was horrified at the idea, and in any case her father held traditional ideas about educating girls. 'If they could dance and sign their name it was all that signified,' was his philosophy. 'For other things he said he could not go to the expense of masters.' Nevertheless, a celebrated dancing master called M. Fouché was sent for, and examined Gertrude 'with a curious eye for business', holding her hand in his large fat hands as she tried out a step or two taught by her grandmother. He gave lessons *au carnet*, giving out a card at each lesson, and after twelve cards, the pupil paid him. Fouché told Mrs Collier that it would be better to teach the little girl as part of a group: they would learn more, and it would be more amusing. And so it was arranged. Gertrude had a new frock made, and was taken to a large room in the Faubourg du Roule, near where her aunt lived. M. Fouché professed to speak English and the lessons would begin with great solemnity. He played a *ritournelle* on his violin, and gave the order 'Commence your beatings [*battements* in the language of dance] and point your fingers.' He meant toes, of course, but Gertrude and the handful of other English girls in the class enjoyed the mistake too much to correct him. She learned *minuettes de la cour*, gavottes and finally the mazurka, all of which would prove very useful as she grew up and went out into society.

Her father was first inspired to consider his daughter's desire for a real education as a result of an unfortunate domestic incident. The Captain wanted Gertrude to run an errand; she had been trying to make figures out of bread and she put them on the back of a book and carried them into the room where he was standing. Afraid of shaking them, she walked very slowly. He was in a dreadful hurry. In a violent passion at her not coming instantly, he gave her a box on the ear which struck her to the ground. The blow caused a vessel to burst and her face was covered with blood. The Captain picked her up, afraid that he had killed her, and sponged her with water and kissed and hugged her as she came back to her senses.

'He assured me I was an angel and so on,' she recalled. 'But I never forgot it and he never forgot it.'

Her father then said to her: 'What do you do all day?'

'I don't know, I amuse myself.'

'I think you would be much better at school.'

'What is a school?'

'Oh!' he said, 'it is a room where girls are kept and taught to read.'

'I *can* read,' Gertrude insisted.

'I think you had better go to school,' he said at last.

Soon afterwards, Gertrude's mother took her to Madame Dobanel's establishment at the far end of the rue de Ponthieu. There were about twenty-five girls, and they were taught history, geography and fables. They were sent outside to play in the garden, where the girls held hands and sang songs. This was amusing, but Gertrude could not get on with her lessons. She couldn't understand what was required of her. They did not follow the English practice of beating children, but the French punishments were humiliating enough. Her curls were cut off and she was required to wear the dirty cap belonging to the daughter of the porter. She was kept in the lodge making pothooks and hangers and passed her days there with the servants; at night she was fetched from the school. Soon after she came home, she was given milk and water and put to bed.

After a few nights, her mother noticed that Gertrude was lying in bed, writhing in an agony of discomfort. 'I have something in my head, it seems to be crawling about,' Gertrude said.

Her mother told her to go to sleep, but the next morning she took a closer look: Gertrude's head was infested with lice. Gertrude's mother was horrified and sent immediately to the school to say she would not be coming back. A doctor was sent for and he advised that the girl should have her head shaved. Gertrude managed to avoid this humiliation, however, and her hair was washed repeatedly until the lice were vanquished. 'And that was the end of my going to school,' Gertrude recalled.

Soon after this incident, the family moved from rue de Ponthieu to the Champs-Elysées. Gertrude remembered an old-fashioned, second-hand sofa in the sitting-room: it had a high back and was suited for two people, with cushions for each, and was covered with crimson brocade. Gertrude's mother and her friends used to sit and chat in this chair, and Gertrude was banished from the room. She found however that she could slip underneath the sofa and, by lying flat on her back, could hear all the conversation. She was particularly fascinated by Lady Cochrane, a former barmaid who had married a famed admiral and lived in the same apartment block: as Gertrude remembered, she was 'handsome, rather vulgar, and very amusing'.[2] Not everyone would receive her in polite society, but she and Gertrude's mother were great friends. Gertrude took great trouble to install herself in the hiding place every time she heard that Lady Cochrane was coming for a visit. 'So [before I was nine] I had the benefit of being perfectly acquainted with all the gossip of Paris,' she recalled, decades later. 'It was like listening to a delightful book listening to all she told my mother.'

Her father took delivery of a package of books belonging to his late brother George. These included a volume of stories about the rakish Regency bucks Tom and Jerry ('Tom was always in blue and yellow . . . his white hat balanced on one side, kept on as if by the winking of an eye!') and a smart illustrated volume called *The Life of Corinthian Kate*, a risqué character who wore a feathered head-dress, for whom she felt great affection. The package also contained less suitable reading material: *Tom Jones*, by Henry Fielding, and a volume of Lord Byron's verse. The roistering novel and passionate poems did not make sense to a girl of Gertrude's age – she was by now nine or ten years old – but she found them diverting nonetheless.

In time, the works of Victor Hugo would become far more important to her than those of Fielding or Byron. She first encountered the name of this towering figure of nineteenth-century French literature, and experienced at first hand the extraordinary impact of his work on his countrymen, on the afternoon of 25 February 1830 – we know the precise date and time because this was the day of the first performance of Hugo's *Hernani* at the Théatre Francais in the rue Richelieu. Gertrude was being driven in a cabriolet with her father on the way to Galignani's reading rooms, when they encountered immense crowds of men gathering outside the theatre. To her childish eyes, it was an alarming sight. What were those strange, wild, ferocious fierce-looking men going to do? Were they armed? She trembled with terror and pressed close up to her father.

Bodkin, the driver of the cabriolet, told her not to worry: 'Don't be afraid, Mademoiselle, they are just people waiting for the Theatre to open.'

'At four o'clock in the afternoon?' asked Gertrude.

'My dear girl they're putting on *Hernani* and they say it will be very beautiful,' he replied.

Gertrude asked her father: 'Who is Victor Hugo?'

'Never heard of the fellow, some French fiddler I suppose,' said the Captain contemptuously. He regarded all poetry as 'd. . .d nonsense,' excepting 'Poor Tom Bowling', a popular song about a drowned English sailor.

Gertrude could not have understood this at the time, but she and her father witnessed that day a historic moment in French cultural history – the battle between classicism and romanticism, fought out, almost literally, by the audience who attended the first night of Hugo's play. In 1827, Hugo had sounded the death knell to the rule-bound classicism of traditional French literature in a stirring preface to *Oliver Cromwell*, a play about Gertrude's ancestor. *Hernani* was a further, deliberate challenge to the government censors who had banned the previous work. Set in sixteenth-century Spain, it is an absurd story; as Lytton Strachey described it: 'a piece of bombastic melodrama, full of the stagiest melodrama and the most turgid declamation'.[3] The censors calculated that there would be no harm in letting the performance go ahead, hoping that the brazenly improbable plot would expose the romanticists to ridicule. But they reckoned without Hugo's stirring verse. 'The story simply does not exist, the invention is beneath contempt,' wrote Balzac. 'But the poetry – ah, the poetry goes to your head. It is Titian's painting, his fresco, on a wall of mud . . .'[4]

The first night was set to be a contest of strength and wills between the two camps. Hugo's many enemies had taken out advertisements in newspapers identifying passages in the play that should be hissed and booed, while his friends assembled a battalion to drown them out with cheers. The allies included a paid claque of mercenary supporters whose loyalty was considered suspect: they might turn classicist for an increase in the bribe. Hence the flower of the younger generation of poets and writers – including Honoré de Balzac, Théophile Gautier (who wore a specially tailored cherry red waistcoat and lime green trousers for the occasion), Benjamin Constant, Gérard de Nerval, Alexandre Dumas and Hector Berlioz – all turned up on the day to show their support, many sporting unsavoury long hair and beards. They waited in and around the theatre for eight hours before the production started; admission was by a ticket printed with the word *hierro* (Spanish for iron, in reference to one of Hugo's poems). Meanwhile, from the roof of the theatre the classicists bombarded Hugo's supporters with rubbish as they queued to get in (Balzac was hit on the head by a cabbage stalk). Once the romantics were inside, they found themselves locked out of the lavatories, with the result that they had no choice but to turn the elegant premises into a *pissoir*. Notwithstanding these unpromising, not to say malodorous circumstances, the evening turned out to be a resounding victory for Victor Hugo and the new romantics. 'Vive Victor Hugo' was written on walls all over Paris, and *hugolâtres*[5] such as Théophile Gautier found themselves astonished that Hugo was a mere mortal, who could be found walking the streets of the city like any other human being. 'It seemed to us he should only have gone out in the city in a triumphal chair, pulled by four white horses . . . with a crown of gold on his head.'

This was more than an obscure, undignified contest over literary conventions; more indeed than the coronation of the 27-year-old Victor Hugo as the living genius of French romanticism. This was a proxy fight for a more fundamental conflict at the heart of post-Revolutionary French society, between reactionary 'ultra' monarchists and more progressive republicans.[6] It pitted young against old, liberals against royalists, advocates of free expression against those who respected authority, in literature as in life. The conflict outside the theatre was thus a foretaste of the July Revolution which took place a few months later, toppling the reactionary

Charles X and bringing Louis-Philippe to the throne. The so-called *trois glorieuses* counts as one of the less sanguinary revolutions in French history. But still, at least 650 people died in Paris during three days of street fighting, in which 4,000 barricades were flung up throughout the city and working-class insurrectionists fought hand to hand with government soldiers in the narrow streets of old Paris. The new King of the French promoted himself as a tolerant and liberal monarch and was supported by the very students and liberal bourgeoisie who turned out *en masse* to support Hugo's play.

* * *

While these historic events were taking place around her, Gertrude was at last making some progress in her quest for a proper education. Shocked by the story of the lice, her aunt Georgina intervened and found Gertrude a governess. Mademoiselle Mercier was an Englishwoman of dubious morals and even more questionable personal hygiene and habits. Her vices were drinking and gambling, and she had been obliged to leave London for unnamed transgressions. She was however a well-born lady who spoke perfect French and Italian, and was said to be immensely clever. Besides, Mrs Aïdé told the Captain, she liked animals: she lived on her own with three dogs. She was hired, and one senses that the Captain was satisfied with the fees she charged, and indifferent as to character references. Gertrude took an immediate liking to Mlle Mercier, whom she described as a tall woman with a very interesting face, and spent four happy years taking lessons from her. These took place in the afternoons and lasted for three hours at a time. Gertrude learned Italian and was encouraged to read poetry and novels such as Samuel Richardson's *Pamela*. As time went on, Mlle Mercier got dirtier and dirtier and drank more. At the end of each lesson she would ask for a drink and Gertrude would obligingly raid her father's drink's cabinet, giving the governess a large glass of Roussillon. One day all of a sudden the governess stopped coming to the apartment and all Gertrude's books and poems were shovelled out of the way. Gertrude later found out that Mlle Mercier had been found dead drunk in the street, and banished from the Collier household.

Let us conclude the chapter with two more cheerful anecdotes that capture Gertrude's girlish enthusiasm for the pleasures that Paris had to offer. Here is her mother's recollection of Gertrude setting out for her first ball:

how she stands before the long glass, how delighted she is with her satin slip and muslin skirt, she thinks it perfect, nothing remains to be wished, for see her leap into the carriage! But oh what vexation! What disappointments await her! Each juvenile companion is graced with a bouquet – negligent, thoughtless mother to subject her eldest darling to such a trial.

Fortunately, the son of Lord Granville, the new British ambassador, asked her to dance, and Gertrude was consoled.

Gertrude also attended the children's balls held by Queen Amélie, wife of King Louis-Philippe. The entire royal family was present at these dances, which took place in the Salle des Maréchaux at the Tuileries Palace, the former Salle des Cent Suisses from whose balcony pre-Revolutionary kings traditionally showed themselves to the French people and where the Duke of Wellington was received by Louis XVIII after Waterloo. The picture presented by the royal family was one of happy domesticity. As Gertrude recalled, the King and the Queen and the young Orléans princes and princesses 'footed it' from eight to midnight, dancing away without a thought of the 'sad stories of the fate of the King'.

At the end of the ball, Gertrude asked the young duc d'Aumale, the King's fifth son, to dance the final *galop* with her:

> It was the most joyous bouncing of all! Dancing as we danced it! He promised me I should be his partner again, and no other – and so away we flew, never dropping to draw breath til midnight pealed from the *Horloge des Tuileries* – the band ceased playing – the Queen came up to speak to the handsome boy, patted my close-cropped curly head – and said – 'venez mes enfants avec moi, vous avez trop chaud' – 'come with me my children, you are getting too hot' – and led us each away by the hand to sit down by her.
>
> At last it was all over . . . I can truly say as I was put in the carriage – I felt for the first time though without realising it what the poets call a pang!

The next morning the French maid asked whether she had enjoyed herself. She began to tell her fairy-tale story – why couldn't she go and live at the Tuileries with the Queen and the duc d'Aumale, she was asking – when the *bonne* interrupted her and brought her back down to earth: 'Bah! vous les reverrez l'anneé prochaine' ('Bah! you'll see them again next year').

CHAPTER 6

GERTRUDE MEETS HER FUTURE HUSBAND

In the summer of 1834, some time after the departure of Mlle Mercier, Gertrude and her family went on an extended holiday to Boulogne on the Channel coast. The Colliers spent their time walking on the beach, riding on donkeys, swimming in the sea and making friends with other privileged middle-class English families. It would have been an unremarkable seaside holiday except that on this occasion Gertrude met the man who would become her husband. At the age of 14, Gertrude was too young to be thinking of marriage; and Charles Tennant, who celebrated his 38th birthday on the first of July of that year, considered the pretty but adolescent Gertrude as no more than a charming girlish companion. In later life, they did indeed make much of their early affection for one another, but at the time Charles was not thinking of marrying anybody and Gertrude was tremendously taken by the entire Tennant clan.[1] Charles, who had recently taken over the management of the family estates in South Wales from his late father, was on holiday with his widowed mother, staying in a château outside the town with three of his sisters, and a variety of their cousins and children. It was a sizeable family – Charles was one of eight surviving siblings – and this summer there were children of Gertrude's age to play with, and cultivated young Englishwomen in their twenties to look up to and learn from, as well as the fascinating Charles to talk to, who was only six years younger than her father, but a different sort of man altogether.

Charles Tennant and Henry Collier were already acquainted: Tennant was by profession a solicitor, and a few years before he had been engaged to carry out some minor legal business for the Captain. Despite their closeness in age, they embodied directly contrary social forces. Collier was a man of the past, whose upbringing rooted him in the Regency period and by birth and training was equipped for a profession that was in abject decline; he had had an adventurous and active youth, but by the time the two met in Boulogne, he had abandoned himself to a life of indolence. Although he had seen much of the world, he was contemptuous of other countries, especially the one in which he was to live for nearly quarter of a century. Tennant, by contrast, was not solely a man of business, but a self-educated intellectual whose interests and enthusiasms were remarkably broad, even for an age of autodidacts and polymaths. By the time he and Gertrude met, he was a published travel writer and poet, an accomplished financial economist and amateur theologian, as well as a former Member of Parliament who managed to play (so he claimed) a decisive role in the enactment of the Great Reform Bill of 1832. Later in life, he would balance his duties as landowner and lawyer by writing a series of popular theses on the big social questions of the day, and became known for his contribution to the new science of economics. He was devout, learned and serious in his outlook on life, but not without a streak of fun. In addition to numerous earnest treatises, he penned a melodrama called *The Cobbler's Hut*. He was partial to a glass of beer, calling Mr Bass the brewer a 'benefactor of mankind' for inventing his eponymous Pale Ale. Through his work with his father, Charles was also a second-generation agent in the latter stages of the industrial revolution that would profoundly change the nature of England and English society in the first half of the nineteenth century. In short, Charles Tennant was a *Victorian*, although of course that label would have been meaningless when he and Gertrude first met, three years before Queen Victoria came to the throne.

Charles was the second son and so perhaps for that reason was not given the benefit of a university education. While his elder brother Henry went up to Oxford and became a fellow of New College, Charles followed the comparatively dreary path of qualifying as a solicitor. At the age of 16 he left Harrow – one of the great public schools that had recently produced both Lord Byron and Robert Peel – and joined his father's firm at 2 Gray's Inn Square as an articled clerk. This was a dignified position in the highly stratified world of the legal profession, for it indicated that someone (in this case his father) had paid a premium to get him the job, and that he was an attorney in prospect; it placed him above the salaried clerk, the copying clerk and the office lads. For nine years, he toiled away in what one imagines was a Stygian office like that of Messrs Dodson and Fogg, as described by Charles Dickens in Chapter 20 of *Pickwick Papers*:

a dark, mouldy, earthy-smelling room, with a high wainscotted partition to screen the clerks from the vulgar gaze: a couple of old wooden chairs: a very loud-ticking clock: an almanack, an umbrella-stand, a row of hat-pegs, and a few shelves, on which were deposited several ticketed bundles of dirty papers, some old deal boxes with paper labels, and sundry decayed stone ink bottles of various shapes and sizes.[2]

Charles's articles finished in 1819, and for two years he took himself off travelling before finally being admitted to partnership with his father. The highlight of his sabbatical was a five-month tour of Switzerland, Germany, the Netherlands, Savoy and France. His adventures were unexceptional, as we know because he set them down at inordinate length: a 900-page account of the journey was published in two volumes in 1824. Like many travellers, he was struck by the stench of Paris when he visited the city. He reached the conclusion that the English nation was indubitably superior to all others, attributing this less to martial or naval valour than to 'that restless spirit of enquiry, the predominant trait in the English character', which he himself exhibited in spades.

After five years back in business with his father, he turned to politics, and in the 1829 general election stood as the so-called 'third man' for the notoriously venal borough of St Albans, in Hertfordshire. Prior to the Reform Act of 1832, most constituencies still returned two members to the House, and the candidates typically had strong family connections or affiliations to the two main parties, Whigs and Tories. With no patronage of this sort, Tennant was surprised to be returned in second place above a Whig. He had gone to the polls professing himself an independent candidate who would be guided by the 'Christian doctrines of our church, which teach universal benevolence and toleration'; he would support a government that 'can combine the greatest portion of individual happiness with the least portion of human distress'. Such lofty thoughts might have appealed less to his constituents than his firm commitment to keeping taxes as low as possible. He told the electors he would support the incumbent Tory government, and yet voiced his support for policies that would put him more firmly in the Radical camp: abolition of slavery, opposition to all monopolies (particularly those enjoyed by brewers and the East India Company) and commitment to alleviating the lot of the working man. 'I . . . will not cease till the oppressions which have bowed down the labouring classes of England have been relieved, until the mists of ignorance are dispelled, and the chains drop from the hands of the slave . . .'

It was a thrilling time to be in politics, as Parliament inched its momentous way towards reform against a backdrop of intensifying public disturbance in the country at large, and later Charles would claim that he had helped make history. 'By [my] vote in favour of the first Reform Bill, under Lord Grey's Administration, [I] made the majority of ONE, by which that second "Bill of Rights" was carried in the House of Commons.'[3] In general, however, his brief parliamentary career was far from illustrious, as he was inclined to bore his fellow members with complex speeches on pet subjects such as the statistical basis for mass emigration. He was also transparent in his self-interested opposition to legislation designed to promote railways at the expense of canals. As we will see, his family fortune derived from a canal, and he would be an indefatigable opponent of railways throughout his life. (There was another reason to dislike this newfangled form of travel: on one of his first train journeys, he had nearly been blinded when he stuck his head out of a carriage window and a splinter of iron flew into his eye.) After the Reform Bill was finally passed in 1832, he did not put himself forward for re-election as he 'did not wish to involve himself in the expense of a contested election . . . against two powerful and wealthy opponents'. He had the good sense to recognise that he was not suited to the cut and thrust of electoral politics.

There was also a romantic side to Tennant's character: he loved poetry and knew by heart thousands of lines of Shakespeare, Milton and Coleridge. In homage to these great authors, he had recently completed his own epic poem. *The State of Man,* published earlier in the year of the Boulogne holiday, was a Miltonic attempt to demonstrate 'a view of the Divine purpose in the creation of man'. It runs to 1,330 lines of indifferent blank verse, accompanied by a hefty apparatus of learned references, and reaches a number of conclusions that now look plain silly. Tennant brushes aside the quickening contemporary debate about the nature of geological time and the implications of the fossil record, with the confident assertion that:

> all the formations of mineral, vegetable and animal matter were severally effected . . . by a mode beyond investigation by any scheme or science or science of man, namely the mode of Creation . . . [and that] by His almighty 'Fiat', He caused the first formations and disposition of all the mineral matter of this globe in one simultaneous operation.[4]

It may not be a great poem, and the science is crackpot, but the rightly forgotten work demonstrates formidable scholarship buttressed by a deep Christian faith. 'Upon the Sacred Gospel, and not upon any human authority, has the author rested his foundation,' he wrote, rather pompously, in the preface to the second edition.[5]

His father George had been an archetypal early nineteenth-century entrepreneur. Born in Wigan, Tennant senior was descended from a long line of North Country lawyers and he too became a solicitor, coming down to London at the age of 12 to take up articles. It was while carrying out legal work for George Child-Villiers, fifth earl of Jersey (1773–1859), a wealthy Whig magnate, that he first visited South Wales and conceived the notion of building a canal to transport the mineral wealth and agricultural goods of the Neath Valley to the docks at Swansea. South Wales was already a powerhouse of the industrial revolution: iron produced there was used to build London Bridge, to construct ships, boilers, cables and machinery, while copper (extracted from imported iron ore) was vital to the shipping industry. South Wales was the world centre of tinplate and copper smelting, and even before the advent of railways its coal was already highly prized for domestic heating and industrial use.

In 1816, George Tennant began his speculations in the area with the purchase of the Rydings estate in Glamorgan, just north of Neath, and thereafter he bought the adjoining property of Cadoxton. He believed that by digging a canal to bypass the River Neath, he could unlock the economic potential of the region and make a lot of money. The project would become his life's work and his son Charles's troubled inheritance. In 1818, George initiated the construction of what would become known as the Tennant Canal, committing his capital with almost complete disregard for the practical problems of cutting an eight-mile waterway through a patchwork of other people's lands. With the recklessness of the true speculator, he went ahead without following the normal practice of getting a private Act of Parliament passed to facilitate the compulsory purchase of all the land along the route of the waterway. (Indeed, along with the Duke of Bridgewater's eponymous creation, this was one of only two major canals to be built without such legislation.) It is a tribute to the power of his vision and his persuasiveness that he did manage to get the canal built, despite inhospitable terrain which obliged him to dynamite cliffs and cut his way through treacherous bogs and quicksand, and the intractable opposition of a number of local farmers and landowners. One notable feature was a 170-foot stone aqueduct of ten arches constructed at the site of the Aberdulais Falls, a beauty spot painted by J.M.W. Turner; at the time of its construction, the poet Robert Southey was troubled by the desecration of the romantic landscape by this visible manifestation of industrial progress. (Southey complained of the 'severe vandalism by which Mr Tennant's quarrymen have destroyed the natural cascade of Aberdulais'.) The canal was completed in 1824, running from Port Tennant harbour at the mouth of the River Tawe, near Swansea, to Aberdulais, just north of Neath ('a navigable line through about twenty miles of country eastward of Swansea and up to the Brecon hills,' according to Tennant's own, self-congratulatory account.[6]) It rapidly became the main thoroughfare for bringing coal and iron from the rich Vale of Neath to the port of Swansea and then on to world markets.

When he died in February 1832, George Tennant was a man vindicated: his speculation had paid off and his canal would be the main artery of the regional economy until the coming of the railways in the 1850s.[7] He possessed extensive lands in South Wales, through which his canal flowed, and a country seat in the form of Cadoxton Lodge, 'an ancient rambling whitewashed manor house lying near the mouth of the Vale of Neath,'[8] some nine miles from Swansea. There were other assets – a large town house in Russell Square, even a theatre in Covent Garden – and he gave every impression of being a man of substance and wealth. He enjoyed an elevated social standing in the county – in 1828 he was appointed Deputy Lord-Lieutenant of Glamorganshire – and the esteem of the local people, some 5,000 of whom turned out to his funeral at the local church of Cadoxton. But there are two sides to a balance sheet. Stripping his new-found social kudos out of the equation, Tennant certainly had a lot of assets, but there were also significant liabilities, in particular a mortgage on the South Wales properties to Child's, the bank owned by Lord Jersey's wife, Sarah, Countess of Jersey. The amount borrowed by Tennant and secured on the estate was £60,000: in 1830, a sum equivalent to many millions of pounds in today's money.[9] 'The debt is appalling,' George lamented in 1831, amid one of his perennial attempts to reduce his outgoings and restructure his liabilities. 'I have no lack of Courage in facing it,' he added, but his heirs did not share this blithe confidence.

One complicating factor was George's troubled relationship with Lord Jersey and his wife the countess, who in her own right had inherited Osterley Park in Middlesex, a magnificent stately home on the main road to the west out of London, as well as an *income* of a staggering £60,000 a year from the bank.[10] George was an adviser to the earl, but had also entered into a variety of property transactions with the nobleman and he owed the family bank tens of thousands of pounds. This engendered what in modern professional parlance would be deemed multiple conflicts of interest, especially when Tennant borrowed money from Child's to finance the purchase of the earl's own land in South Wales (as took place in 1828). After this deal was done, George indelicately suggested to the countess that she needed to make economies to finance her extravagant lifestyle; she never forgave him or his heirs for this rebuke, and the transaction would haunt the Tennant family for at least a generation.

A further complication was the haphazard way that George carried on in business. He preferred not to write anything down, and as a result, the multiple agreements he had entered into during the construction of the canal were never properly documented. The local resentments caused by George's habit of digging the canal with little respect to others' property rights, together with the complex web of mortgages and remortgages taken out to finance the project, set the scene for decades of dispute and litigation.

It was originally intended that two of the Tennant sons would take over the family business: Charles would become a partner in the law firm while his younger brother William would run the canal and the estate. Charles spent the years after he returned from his Grand Tour working in London to make sense of his father's chaotic affairs, wading through the 'heaps of papers tossed almost indiscriminately into large boxes'. He took on some of his father's clients (including Lord Jersey) and engaged in interminable lawsuits on his father's behalf. William stayed in South Wales, helping his father to build and operate the canal: chasing debtors, negotiating contracts with suppliers, organising building work and repairs, paying the workforce and wrangling with local landlords. William took over full responsibility for the estate only in 1831, the year before his father died, when matters were still so vexed that he had to write to his father daily. The pressure of running the estates, servicing the debts and fighting innumerable lawsuits did more than grind him down. Within eighteen months of George Tennant's death, William joined his father in the family vault in Cadoxton Church. Charles Tennant was thus not born to inherit the full responsibilities of the estate, but had the role thrust upon him at the age of 36 after his father and brother died in rapid succession. When he met Gertrude in Boulogne, he had spent the previous year in Wales attempting to get to grips with the practical problems of the canal. It would be twelve further years of toil before he and Gertrude met again.

CHAPTER 7

GERTRUDE ENTERS SOCIETY

Shortly after her return from holiday, Gertrude was reading an English newspaper in Lady Cochrane's apartment. Contact with the cultivated Tennant family had left her more than usually conscious of her educational shortcomings and she was intrigued to read the following advertisement in a corner of the journal:

> Monsieur Colard, tutor to the duc de Bordeaux, has established in the rue de l'Arcade cours for young ladies on interesting subjects. Apply for information No 12, rue de l'Arcade.[1]

Resolved to improve herself, Gertrude walked by herself to the rue de l'Arcade (which now runs from the Boulevard Malesherbes to the Boulevard Haussmann) at the back of the Madeleine. On arrival, she rang and said to the porter: 'Ask M. Colard if he will see a young English girl who wants to consult him.'

She was shown into a stately library where she encountered a fierce-looking, ill-tempered gentleman. 'Will you let me know something about your *cours* for young ladies,' Gertrude ventured. 'I want to know what you teach. I think I want to join them.'

'Oh,' he said. 'Who are your parents?'

'My father is a Captain in the King's Navy,' she replied. 'My mother is a descendant of Oliver Cromwell, and I am a lady.'

'Hmm!' he said. 'What do you know?' She said she did not know much, but was anxious to learn.

'Well, I should like to see your parents,' he said. 'Give me your address.' Gertrude gave him her address and asked when he would call.

'I will call tomorrow at twelve o'clock,' he told her. 'My time is very valuable and I hope your mother will see me.'

'I hope so, but I do not think it quite certain,' Gertrude replied. She bowed and was shown the door. The difficulty was how to break the news to her mother, who still thought schooling for Gertrude was unnecessary and ridiculous.

At twelve o'clock, M. Colard was announced. Gertrude was relieved to see that her mother was on her best behaviour, evidently convinced that it would not do to treat him like a shopkeeper. The interview went well. It became clear that the other girls attending this Parisian finishing school were all members of the *haute noblesse*, living in the Faubourgs Saint-Germain and Saint-Honoré, bearing grand surnames such as: de Sainte-Aldegonde, Berthier, de Praslin, de Molinis, de Foucault, de St-Aubyn, de Bréteuil. [2] Mrs Collier was impressed and before too long she was asking M. Colard if there was a place for Gertrude. He said there was, explaining that the classes took place in the mornings, for five or six months of the year only, during the autumn and the winter. (In the summer, aristocratic families were in the habit of leaving Paris for their country estates.) Gertrude went the next day, together with a maid, and discovered that she was the only English girl in a class of twenty. When the time came she put on her best clothes and tried to make herself as smart as possible. She and the other girls were shown into a large, airy room with a long table running along it covered with green baize. Each person had a stool and a box in which there was a slit, into which you dropped a counter if you answered a question correctly. When the lecture was over, the person who had won the most counters had a card which would have written on it, for example, 'Mademoiselle de St-Aldegonde, première précédence.' There was great excitement and competition to get these counters, and an enormous desire to learn.

It was a highly charged atmosphere, and after initial trepidation Gertrude enjoyed it immensely. At last, she was being stretched and stimulated, and soon she was top of the class, carrying off the prizes given out at the end of each *cours*. The literature lessons made the deepest impression. The girls were encouraged to take sides, like the crowds outside the Théatre Francais, in the great battle between classicists and romantics. They were obliged to analyse, memorise and recite lines of verse from the great French poets, especially Victor Hugo. Gertrude developed a passionate attachment to the intoxicating, dithyrambic verse of this most romantic of poets. She wasn't satisfied with the gobbets they had to learn for the lessons: 'I went out and read, and raved about Victor Hugo,' she recalled, acquiring and committing to memory as much of his work as she could afford. (Two of his great works were published in 1831: *Notre Dame de Paris* and *Les Feuilles d'automne*. He was still not yet 30 years old.)[3] The attachment to Hugo would prove deep and lasting, but her first meeting with the great man came about when she was a schoolgirl.

Gertrude's closest friend at the school was an 'enchanting piquante Parisienne' with the name of Euphraisé Davidal. Fraisé, as she was nick-named, was not merely a fellow Hugo fanatic, she was actually related to him in some distant way, and could pull strings to effect an introduction. Fraisé's mother promised to take Gertrude and Fraisé along next time she paid a visit to her remote cousin at his grand apartment in the Place Royale (now Place des Vosges) in the Marais. One hot afternoon in the summer of 1837, the girls crammed into a one-horse coach called a *demi-fortune*, which was like a melon inside, circular and lined with faced yellow satin, and painted green on the outside, and made their way across Paris to pay homage to their idol, feeling just like Cinderella on the way to the ball. The official purpose of the visit was to admire a picture that Hugo had just been given by the young duc and duchesse d'Orléans, a tribute from the ruling family. Hugo would return the compliment in *Les Misérables*, dedicating a eulogistic chapter to the virtues of King Louis-Philippe.

The door opened and at first they could see nothing of the house. There was no light in the apartment and they were blinded after coming in from the glare of the midday sun. Gertrude remembered that it was deliciously cool. As they regained their sight, they began to make out the gorgeous decorations and treasures that filled the house. They were led through a large dining-room, decorated with old furniture, the walls hung with valu-able, ancient tapestries and inlaid with Arabian bronze medallions and porcelain. Every corner of the room was filled with *objets d'art* – there was a dark wooden buffet and the sheen of arms and armour – as they moved forward past the entry to Madame Hugo's salon, a finely proportioned room shaped like a T, with three corridors and a balcony giving directly on to the square below. The walls of this room were lined with family portraits – two life-size paintings of M. and Mme Hugo by their friend Boulanger – and a picture of Peter denying Christ, by Caravaggio. They moved on into the drawing-room, where a group of exquisitely dressed *parisienne* friends of Mme Hugo were gushing over the gift. Gertrude and Fraisé were not impressed by the painting. It was a picture of the disinterred corpse of Inez de Castro being crowned posthumously by her husband Pedro the Cruel of Spain (the caption was: 'trop tard' – 'too late') – a reference to one of Hugo's early works. A more gruesome subject could hardly be imagined, and the girls recollected a lugubriously appropriate poem by the master, 'La Tombe dit à la Rose' (in which a tomb and a rose engage in conversation) that they had learned by heart at school. But where was the great man himself? The girls looked at each other: there was not a man in the room! They stood there, feeling awkward and ignored: Fraisé, a mere *charmant enfant*, and Gertrude feeling herself too young and insignificant to join the polite conversation, acutely aware that she was ill-dressed, wearing a pink dress, straw bonnet and cotton gloves, in marked contrast to the magnificent attire of the society ladies.

The visit was drawing to a close – as Gertrude recalled many years later she was near to tears of disappointment – when in walked Victor Hugo at last:

> He looked hot, and tired, and passed his handkerchief over his face . . . he was always very simple in his dress and wore his shirt collar down, which was not the fashion in those days . . . he wore no beard or moustache, but was closely shaved, his thick brown hair brushed completely back from his massive square forehead on which I noticed a scar. His eyes were brown but they looked in the full sunlight of an orange reddish colour . . . [they] . . ., were very deep-set shadowed by the heavy brows – the absence of eye-brow or eye-lash rather added, than took away from the expression of those not very kindly eyes – his mouth was severe, finely modelled – and his teeth faultless, his laugh merry and manly, everything about him was vigorous – his extreme courteousness kept people at a distance.

The master greeted one of the ladies, a Mme Beaumont, in a coldly formal way, enunciating the words of greeting in polite, measured tones and taking her gloved hand and raising it to his lips, before turning to Fraisé. He pushed the girl's straw hat back, kissed her forehead, and said she resembled her father. Then Fraisé, 'with the grace of true kindness', put Gertrude's hand in his, with the introduction: 'C'est mon amie anglaise'.

Gertrude's heart beat fast, she looked up at the great man, and met the full blaze of his penetrating eyes.

'Mademoiselle is English?' he enquired.

'Yes, she's called Gertrude,' answered Fraisé.

'Ah, she's not German,' he said.

Gertrude spoke, to say that her Christian name was Spanish.

Hugo brightened up: 'Oui, c'est vrai, mais c'est avec un H, Hertruda . . . avez vous été en Espagne?' ('Yes, that's right, but it is normally spelt with an H. . ., have you ever been in Spain?').

She said yes, she had been to Corunna as a child.

'Moi aussi,' he said. 'I too was in Spain and spoke perfect Spanish when I was a child.

'Gertrude est un nom qui n'a jamais été populaire en France,' he then added, to Gertrude's immense mortification, and turned away in search of his wife Adèle. Gertrude desperately wanted to be called Adèle, which from Hugo's lips sounded like the most beautiful name in the French language, or any other name that he might have liked. The girls took their leave, and Gertrude felt sorrowful:

> I had expected . . . I hardly knew what. I felt small, I had looked forward so long to this visit, and had arranged in my own mind that he was to say certain things, and I was to reply to them, most brilliantly! And it had all ended in nothing but an uncomplimentary remark on my Christian name!

Gertrude was vexed that she hadn't had a chance to peep into Hugo's study, the inner sanctum of creativity, filled it was said with sculptured oak furniture, hangings of antique brocaded silk, rare pictures and statuettes. Fraisé and her mother tried to console her with the thought that it was quite something to have seen Victor Hugo in person, for in those days he did not often go out. It would be nearly thirty years before Gertrude would properly renew her acquaintance with the great man of nineteenth-century French literature.

* * *

Meanwhile, she was going out a great deal. Her school connections ensured that she was one of the few foreigners who could enter the *portes-cochères* of the grand *hôtels* occupied by the most ancient families. What she found behind these thick, nail-studded gates was sometimes chilling, as when a school-friend invited her to meet her grandfather, a survivor of the Revolution. He showed her his collection of curiosities, which included the preserved head of a woman: 'The eyes were closed. It was not seen full face but sideways, and it showed the most beautiful profile. Of course it had been drained of all the blood so that it was not white. It was a sort of pale brown or cream colour, and it was quite beautiful to look at.' Gertrude demurred when the old man asked whether she would like to touch this gruesome souvenir. This was said to be the head of Charlotte Corday, the young woman guillotined after she assassinated Jean-Paul Marat in his bath.[4]

Gertrude's familiarity with the aristocratic French families of the 1830s left a more enduring impression, for the 'at homes' that Gertrude would hold at 2 Richmond Terrace fifty years later were modelled on these early experiences of French high society. Consciously or unconsciously, she would seek to import the quintessentially French notion of a *salon* to late Victorian London. The word *salon* simply means room, and although debased in modern English usage to suggest a place where hair is expensively cut, it carries with it considerable cultural baggage. The first salons originated in the seventeenth century as an alternative to the stifling society of the court at Versailles. They proliferated in the decades leading up the French Revolution, as society hostesses such as Mme Geoffrin, Mlle de Lespinasse and Mme Necker (the mother of Mme de Staël, possibly the most celebrated *salonnière* of all) turned their homes into places where philosophers, social theorists, writers and artists could mix with aristocrats (i.e. those who held the power under the *ancien régime*) to discuss ideas of social reform in a relaxed and informal setting. It is not going too far to say that by promoting the spread of the ideas of the Enlightenment, they helped foment the intellectual climate that made the French Revolution possible; when revolution led to the Terror, however, many hostesses and their *habitués* were exiled or beheaded.

Salons revived under Napoleon, but Mme de Staël fell out of favour with the regime, and she and her salon were banished from Paris. They came back into their own with the Bourbon Restoration, when the *grandes dames* of the Faubourg Saint-Germain, freighted with Proustian surnames such as de Ventimille, de Beaumont, de la Broche, de Rumford and Récamier, sought to recreate the exquisitely civilised social life of the pre-Revolutionary era. 'I cannot help recall the charm of these salons,' recalled one French aristocrat, 'which as it were marked a return to life . . . [after] denunciation, exile and the guillotine.'[5] He went on to make a distinction between the aristocratic values of the true salon and the ostentatious celebrations of the *nouveaux riches*:

A great simplicity marked these receptions. Brilliancy, wit, conversation were the only contributions that they levied. Simple dances, modest suppers . . . those who wished to see the luxury of sumptuous festivals sought it in the mansions of the contractors who had been enriched by the Republic.

By the mid-1830s, when Gertrude was beginning to go out into society, the reality of Parisian salons fell below this patrician ideal. As chronicled in Balzac's *Comédie humaine*, this was a time of strife and contention, as much between nobles and the *nouveaux riches* spawned by Louis-Philippe's business-friendly regime, as betwixt the myriad political factions and subfactions that sprung up in the aftermath of the July Revolution. In 1832, the mutual hostilities even spilled over into a 'war of the salons', when the society *grandes dames* refused to invite guests from opposing factions into their homes, and foreign embassies cancelled their balls, for fear of exacerbating these political tensions (Austria was thought to be intriguing in support of the Carlists, as the legitimists were called, while the English were supporters of the Anglophile Louis-Philippe).[6] According to Madame de Boigne, it was a time of 'unimaginable vituperation'. The duchesse de Dino, niece of the statesman Prince Talleyrand and a *salonnière* in her own right, holding court at her uncle's *hôtel* in the rue Saint-Florentin, declared herself horrified at the turn of events. She characterised the ladies of the Faubourg as 'indescribably insolent . . . and more irreconcilable than ever'. A veneer of *politesse* was restored by the time Fanny Trollope visited the city in 1835, and she describes how each society hostess had her very own group of 'remarkable people' she wished to introduce. At the house of Madame A, one might meet 'some one who has been a marshal, or a duke, or a general or a physician, or an actor, or an artist to Napoleon'; chez Madame B, on the other hand, one would meet doctrinaire Orléanists, while Madame C could introduce one to 'an ex-chancellor, or chamberlain, or friend, or faithful servant of the exiled dynasty. . .' and so on through an alphabet of social possibilities.[7]

Debased or otherwise, the salons were striking on a number of counts, even in the 1830s. As in their pre-Revolutionary heyday, they still brought together remarkable men from all walks of life, and they continued to be run by women, who were otherwise excluded from the power structures of French or indeed European society. Brilliant and powerful men came to pay homage to them. Benjamin Constant had attended Mme de Staël's salon, for example, while François-René Chateaubriand was to be found *chez* Mme de Duras, and the statesman Francois Guizot was inseparable from princesse de Lieven. The ageing Charles-Maurice Talleyrand held court at the salon of the duchesse de Dino, and it was there that Gertrude met him. One evening, she and a friend were ushered into a small, lofty salon, where they found the old man sitting by a large wood fire, in a straight-backed armchair, with both his small hands partially hidden by lace ruffles, and the duchess standing behind the chair: 'He was muffled in yards and yards of soft, snowy white muslin, on which his small well-made chin rested . . . his hair was as white as the muslin, very fluffy, slightly powdered and divided down the middle.'

Talleyrand turned to the duchess and exclaimed: 'How wonderfully this young girl reminds me of my first love – she was an actress.' What the duchess was supposed to make of this flattering remark directed at the obscure English girl is not recorded: she herself was the long-standing mistress of her uncle (not as incestuous as it sounds: she was married to his nephew and was not a blood relation).

The *salonnières* often compared themselves to musicians or artists, skilled in creating harmony among their distinguished guests from all walks of life. They saw themselves as moderators of intelligent conversation rather than mere hostesses. They were highly assertive, and this point was noted by English visitors to France. 'Woman is Queen in France,' proclaimed Bulwer-Lytton in 1834, and Mrs Trollope declared Paris to be 'le paradis des femmes'.[8] Two decades later, George Eliot wrote a risqué article about the salons, suggesting that as they brought together clever women and men of genius, they fostered 'that marriage of minds which alone can blend all the hues of thought and feeling in one lovely rainbow of promise for the harvest of human happiness'. Readers of the *Westminster Review* who knew of the author's cohabitation with George Henry Lewes, a married man, saw the article as a none-too-coded defence of scandalous French morals.[9] It was part of the dangerous fascination of Paris for the English, who were not used to seeing women take so prominent a role in social life.

If the dominant institution in French high society was the salon, in England it was the gentlemen's club, where men could gather together to eat, drink, smoke cigars, read newspapers and play billiards, or simply doze off in deep leather armchairs, waking (as Henry James observed much later in the century) to find 'amiable flunkies in knee breeches presenting them the divinest salvers of tea and toast',[10] all without the distraction of female company. The 1820s and 1830s saw the opening in the west end of London of such famous clubs as the Athenaeum (1824); the Garrick (1831) and the Reform (in 1836). The Jockey Club, founded in Paris in 1833, was directly modelled on the English institution of that name. This raffish establishment was frequented by rich and aristocratic men who wanted to escape the high-falutin' conversations of the salons, and their intimidating hostesses. They could gossip about horses or *grisettes*, and smoke cigars without giving offence.

It is an irony that one or two of the most fêted society hostesses in the Paris of the 1830s were Englishwomen. Mary Clarke, the daughter of an Anglo-Irish builder who had come to social prominence through her association with Mme Récamier, held a famous salon on Friday nights, attended by Chateaubriand, Prosper Mérimée and Victor Hugo (and on one occasion by the visiting Florence Nightingale).[11] More important for Gertrude and her family was Lady Granville, the chatelaine of the British Embassy for most of the decade.[12] The daughter of the fifth duke of Devonshire, and wife of Lord Granville, the salon she presided over at the embassy was if anything more chic than French high society. When she and her husband had undertaken their first tour of duty in Paris in the 1820s, she had been intimidated by the insolence of the French ladies, describing them as 'profligate heartless hardened and false to a degree that makes one shudder'.[13] Together with Madame Appony, the wife of an earlier Austrian ambassador, she used to shed 'real hot tears . . . [over the] impenetrable coldness and rudeness of the French'. But now she was socially supreme, and Gertrude's aristocratic French friends like Mlle St-Aubyn were desperate to receive an invitation to a ball at the British Embassy. 'There was nothing on the face of the earth that she would not give me if I could manage to get her an invitation.'[14] Gertrude's father regularly attended the Friday night soirées at the embassy, and as she grew older, he took her along. (Later, when he fell out of favour, she took *him* along.) She would have entered the ballroom on his arm, before her a sea of diamonded necks and stomachers, gold-embroidered epaulettes and amply padded chests ablaze with orders. Wearing a smart new dress in the latest fashion, perhaps with her hair *en coque* (high on one side of the head over a tall comb and with falling ringlets) and a touch of rouge applied to her cheeks, Gertrude would have impressed the old generals and marchionesses with the quality of her French and captivated the visiting English with her repartee. Her dancing lessons certainly proved their worth. At one of Lady Granville's parties, she was the only girl at the ball who could dance the mazurka with Count Esterhazy, the Austrian statesman.

There was more to Lady Granville's salons than dancing: they had an undertone of moral seriousness and religious piety that anticipated the coming of the Victorian age on the other side of the Channel. In England, this was the decade of the Oxford Movement, when educated Englishmen (and women such as Florence Nightingale) experienced the attractions of revitalised religion. Some of this fervour was transmitted to the embassy, and in later life, Lady Granville became known for her piety while her daughter Lady Georgina Fullerton (1810–85), a successful novelist, was a prominent convert to Catholicism. Although Gertrude's religious experience was not intense, she attended the English church in Paris and became a sincere believer. That much is evident in the New Year's resolution she wrote for herself in her late teens, when she pleads for spiritual strength. 'May I be more kind, gentle, resigned and forgetful of myself . . . May I be better, and should I have no reward on earth, God will surely recompense the good in heaven . . .'

What kind of picture can we paint of her as a young woman, her childhood behind her, her future uncertain? Having come late to formal schooling, she spoke flawless French and passable Italian, and was well read in the classics of European literature. Cut off from the little that girls of her age and class were learning at home, she had more than made up for what she had missed. She had met many historic figures, and witnessed momentous events. She was pretty and vivacious, with penetrating blue eyes, red-brown hair and a creamy complexion, her sociable temperament more than adequately stimulated by all that Paris had to offer. At home, meanwhile, Gertrude was at the centre of a bustling household. In one of the earliest letters preserved in the archive, we see a touching picture of the domestic life of the Collier family in Paris (the letter is dated 6 August, 1837, when Gertrude is away in England). Gertrude, now 17 years old, has been ill and her mother and sisters rally round. 'How odd it seems going to bed without you and [how] wretched the organ [which played outside the apartment in the Champs-Elysées] makes one [feel],' writes Henrietta. 'I miss you very much we all wish you were here,' adds Adeline. Clem, who is only eight years old, scribbles a note in a childish hand. The seven-year-old Clarence is too busy to write, but sends his affectionate good wishes. They tell her that her pet bird is being properly looked after and they ask after their brother George (by now a fledgling naval officer), whom Gertrude is set to meet for the first time in many years. Her mother pens her own chatty, affectionate note, literally on top of the children's writing.

For all the apparent gaiety of her social life, and the warmth and good humour of the family scene, Gertrude would look back on this stage of her life with sadness, even bitterness. She was now of marriageable age, and she would eternally resent her parents' machinations to get her off their hands and into the arms of a suitable, that is to say an English, husband.

CHAPTER 8

THE MARRIAGE MARKET

One has to have some sympathy for the Collier parents: they had four girls, all of whom had to be propelled into matrimony without the benefits of fortune or a title, and three sons who could be launched into their careers only at considerable expense. In the late 1830s, by which time Gertrude was coming to the end of her teens, the Colliers decided to introduce their eldest daughter to English society. In Paris, she was meeting Frenchmen by the score, many of them titled and wealthy, but the xenophobic Colliers could not countenance their eldest daughter marrying anyone but a compatriot. And while many raffish Englishmen passed through Paris, they were not suitable, either. 'Englishmen do not come to Paris to marry,' observes a character in a contemporary novel. 'They come to amuse themselves – opera-dancers and ball-room flirtations – and every girl here they consider fair game.'[1] A romantic dalliance was one thing, but no Englishman would commit the folly of actually *marrying* a penniless English girl in Paris.

Gertrude was sent back to England for the first time in the summer of 1837, a matter of weeks after Queen Victoria came to the throne (she succeeded on the death of William IV on 20 June), leaving her mother and siblings in France and accompanying her father on a visit to his niece Julia Augusta Pitney Martin, daughter of George's elder and heroic brother Admiral Frank or Francis Collier. Unlike the Colliers, the Pitney Martins were exceedingly rich and divided their time between their town house in Charles Street, just off Berkeley Square in Mayfair, and a country home in Hampshire.[2] One senses that that this was a reconnaissance visit for the Captain to assess Gertrude's chances in the London marriage market, and who better to ask than a wealthy family connection? It was not the best time for Gertrude to meet actual suitors, however, as she was in London out of season and fashionable families had dispersed to the country or to the continent on holiday. The visit lasted six to eight weeks and all we know about it from Gertrude's perspective is the note she confided to her diary twelve years later: she had a 'wretched time of it'.

Some time after Gertrude's return to Paris, no closer to finding a spouse, her father introduced her to Elizabeth, Lady Aldborough, an aged Irish peeress who enjoyed a mixed reputation in European society. One of the first people Lady Aldborough wanted to introduce to Gertrude was 'an Irishman of extraordinary talents, famous they say in former days for putting young ladies to sleep, and taking improper advantage of it . . .' With these kinds of friends, it is difficult to see how the countess could have been considered a good influence on the young Gertrude, but one suspects that Gertrude's moral well-being was not a paramount consideration when her father decided to foster the association. Born around 1755, Lady Aldborough had married John Stratford, third earl of Aldborough, in 1777, but she subsequently deserted him, and lived the rest of her life travelling between homes in Brighton, Dublin and Paris. When, aged around 70, she was asked by a French customs officer whether she was really 25 years old, as stated on her passport, she replied: 'Monsieur, you are the first Frenchman who ever questioned what a lady says about her age.' No one knew her exact age, but she must have been in her early eighties when she befriended Gertrude, and she soldiered rudely on into her ninetieth year. 'Lady Aldborough's language was plain and unvarnished,' recollected the normally unshockable Captain Gronow, 'and many hardened men of the world have been known to blush and look aghast when this free-spoken old lady has attacked them at her dinner table.'[3] Wearing clothes that were considered thirty years out of date, Lady Aldborough still enjoyed a certain social cachet in Paris, if not in London (where she had been excluded from court by Queen Adelaide, wife of King William IV). Gronow leaves a most unflattering portrait: 'Her features were regular in outline, but somewhat sharp,' he wrote, 'and the expression of her countenance was stern, hard and restless. Her voice . . . [was] harsh and loud [and] her manner was abrupt and unequal. Her wit . . . fluctuated between levity and sarcasm.'

There is a robust, unstuffy charm to her witticisms, however and one can see how she managed to amuse as well as offend. On hearing that the princesse de Léon had been burned to death, for example, and learning that the Prince had been more of a brother than a husband, Lady

Aldborough had exclaimed: 'What, a virgin as well as a martyr, really that's too much.' In her distant youth, she had taken an obscure officer by the name of Lieutenant Wellesley to a ball at Dublin Castle; bored with his company, she abandoned the future duke of Wellington, leaving him to make his own way back to barracks with the fiddlers who had played at the ball. Years later, when she encountered the duke in Paris after Waterloo, she apologised: 'I never thought when I left you to travel with the fiddlers, that you would come to play first fiddle yourself.' In Paris, she was invited regularly to the Tuileries where she went up to King Louis-Philippe after a failed assassination attempt. 'Sire, I congratulate you,' she said, poking the unfortunate monarch in the belly, 'I see you have been under ordeals of both fire and water.' (The reference to water was an allusion to a chronic stomach complaint.) The diarist Charles Greville recorded that at a dinner party in London in 1830 she rushed up to Marshal Marmont, the general who had tried in vain to hold Paris for Charles X, and exclaimed: 'Ah, mon cher Maréchal, embrassez moi.'[4] At which Greville tartly observed: 'And so after escaping the cannon's mouth at Paris, he was obliged to face Lady Aldboro's mouth.'

The Captain had somehow fallen out of favour with Lady Granville – the correspondence preserved in the attic alludes darkly to enemies that were agitating against the interests of the Collier family – and he enlisted Lady Aldborough's support to get back on good terms with the embassy.[5] 'It is evident to me that Lady Granville thinks of Mama as on the sick list,' the countess wrote. 'I am so glad my interference has brought about that attention to your family which never ought to have been wanting.' 'I hope, and shall be curious to hear, if Lord or Lady Granville make an apology for their late neglect,' she wrote a few days later. Gertrude became her confidante and companion, the recipient of endless detailed briefings on the old lady's ailments. 'My cold is very, very bad, I wish you would come and beguile the tedious hours of solitude,' the old lady implored. *La grippe* would keep her in her bed at her Place Vendôme apartment for days at a time, worsted socks the only proven relief for her cramps. It was not all so dismal: she issued numerous invitations to balls and *soirées dansantes*, scribbling peremptory instructions for Gertrude to be ready, dressed in her finest toilette, to attend a ball or simply to accompany her on a ride through the Bois de Boulogne. The old lady would send the barouche, and whisk her young friend off with her to visit princesses, duchesses and the *crème de la crème* of expatriate society.

'I think dear Gertrude your shape would be improved by making yourself less voluminous in the bust,' she wrote to her young protégée, ever free with her advice. 'The present size takes from the youthful appearance. I know you never take amiss any little hint, or opinion I take the liberty of giving you on this subject . . .' Wear a turban for the dance, the old lady commands, it will suit you. 'You can come with me on Thursday morning to see Lady Hamilton and thank her for her attention.' 'I hope you are not coming out in flounces and furbelows,' she went on. 'Your own simple style is so much to be preferred.' She told Gertrude she had heard of a young English lady who had celebrated her impending marriage by ordering the handsomest chariot that money could buy. 'All this to prove the liberality of the future,' Lady Aldborough observed. 'I wish a ditto bill of fare for you.' Perhaps she intrigued with Gertrude's father to find her a husband; she certainly expressed her hopes that the young girl's friendship with a much older, and married, French aristocrat would one day lead to a felicitous match. 'I give you my dear Gertrude brilliant prospects of being Madame le Préfet de la Seine,' she observed of the comte de Rambuteau, a family friend of the Colliers. 'For if the old fat lady [the countess] were to slip her wind I think it appears you have a good chance of the succession. He is a very amorous old man and like to take warmly to a pretty young girl.'

As Prefect of the Seine, the *Département* which included Paris, Claude Philibert Barthelot, comte de Rambuteau, was one of the most distinguished men in Orléanist France. He was an aristocrat of sinuous political talents who survived the Revolution as a child, grew up to serve Napoleon, returned to the Royalist cause after the Emperor was deposed, and reverted to Napoleon during the Hundred Days between his return from Elba and the Battle of Waterloo. After this ill-advised move, the count felt compelled to absent himself from the court, retiring to the country to cultivate his garden (quite literally – he planted tens of thousands of trees on his estate in Burgundy). In 1826, he judged the time was right for a return to political life and he was elected to the Chamber of Deputies, where he deftly aligned himself against the extreme conservatives who supported Charles X, thus endearing him to the future King of the French, Louis-Philippe. He was rewarded in 1833 with the Prefecture of the Seine (a job nearly equal in stature to that of a government minister), where he was charged with improving public hygiene in the light of the severe cholera epidemic of the previous year. A precursor of Baron Haussmann, he carved wide, modern roads through what was still a pestiferous, medieval city centre; one of which cuts its way from Les Halles to the rue des Francs-Bourgeois in the Marais and bears his name to this day.

There is no doubt that the count took a lively interest in the young Gertrude: at least a hundred letters from him to her survive. Barely decipherable, the letters provide unexceptional accounts of his daily routine. However anodyne the content, however, his lavishing so much attention on an unmarried young English girl from a relatively obscure family suggests that there was something to Lady Aldborough's theory. In the event, Gertrude's friendship with this distinguished Frenchman outlasted her close association with Lady Aldborough, as at some point late in 1840 she decided to make the break with her patroness. Gertrude liked parties and balls, and must have been quite taken by the old lady, too – for all her coarseness and love of social intrigue, Lady Aldborough was tender-hearted and good-humoured, qualities that would have endeared her to her protégée. But Gertrude bridled at being constantly at the old lady's beck and call, and besides, she was a serious-minded person, quite religious by this stage, and found it too much to devote herself morning, noon and night to frivolous socialising. Gertrude began her revolt by turning down invitations to fashionable events – unforgivable and shocking behaviour, in the eyes of Lady Aldborough. ('I will not urge you to act against your feelings, dear Gertrude,' frets the countess, 'but I am persuaded that Lady Granville expects to see you at her ball, and I have only heard of two persons [ever] having refused invitations.') Gertrude was obliged to take more extreme action. She wrote to break off relations, pleading that since she was obliged to look after the education of her younger brothers, she could no longer accept the countess's many invitations. 'I may have misconstrued your note,' the countess wrote back, plainly hurt. 'Am I to understand, not only [that] you decline all future association (as far as I am concerned) with society in general, but that you give up with one stroke of the pen all friendly intercourse, which subsisted between us?' Gertrude had worked out for herself that the influence of this lady was not wholesome, even if the association continued to be encouraged by her parents. Eventually, Lady Aldborough transferred her attentions to Henrietta, presenting her with a necklace that would long be a source of rancour between the two sisters.

In the spring of 1841, Gertrude was sent once again to stay with the Pitney Martins in England. She was 21 years old and might by now have been expected to enjoy the London season and the company of her older cousin. Yet, years later, she wrote in her diary: 'had a miserable, wretched time of it, tossed about [from one set of relations] to another'. Gertrude gave no further details, but a hint as to the underlying motive for the visit is contained in an undated letter from her mother:

[in England] you are more likely to make more advantageous acquaintances than here . . . if you mix only with French Princes and Princesses, I see no good in them, nor in such English as were here last winter. [If you come back] you know pretty nearly what your life here will be, with the addition of a few balls, a few more operas and few more dinners . . .

Harriet urges her daughter to stay in England under the wing of Lady Aldborough, going so far as to offer advice on how to rebuild relations with the old lady and to warn of the dire consequences of rejecting her hospitality, especially when Captain Collier has invested so much time ingratiating himself with her ('your father as usual saying yes, yes, to everything she says'). In another letter, her mother is still more direct: 'Do not imagine, my dear girl, that you are wanted here, much as we love you . . . you cannot possibly do yourself or others good here. At least where you are you have a chance – and what is for your advantage is for theirs' (i.e. that of her brothers and sisters).

If this maternal indifference sounds callous, it was no more than a statement of the facts. Earlier in the summer Henrietta had been taken ill with a mysterious affliction of the spine, a debilitating illness that started when she got her feet wet after dancing, developed into what her mother called a 'low nervous fever', and by now caused her great pain and rendered her an invalid. While Gertrude was away in London, given a chance to experience the delights of fashionable English society, the rest of the Collier family were plunged into a crisis as they had to look after the immobilised Henrietta and deal with a succession of doctors and quack cures, all to no avail. A pitiful letter to Gertrude from Henrietta herself explains how she was forced to eat a special diet of fresh eggs mixed with calomel, a laxative. ('I can only walk from my bed to the sofa,' the ailing sister wrote in spindly, child-like lettering.) She was treated by the painful, nightly application of blisters to her back. Her mother felt that Gertrude would get in the way if she returned to Paris, a sentiment echoed by her sister Adeline in another, more forceful letter. We know very little about Adeline, but here for an instant a no-nonsense personality emerges from oblivion, writing in a bold, purposeful hand, telling Gertrude in forthright terms to stop burdening the family with her complaints:

Your letter arrived this morning [Sunday, 23 May 1841] [Henrietta] joyfully opened it but put it down with very different feelings. How can you dear Gertrude write to her who is ill such melancholy letters. Your

letter was one that would have [disappointed] a person in perfect health
. . . receiving such a melancholy account from one of the persons she
loves best in the world does her no good. She used to indulge in all kinds
of happy illusions and it is a pity to destroy them all. . .

Adeline urges her sister to write a charming, superficial letter about the
little adventures of the day, about what she was wearing, who she met and
where she went, but not to add to Henrietta's troubles by telling her about
how little success she was having in her search for a husband. Only this
morning, Adeline recounts, she was combing Henrietta's hair when the
invalid looked at her reflection in the mirror and said plaintively: 'If
nothing lucky happens to Gertrude then what will it be for us?' Adeline,
having castigated her elder sister for her self-pity, now offers a few
consoling words: 'besides, how is it possible for you to know what will and
will not happen? Happier things may be in store for you than you may
know of . . . you must take the world as you find it.'

    How Gertrude responded, we do not know. But at some point she
decided enough was enough. She went back to Paris under the escort of
her elder brother George. 'Returned to Paris, had a miserable winter,' she
wrote of this time, many years later.

CHAPTER 9

PHANTOMS OF TROUVILLE

The next summer the extended Collier family – all of the six children based in Paris and their parents, together with Aunt Georgina and her son Hamilton – left the capital as usual for a long holiday. Their destination was Trouville, then a remote fishing village in Normandy on the estuary of the River Touques. Later in the century, Trouville and nearby Deauville were developed into full-scale resorts that became popular with the haute bourgeoisie of the Second Empire. In 1842, however, there were none of the pompous villas, hotels and casinos that line the sea-front and give the place an air of grandeur even today, nor the elegant and fully clothed Parisian tourists promenading and picnicking on the sands, as captured in the paintings of Eugène Boudin. As Gustave Flaubert described it in *Mémoires d'un fou*, it was an unspoilt village of around one thousand inhabitants, a huddle of black, grey, red and white hovels, piled higgledy-piggledy on top of one another, facing every direction like a heap of shells and pebbles thrown up along the shore by the waves, the motley collection of houses blossoming 'like a flower garden in colourful disarray'.

The main attraction for holiday-makers was the silver-grey, sandy beach, which stretches for a mile and a half beneath a backdrop of steep, rocky cliffs and sharply rising hills. In those days, there was just one restaurant in the port and a handful of fishermen's cottages and villas on the cliff-tops. It was a primitive and isolated location for the gregarious Collier family, and the fact that they went there in preference to Dieppe or Boulogne, where they would have been assured of some sophisticated expatriate company, indicates how worried they were about Henrietta.

She was showing no signs of recovery from her still undiagnosed illness and they needed somewhere where she could sit out in the open air, undisturbed by the crowds they would find at more fashionable resorts. While she was confined to her bed, or carried out into the open air on a couch, the rest of the children could run wild on the beach, without much in the way of supervision from the parents. The scene was thus set for an unexpectedly momentous summer holiday. Instead of meeting no one at all at this sequestered spot, Gertrude and her invalid sister both met and fell in love with a future literary genius, namely Gustave Flaubert – at the time a confused and dreamy but spectacularly handsome law student more than a decade away from public recognition for *Madame Bovary*, the first of his great novels. Flaubert spent the summer toying with the affections of each of the sisters in turn, and while he might have given both the impression that he was head over heels in love, his mind was elsewhere: he was writing a pornographic and partly autobiographical novel about a prostitute working in a high-class Parisian bordello. The triangular relationship between the two very proper English sisters and the debauched French drop-out was encouraged by Flaubert's younger sister Caroline, who was hoping in vain that her brother would settle down with one or other of the respectable English girls. Gertrude's parents also gave their tacit blessing to the liaison: under the mistaken impression that Gustave Flaubert was a gentleman, they relaxed the rules requiring their daughters to be accompanied by a chaperon.

'We were very young, accident threw us much together,' Gertrude wrote decades later, but of course, at the age of 22, Gertrude was not so very young, nor was she 'on the verge of womanhood', as she later claimed: she was a young woman of marriageable age, prey to deep emotions and hungry for the sort of intellectual stimulation that Gustave Flaubert was well qualified to provide. She tried to cover up the intensity of her feelings for Flaubert throughout her many years of married and widowed respectability. The other characters in this tangled holiday romance were also at a much less innocent age than one might suspect from reading Gertrude's various sanitised accounts of the summer: Henrietta was 19, while Flaubert was 20 and his sister Caroline was 18. Gertrude's cousin Hamilton Aïdé, then 16, developed a teenage infatuation with Caroline Flaubert, but was too young to be taken seriously by this beautiful and accomplished young French girl.

Flaubert is now acknowledged as one of the great writers of the nineteenth century, his reputation founded on four novels, a handful of stories and fragments, a compendium of clichés, and his voluminous correspondence. Every detail of his life and work has been analysed by scholars who regard even the most trivial incident, and the most inconsequential jotting, as charged with an almost supernatural significance. Such reverence is justified, for Flaubert can be said to have invented the modern novel, setting the standard for heroic, painstaking dedication to his art, spending hours if not days over his efforts to produce the perfectly crafted sentence ('May I die like a dog rather than hasten the ripening of a sentence by a single second,' he wrote.) More than this, his correspondence demonstrates a compelling personality, by turns funny, crude and lyrical, warm-hearted with his friends, contrasting with the chilly, impersonal style of his fiction. In the summer of 1842, however, there was little to suggest that he was a genius in the making. Under pressure from his father, a distinguished surgeon, he was going through the motions of entering a respectable profession. In early July, he had moved from the family home in Rouen to Paris intending to mug up for his first law exams. He quickly became lonely, homesick, profoundly bored with his studies, and prey to all manner of temptations. He rose at four in the morning and read pages of Homer or Tacitus in preference to the unremittingly turgid *Code civil*. He tried to turn his mind to his studies, but his thoughts would wander, as he smoked a cigarette and watched the sun rise over the rooftops. He would day-dream about women – ever since he had been deflowered by his mother's chambermaid at the age of 16, he had been enthusiastic in his pursuit of carnal adventures. He spent his evenings drinking with his childhood friend Ernest Chevalier, who had taken a mistress and moved to the *louche* Latin Quarter. And he visited brothels, useful field research for the story he would finish later that summer. (As Benjamin Bart, Flaubert's distinguished biographer explained, it was a good time to be a dissolute young man in Paris: 'In the 1840s the *jeunesse dorée*, or gilded youth, of the Bourgeois Monarchy under Louis-Philippe joined with the prostitutes created by the Industrial Revolution to establish in Paris some of the most lascivious haunts this capital of gaiety has ever known.'[1])

To alleviate his homesickness, Flaubert and his sister exchanged letters almost daily: they are intimate, playful, teasing and full of mutual love and affection. 'My dear Gus,' is Caroline's endearing address to her brother; he writes to his 'little rat' or 'dearest Carolo' in reply. Throughout the summer of 1842, the letters went backwards and forwards from Trouville to Paris. In mid-July, Flaubert was intrigued to read Caroline's impressions of the Colliers:

We have got to know an English family that is living in the house with green shutters . . . They consist of four girls, one of whom is ill, I think, with an ailment of the spine; she comes and sits every day in the park [outside our house] and stays there for hours at a time. We offered her a couch and some cushions and this is how we got to know them. The second girl [Gertrude] is very pretty, speaks perfect French and adores [the French actress] Mme Rachel and knows the whole of Shakespeare by heart. You would like her a lot. The two others are quite nice, they hardly say anything, and they walk along the sea-shore from five in the morning until ten at night. Their father is an old captain in the English Royal Navy, who would perhaps be interesting to listen to, if he didn't stutter so much, even in English.[2]

There is a tone of *espièglerie*, or gentle waspishness, in Caroline's description of the family, and the gallant Captain would have been dismayed at being described as a stuttering old man (he was only 52, after all). But Gertrude comes out well under the French girl's mildly sardonic gaze: she is seen to be intelligent, well read, beautiful and passionate, very different from the kind of women Gustave Flaubert was used to consorting with. Caroline's letter seems designed to pique Gustave's interest in these attractive English girls, one a little older than he, the other a little younger, distracting him from the dreariness of his studies, before she turns to other subjects, for example the difficulty of practising the piano on an instrument where half the notes are broken or out of tune.

Gertrude was deeply impressed by Caroline. The French girl was exceedingly beautiful, so beautiful that the Captain said she could almost be English: the ultimate compliment from this ultra-patriot. Gertrude agreed with this assessment: 'She was of an English type of beauty. She was so fair, and had that exquisite and very rare charm of the colour in her face coming or going with every emotion of pain or pleasure.' The French preferred to say she had a fresh Norman beauty: high cheekbones and a well-structured face, large, bright blue-green eyes and blond hair curled in fringes over the front of her face. According to her brother she was 'a spectacle made to give great pleasure to the eye'. Gertrude was used to mixing on formal terms with members of the Parisian high aristocracy in salons and ballrooms, but Caroline was bourgeoise like herself. (Despite her mother's aristocratic background, Gertrude was closer to Caroline Flaubert in terms of social class than to the members of the *haute noblesse* she knew in Paris.) But how different in so many ways! If Gertrude felt herself neglected and uneducated, Caroline was cherished and pampered in the bosom of a close and civilised family. Gertrude had had to fight to go to school, while Dr Flaubert made sure that his own daughter had the best that money could buy. She spoke fluent Italian and English. Her piano teacher was himself a pupil of Chopin (who lived in Paris from 1831 until his death in 1849), and she was taught painting by Charles Mozin, an acknowledged master who had his atelier at the top of the cliffs just outside the entrance to Trouville harbour. They took painting lessons together and after overcoming Caroline's initial *froideur*, the two became firm friends.

A few weeks after Caroline's letter, it was time at last for Gustave to rejoin his family. Certain he had failed his law exams, he took the public carriage to Pont l'Evêque, a village ten miles from the coast, and in the small hours of the morning walked alone through the deserted lanes to Trouville. The moon shone brightly as he trudged gaily along, dressed in a cloth jacket and carrying a white walking stick. He was sweating despite the chilly night air. His heart lifted as he approached the coast and caught the first scent of the sea in the air. It was a place full of childhood memories: here as a child Gustave had ridden on a donkey with his sister, and gone for long walks along the beach or along the cliff-tops to nearby Hénnequeville. When he was older, he had explored the streets of Trouville, strolling along the pebbled road that led through the village, staring at the half-naked children and the fishermen working at their nets, waiting excitedly for the twice-weekly arrival of the fishing fleet.

Trouville had already been the scene of one of the more significant romantic encounters of his life. In 1836, as an impressionable 14-year-old, he had rescued a black-and-red striped *pélisse* that was about to be overrun by the rising tide. The owner of the shawl was Elisa Schlésinger, a married woman twelve years older than Flaubert, and she came up to him later that day to thank him. The boy became drunk with infatuation at the sight of her dark eyes and the downy hair on her arms. A glimpse of a bare breast would ensure that he remained obsessed with this woman for much of his life. (She became the model for Mme Arnoux in *Education sentimentale*, the older woman all the more alluring for being unattainable.) There had been other holiday romances, some of which were decidedly less chaste than the early infatuation with Mme Schlésinger, and they exerted so powerful an influence on him that many years later, his mistress Louise Colet lashed out at his preoccupation with the various women he had met on the beach; sometimes, she complained, these ethereal 'Phantoms of Trouville' were more real to him than a living, breathing, passionate creature such as herself.

Walking on the beach one day, Gertrude and Caroline caught sight of Gustave in the distance. Ever since his arrival, he had taken pains to be elusive and to avoid his sister and the English family staying nearby: he stalked about the beach with his black Newfoundland dog Néo, treating everyone else with what Gertrude called 'magnificent disdain'. He spent most of his time wallowing in the waves with his dog or pacing up and down the beach dressed like a fishermen from the village: he wore a red woollen shirt, dark blue woollen trousers, a dark blue scarf tied around his waist, and a slouching hat on his head. Catching sight of the girls, he immediately turned his back and headed off in another direction. Caroline apologised for Gustave, saying: 'My brother is very wild'.

A few days later, Gertrude was again walking down the beach, this time with her little brother Herbert, who was amusing himself throwing pebbles into the sea. A stone must have hit Gustave's dog, for the maddened creature came rushing out of the frothy waves and ran towards Gertrude, barking ferociously and whisking about in circles. In a scene charged with Freudian imagery, Gertrude staggered back; her straw hat was carried off by the wind, and she was covered from head to foot by spray from the sea. Gustave ran out from the waves, called off the dog, apologised for its behaviour – and rescued the hat. As he emerged half naked from the waves, Gertrude acknowledged to herself that she had never before seen a more beautiful man. (Although it was still entirely normal for men to swim naked in both England and France at this time, Flaubert was probably wearing the newly fashionable striped flannel bathing shorts.) He was tall, slight, and elastic in his movements – with the most faultless limbs. 'He had the great charm of the utter unconsciousness of his own physical and mental beauty, and [was] perfectly indifferent to all forms and ceremonies,' she recalled decades later, still under the spell of this arresting first impression.

From that moment, Gustave no longer avoided the English family, but he was hardly a model of courtesy. He treated Gertrude's mother and aunt with perfect indifference, laughed at her father's French, and outraged the older generation by calling Gertrude by her Christian name. He ridiculed the Colliers' observance of Sunday, teasing Gertrude when she put on her bonnet to go to church: 'You call that proof of religious sentiment – do you really think the good God cares what kind of hat you're wearing?'

He was the archetype of the romantically self-absorbed creative artist, contemptuous of the norms of society and quite ignorant of the world and its ways. Gertrude did not appreciate the irony that Gustave's posturing was underwritten by a thoroughly bourgeois background: his father made a fortune by buying up land and holiday homes on the Normandy coast, and it was the income from this property portfolio which ensured that Gustave could dedicate his life to his writing. The difference in outlook was not an obstacle to friendship with the English girl; it rather stimulated a flirtatious badinage in which Gertrude would express her horror at the pointlessness of Gustave's existence, goading him in return to utter still more provocative imprecations against the middle classes:

> I used to think his life purposeless, and [told] him so – he would then with infinite fun and drollery describe all the various small, vulgar, *épicier* bourgeois lives which he declared I admired. He would say he wanted nothing but to look at the blue sky – green waves and yellow sand – I talked to him of possible celebrity and great influence as to what I should prize ... he listened, smiled, and seemed supremely indifferent. He admired what was beautiful in nature, art and literature – and would live for it, but quite out of himself – he did not think of gaining anything for himself – it was quite sufficient for him that a thing was true and beautiful ...

They found common ground in their mutual obsession with Victor Hugo, the master whose heavily rhythmic verses had the same intoxicating effect on French youth as Byron on the English. As summer gave way to autumn, Gustave and Gertrude, together with Caroline, sat out on the sands from dawn to dusk, reading and reciting Hugo's plays and poetry, acting them out and raving about Hugo. The first work Gustave read aloud was *Hernani*, followed by the famous preface to *Cromwell*. Gertrude thrilled to the poetry of the former but did not understand the subtle arguments of the latter; still, she was entranced by the sound of his voice.

> It was a rare pleasure to hear French as he read it – nothing ever came up to it except for the reading of [certain actors] of the *Comédie Française* ... Gustave was conscious of the gift and liked to exercise it – and many were the beautiful things he read to us – indeed he made poor poetry sound grand and harmonious by the understanding [and] the passion, the feeling he threw into it ...

In these *lectures*, Gustave tried hard to transmit his own enthusiasms into the hearts and minds of his sister and her English friend, to educate them to understand his views. She remembered his central doctrine as follows:

Style for him was everything – and *la forme* was of supreme importance, and never to be lost sight of. It was the beginning of the end. Nothing could be beautiful and harmonious without order and form – and that was style. All ideas however grand – were nothing without style. And no thought could be beautiful unless beautifully expressed.

It is the kernel of the doctrine to which he would devote his life.[3]

* * *

Meanwhile, Gertrude tried to persuade Gustave to take an interest in English poetry. He knew a little Byron, and had read some Shakespeare in translation, but that was all. This irked Gertrude, who was as passionate about English literature as Flaubert was about the great French or classical writers. Also, Caroline spoke fluent English, and while she would enter into all her brother's wild vagaries and admiration for the literature of the ancient world, she seemed to have no influence on his reading. Gertrude decided that it would be good for Flaubert to become acquainted with more works of English literature: 'it would have been of inestimable benefit to him mentally and would have enlarged his horizons'. She proposed to read to him – and to translate as she went along – Coleridge's poem 'Christabel'. She began thus:

Tis the middle of the night by the castle clock,
And the owls have awakened the crowing cock;
Tu—whit! Tu—whoo!!

Flaubert listened intently for a while, before bursting into a fit of Rabelaisian laughter. 'But you don't understand a word of this yourself,' he said. 'This story of Christabel, it's meaningless!'

Gertrude was mortified, and secretly acknowledged that he was right: she didn't understand Coleridge's mysterious poem. When she didn't see Gustave for the next few days, she was worried that she had deeply offended him, and asked Caroline what was the matter with her brother. Caroline told her that at home in Rouen he often disappeared to his room for long periods without seeing anybody. This was considered quite natural and permissible, and during these absences he read and wrote.

Gustave did not talk about the story he was working on, a fantasy novella entitled *Novembre*. It is, as a recent biographer describes it, 'a vividly inconclusive first person singular poem of sexual initiation.'[4] This piece of

Flaubertian juvenilia had literary influences – chiefly Théophile Gautier's *Mademoiselle de Maupin* and Chateaubriand's *René* – but was also grounded in Gustave's own sexual experiences in Parisian bordellos and in the arms of a certain Eulalie Foucaud de Lenglade, the 35-year-old daughter of a hotel manager who had seduced him when on holiday in Marseilles two summers before. Eulalie is supposed to be the model for Marie, the prostitute in the story whose passion surprises the adolescent Flaubert figure into the realisation that he can inspire sexual desire as well as feel it; but Marie was also modelled on Flaubert himself. 'She had Flaubert's erotic desires, his morbid curiosity about sex, his need to find the infinite fully realised in his passions – and his irritation and disgust when the universe refused to oblige.'[5] This was an early example of Flaubert's talent for projecting his own experiences into the life of a female character. The most celebrated example of this gender transposition would be Emma Bovary herself. Years later, Flaubert declared: 'Madame Bovary, c'est moi.'

Gustave also found ways to conduct further research for the story in a brothel near Trouville, where he overindulged to the extent that he could no longer perform. He wrote an anxious letter to his companion in debauchery Alfred le Poittevin who told him there were many possible causes for his temporary impotence and he should not be alarmed. The images of depravity contained in the story are counterbalanced by passages describing the memory of boyhood days at Trouville: the boy walks across the fields at sunrise; he lies in the corn, listening to the sound of the waves below, and in the intervals between the waves he hears the call of the quails. In the end, the narrator dies, revolted at the idea of pursuing a conventional bourgeois existence. The story tells us a great deal about the evolution of Flaubert's literary talent, but reflects only indirectly on the events of the summer. It seeks to dramatise the competing claims of innocence and experience. On the deserted sands of Trouville, the Collier girls were transparently innocent. There was a tremendous gap in experience between Gustave and his new English friends, and indeed between brother and sister. It was normal for such double standards to apply: it was part of the romantic artist's education to steep himself in depravity, while the girls had to be content with the chaste pleasures of listening to Gustave reading passionate poetry.

* * *

One hot night, the windows were left open in Henrietta's bedroom and the sea breeze blew the muslin curtains into the lighted candle. Within moments, the curtain was ablaze, and with the flames threatening to engulf the bone-dry timber of the house, the bedridden Henrietta was in danger. The Flauberts saw the flames from their windows, and father and son ran across to offer their assistance. Gertrude was woken by the cry of 'Fire!' and the smell of smoke and went out of her room to find Gustave carrying Henrietta down the rickety stairs to safety, wrapped in a blanket. He had gone directly to the upper room from which the flames were issuing; on the way down, he instructed Gertrude to go back up the stairs and shut the bedroom door to stop the draught fanning the fire. By the time she had closed the door and come downstairs, fishermen from the village had arrived and the fire was soon put out. Dr Flaubert expressed his concern that the shock of the emergency might have seriously affected Henrietta, and he insisted that she be carried to their house for closer observation. She stayed there overnight.

In due course, the Colliers decided to place Henrietta under Dr Flaubert's medical care, but the incident had the immediate effect of intensifying the relationships between the youngsters. Gertrude and Caroline became constant companions, seeing each other almost hourly. Gertrude deepened her intimacy with Gustave, while Gustave himself made friends with Henrietta. Alone of the four characters involved in this innocent drama, Henrietta left no records of the summer of 1842, but it is not going too far to suggest that she admired Gustave Flaubert, if not for his theories on art and life, for his good looks and heroic action in saving her life. All the girls adored Gustave Flaubert, and he and the two English girls adored Caroline. But which of the two English girls did Gustave adore in return?

In later life, Gertrude wrote several different accounts of the summer. In one of them, a lightly fictionalised story about a love affair between an English girl called Nelly and a Flaubertian figure she calls César, Gertrude relates the incident in full: but says that the person rescued from the top floor bedroom was her mother, not Henrietta.[6] Gertrude clearly resented the attention that Henrietta's status as an invalid brought the younger sister, and one can detect an unmistakable note of jealousy, as if she is writing Henrietta out of the story as a way of taking belated revenge for the hold the beautiful invalid had on the young Frenchman. Elsewhere, Gertrude is dismissive of her sister's illness. 'My sister was supposed to have something wrong with her spine,' she wrote, a remark that would be downright cruel but for the benefit of more than forty years of hindsight, during which time it became clear that there was nothing fundamentally wrong with Henrietta's constitution: she grew up, married a Scottish baronet, produced an heir and several children and lived almost as long as Gertrude herself (she died in 1909 at the age of 86). As Gertrude tells it, she and Gustave were on the same intellectual wavelength, but perhaps Gustave preferred the quieter girl, the one nearer his own age, who would lie passively on the sofa, a coat of ermine over her legs to keep her warm, as he read aloud from the romantic poets?

For evidence of the true state of Flaubert's feelings, we need to look to fragments of another work of juvenilia. Buried deep within his literary archive at Rouen, are two manuscript pages on which he tried, without success, to write a short story about an artistic young man (who wears a fine lace shirt beneath his coarse, peasant's jacket) who is sitting by a windswept coast when he notices a beautiful girl. There is no attempt to conceal the real-life object of his feelings and the name on the manuscript is unequivocally that of Henriette. Feeling the inappropriateness of so direct a betrayal of his emotions, Flaubert leaves a note to himself that he must change the name of the heroine. He never did, and he never returned to the story. But unlike many of his more intimate papers, these pages were not destroyed. [7] Gustave finished *Novembre* at Trouville on 25 October, 1842; shortly afterwards, Gertrude returned with him and his family to Rouen, together with the invalid Henrietta and their mother.

CHAPTER 10

AT HOME WITH THE FLAUBERTS

Henrietta had been treated by many doctors during the three years that she had been ill. First, there was Dr Richard Verity, attached to the British Embassy, who prescribed bleedings and cataplasms; then there was his nephew Dr Robert Verity, whose ministrations succeeded in turning a low fever into a spinal complaint; then Dr Rue, who recommended cautery, a technique whereby a branding-iron was applied to the unfortunate patient's flesh (hence the blisters in the letters to Gertrude). Dr Rue also prescribed the holiday in Trouville, but the fresh air did her no good. 'The pain being severe and augmenting at Trouville where she passed the summer', she was then, as we have seen, put in the care of Dr Flaubert. He insisted that she return with him to Rouen, where she and her sister would become daily visitors to the Hôtel-Dieu, the imposing neo-classical complex of public buildings in the centre of Rouen which had been a prison, barracks and a warehouse before becoming the municipal hospital and home to the Flaubert family.

Dr Flaubert was medical director for the City of Rouen – the presiding professional deity – and it was in these forbidding buildings that Flaubert had grown up. Biographers tend to stress Flaubert's delight in watching his father dissecting corpses in the operating theatre (prompting acidulous comments on the scalpel-like quality of his prose – as when Flaubert wrote to a friend in 1837: 'the loveliest of women is not very lovely on a dissecting table, with her intestines on her nose, one leg skinned and half a cigar lying on her foot')[1] or viewing the lunatics in the public asylum (hence his fascination with the grotesque in human behaviour, it is argued). But to counter the ghoulish aspects of his upbringing, there is the picture of the little boy, hand in hand with his sister, exploring the seemingly endless sequence of courtyards, cellars, attics and gardens, or of the gregarious youth staging plays, scripted and acted out by himself, on the billiards table, in front of admiring members of his family.

Gertrude tells us that she, together with her mother and sister (there is no mention of the other children – perhaps they went back to Paris with the Captain and Aunt Georgina?), spent 'several months' in Rouen, staying at the Grand Hotel. This is an exaggeration: they went there in late October and were back in Paris for a medical consultation on 4 December. 'I found it very dreary being shut up all day with my mother and sister,' she recalled, 'and . . . I was always welcome at the Flauberts' . . .' She leaves a poignant account of a tight-knit family whose rudely frank manners and mutual affection contrasted so sharply with the emotionally buttoned-up environment in which she had grown up. Gertrude took particular delight in joining the family for *déjeuner*, taking tremendous pleasure in telling Gustave's father all about the outlandish habits of the English. The family had an English nanny, but she was on holiday in England, so there was no one to contradict her, and she delighted in startling father and son into loud discussions:

> what surprised me was the noise, loudness and want of courtesy with which they carried on their conversation, particularly Gustave [who] lost all measure, and thus missed his mark . . . his voice seemed to drown every other voice, he looked at this passing scene with such passionate earnestness, that he threw into it his voice, and manners and into every- thing he said and did! He never repressed any feeling, and this side of his existence was so much to him, that he was carried out of himself, when really interested, and was wanting in dignity and calm – at least from an English point of view!

The family treated her as one of their own, and talked over their joys and sorrows and gossiped unreservedly about their friends. They talked a great deal about Dr Jules Cloquet, a physician friend of their father's who they were all hoping would come from Paris to pay them a visit, and 'many little references to his tastes and habits were unconsciously dropped by them in my presence'. (Cloquet became a close friend of Gustave and would have a vertiginous professional career, culminating in his ennoble- ment and his appointment as personal physician to Emperor Louis- Napoleon.) This allowed Gertrude to play a practical joke on her hosts. She had assured Gustave that she had a gift for deducing the character of any man or woman simply by studying their handwriting. Over lunch one day, Dr Flaubert decided to put her to the test, producing a letter from his pocket which he declared gave him infinite pleasure. Gertrude knew that the post had just arrived from Paris that morning and worked out that the letter must have come from Dr Cloquet, announcing his intention to visit. As Gertrude recounts:

> On that conjecture I launched out – I astonished them all by my admirable analysis of their friend's character, all the facts and details they themselves had unconsciously furnished me. This – followed on by two or three other lucky hits – firmly established in their minds my extraordinary gifts.

Gustave talked so much about his college friends Le Poittevin and D'Arcey that she had no difficulty in describing the character of these correspondents. One day he gave her another script and asked her 'with feverish earnestness' to give the character of the writer. Having no clues, and concerned not to damage her reputation,

> I paused and paused and Gustave got more and more noisy and impatient – suddenly it struck me it might be his own writing – and it was – and acting on the thought – I described him as I knew him to be – and delicately balancing admiration and blame and pretending to shew by the writing the curious deficiencies in his character I made père Flaubert, and all the family believe in my gift!

Gertrude makes no reference to her sister's sufferings, but we know that while she was enjoying herself, Henrietta was subjected to a peculiarly unpleasant treatment called 'setons', whereby the flesh was cut open and a thread drawn through the skin in order to maintain an opening for discharges. According to her medical records, the wounds were 'kept open until their inutility became too evident'. On 4 December, Dr Flaubert convened a conference in Paris of 'Drs Brachy, d'Angers, Clocky [*sic* – evidently Dr Cloquet] and Amusot'.[2] Dr Flaubert thus joined the long line of physicians who were unable to find a cure for poor Henrietta.

When the visit came to an end, Gustave gave Gertrude a large box of Rouen cakes called *mirlitons*, and a beautiful Newfoundland puppy, which Gertrude named Néo after Gustave's own dog. The puppy lived with the Colliers for a short period of time in their apartment, where it constantly annoyed Gertrude's mother and sisters by peeing in the sitting-room, and ran uncontrollably up and down the Champs-Elysées, before Mrs Collier insisted that the creature be given up to the safe keeping of the comte de Rambuteau, her distinguished friend who possessed a country estate where the dog would be more at home.

In the memoir she wrote for Caroline's daughter many years later, Gertrude suggests that the intimate friendship with the Flaubert family, and with Gustave in particular, ended soon after they returned to Paris: he to resume his studies, she to her busy round of social engagements:

> When Gustave came to Paris to study his *droit* – we saw less of him – I was growing into womanhood – and his eccentricities were more notice-able – in the drawing room in Paris – than on the plage of Trouville – he ridiculed all the conventionalities of fashionable life – *les plaisirs sans bonheur si pleins d'un vide immense* – pleasures without happiness, filled with an immense emptiness – he never attempted to take part and ridiculed me for doing so . . .

She conflates the events of the next four years into one paragraph:

> A joyful letter came one day announcing [Caroline] was to be married – but I felt she would never be on the same intimate footing with me again. Then another letter came announcing the birth of her daughter [the future Mme Commanville]. Then, soon after, too soon alas! A letter announcing her death – Gustave I saw only at long intervals – but the affection was too deep, too sincere for time – or circumstances – or death – or anything that can happen in this sad world – in any way to affect it.

Poignant though this is, it is also disingenuous: Gustave saw a great deal of Gertrude and Henrietta when they were all in Paris, and his affection for the girls went deeper than one might suspect from this account. Shortly afterwards, he considered marrying one or other of these English girls – the first and only time in his life he thought about taking a wife.

Gustave returned to Paris in early November 1842, and quickly found his own apartment in the rue de l'Est, on the south bank. (The street was demolished when the Boulevard Saint-Michel was constructed during the Second Empire.) He was preparing to retake his exams at the end of December. His windows looked out over the greenhouses and nurseries of the Luxembourg Gardens. Gustave began once again to write to his sister, and the reprise of this correspondence shows us just how important the Colliers were to him at this time. On 12 November, just days after he moved into his apartment, he wrote that he had been a guest at the Colliers' in the Champs-Elysées. They received him with 'perfect politeness' and great affection: little Herbert jumped on to his shoulders with 'great transports of joy'. (Elsewhere, he tells us that Herbert had become so fond of him that he called him *papa*.) He notes that the Colliers' residence was better than he had expected: in fact, the English family seemed to be quite well off (*cossu*); they must have come across as rather shabby in Trouville. A few days later, on the 16th, he explains that he is already in the habit of crossing the river once a week to visit the Colliers; he noted that Henrietta was still confined to a couch ('she never gets up; they have to bring her meals to her').[3] On one occasion at least, Captain Collier and Herbert had made the journey in the other direction to see him. Gustave was out, and the Captain had left a visiting card with the portentous words 'Captain of a Vessel in her Britannic Majesty's Navy'. Collier still laid great store by his rank, even if it was now twenty years since he had commanded a ship.

The chatty letters to his sister contain the usual student's complaints: he was suffering toothache and other ailments – doing too much boring work – smoking too many pipes – he had too little money — he was dining in seedy restaurants on tough beef and bitter wine tempered with water. He was missing Caroline dreadfully; he told her he could hear her gentle laugh in his ears, and 'would jump to his feet to go over to the mirror and make the faces he used to make for her'. His visits home were slightly alarming: he would run up the wide curving staircase of the Hôtel-Dieu to the family apartments on the first floor, and would shout for joy, hugging them all with 'reckless exuberance'. His clumsy kisses were so 'rough and noisy' that his mother had to pull her children apart. He did not tell Caroline that he was also in love with one or other of the Collier sisters, but he wrote to Le Poittevin later in November (in a letter that is now lost), speaking darkly of his loneliness and his desire to get married. His friend wrote back that he had never supposed Gustave incapable of falling in love, and 'time alone would tell what the outcome would be'.[4]

As his exam approached, he restricted his visits to the Colliers to once a week. In his letter dated 21 December, he describes how on one such visit he said farewell to Captain Collier and Herbert (who were about to set off to England) and found the girls 'toutes dans les arts' (all engaged in the arts).[5] They had painted a portrait of Henrietta (to send to her elder brother in England) and were going to paint one of Henrietta and Gertrude together. Adeline was modelling in putty and Gertrude was painting a picture of the cook. The girls suggested that he had his own portrait painted, so it could be sent to Caroline. 'At the mention of the word portrait . . . I came out in a cold sweat like 100 Articles of the Code Civile,' he notes. They had to banish the dog from the apartment because it had again been peeing in the living-room.

This laconic account gives no hint of the emotional turmoil he described to Le Poittevin. But he continued to see a great deal of the Collier girls when he returned to Paris in the New Year, and there are various sources to help us reconstruct the events of the next few months: the letters Gustave wrote to his sister; letters written very much after the event to Louise Colet and to Henrietta; some letters from Gertrude to Gustave, rediscovered in a Paris library by Jean Bruneau, the great Flaubert scholar, in the 1980s and even Gertrude's own lightly fictionalised account of their relationship (entitled 'Written by Request' this is to be found in the attic with Gertrude's other papers).[6] There are also two unknown and hitherto unpublished letters from Flaubert to Gertrude dating back to 1843–44. In the first of these, Gustave writes briskly that he would be delighted to attend Gertrude's party, if the Captain and Henrietta's back allowed it, as it would be an excellent distraction from the tedious work of preparing for his exams. To say that a visit to the Rond-Point would be a way of countering the boredom of his studies is not a romantic statement: it is a letter from a friend, not an impassioned lover.

To his sister, he maintains the tone of mild irony, particularly at the expense of Captain Collier. After one visit in early March, the Captain has flu and is wearing some enormous leather boots – Flaubert comments that the squeaking of the boots harmonised perfectly with the terrible noise of his unintelligible voice. 'That completes the picture!' he writes, before describing how Gertrude is leading a giddy social life. 'She only goes out for balls – it is a duty for her not to miss a single one.'[7] A few days later he writes again, drawing a contrast between Henrietta (who 'was wearing a large pink dress which made her look more pretty and gracious') and Gertrude. Henrietta is described approvingly as being 'always the same and even tempered', while Gertrude is more excitable: 'she always has some news to tell you'. On the day of this particular visit, Gertrude is desolate at the death of the duc d'Orléans, prompting some wry remarks about the staunch royalism of the Collier family compared to the almost republican indifference of the Flauberts. He quickly moves on to other subjects, including the forthcoming publication of a new play by Victor Hugo. '*Les Burgraves* hasn't appeared yet. I'll bring it to you as soon as it does . . .'[8]

The writings of Victor Hugo brought Gertrude and Flaubert together on the beach of Trouville, but in Paris *Les Burgraves* drove them asunder.

As Gertrude tells the story, Gustave one afternoon insisted on reading the preface to this now-forgotten play:

> In [the preface] Hugo displays the most wearying and pompous learning
> . . . and it is all so tiresome and bombastic that I begged Gustave would
> pass on the *Burgraves*. He would not – so I determined to be as disagree-
> able as possible – opened and shut the door – opened the window –
> coughed – Gustave bore it all quietly for some time, at last the blood
> rushed up into his face – his eyes flashed – for 'abused patience becomes
> fury' – the proverb says – and stamping he shrieked out 'comme vous
> m'impatientez' – 'how you try my patience' – tossed back his hair which
> he wore very long, closed the book with a loud clap and left us all
> flabbergasted.

As she confesses in her novella, she was 'always trying to contradict' Flaubert, a form of coquetry designed to grab his attention. But there was a special sensitivity about *Les Burgraves* (a play set in the Rhineland of the Middle Ages which failed to repeat the success of *Hernani* when it was put on at the Théatre Français on 7 March) and she gives several different accounts of the argument the reading inspired. In none does she mention her sister, but Henrietta seems to have listened more receptively to Gustave's readings, and this must have rankled, especially when it becomes clear that Caroline was gently intriguing to bring Gustave together with Henrietta. In a letter dated 30 March, Caroline tells her brother that she has received a plaintive note from Henrietta, whose condition was getting worse as the year progressed:

> She only wrote a few lines, and in the few lines she talked to me about
> you, she is hoping that you will have the kindness to read *Les Burgraves* to
> her, and I am sure that you will have this kindness, because how can one
> refuse anything to Henrietta, when she says to you: 'You are so good!' It
> seems that I can hear her saying these words again now . . .

Caroline thus encouraged Gustave to read Hugo's poetry to Henrietta, and this he certainly did. He spent many long hours reading *Les Burgraves* and other romantic stories such as Chateaubriand's *René* and *Atala* as she lay motionless and no doubt entranced on the sofa. 'How I wish we could once more be at the Rond-Point,' Flaubert wrote to Henrietta many years later, in November 1851, by which time he had lost touch with Gertrude. 'How I would love to see you! And what a good afternoon we would spend together, you lying on the sofa, near the window, your head on the pink cushion, and me sitting on a chair at your side.'

Gertrude wasn't present when Gustave was reading to her sister, but she too was playing a role in what Gustave mockingly referred to as a 'comedy of love'. At the beginning of April, she wrote a letter to Gustave wishing him well on his journey home to Rouen:

> I wish you *bon voyage*. This is the grocer's way of speaking, as if the journey from Paris to Rouen really counted as a voyage. Be sure to say a thousand affectionate things to Caroline the beautiful and good xxxxxxx ... Henrietta, Mother, Papa, Clem and Ad send you a thousand friendly greetings.[9]

As Professor Bruneau notes with academic scrupulousness, the seven 'x's' are to be interpreted as kisses, and whether they were directed at Gustave or at his sister, he is surely right to detect that the tone of the letter was 'un peu flirt'. In May, when Gustave was back in Paris, Caroline tells him that it has become a standing joke among his friends that he has been spending so much time in the company of the Collier girls.

At this point Flaubert was remembered by contemporaries as looking like a Gallic chieftain of long ago: strikingly good-looking, with long flowing hair and a heavy, golden blond beard, large, sea-green eyes, and exaggerated gestures and uproarious laughter. Gertrude made it her mission to civilise him by inviting him to a tea party at the Champs-Elysées. Caroline tells Gustave that she has received a letter from Gertrude in which she told her all about the tea party: it was a stupid evening, but she boasted of *having imposed a role on Gustave*.[10] This has been taken by Flaubert's biographers to mean that Gertrude forced Gustave to behave as if he was her suitor; but there is a more innocent explanation: she twisted his arm so that he would observe for once the hated *convenances de société*, and make an effort to be civil to the other girls at the party by praising them for their *toilettes* and their singing. 'You see my dear friend,' writes Caroline, 'despite your desire to pass yourself off as churlish, Gertrude is giving you a reputation on the contrary of being gallant and amiable.'

As spring turned to summer, Henrietta's condition worsened (Gertrude wrote several letters to Flaubert asking him to arrange urgent appointments with Dr Cloquet) and the Collier family removed to Chaillot, a village on the other side of the Bois de Boulogne. Of necessity, they saw less of Gustave, who had in any case discovered new friends – chief among them the rakish Baron Maxime du Camp – who encouraged him to indulge his taste for booze and bordellos. He was also seeing the Schlesinger family, thereby renewing his chaste passion for Mme Schlesinger and gathering raw material for what would become *L'Education sentimentale* (he had already started writing the first version of this novel). He had little money (a begging letter prompted a reprimand from his stern father), was smoking forty pipes a day, but drinking and eating enough to start putting on weight. He was working towards the next stage of his exams, and in the confident expectation that he would pass, his family arranged to come and see him in Paris. In mid-August Gertrude wrote from Chaillot to Gustave asking him on her mother's behalf to come to the opera (where the Collier family had the use of Count Rambuteau's box). The stage was set for a reunion of the two families, and perhaps for a romantic encounter with Gertrude.

Later, she wrote in her novella how her heart beat when she learned that the Hébert-alias-Flaubert family was invited to dine at their Champs-Elysées apartment, before she and her father accompanied César-Gustave and Marguerite-Caroline to the opera:

> My toilette arrived in time, it was snowy white, and faultless! So clinging and yet so vapoury! The Héberts arrived very early, I heard Marguerite's voice, pushed open the . . . door and rushed out with my dress half on, half off. 'Oh Nellie, comme tu est belle!' was Marguerite's first exclamation.
>
> César walked straight up to me, holding out both his hands, into which I put both mine, and looked up into his eyes, he looked down into mine and neither of us spoke! 'Inaltérable affection' was written there!

The words 'inaltérable affection' seem hyberbolic, but they are not a fantasy. In her story, Gertrude states that Gustave gave her his treasured copy of Montaigne's *Essais*, with the dedication: 'en souvenir d'un inaltérable affection' – in remembrance of an inalterable affection – inscribed in it. We know that Flaubert did indeed give this cherished book to Gertrude, with an identical inscription, when she left Paris for good (which was not until 1846). Later in life, he used a similar form of words to her when he presented copies of *Madame Bovary*, *Salammbô* and *Trois Contes* to her. The words speak of a deep emotional attachment that goes beyond the boundaries of mere flirtation. Gertrude would seem to be conflating the later parting with the momentous visit to the opera.

> The carriage was announced, he offered my mother his arm, and we departed . . . my heart was very full, and I was deeply grieved at the thought of leaving France tomorrow – so this was my last day . . . [sitting in the box listening to Spohr's *Faust*] I was sorrowful beyond words! I felt as if something was passing away out of reach – was it my youth passing away? Was it my happiness? I thought of a song Marguerite used to sing – 'c'est l'amour qui est passé!!!!'

The manuscript has three crossed-out versions of what happened at the end of the opera. This is the one Gertrude was happy with:

> I slowly rose from my seat – the box was empty – and turned to César to ask him for my cloak. He looked like a person in a dream, I walked towards him, and again asked him to unhook my cloak – he started, roused himself mechanically, wrapped my cloak around me, then in a moment I found myself passionately folded in his arms, his head bent down to mine, which he kissed rapturously, I felt his heart beating, but I dared not speak or move, till he released me! So ended my first evening of what is called – Pleasure!

Two days later, the fictional Nellie is obliged to leave for London, where her grief at the parting is tempered by the thought that she would never have been happy marrying a heathen like Flaubert. We know that when the Colliers paid a visit to the Flauberts at their hotel during this visit, Gertrude was intending to present Caroline with an engraving of the head of Jesus Christ, prompting a sharp response from old Dr Flaubert: 'Vous croyez donc au crucifixe?' As she told Caroline's daughter many years later:

> I understood [the Doctor] to mean 'you believe in that impostor?' – though he certainly did not use these words – I murmured oui Monsieur, fearing I know not what. I rolled up and hid my engraving and never shewed it to Caroline – I feared too that she might disbelieve.
> This incident, trifling as it was, had a very extraordinary effect on my intimacy with the Flauberts – I felt that to renounce my ideal, my hopes of a future life, my belief in Christ, would be to me so terrible a loss – no

love, no friendship could make up for it, and I secretly feared their silent influence over me – I am sure Gustave never thought about it – but I did – and I wondered he did not . . .

This is the voice of the pious High Victorian widow reflecting on events that took place decades before. We have to ask ourselves: so what actually happened in Paris in the summer of 1843? So much of her novella is indeed fantasy that the embrace at the opera could theoretically be no more than a form of retrospective wish-fulfilment – or a form of revenge on her sister, who was certainly the recipient of Flaubert's amorous advances. I tend to think, with the distinguished Professor Bruneau, that the kiss did indeed take place. The depth of feeling that Gertrude shows in her memoirs – and that was to come to the surface at intervals in her remaining years in Paris – together with the tone of Flaubert's letters in later years, suggest that the 21-year-old law student was romantically attached to *both* sisters. But he was a man who was already demonstrating what Julian Barnes has called 'kaleidoscopic shifts of temperament' in his life as he would later in his novels. This part of the story is not yet complete, but my judgement is that the young Gertrude was more important to Flaubert as a young man than has hitherto been acknowledged. Certainly, Flaubert was more important to Gertrude than *she* ever directly acknowledged. In a later diary, her comments on the two years are perfunctory:

> 1842 – went with poor Henriette to Trouville in Calvados, was joined there by Mrs. Aïdé and Hamilton
> 1843 – spent the summer in a large house in Chaillot

* * *

The late summer of 1843 marked a turning point for Gustave. Predictably, he failed his exams. Whether because of that, or because of the night at the opera with Gertrude, or simply because he was sated with debauchery, he took a vow of chastity, which he was to honour until after the death of his father and sister three years later. He returned to his studies; the Colliers are mentioned less and less in the letters to Caroline. In December, he notes that he caught a glimpse of Gertrude at the studio of James Pradier, the sculptor, and that she departed the moment she saw him enter the salon. (He was left with the consolation prize of meeting Victor Hugo in the flesh for the first time.)[11] When Gertrude wrote towards the end of the year asking Gustave to join the family for Christmas dinner, there is a note of polite cordiality which suggests that their relationship has moved to a different footing. However, the second hitherto unpublished letter from Flaubert to Gertrude (and Henrietta) betrays the incoherence of true feeling:

> I am really angry that you doubt me and that the friendship you have for me has been shaken not by my negligence but by the appearance of my negligence. I believed myself to be too deeply rooted in your esteem and I like to think that Miss Gertrude's practical spirit has exaggerated a sentiment that perhaps in reality she doesn't really feel. At the time that you cursed me I was in an extremely pitiable state with bad nerves and a congestion of the brain which is subject to many remedies which I am continuing to endure . . . thus I am not ready dear girls to start once again my visits to the Champs-Elysées – I would love to prolong indefinitely the [hours at the Rond-Point] the declamation, exaltation, inspiration and a thousand other beautiful things are formally forbidden to me. I am obliged to live a calm bourgeois life like a grocer or a notary. I am sorry that I have not been able for so long to read the verse of the poets who ravish you and which you understand so well . . . We'll talk about it one day when I'm in Paris, in the full expectation that I wish everything that you desire.
>
> Adieu
> Your friend Gustave Flaubert
> A thousand affectionate respects to Mrs and Mr Collier

Gertrude has evidently rebuked him sternly for not keeping in touch, and the wounded tone of the response suggests that he acknowledges the justice of her criticism. The letter is undated but the reference to his ill health puts it in early 1844. A few days after his Christmas dinner with the Colliers – at which he read from *Hernani* – he suffered an epileptic fit that marked the beginning of a long period of serious illness. His father was so concerned about his son's health that he was allowed to give up his legal studies once and for all. From this point on, Flaubert retired to Normandy, and that summer his parents bought the country house on the bank of the River Seine at Croisset where, but for intervals of travel, he was to spend the best part of his life.

* * *

In March 1845, Gustave returned to Paris for the second time since he had fallen ill and abandoned his legal studies. It was only three years since he had first come to the city, he wrote later, but it felt as though a century had gone by: it was as if he were going back up the stream of his past like a man struggling against a torrent. Catching up with his old friends, he paid a visit to the Colliers at the Rond-Point of the Champs-Elysées, where Henrietta was still lying on a sofa with the same smile and voice, the girls still seemed keen to listen to his readings of *René* and *Hernani*, and outside the window an organ-grinder was playing in the street, just like in the old days. Although little seemed changed in the Collier household, the circle of friends who had met on the beach at Trouville had drifted apart in the intervening years. Gustave was ill and no longer lived in Paris. A still more radical transformation had befallen his beautiful and accomplished sister: she had got married! Much to Gustave's chagrin, he had inadvertently brought her together with Emile Hamard, a fellow law student, who had been given the task of carrying Gustave and Caroline's letters backwards and forwards from Paris to Rouen. Emile and Caroline fell in love and married on 3 March, 1845, an event which of necessity meant the end of Gustave's especial intimacy with his sister. Days after the visit to the Colliers, he and his parents, together with the newly married Hamards, set off for the south of France and Italy. For Gustave, it was awkward to accompany Caroline on her honeymoon, and he wrote many letters to Le Poittevin saying that he had given up all idea of love. He consecrates himself to art and condemns the bourgeois and *épicier* institution of marriage.

On his return, however, there was a reprise of his flirtation with the Collier sisters. He visited the girls three times a week, writing later that he saw them on Sundays, Tuesdays and Wednesdays. 'How wonderful is the story of these visits!' he wrote. 'I saw there the chink in the armoury of my soul – just like other people's'.[12] He was, for now, recovered from his illness. He leaves a telling account of intimate moments spent with one of the sisters, in a letter written to Louise Colet in September 1846:

You wrote something very true: 'love is a great comedy, and so is life, when you're not playing one of the roles'. Only I won't concede that it makes you laugh. About a year and a half ago, I experienced a living illustration of this . . . At that time I often visited a family in which there was a charming young girl, marvellously beautiful – of a Christian, almost Gothic beauty, if I can put it that way. She was a pure spirit, easily susceptible to emotion; one moment she'd be crying, the next laughing, like sunshine after a shower. The feelings of this lovely, innocent creature were entirely at the mercy of my words. I can still see her lying against her pink cushion and looking at me, as I read, with her great blue eyes. One day we were alone, sitting on a sofa; she took my hand, twined her fingers in mine; this I let her do without thinking (most of the time I'm a great innocent), and she gave me a look which still makes me shiver. Just then her mother entered, took in everything, and smiled at what she thought was the acquisition of a son-in-law. I'll not forget that smile – the most sublime thing I've ever seen. It was a compound of indulgent benevolence and genteel vulgarity. I am sure that the pure girl had been carried away by an irresistible affectionate impulse, one of those moments of mawkish sentimentality when everything within you seems to be melting and dissolving – a voluptuous anguish that would fill you with delight if only it didn't bring you to the verge of sobs and tears. You cannot conceive the terror I felt. I returned home shattered, reproaching myself for being alive. I don't know whether I exaggerated the situation, but even though I did not love her I'd gladly have given my life to redeem that sad, loving look to which I had not responded . . .[13]

Here, Flaubert is at his most Flaubertian: wielding the scalpel of his prose to lay bare illusion and weakness. He is merciless in his description of Mrs Collier (this, after all, would have been the first of the four girls off her hands) and in his dissection of Henrietta's innocent passion. There is no record of what if anything he felt about Gertrude, although he certainly resumed his visits to the Collier household early the following year.[14] She no doubt told him the story of how one winter's evening, shortly after he had left Paris, she and her maid were on the point of crossing a bridge across the Seine when out of the shadows a gruff watchman demanded payment to let them pass. They had no money and were reduced to asking a passer-by to produce the few sous necessary to pay for the crossing. 'As I spoke the words and looked up into his face, I recognised in the dim light . . . Victor Hugo,' she wrote later. 'I exclaimed with astonishment and uncontrolled delight – Victor Hugo – as if I had known him all the days of my life and was meeting him again after a long absence.'

Gertrude would have been able to tell Gustave how she and Hugo had walked across the bridge together. 'Evening was fast closing in, and clouds were gathering, a cold wind was sweeping them along the sky – his favourite expression – a *grandeur crépusculaire* – a twilight grandeur –

came to my lips – he gave me a kindly look as a reward for the quotation – he seemed reluctant to move, lingered looking round and down at the swift flowing water of the Seine – and said in a half apologetic tone it always gave him a strange sensation of pleasure standing on a bridge . . .'

* * *

After his sister's honeymoon, Gustave returned to Croisset where he had to come to terms with the fact that Caroline was not merely married, but pregnant. On 21 February 1846, she gave birth to a little girl, also called Caroline. This should have been a joyful event in the Flaubert household, but it was overshadowed by the death of Dr Flaubert a few weeks before, and prefigured the tragic death of Caroline herself on 22 March, at the age of 21, from puerperal fever (or post-natal septicaemia as it is known today). Flaubert's descriptions of his sister's decline and death are harrowing. Gustave's so recently widowed mother was more like a crying statue than a human being, he recorded. 'Quelle maison! Quel enfer!' ('What a house! What hell!'), he wrote to Maxime du Camp.[15] He kept a vigil by her deathbed as her agonised screams gave way to murmurs of pain and finally the silence of death. In the background the baby was screaming and Emile Hamard was sobbing, speechless with grief, beginning the journey to madness. Gustave watched over his sister's body as she lay robed in her wedding dress and holding her white bouquet. He remembered their childhood games – recalled watching their father dissecting corpses – and read Montaigne's *Essais*. He re-read the lubricious letters of Eulalie Foucaud. The next morning Caroline was buried – in her wedding gown and holding a fresh bouquet – and still his sister was not free from indignity. The grave was too narrow for the coffin. The gravediggers pushed this way and that. Finally, one of them stood on the coffin at its head to force it down into the earth.

Three letters in the attic give another poignant perspective on the events of March 1846. Here is how Maxime du Camp announced to Gertrude the news that Caroline had only hours to live:

Madame

I am charged by Gustave Flaubert, my intimate friend, to give you news of his sister: her state has become worse and worse, and it is probable that in only a few hours she will cease to suffer: the last letter I received, yesterday evening, told me she hadn't more than an hour to live . . .

Your humble servant
Maxime du Camp

Caroline's death was announced in a letter from another friend, addressed simply to Madame Collier, Avenue de Champs-Elysées:

Madame Caroline Hamard died yesterday at the age of 21, she was torn from the arms of a family of whom she was the hope, and of a husband who adored her. You will understand easily that the people who are more closely touched by this terrible news are not able to have the courage to announce it to you, so it is thus in their name that I speak . . .

A few weeks later, on 3 May 1846, Caroline's widower Emile wrote in distraught terms from Croisset. The letter encloses a lock of Caroline's hair. He asks plaintively if she could return to him some of her letters from Caroline, as he has so few of his own. He says that on this very day he has learned from Gustave of Gertrude's imminent departure to England.

For Gertrude, leaving for England was a conscious act of will rather than a bowing to circumstances or parental pressure. In her diary, she wrote quite emphatically that she herself 'took the decision to leave for England'. She had given up on Gustave and on any thought of finding a husband in Paris. Caroline's death was a brutal reminder that time was moving on and that her youth was coming to an end. More cheerfully, there was at last a precedent from within the Collier household: Adeline – the strong-willed third daughter who some years before had not been afraid to voice her criticism of Gertrude – had managed to conjure a respectable marriage out of the unfavourable circumstances of the Champs-Elysées. Somehow – the records do not show how – Adeline had met an army officer serving in India, by the name of Lieutenant Gordon, and in January 1846 she set off alone on the long and arduous sea voyage to Madras to join her husband-to-be.

As Gertrude embarked on the no less momentous journey to England, she promised herself that if she could not find a suitable spouse, she would take matters into her own hands. She wanted to lead a purposeful life, to do good and to be useful to other people. Deeply affected by her close friend Caroline's death, and inspired in part by the spiritual earnestness of the times, as well as by the frustrations of her unmarried status, this vivacious woman of the world somewhat improbably vowed to herself that she would enter a convent if she could not find a husband. She even gave herself a deadline: she would take her vows unless she married within three years (by which time she would be coming up to 30 years of age). In the event, she would find a husband within a matter of weeks of returning to England. The obstacle to her happiness turned out not to be the absence of a suitor, but the objections of her parents.

CHAPTER 11

AN IMPROBABLE ROMANCE

A few days after leaving Paris, Gertrude was in England. She and her parents went first to the Isle of Wight, where they rented a house overlooking the sea in Ryde, and from there to stay with friends in London, where by chance they met their former family solicitor in Gray's Inn and blithely accepted an invitation to tea at his home in Russell Square.

Charles Tennant, now nearly 50 years old, bewhiskered and hard of hearing, was far from being a romantic figure in the mould of the wildly good-looking Gustave Flaubert. In the years since they had met at Boulogne, he had become the model of pious, middle-class and middle-aged Victorian rectitude: he was sensible, earnest, learned, inclined to be self-righteous, and at nearly twice Gertrude's age, old enough to be her father. He and Gertrude were, on the face of it, so ill suited in terms of age and temperament that the question of their being romantically interested in one another didn't occur to Gertrude's parents when they took their daughters to tea. Neither, for that matter, did Charles suspect that his own comfortable, bachelor's existence was about to be turned upside down. Tennant had never known what it was like to be in love, had never so much as kissed a woman, was exceptionally close to his mothers and sisters, and he would be flabbergasted by the intensity of the ensuing love affair.

Charles Tennant kept a detailed diary for much of his life. His normal entries for the year 1846 relate to his interminable court cases, or minor emergencies in Wales such as when a horse fell into the canal or the docks flooded after a severe tide. All of a sudden, following a flirtation over tea and cakes, there is a different, urgent tone: he is a man pierced by Cupid's arrow. Shortly after the tea party, he followed the Colliers down to the Isle of Wight, taking the train from Charing Cross at 10 a.m. on Sunday, 4 July, and arriving in Ryde at 5 p.m. The next night, he: 'dined with Captain and Mrs Collier and family at their lodgings, and there met my Gertrude after an absence of many years'.

'At Ryde, could not get away, ought to be in London, Gertrude's fault,' he scribbled the next day in his diary, the brevity of the entry concealing the immensity of the emotional storm ahead.

On Wednesday the 7th, he went for a long walk with Gertrude on the seafront. No doubt Gertrude's parents remembered Charles's avuncular interest in their eldest daughter from the holiday in Boulogne, and thought there was no need for a chaperon. This was a miscalculation: as they walked along, Charles and Gertrude argued, and then fell in love. They talked about the past – her life in Paris, their holiday together in Boulogne – and then the conversation turned to the future. Gertrude said she intended to pack herself off to a nunnery. Charles declared that he was horrified. She replied that her resolve was made, and that no earthly power could turn her from this intention. 'She saw no other prospect of directing her life to any useful purpose,' he recalled later. Charles decided that in no circumstances could this noble-hearted girl cast herself away and 'wander through the rest of her life, a downcast, wretched creature, wrapped up a blanket, or a white dressing gown!' It dawned on him that it was his mission to rescue her from this folly. He argued with her in his pedantic, lawyerly fashion:

I did not agree with all she said, but even then I loved [he wrote to his sister a few weeks later]. I even chided some of her thoughts and views as serious errors, until I brought a tear to her bright full eye, but for all these errors, I loved her not the less, but every moment more and more, and before my first visit was terminated, the void in my desolate heart was filled, and with true, devoted and eternal love was overflowing. I have never from the first, felt a moment's hesitation, doubt or misgiving, and this is what I never could imagine possible with me! Though I never before knew what this love was, but in idea, yet now I know it to be a pure and holy love, for I feel as if . . . my soul were already united to another.

He dined again that evening with the Colliers. The evening 'held an attraction before unknown'. Still, Captain Collier and his wife had no inkling of Tennant's intentions; still, he had not asked Gertrude to marry him.

On Thursday, he returned to London, without having asked the question. 'Ah, how desolate,' he wrote that evening, wondering how he would ever bring matters to a head. On Friday night, he wrote the following letter, which babbles with the bewilderment of first love as experienced by a 50-year-old bachelor:

> I ought to commence with a thousand apologies for troubling you so soon with a letter, but, really, I left Ryde in such a state of confusion, or absence of mind that I seem to have forgotten everything I ought most to have remembered . . . This is the more strange to me, as nothing of the kind ever occurred to me before in all my life; – I have obtained, deservedly I hope, a pretty good character for being cool, calm and deliberate – by no means subject to absence of mind. I have a vivid recollection of parting with you at the pier-head, but for some time before and after that event my recollection is extremely indistinct; except that while cutting the bright blue waters, I felt so very little interest in anything in the direction of Gosport – and so very much in the opposite shore which was receding that, whilst I was talking to your respectable parent (about sea-faring matters, I believe) though without the least consciousness of what I was saying, I was, all the time, sensible of a very strong impulse to walk over-board, under the notion of running back, just to say to my dear Gertrude a few parting words which I had so strangely left unsaid. Why I did not walk over-board is, to me, rather a wonder than otherwise, considering my position and state of mind. But it so happened that I did not and, on landing at Gosport, I walked away without thinking of my carpet bag, and therefore very nearly lost it; and on arriving at the station, I walked away with my carpet bag in my hand, but forgot to pay, – and therefore the man very nearly lost his fare, though he at last, and at the last moment, discovered me ensconced in a corner of the railway carriage, looking with vacant eye upon his streaming face and agitated features, perfectly unconscious, and therefore wholly undismayed. Having protested my profound penitence, and having purchased my pardon with pence, I was permitted to depart in peace and, without further adventure, reached my lively home in the enlivening period of expiring twilight, and presently afterwards I was singing to my tea-pot the cheerful air 'By the Waters of Babylon we sat down and wept' – and so you see, most charming and amiable Gertrude, I am entirely in your power and at your mercy; and as I feel it quite

impossible for me to write half that I have left unsaid, I must, as soon as possible, if I can obtain your permission, and your good parents' leave, come back to tell you, if I can find the words.

The letter continues, still without getting to the point, and gives her an 'opt-out clause':

> But, dear Gertrude, the sun of worldly prosperity, as it is called, is not shining upon me, and I must just now confess to you . . . that my experience of unclouded sunshine is rather of a distant date, and though I do my best to bear my burden merrily before the world, and really am by nature joyously inclined, and much given to trifles, yet that I have, of late especially, felt my burden press upon me sorely . . . You may remember my telling you that I thought it a good rule to observe, in a case of difficulty, when you could not clearly see your way, – to stand still, until the way became more clear. – But I feel now, for the first time in my life, as if it were quite as difficult to stand still, as to move forward . . .
>
> If we should meet again, which I must hope as I hope to live; then if I may with my dear Gertrude's leave, I will try to speak more plainly to her.
>
> Meanwhile – farewell – farewell –
> My summer love, farewell!
> Yours with all affectionate regard
> Chas Tennant

Gertrude wisely interpreted this impassioned but equivocal letter as a proposal of marriage, and replied in the affirmative. On Tuesday of the following week, Charles Tennant wrote back to her in a different vein:

> July 14th
>
> My Dearest, best beloved, nearest to my soul's ideal for my wife, and far beyond my fondest hopes to find – how shall I express my thanks for your most precious letter? How shall I attempt to express what I feel so very far beyond the power of my earthy expression, my boundless and mysterious love for my beloved darling Gertrude? I call it mysterious because I cannot account for it – I know it to be a pure and holy love . . . and yet . . . I must now admit, I have not yet been able so carefully, and clearly to analyse my own thoughts, as to see precisely the why and the

wherefore I do so wonderfully, so profoundly love thee. I never felt until now the full force of that most expressive and oft quoted line

Perdition catch my soul
But I do love thee

Because I have never before in all my life, felt the slightest sentiment of earthly love, as I now know it, and because I never could bring myself to believe that I was capable of it . . .

Her answer, he confided to his diary, 'binds me to her body, soul and spirit, here and hereafter, forever. And God's blessing be upon her, now and forever, Amen.'

He sought God's blessing, but needed that of Captain and Mrs Collier. Two days later, a letter arrived at Russell Square in which Mrs Collier refused her consent to the marriage. 'Also received a short letter from Gertrude embarrassed and bewildered by the entreaties and distress of her parents and sister.'

* * *

As an experienced advocate, Charles Tennant had a high regard for his powers of persuasion, and made haste to return to Ryde so that he could plead his case in person.

'My dearest Gertrude,' he wrote to his intended on Friday,

As I can be safely absent on Sunday next from any worldly duties here, I propose to escape from here tomorrow morning, and to fling myself at your feet – not to ask anything further of you, but to pour out to you my overflowing gratitude, as far as words can express it, for your most generous and heroic confidence in me your declared and devoted lover; – and then to make all those communications to your kind and excellent parents, which they must require and ought to receive from me, before they can be expected, freely and willingly, and with no heavy misgiving, to yield up their heart's most precious treasure to my safe-keeping.

Oh, Gertrude, my beloved! Truly said I in my letter to your mother, what most truly I do feel that, the first and only question here should be your happiness . . .

In the only ground assigned by your dear mother, I must confess I do not see any ground of reason for the doubts expressed by her; nor can I

feel any doubt, my dearest Gertrude that, with your confiding love, freely
and fearlessly bestowed, our lot in life together would be a very happy
one. . . ..

Wait, dearest, until you have heard from myself the uttered words
which the heart can speak, much better than the pen can write . . .

As he was to discover at the weekend, Captain and Mrs Collier, together
with Gertrude's elder brother George and her younger sisters Henrietta
and Clemmy, were united in outrage at the impending match. This was
not because of the difference in age, which might be an affront to modern
sensibilities but was no obstacle in the mid-nineteenth century, but because
of his social standing: they felt that he simply wasn't rich or upper-class
enough marry a member of the Collier family.

Their hostility casts an interesting light on questions of class and social
standing in early Victorian England. Although Charles Tennant was a
distinguished professional gentleman, who stood to inherit large, admit-
tedly encumbered estates, he was still considered by the Colliers to be so
far beneath them in status for it to be almost an offence against nature
for him to propose to their daughter. The fact that Collier had been
professionally idle for decades – and in December 1846 would be
pensioned off as a non-working 'yellowed' admiral – was of no consequence in these socio-economic calculations. Captain and Mrs Collier
would have preferred Gertrude to run the risk of becoming an old maid
rather than marry someone who was not titled or rich. They thought
very highly of themselves. Charles found their attitude baffling:

> I am vain enough to believe that no fault is found with me [he wrote
> to Gertrude later], but with my worldly position; that there is no dislike
> of me personally; and that I may be (it is hardly correct to say that I am)
> the cause of disappointment. I am aware that no objections would
> have existed, and that all would now, at once, be removed, if only I
> possessed a much greater share of worldly riches. It is because I am so
> well aware of this that I have no hope that I shall ever be <u>sought</u> for
> by your family, and that, therefore, to bid me wait for this, is to bid me
> wait for ever . . .
>
> But very true it is I think that you would adorn the highest station,
> though what might be the grounds of your fond mother's lofty expecta-
> tions on your behalf, beyond your own high personal merits, of course, I
> do not know.

There is no record of the awkward conversation that took place on the Sunday, but he was able to persuade her parents that the only consideration should be Gertrude's happiness. Reluctantly, Captain and Mrs Collier acknowledged the force of his argument and lifted their veto, but they gave their consent with uncomfortable conditions attached. They required that the wedding should take place at some indefinite time in the future, and ruled that Charles would be 'tolerated' if he visited Gertrude in Ryde, but would not be made welcome. Mrs Collier – there was no doubt in Charles's mind that she was the author of this stratagem – thus imposed a *de facto* cooling off period in which time Gertrude's parents and siblings would try their hardest to persuade Gertrude of the folly of her choice and unite in intrigues to find her a more suitable husband.

Charles returned to London at the beginning of the following week 'happy in confirmed hope that Gertrude will stand the trial imposed on us both by her mother, and then be mine forever'. But he had no sense of when the marriage might take place, or even how often they might see each other. The scene was set for twelve frustrating months during which Charles and Gertrude became ever more certain about the depth of their love for one another, despite the persistent ill will of the rest of the Colliers. They took to pouring out their thoughts and feelings in letters that went backwards and forwards between Russell Square and Ryde two or three times a day for the entire period. The post was highly efficient in those days, and a letter written at lunchtime on one day could receive a reply less than twenty-four hours later. Although Gertrude's half of the correspondence has not survived, she kept all the hundreds of letters she received from Charles, and they paint a vivid picture of this improbable early Victorian love affair:

> . . . my Gertrude must not expect any more sane answers from me [he wrote in a long letter on 11 August], I am too far gone in the delirium of love to be any longer accountable for what I write.
>
> You are a most rare girl! And your letters are like yourself – rare, charming, piquante. What pictures you present to me in a few words! How graphic! How full of life! How true to nature! How felicitous in expression! How full of subject for reflection! And for improvement, how profitable! I mark with admiration those fine characteristics of your mind, that freshness of originality and truth which many years ago so pleased me, and have now so entirely captivated me – you realise to all my senses an object for my everlasting love.

When I think of you as my bright-minded, highly intellectual companion for life – the partner in all my fortunes, to share with me all my joys and cares, all my hopes and fears – when I think of you as the charming girl with the large bright dreamy eyes, in the full tide of life and health, who may, before long, be mine – my own for ever – whom I may clasp within my arms, hug to my heart, cover with kisses, love, and hope to be loved, for ever; – Oh! My dearest darling Gertrude – when I think of all this I am wild with delight! And this I suppose is love! For the first time in my life I have found out what it is to be in love. I who, in all my life before, have never felt for woman, other than a son's or mother's love, now feel for you a love so far surpassing even this, with all its strength, as to be like something different, and beyond compare.

* * *

Later in the year, when the Colliers returned to Paris for a short visit, the news reached Gustave Flaubert that Gertrude was to be married. He wrote a letter of farewell, in which he asks repeatedly whether he will see her again, says she is mixed up in some of the most intimate events of his life, curses the effect of time that destroys everything – like drops of water that erode the hardest marble and destroy the most solid of sentiments — may the heavens ensure that she be happy – it would be a great joy to see her again. 'How we will talk!' he declares.[1] However poignant this adieu from a man whose letters are considered to be among the great works of European literature, those from the middle-aged English solicitor were far more romantic:

'I am bewitched, you have bewitched me,' Charles wrote in January of the following year.

When I think of myself seated by your side, with my arm around your lovely waist, and my lips upon your soft warm cheek I am absolutely lost in astonishment at my own presumption! But at the same time I am fully sensible that I am not, and never can be again, the same as I was before – that I am changed, and that you have made the change, a change which I had long ceased to believe any human being could have made in me – that it is essential to me for any joy in my earthly existence that my arm should be ever around you, and that I should ever feel the warmth of your soft cheek upon my lips, that the liberties which have once been permitted should be continued . . .

On occasions, the quasi-mystical tone of his admiration gives way to expressions of more earthly desires. 'When the glorious sun shines brightest in the heavens,' he writes from Russell Square one spring evening,

> – when the green leaves are young and fresh upon the trees, and the sweetest blossoms are just bursting into flower, why am I shut out from all these joys, and left alone in solitude to feel how very joyless are even nature's charms, without the highest charms of life, where, in another's joy, we share, and find our own? . . . why shut me altogether out from my best worldly help and comfort? Why make me feel in this warm sunny time of spring, that it is but the winter still to me? Why say I shall not see the light of your bright eyes? Why keep me from the music of your voice? Why urge me on my way and yet not help me by the warm touch of your soft cheek on mine! O, my sweet lovely girl! If I must longer wait for all your charms, yet why deny me these? Why shut me out from your sweet face, the sun which warms my soul?

And, a few weeks later: 'I go on dreaming half my time both day and night – and often in the early morn I wake, believing that I hold my darling in my heart, and find my pillow only in my arms.'

Gertrude sat on the steps of the pier just outside the family house, reading these impassioned letters and others – some full of poetry, some with earnest reflections on Christian theology, others containing more mundane accounts of his professional work, still others reflecting on how many children they would have – wondering when and if they were to be united, all the while suffering the barbs of her parents and siblings. In the spring of 1847, it must have seemed as if they would never be together, as Mrs Collier imposed an outright ban on Charles coming to visit. Charles had taken on some legal work for the Captain and a squabble had ensued; and there were other complications which sowed the seeds of longer-term estrangement between Gertrude and the rest of the Collier family.

Henrietta, who it seems had also been engaged to be married in the autumn of the previous year, had been jilted, and had taken to her bed. The old symptoms returned and once again she was an invalid. Charles could not resist offering his advice: he told Mrs Collier that her daughter's condition was not one that admitted of being treated by a physician. (In modern parlance, he believed that her illness was psychosomatic, and he might well have been right: it was not abnormal for young women to offer 'passive resistance to family authority' by falling ill, or becoming excessively religious.[2]) He urged the Colliers not to spend £50 on a consultation with a fashionable West End doctor, and recommended instead his good friend Dr Cronin. This hapless professional gentleman, who had operated on Charles in an attempt to cure his deafness, was of the opinion that exercise, fresh air and a good diet would restore Henrietta's health. However sound the advice, the Colliers were reluctant to allow Dr Cronin anywhere near their daughter, and for good reason: the doctor was facing trial for murder after one of his patients died following a course of treatment. (The patient had, it seemed, misread the dosage on a prescription of prussic acid, with fatal consequences.) Charles acted on his friend's behalf, and managed to get him acquitted, but this is one instance where Charles might have been more diplomatic in pressing his own remedy to a Collier family problem. Poor Henrietta was soon subjected to another course of painful bleedings.

Charles was bemused when others could not follow his line of reasoning, even when he found it self-evidently to their advantage that they should. When, for example, he urged Gertrude's older brother George to reconsider his decision to retire from the Navy ('a retired half-pay navy lieutenant, oh miserable termination to a career so promising as his was and might have been . . . [he is] sneaking away from the active duties of his life and station, to sink into inglorious sloth') or when he exhorted the Colliers to take a house in Russell Square rather than the fashionable West End, his well-intended interventions were interpreted by his in-laws as meddlesome interference. He did manage to bring about a reconciliation between the now Admiral Collier and his elder and much more active and successful brother Frank, who was home on leave. Charles Tennant's diplomacy ensured that Admiral Sir Frank was invited to the wedding, which after more than a year of separation and vicissitudes, was at last set for 11 September.

The prospect of the imminent fulfilment of all he had so long desired made Charles jittery: in the late summer of 1847, the rhapsodic tone of his letters gave way to a morbid note as he compared the impending event to death. ('My weak senses are almost bewildered when I contemplate as a reality an event which I have always regarded as so awful and mysterious that my mind could never dwell on it as possible to be ever realised by me! I can imagine the condemned one counting away the hours. . .') Perhaps, he urges, the wedding could be postponed until the following spring, when they might visit Scotland on their honeymoon? Even days before the wedding, he was suggesting that they push the service back a week to the 18th ('tell your friends I have toothache,' he wrote).

Gertrude may have resented her mother, but she inherited her strength of character: she brooked no nonsense, and the marriage finally took place on a sunny day at the Church of St. Thomas, in the parish of Newchurch, Ryde. Here is how Gertrude recorded the event in her diary:

Changed my name this day from Gertrude Collier to Gertrude Tennant ... Charles and I spent our wedding day – which was one of glorious sunshine – though there must be something sad in a wedding day! – at the Matchams Hotel in Southampton ... we arrived in time for dinner. I had on my lilac silk pelisse and a straw bonnet – we dined, Charles and I, on some mackerel, roast chicken, French beans and an apple tart.

Marrying Charles was driven by the imperative of mutual love – but (as one well-wisher observed) it was for Gertrude a conscious decision to abandon her 'poetic existence' in Paris and settle down and become 'a good steady Englishwoman'. She had no hesitation in turning her back on the bohemian circumstances of her childhood and youth and distancing herself from her raffish parents. She adapted rapidly and happily to her new role as a thoroughly English and unashamedly (upper) middle-class wife.

CHAPTER 12

PORTRAIT OF A MARRIAGE

During more than a year of enforced separation, Charles and Gertrude had corresponded extensively, on all manner of subjects, but in reality they barely knew each other when they became man and wife. They had spent little time alone together: perhaps a stroll on the beach under the reproachful eye of Mrs Collier or a polite kiss on the cheek at the ferry as Charles made his way back to London after a weekend visit. Now, married at last, they had ample time to make up for that as they embarked on a honeymoon destined to last a leisurely four months. Their ultimate destination was Cadoxton Lodge, Charles's family home near Swansea in South Wales, but there was no hurry to get there and Charles had arranged to visit a succession of friends and relatives on the journey westwards.

After two nights in Southampton, they took the train to Dorset, where they would stay a few nights at Kingston Maurward, an imposing country house three miles from Dorchester recently acquired by Gertrude's rich cousin Julia Augusta Pitney Martin and her husband Francis. They arrived late in the afternoon and were shown straight up to a sumptuous bedroom which was perfumed with nosegays of fresh flowers. They dined alone in their host's study, the very room where Julia Augusta was in the habit of dandling the young Thomas Hardy on her knee,[1] before retiring for the evening. The next day, they walked through the grounds of the estate, watching the swans and geese on the magnificent lake and the speckled trout darting about in the chalk streams, as the visitor to what is now an agricultural college can do to this day. On the way to the nearby village of Lower Bockhampton, Charles told Gertrude about his own victories and reverses: his endless struggles over the Welsh estate; his disputes with his brothers and in-laws over the inheritance; his quarrels with the trustees of Swansea Harbour and neighbouring landowners; his battles to hold back the invasions of the sea and to build a road up to the front door of Cadoxton Lodge and render the house habitable after his father died.

As a 14-year-old girl, Gertrude had met many of Charles's relations and they had made a good impression, but much had changed over the intervening years. Charles still idolised his mother, who was now in her 79th year, and adored his sisters Margaret and Fanny, but he was barely on speaking terms with his brothers George and Henry and their respective spouses. George, his surviving younger brother, had once turned up two nights in a row at Charles's house in Russell Square and threatened him with physical violence. Henry, his elder brother, had been even more outrageous: he and his wife Ellen[2] had taken advantage of Charles's generosity and moved into the house with their children at the beginning of 1844. This was supposed to have been a temporary arrangement, but they were hard up and they had tried to force Charles out of his own home by making his domestic life a misery. They locked him out of his dining-room, denied him access to his servants and obliged him to lay in his own stock of tea and sugar. Charles retaliated by dividing the house into two, moving his brother's furniture to the drawing-room on the first floor and keeping the dining-room to himself. He eventually threw them all out, whereupon they followed Henry Collier's example and emigrated (temporarily) to France.

There would be plenty of opportunity for Gertrude to become properly acquainted with the byzantine details of the Tennant family quarrels. For now, one imagines, she listened with trepidation. None of her husband's family had attended the wedding and she was set to enjoy the dubious pleasure of meeting the clan later in the honeymoon. On the walk through the park, Gertrude told her husband more about the unusual circumstances of her upbringing in France, sparing nothing in her account of her father's ignominious flight across the Channel after he lost his fortune. There was little in these stories to change Charles's low opinion of the snobbish Collier parents and siblings. Gertrude was delighted when Charles took her side in an ancient dispute with her sister Henrietta over the gift of a valuable necklace by Lady Aldborough, Gertrude's patroness. Charles considered the facts and delivered his loyal but perhaps less than impartial judgement: the necklace should have been given to Gertrude, not her sister. Gertrude loved dear Charles all 'the more for his reflexion on this injustice, felt that he indeed had a noble soul.' She said nothing of another contest with her sister, for the affection of Gustave Flaubert, which one suspects was more deeply at the root of the sisters' lifelong estrangement. It would be many years before Gertrude and Gustave re-established contact; for now, he belonged to a chapter of her life that was firmly closed.

Overwhelmed by the unaccustomed luxury of the house, Gertrude was trying to come to terms with her new position as a married woman. She felt content and peaceful but also a touch melancholy, in keeping with the blustery autumnal weather. 'I am now seven and twenty, and married! A human being's entire happiness depends on me,' she wrote in her diary at the end of the first day at Kingston Maurward: 'the confusion and riot of the wedding is over, [and] I mean now to live in earnest, not merely to dress, be admired, fritter year after year away.' The days of aimless social-ising were past; now she could find fulfilment in dedication to her husband and to the longed-for children. It is difficult to overestimate the changes experienced by a young woman such as Gertrude in the days after marriage: she left her parents and siblings for good and threw herself on the mercy of a much older husband and his as yet unknown family. After a night in the bridal bedroom, she was earnestly hoping that she and Charles would soon have 'one of our own, to love, and be loved by.' They had already decided that if they had a daughter, she would be called Alice after Charles's paternal grandmother.

They stayed at Kingston Maurward until 27 September, before heading further west in their chariot (this had been brought down to Dorchester station on the train). They passed a night or two at Bloxworth Rectory with friends of Charles; a day in Bath where Gertrude took the waters and rode on a donkey while Charles had his hair cut, then on to Bristol, where they were unimpressed by the High Church chanting of the liturgy at the cathedral service. They spent a long day in Chepstow, and moved on to Monmouth with a quick stop at Tintern Abbey, then deeper into Wales, to Abergavenny and Merthyr Tydfil, where they stayed a few nights at Dowlais House, the home of a local ironmaster and his wife.[3] They arrived late. A dinner party was in full swing and Gertrude was obliged to rush upstairs and change for the rest of the evening's entertainment. This veteran of Lady Granville's Parisian soirées was not impressed by the provincial hospitality: she found the whole party insufferable and went to bed exhausted and hungry after eating little more than iced pineapple. The next day, they visited the nearby ironworks and Gertrude was over-whelmed by the raw physical power of the furnace: it was her first encounter with industrial Great Britain, which had so dramatically changed the character of the country in the decades Gertrude had been living in France and was the basis of the nation's wealth during the prosperous mid-century decades.

She also caught an unmarried woman who was one of the party 'deeply occupied in studying Charles'. Gertrude could only guess at the young woman's thoughts, drawing the conclusion that her new friend 'would rather belong to one like him, than to any of the empty worldlings she was surrounded by and expected to settle with'. She heaved a sigh of relief that she herself was at last out of the marriage market, and had found a sensible and serious husband.

On Tuesday, 12 October, they set out late in the morning to complete the last leg of their journey to Cadoxton. It was a beautiful day and Gertrude tried to share her husband's admiration for the verdant valleys and hills, the waterfalls, woods and rivers of the spectacular South Wales countryside, as well as the foundries and mines which were less lovely to look at but testified to the prosperity of the region and produced the goods conveyed along her husband's canal. She was, however, preoccupied with the imminent prospect of meeting her mother-in-law and a host of other new relations for the first time since that childhood summer holiday in Boulogne, hoping that she would cut a good figure in her dark blue dama-scene silk dress and her drab-coloured bonnet trimmed with lace. At three in the afternoon they reached the house and were shown straight into the music room. There Gertrude found the ageing Mrs Tennant waiting for her. The old lady was overcome with emotion and burst into tears, unable to rise from her seat. In trooped a succession of other Tennants, a multi-tude of brothers- and sisters-in-law and their children. Gertrude rushed upstairs to change into a white muslin dress; then her husband led her out on to the lawn at the front of the house where the estate workers were gathered to toast the squire and his new bride. Charles had sent ahead instructions that they should raise three cheers for the new Mrs Tennant, and a further cheer for his mother, the honoured lady of the lodge, as he called her. The men were in good spirits, as Charles had ordained that they should all receive a full day's pay for a half-day's work, but not as cheerful as they might have been, as Charles had banned fireworks and drunkenness.

We can guess at Gertrude's thoughts as she stood on the lawn in the dusk of an autumn's day in South Wales. She was flattered, no doubt, by the attentions of the men and the change of status that all this signified. Charles might not have been smart enough for her parents, but this was the first time she had experienced the deference due to a future landowner's wife. In a different vein, she was trying to get the measure of all her new relations: after what her husband had told her, how many of them could really be trusted? Could their protestations of affection be taken at face value? Raising her eyes beyond the garden and meadows in front of the house, she studied the landscape. She saw the Vale of Neath spread out before her in the twilight, encircled by a ring of low-lying hills. The tall spire of St David's Church, together with the smokestacks of numerous factories and ironworks, rose from the town of Neath, one mile to the west. Behind the house, to the north, rose the steep slopes of Mynydd March Hywel, a hill more imposing than its altitude of 1,400 feet might suggest. In this direction the country was bleak and grey, home to sheep and curlews: a landscape that she and later generations of Tennant children would come to appreciate as a wild, Brontëan wilderness.[4] On her first visit, however, she was not impressed by the house or by the boggy Welsh scenery. 'Felt a general . . . disappointment in the place,' she wrote in her diary the next day. 'Thought it dismal, dark and dreary, thought the mountains small, and the whole place wretched.'

As the nights drew in, and the weather grew wet and wintry, it was hardly the best of times to be in South Wales, but Gertrude did eventually relax in the company of her husband and his family. Charles rode out with her to inspect the lands and the canal. They visited the salient features, including the Aberdulais Aqueduct: with ten arches and 340 feet long, this was an impressive feat of engineering. There was the occasional distraction of a visit to nearby gentry, but for the most part she occupied herself in painting, sewing and making conversation with her mother-in-law, and playing with her husband's nephews and nieces. Charles and Gertrude also began the lifelong habit, common in middle-class families of this time, of reading aloud to each other in the evenings. Like tens of thousands of other couples of all social classes, they read with delight the novels of Charles Dickens as they were published in monthly parts (*Dombey and Son* would reach its conclusion early in the following year, to be followed by *David Copperfield* in 1849). From these earliest days of their marriage they read French literature to each other as well.

Gertrude and Charles spent more than three winter months at Cadoxton before leaving for London towards the end of January. Thanks to the railway, the journey eastwards was brisk when compared to their stately honeymoon in the other direction – but still far from comfortable. Leaving the house early in the afternoon on Wednesday, 26 January, they drove six hours in Mrs Tennant's carriage to reach Cardiff, where they stayed the night. The next day, they took a steamboat to Bristol and then the train to London, reaching 62 Russell Square late in the afternoon on

Thursday. It was a journey that Gertrude would make scores of times over the next six decades.

* * *

'Never mind if Russell Square be not the first chop in fashion,' Charles had urged midway through the year of separation. 'My lovely Ger has only come here to bring it into fashion.' This romantic line of argument cut no ice with the Colliers: Gertrude's parents and sisters deemed Bloomsbury a social no man's land and urged Gertrude and her husband to reside in Belgravia or Mayfair. Using the same arguments as Mrs John Knightley in Jane Austen's *Emma*, Charles tried to talk them round by urging that the air was so much fresher than in the west, where the modish streets and squares (including Belgrave Square, the grandest of them all) had been built on former swampland under the level of the Thames and were miasmal and unhealthy; or that 'dear old Number 62', as he called the house he had inherited from his father, was in a felicitous location in the south-east corner of the square, streaming with light and secluded from its neighbours by gardens and trees. [5]

If not the height of fashion, Russell Square was one of the largest residential squares in London, known for its open aspect and its fresh, breezy air. It had been laid out in grand style by Humphry Repton at the beginning of the century: tall Georgian houses on three floors overlooked the bosky delights of many acres of landscaped parkland. The hereditary owners of the area, the ducal Russell family, protected Bloomsbury from the excesses of uncontrolled development, ensuring that the squares were all laid out in a pleasing Georgian uniformity and the neighbourhood was kept free of noisome distractions such as shops and pubs (as a visitor to Birkbeck College or Senate House will note to this day). It was not too far away from the noxious rookeries of mid-Victorian London, chiefly the notorious St Giles-in-the-Fields and Seven Dials to the south, where tens of thousands of the poorest of the poor lived (as one social inspector described it) 'in all the filth attendant on improvidence, crime and profligacy'. But the stink and hubbub of 'Dickensian' London seemed a world apart from their new marital home. By virtue of its pleasant aspect and its central location, a short cab journey from the City to the east and within walking distance of Fleet Street, Chancery Lane and the Inns of Court – and not at all far from Oxford Street and Mayfair to the west, especially after the construction of New Oxford Street in 1847 – Russell Square was a congenial, practical place for busy barristers, journalists and City merchants to live. However, it was not where the socially ambitious would choose to reside and as Roy Porter puts it, the square 'did not gain aristo-cratic éclat, being solid rather than scintillating'.[6] Its association with money-making and honest professional labours made it faintly vulgar in the eyes of not just the Colliers, but also the contemporary satirist William Thackeray. It was in Russell Square that he chose to locate the homes of the Sedleys and Osbornes, the well-off but distinctly vulgar stockbrokers, in *Vanity Fair*. Although set in the latter years of the Georgian era, this popular and irreverent novel was being written and published in monthly parts during the first year of the Tennants' marriage.

'Felt strange at coming to my future home for the first time,' Gertrude wrote in her diary on her first night at No. 62. She was tired after the long journey, and bewildered at arriving at the house which would be her home for all but the last four years of her married life. Long since demolished and now the site of an unprepossessing modern hotel,[7] it was a substan-tial residence on three floors, with a splendid first-floor drawing-room extending the full length of the house, tall windows giving on to the land-scaped square at the front and the lovingly tended gardens at the rear; on the ground floor there was a richly furnished dining-room for formal entertaining, and a parlour for the family. The bedrooms and future nursery occupied the second and third floors; the kitchen and scullery were in the basement. There was no time now, though, for looking around, or for dwelling on the fact that, for all her family's snobbish disap-proval, this was a more substantial residence than any of the Parisian apartments she had lived in for most of the first twenty-five years of her life. The servants – two maids, a butler and a cook who had catered to Charles' domestic needs during his many years of bachelorhood – lined up to greet her in the handsome entrance hall, no doubt intrigued to know how the new chatelaine of the house would ring the changes. She went to bed alone, in a bed made up in her husband's former study at the back of the house, after nearly overdosing on sal volatile (smelling salts used at the time to revive those who were feeling faint). Beyond the rigours of the journey, there was another reason for her fatigue and sickness: to the great joy of this newly married couple, it was soon confirmed that Gertrude was pregnant. The first of six children, a daughter called Alice (always known as Elsie) would be born on 3 September 1848, eight days before their first wedding anniversary.

* * *

While the Tennants busied themselves in domestic duties and in preparation for the child, the world at large was undergoing momentous changes.
On 23 February 1848 Charles noted in his diary the fall of Louis-Philippe,
the king who had spoken to Gertrude as a child; he and his arch-
conservative Prime Minister Guizot were deposed amid bloody riots.[8] A
week or two later, the hated Prince Clemens Metternich, Chancellor of
the Austrian Empire, was overthrown. Across Europe, decades of social
tension and oppression spilled over into violent revolution and repressive
counter-revolution. There were many who thought that Great Britain was
a natural candidate for a similar social convulsion, not least Karl Marx
and Friedrich Engels, whose first Communist Party Manifesto was
published earlier in the month. Britain was the richest, most powerful
nation on earth, but the country laboured under extremes of wealth and
poverty. 'The condition of England . . . is regarded as one of the most
ominous, and one of the strangest ever seen in this world,' thundered
Thomas Carlyle in the opening lines of *Past and Present* (1843): 'With
unabated bounty the land of England blooms and grows; waving with
yellow harvests; thick-studded with workshops and industrial implements';
yet 'in the midst of plethoric plenty, the people perish.' In Benjamin
Disraeli's famous phrase, there were 'Two Nations of England, the Rich
and the Poor' (*Sybil*, 1845), and the contrasts between the two were the
source of appalled fascination for novelists like Dickens or Elizabeth
Gaskell, and for reformers like Robert Owen or social observers like
Henry Mayhew, whose first portraits of *London Labour and the London Poor*
began to appear in 1849. The schism between rich and poor was nowhere
more acute than in London itself, where the wealthy lived cheek by jowl
with the extremely poor.

The fizzling out of what might have been the English revolution of
1848 took place in part in Russell Square, within sight of the Tennants'
gracious first-floor windows and balconies. The Chartists gathered more
than a million signatures to a petition calling for universal male suffrage
and named 10 April as the date for a mass march to deliver it to the
Houses of Parliament. This was to be the third, and last, unsuccessful
attempt to move Parliament to legislative reform by means of direct
action. Although the march was intended to be peaceful, and the
Chartists' six demands look moderate by today's standards (in addition to
votes for all men, they wanted for example annual parliaments, and the
removal of the requirement that MPs should be property owners), the
threat of stampeding hordes of malodorous and hungry working men
prompted panic in the metropolis. The Whig government under Lord

John Russell recalled the Duke of Wellington from retirement to take charge of counter-measures.

The ageing victor of Waterloo rose to the occasion, saving the nation from its lower orders just as from the Napoleonic menace more than thirty years before. He ordered 8,000 troops to the capital and thirty guns to the Tower of London, where they could be shipped down the river to Westminster if the protest turned into insurrection on the continental scale. Wellington hit upon the masterful idea of sealing off all the bridges across the Thames. This stratagem ensured that the main body of 50,000 protesters, gathered on Kennington Common to the south of the river, could not get close to Westminster, and were reduced to sending a small, subdued delegation to deliver the petition. Several thousand marchers gathered at other locations, including in Russell Square, where protesters who had travelled down by train from the great industrial cities of the north gathered at eight in the morning after debouching from nearby Euston station. They then marched down Southampton Row and along Upper King Street and Holborn and down Farringdon Street, crossing the Thames at Blackfriars Bridge before making their way to join the main body of protesters at Kennington. Gertrude and Charles must have watched the procession with interest (but regrettably did not choose to record the event in their diaries). The Chartists were defeated as much by the presence of the troops as by tens of thousands of volunteer special constables, drawn from the same or ever so slightly higher social class as the protesters and vividly demonstrating the essential conservatism of the English proletariat. Despite the promising circumstances adumbrated in the Communist Manifesto, conservative Britain prevailed, the Chartists were defeated as a mass movement, and the process of social and constitutional change in England reverted to its traditional, that is to say very gradual course.

Although at the time the march would have seemed the culmination of years of famine and economic depression, the year 1848 in fact marked a watershed and the country was on the cusp of decades of unprecedented peace and prosperity. The conditions that had given risen to the social unrest of the 1830s and 1840s had abated: bread was cheap after the repeal of the Corn Laws; demand for British goods was high, and wages were rising. Over the next two decades, Britain's foreign trade would grow to eclipse that of France, Germany and Italy combined, while real incomes continued to climb. Already, under the tutelage of Prince Albert, planning had begun for the Great Exhibition, this defining expression of mid-Victorian self-assurance only three years away. Even the traumatic experience of the Crimean War in the middle of the next decade delivered only a temporary blow to national self-confidence; it proved a catalyst to self-improvement and had no lasting impact on Britain's ascendancy in world affairs, commerce and manufactures.

The rising tide of prosperity did not carry all with it – least of all, the urban poor, who would be just as much as feature of London life decades later when Gertrude's artistic daughter Dolly ventured across the river from the family mansion in Whitehall to Lambeth to paint street urchins. Even the middle classes who benefited from the surge in material prosperity tended to be mired in self-doubt and uncertainty, perhaps because it was a ferociously competitive society, where, as one contemporary observer noted; 'every man's hand [was lifted] against his brother, and each struggling to exalt himself, not merely by trampling on his fallen foe, but by usurping the place of his fallen brother'.[9] There was an alarming degree of social mobility, with great families cast down by 'the failure of some bank or mercantile speculation,' while tradesmen attained aristocratic pretension simply by virtue of having money. It is as if the gains in material prosperity were at the expense of spiritual well-being, and the literature of the mid-century sees a marked move away from the hard-headed social and economic analysis of the 1830s and 1840s. A note of plangent introspection creeps in. 'These are damned times,' lamented Matthew Arnold, author of some of the most expressive poetry of the period. 'Everything is against one, the height to which knowledge is come, the spread of luxury, our physical enervation, the absence of great natures, the unavoidable contact with millions of small ones, newspapers, cities, light profligate friends . . .'[10] The most popular poem of the mid-century was Tennyson's long and melancholy *In Memoriam*, which reached the tentative conclusion 'that somehow good/Will be the final goal of ill'. For all this agonising, the social tensions of the 1830s and 1840s abated and the more flagrant injustices were gradually addressed by legislative reform. Gertrude and Charles lived their entire married life in this outwardly buoyant, self-confident mid-Victorian era, the so-called 'Age of Equipoise'.[11]

* * *

'A dear round faced, fat healthy baby,' Gertrude wrote in her diary in the morning of Sunday, 3 September 1848, after Alice was born. 'No sound that ever reached my ear equalled the thrill and astonishment produced by her first infant cry!' Just over a week later, on her first wedding anniversary, she wrote: 'we have been as happy in each other as it is possible for two human beings to be! I can see nothing in Charles that I would wish to alter! He is perfect in my eyes! And when I compare him with other men, I feel myself blessed indeed!'

On the same day, in his own diary, Charles sought to express the intensity of his emotions by citing Shakespeare's *Two Gentlemen of Verona*:

She is mine own
And I am as rich in having such a jewel
As twenty seas, if all this sand were pearl
The water nectar, and the rocks pure gold.

Their diary entries became more prosaic over the years, but throughout the entire quarter-century of marriage their love remained touchingly intense. Gertrude was always 'my darling Ger' to Charles, while to Gertrude he was 'my dear Charles'. There was never any indication, in word or deed, that Gertrude regretted throwing in her lot with the prematurely deaf solicitor, no hint that she would have preferred an alternative existence in France, or indeed a robust upper-class match in England with someone whose finances might have been more stable. Although family life had its fair share of strains and would be touched by tragedy on more than one occasion, the marriage proved to be exceedingly happy, characterised by an affection and mutual respect that is rare at any time but was – if conventional wisdom is anything to go by – especially unusual in early Victorian England.

CHAPTER 13

CHARLES'S ANGEL IN THE HOUSE?

Both Charles and Gertrude had conventional notions of the role of marriage. It was, first and foremost, holy matrimony, a union undergirded by the principles of the established Christian religion. Charles had urged Gertrude to take communion on the day before their wedding, 'so that the Lord's blessing may be with us both when we meet to celebrate together, in his name, the holy sacrament of marriage'. On the day after the wedding, they attended the afternoon service together and, with rare exceptions, they went to church on every Sunday morning of their lives. At a more worldly level, Charles sought in marriage a haven from the toils of business life and from the ceaseless conflict within his own family. Gertrude would hold sway over the domestic sphere: bear and raise children, run the household budget, hire servants and provide companionship and consolation after his brutally combative days in the office or in court.[1]

'To men belongs the potent consideration of worldly aggrandisement,' wrote Sarah Stickney Ellis, the influential author of numerous conduct and child-rearing manuals; while women were supposed to stay at home, 'clothed in moral beauty'. This doctrine of the 'separate spheres' was celebrated by Coventry Patmore in his immensely popular poem *The Angel in the House* (1854–62) and elaborated later in the century by John Ruskin in a florid and oft-quoted address to the burghers and matrons of Manchester:

> The man's power is active, progressive, defensive . . . He is eminently the doer, the creator, the discoverer, the defender . . . The man, in his rough work in open world, must encounter all peril and trial: – to him,

therefore, the failure, the offence, the inevitable error: often he must be wounded, or subdued, often misled, and always hardened. But he guards the woman from all this; within his house, as ruled by her . . . need enter no danger, no temptation, no cause of error or offence. This is the true nature of home – it is the place of Peace; the shelter . . . from all terror, doubt and division . . . a sacred place, a vestal temple . . .[2]

The notion of home as a sanctuary insulated from the brutality of competitive modern society was deep-rooted and derived originally from the pieties of evangelicalism earlier in the century. 'The home was a microcosm of the ideal society,' explains the historian Judith Flanders, 'with love and charity replacing the commerce and capitalism of the outside world . . . this idea was so useful that it was internalised by many who shared no religious beliefs with the Evangelicals, and it rapidly became a secular norm.'[3] It was the woman's job to preserve the sanctity of home life, and this is where it was helpful to have self-denying qualities. The idealised mid-Victorian housewife was obliged 'to excel in the difficult arts of family life. She sacrificed herself daily. If there was chicken, she took the leg; if there was a draught, she sat in it – in short, she was so constituted that she never had a mind or a wish of her own.' Thus Virginia Woolf, looking back on her own late Victorian upbringing in a sardonic address to a later generation of students.[4] Woolf told her audience that she first had to strangle the domestic angel before she could embark on her career as an author. 'Had I not killed her she would have killed me.' Women of Gertrude's generation had little choice but to coexist with the angel.

The flowery language from Ruskin and other of Gertrude's contemporaries masked the brute reality that mid-century middle-class women were very much second-class citizens; in fact, barely citizens at all. Once Gertrude married, she was defined legally as the possession of her husband, and she lost the right to enter into contracts or to dispose of whatever property or income she might have brought with her into the marriage. After marriage, she and her husband became one flesh, 'and that flesh became the husband's', according to Sir William Blackstone, the great eighteenth-century legal authority.[5] Charles thus exercised complete dominion over his spouse and the family: a husband was entitled to dispose of his wife's income and inheritance as he saw fit, and free to beat his wife to the point of 'reasonable chastisement', and he could do what he liked with his children, as illustrated by the notorious case of Caroline Norton (1808–77), a society beauty and successful author whose three young sons were snatched from her after the breakdown of her marriage to a brutish nobleman. The main events of this sad saga took place in the 1830s, but in the early 1850s she was once again in the headlines, and it is likely that Gertrude read newspaper accounts of Mrs Norton's fight to prevent her husband ripping away from her what remained of her income and assets – in vain, as married women were not allowed to make contracts. (Later, Mrs Norton and Gertrude became friends, and the Norton grandchildren played with Gertrude's daughters.) Neither Mrs Norton, nor any other woman could seek divorce in such circumstances, and it was not until the Matrimonial Causes Act of 1857 that women's legal status began to improve.[6]

At the time when Gertrude and Charles married, middle-class women were not merely legal nonentities. Typically, they were ill-educated; Gertrude's frustration at her parents' neglect of her education in Paris was shared by tens of thousands of intelligent young women brought up in England, from Florence Nightingale to the Brontë sisters. They were expected to be passive, subordinate, and content with their lot. 'The first thing of importance is to be content to be inferior to men,' counselled Sarah Ellis, 'inferior in mental power in the same proportion that you are inferior in bodily strength.' A new wife needed to recognise 'the superiority of [her] husband, quite simply as a man'. Accordingly, she should take care to minister to his every need: if he likes a cheerful welcome and a clean hearth and blazing fire when he comes home, make sure it is just so, even leave the coals ready for him to poke if that gives him pleasure. 'Let the master be entitled to the choice of every personal indulgence.' If you are cleverer or more talented than your husband, don't let anyone be aware of this, least of all him, for exhibiting your gifts and thus showing up your husband can be fatal to happiness. Make sure that your conversation is light and varied, and don't 'talk about the stars when your husband wants his slippers'. In words that will be balm to a modern male chauvinist, and horrify everybody else, she says: 'to be permitted to dwell with the influence of [a good man], must be a privilege of the highest order; to listen to his conversation, a perfect feast – but to be admitted to his heart, it is difficult to say whether humility or gratitude should preponderate in the feelings of the woman thus distinguished and thus blessed.'[7]

There were very limited opportunities for women to pursue a profession or to work at all outside the home. According to the 1851 census, only 7 per cent of middle-class women actually had a job, and they were typically small farmers, governesses or writers. It was different, of course, for working-class women, who were obliged to work in factories or the fields, and at the other end of the social scale there were spectacular exceptions in the upper classes, the most prominent of whom was the Queen of England – born a matter of months before Gertrude – whose preference for a respectable domestic life helped promote a revolution in social manners and marked a decisive break with the *louche* ways of the Regency. Sarah Ellis went so far as to dedicate her seminal work *The Wives of England* to the new monarch. 'Let us not forget,' she wrote, 'that in the person of our beloved Queen we have the character of a wife and mother so blended with that of sovereign, that the present above all others ought to form an era in British history, wherein woman shall have proved herself not unworthy of the importance attached to her influence and her name.'

Other remarkable women of the era included Marian Evans, born in the same week as Gertrude, who in 1851 moved to London to start her career as a journalist and writer (but who would not use her *nom de plume* George Eliot until later in the decade). Florence Nightingale (1820–1910), a near contemporary drawn from moneyed upper middle-class stock, would soon find fame, and an outlet for her formidable talents as an administrator, in the Crimean War. Less well known today, but prominent at the time, were the articulate and well-connected ladies who in the late 1850s formed the nucleus of the Langham Place group. Harriet Martineau, Barbara Leigh Smith Bodichon and Bessie Rayner Parkes fought for improvements in women's legal rights, recognising (as George Eliot put it) that their early achievements were but 'one rung of a long ladder stretching far beyond our lives'. It was only much later in the century that women could enter the professions, and we will see how two of Gertrude's daughters pursued independent careers before and after they married, taking full advantage of the more liberated environment of the 1870s and 1880s.

George Eliot, Charlotte Brontë, Florence Nightingale and the vocal ladies of the 1850s were of course exceptional, unrepresentative of the vast majority of mid-Victorian gentlewomen. Millions of Gertrude's contemporaries accepted that their destiny was to marry and raise children. But were they necessarily obliged to 'suffer and be still', as Sarah Ellis counselled? Were all Victorian marriages as lugubrious as those endured in literature by such monumentally unhappy and ill-suited married couples as Paul and Edith Dombey in Dickens's *Dombey and Son* or the Lydgates and Casaubons in George Eliot's *Middlemarch*? Until relatively recently, historians argued that the institution of marriage deteriorated from an idealised state in the eighteenth century. Intimate, personal relations are supposed to have given way to an oppressive system in which women were condemned to groan under the weight of patriarchal oppression and injustice. As Gertrude's experience helps us understand, the reality was more nuanced. Most women assumed that marriage was better than the alternative of remaining single: it was a dreadful dependent fate to make one's way as a governess or a teacher. Staying at home to look after one's aged relatives was little better. 'Being married gives one one's position like nothing else can,' stated Queen Victoria herself, in a letter to one of her daughters in 1858. Once married, a woman's chances of happiness might depend as much on social class as on gender; for the poor, life was a struggle to survive, while the prosperous upper and upper-middle classes had the luxury of seeking self-fulfilment. Well aware of their position near the top of a highly stratified society, upper-class women could remain blissfully 'indifferent to the severe constraints under which women less fortunate than they had to live', demonstrates M. Jeanne Paterson in her study of three generations of the women of the upper middle-class Paget family.[8] Money aside, common sense dictates that wherever you stood in the social pecking order, the most important ingredient in a marriage was personal compatibility between man and wife. 'What marriage may be in the case of two persons of culti-vated faculties . . . between whom exists the best kind of equality, simi-larity of powers and capacities . . . so that each can enjoy the luxury of looking up to each other . . . I will not attempt to describe,' wrote John Stuart Mill in his classic essay *The Subjection of Women* (1869), which is as much an understated celebration of the philosopher's supremely happy marriage to Harriet Taylor as a denunciation of the inequality of the sexes.[9]

It is aggravating, from our point of view, that Gertrude left compar-atively few records for this central period of her life, as if she regarded her marriage as being less worthy of documenting than her picaresque youth. But enough survives to reconstruct an intimate portrait of this successful mid-century marriage. Gertrude, a feisty and independent young woman, accepted the constraints of marriage as a kind of libera-tion, rather as a poet or composer finds freedom of expression within the confines of rigid convention. She was dependent on Charles, but at least she was dependent on her own terms. At last, she was free from her impe-rious parents and the sniping of her siblings; the balance of domestic power shifted significantly in her favour – she had a home to maintain, a husband to look after, and in time a brood of children to minister to. In short, she embraced marriage with heartfelt enthusiasm, and for the best part of the next quarter-century she was a privileged member of the so-called 'silent sisterhood' of middle-class women who sought and found happiness as wife and mother.

In due course, as we will see, Gertrude and Charles came to understand each other so well that there was a blurring of the boundaries between public and private life, between the masculine and feminine spheres of influence: he confided every detail of his business affairs to her, and when she was eventually widowed she was so well prepared that she was ready to take on much of the responsibility for managing the estate. But for now, Gertrude would conform to the caricature. 'You are to me the angel of my long dream of life,' he had written during their courtship, 'the angel of my life and spirit.' She was quite content to be possessed by him, to be literally and legally 'his Ger'.

CHAPTER 14

BIRTHS AND DEATHS

One evening shortly before Christmas 1849, Gertrude was sitting in the music room at Cadoxton with a companion, reading out excerpts from *The Times*. Now thirty years old and three months pregnant with her second child, she was spending a few weeks in South Wales with her husband's family. The following lines from the newspaper's Hong Kong correspondent caught her eye:

> We regret to have to announce the death of Rear Admiral Sir Francis A. Collier, Commander-in-Chief of Her Majesty's Naval Force in the east.

'Thus,' Gertrude wrote in her diary later that night, 'was the manner I received the first, sad intelligence that the head of my father's family, and the most distinguished member of it, was dead.' The next day, she sent out for a copy of the *United Service Gazette*, which carried a more extensive obituary of her uncle. The article chronicled his valiant career, from his days as a protégé of Nelson to his more recent role as defender of British mercantile interests in the Far East. The obituary offered a jocular appreciation of Sir Frank's rough and ready personality ('his full, rich bluff humour amused and delighted his companions in arms and his social acquaintances') and ended up by hinting, hyperbolically, that there was something Christ-like in his determination to press on with his last mission despite ill health

Thus portrayed, Gertrude's uncle was the perfect embodiment of the heroic values and gruff manners of an age that seemed very remote from mid-century Victorian England. But more than that, his entire career was an implicit rebuke to her father's manner of existence. Far from hiding away on the Isle of Wight, Admiral Henry Collier had found the funds to relocate his wife and two remaining unmarried daughters to the metropolis and was now living at 25 Upper Grosvenor Street, in Mayfair. This was exactly the fashionable address that had been so long beyond his reach. Somehow, in the two years since Gertrude and Charles had been married, her father had managed to restore his fortunes and swagger. Gertrude had a theory that the money came from her elder brother George, with whom she had lost all contact but who in the years since leaving the Navy had married an heiress and come into possession of £20,000, a very considerable amount of money in those days. Perhaps George helped out in order to bolster his father's social standing and to give Clementina and Henrietta a better chance in the marriage market? Wherever the money came from, the newfound wealth was certainly not the product of hard work and self-sacrifice, and the contrast between her father's idle existence and the heroic life and death of her Uncle Frank was acute. 'I knew [Admiral Sir Frank] and admired him as the noblest of his race,' reflected Gertrude. 'I feel that truly the glory is departed from our family.'

The Colliers were living barely two miles to the west, close enough to be on visiting terms with the Tennants in Bloomsbury; but neither her parents nor her sisters had relented in their disapproval of the marriage and they kept a frosty distance. Gertrude was not unduly concerned by this rupture: her loyalties were transferred from father and siblings to husband and children, and she busied herself in domestic duties, managing the house and bringing up the children.

With three or four servants at hand, Gertrude would not herself undertake the back-breaking work of keeping the large house clean and warm and its inhabitants fed, so she had to learn to delegate. Most newly married women turned to their mothers for advice on how to master their new responsibilities, but since Gertrude and her mother had so little to do with one another, one imagines that Gertrude undertook a crash course of reading to master the art of household management. There was a flourishing of woman's magazines in the 1850s, as publishers responded to the growing prosperity of the age, and many hundreds of fully-fledged self-help books for women were published. The most famous of these was *Mrs Beeton's Book of Household Management*, with its arresting opening sentence: 'As with the Commander of an Army, or the leader of any enterprise, so it is with the mistress of a house.' This useful tome, with its hundreds of recipes and chapters on children, servants, doctors and lawyers, would not appear until 1859–61, so perhaps Gertrude turned to Sarah Ellis. 'In a well-regulated household,' this writer stated, 'even where the mistress takes no part in the executive business herself, there must still be a constant forethought, accompanied with a variety of calculations, plans and arrangements, which to an indolent person can be irksome in the extreme.' Get up early, Ellis advises, and start the day by reviewing the actions and events of the previous day, and 'ask for divine assistance to make sure the day [ahead] goes better'. The mistress of a house should 'appear calm, and perfectly self-possessed, whether she feels so or not'. Above all, Ellis warns, keep clear of the kitchen: 'don't plunge head, heart and hand into the vortex of culinary arrangements. That would best be left to servants.' One of her first tasks, we learn from Gertrude's diaries, was to replace the furniture in the house: this was of great antiquity as it belonged to her husband's long-deceased father. She waited until Charles was away on a business trip before introducing so radical a change. There was some rebellion and turnover among the servants, especially when she introduced mandatory morning prayers for all the household, but there is no reason to doubt that in time she managed to introduce the 'principles of order, justice and benevolence' to 62 Russell Square, just as Sarah Ellis advised.[1]

In the early years of her marriage, Gertrude looked after her infant daughter and prepared for the birth of the next child. Blanche was born in June 1850, and from then on she was pregnant or nursing a young infant throughout the entire decade. Charles, the only son, was born next (30 July 1852), then Dorothy (always known as Dolly – 22 May 1855) and Eveleen (on 21 November 1856), and finally baby Gertrude was born on 21 September 1859, just after her mother's fortieth birthday. Chloroform dulled the pain of the later births: the wonder-drug of the mid-century was introduced in the late 1840s and became increasingly socially acceptable after 1853, when Queen Victoria took it during the birth of Prince Leopold, the eighth of the monarch's nine children. Gertrude and Charles would have been delighted to produce a whole alphabet of children, but that was not to be.

In these early years, they preferred each other's company to that of 'society' at large. They did not go to balls or to fashionable soirées. They entertained modestly: children's parties in the square, a trip to the pantomime, dinner parties with her husband's stolid professional friends. ('Dined with Mr and Mrs Fletcher, a clergyman [and his wife],' Gertrude lamented after one dreary supper party. 'Heavy! Made the best of it.') Charles became stiff and formal when in company, 'never so natural' as when at home; one cause of this stiffness was his increasing deafness, which made it difficult for him to enjoy the cut and thrust of dinner party conversation. There were a few special friends, with whom they enjoyed intimate evenings: chief among these was Hamilton Aïdé, who came to visit his cousin when home on leave from the Army: one imagines that he and Gertrude spent many an hour talking over the shared circumstances of their exotic youth in Paris. Another family friend from these early days of the marriage was John Everett Millais, the Pre-Raphaelite painter who lived not far from the Tennants at 83 Gower Street, and achieved prominence when *Ophelia* and other of his works were exhibited at the Royal Academy in 1852. It is not clear how they became acquainted, although by 1853 Millais was a regular guest in Russell Square, and the friendship would deepen later in the decade after Millais fell in love with John Ruskin's wife Effie. She and Ruskin were granted a divorce on the grounds that their marriage had never been consummated, and she eventually married Millais. The love affair scandalised society at large, and from the mid-1850s Millais and Effie spent much of each year out of London. Decades later, the two families took holidays together and Millais would paint portraits of two of the Tennant daughters. Gertrude was fascinated by Millais and wrote an account of their friendship which is now sadly lost.

As well as reading to each other in the evenings, at weekends Charles and Gertrude went to hear Frederick Maurice preach his sermons at Lincoln's Inn Chapel,[2] and strolled through the streets of Bloomsbury to nearby art galleries, or round the corner to the British Museum, which was completed in 1852. The streets were thronged with cabs and horses which clattered along the cobbled streets; there was dung, mud and straw everywhere; hawkers touted their wares noisily. They must have visited Mudie's Select Lending Library, which moved to 512 New Oxford Street, perhaps ten minutes' brisk walk from their home, in the same year. Although prosperous enough to buy their own novels, they would certainly have paid their deposit of one guinea a year in return for unlimited loans of the three-volume 'triple decker' novels that were a defining feature of the age (virtually all novels from the 1850s to the 1890s were published in this format). While Mudie's is long gone, James Smith and Sons moved to 53 New Oxford Street in 1857, and is there to this day: an emporium of umbrellas and swagger sticks beneath mid-Victorian mirrors and gaudy adverts. The establishment has barely changed since Gertrude's day, even if swordsticks, Irish blackthorns and malacca canes are no longer available as advertised on the shop-front. Sometimes they took a cab or walked further afield, to Covent Garden to see the fruit and vegetable market, or even to the West End, to shop for luxury items not available in Bloomsbury or Holborn.

For anyone tempted to retrace their footsteps, neither Charing Cross Road nor Shaftesbury Avenue, the main thoroughfares from Bloomsbury to Trafalgar Square and the West End today, existed when Gertrude and Charles were living in Russell Square. They were constructed in the 1880s, carved out of some of Victorian London's poorest and most overcrowded slums. New Oxford Street, on the other hand, cut through the same rookery of St Giles in 1847, really was new when the Tennants first lived in Russell Square. They visited attractions such as the Diorama, a forerunner of the picture show, at which they enjoyed animated vistas of the Nile or of Mont Blanc, and like many millions of their countrymen, they paid a visit to the Great Exhibition of the Works of Industry of All Nations, which opened amid much pomp and ceremony on May Day 1851, under the dome of Joseph Paxton's Crystal Palace in Hyde Park.

'The progress of the human race, resulting from the labour of all men, ought to be the final object of the exertion of each individual,' urged the catalogue to the Great Exhibition, in a quintessential statement of the spirit of the age. 'In promoting this end we are accomplishing the will of the great and blessed God.' Visitors to the exhibition, from Queen Victoria (who attended several times even before the exhibition officially opened), to the hundreds of thousands of surprisingly well behaved members of the working class, to foreign visitors from all nations (including Gustave Flaubert), were bowled over by the vast, cathedral-like building, and all that they found inside. Fountains plashed and the great elms of the park flourished within the enormous greenhouse. There were treasures, such as the Koh-i-Noor diamond lent for the occasion by the Queen herself; wondrous exhibits such as Mr Osler's 27-foot-high crystal fountain; marvels from abroad, for example the Bavarian Lion or the Stuttgard (*sic*) horses; even a collection of meerschaum pipes from Austria. But most tremendous of all was the display of wares from Britain and her colonies. 'The long rows of iron frames [produce] a striking effect,' gushed *The Times*, 'and the vast mass of contributions [leaves] upon the mind a profound impression of the capital, the energy and above all the mechanical genius of the country.' It was also a celebration of the consumer culture of the mid-century: never before had so many had so much money to spend on shopping. Flick through the catalogue today, and one is immediately taken back to that energetic, practical and endlessly inventive age. To name at random a few of the exhibits: Montgomery's self-acting railway brake; Barber-Beaumont's patent locomotive equipment, for working up or down steep inclines from or to wharfs, etc.; W.P. Stanley's steam-powered cake-breaker for sheep, cattle and manure; numbers of thrashing and threshing machines; G. Phillips's improved collateral beehive; an electrical table lamp; a Telekouphonoun, or speaking telegraph, from F. Whishaw of John Street; infinite varieties of woollens, cottons, ginghams and worsted, silks and velvets, cambrics and hemps; leathers, skins and furs; lace and embroidery; locks and grates; works in glass, mosaic, papier mâché and gutta-percha and so on through 320 pages and eighteen acres of *things*. As Karl Marx acidly observed in *Das Kapital* (written round the corner from Gertrude in the British Museum Reading Room), 'the wealth of society in which the capitalist mode of production prevails appears as an immense collection of commodities'. He went on to denounce capitalist society's apparent *fetishism* of such commodities. Charles Dickens was another sceptic who bridled at the complacency of the exhibition and all that it stood for; in late 1851, he duly began work on *Bleak House*, a novel conceived as a 'great display of England's sins and negligence'. Gertrude started reading this book out loud to Charles in March 1852, and could not fail to have been struck with the parallels between the novel and her own family's situation.

* * *

Gertrude rapidly became aware that Charles's pre-marital grumblings about the perilous state of the family finances were far from exaggerated. 'I feel greatly deteriorated in one respect since my marriage,' Gertrude confessed to her diary on 14 October 1849. 'My mind dwells so on money! Money! I feel as if that one thought engrossed my being. I shudder to think of the hideous crimes that one feeling leads to! [I] dread my mind becoming degraded by wanting money – and by the thinking of it!'

Charles had a number of sources of income, chiefly the steadily increasing rents and tolls from the Welsh estate (the peak of traffic on the canal was 1866, when 225,000 tons of goods passed along the canal) and the fees from his professional practice. His gross income, before the cost of servicing his considerable debts, was in the region of £2,000 a year – by no means enough to put him in the category of the incontestably wealthy (for that, he would have needed £5,000 a year), but still a very considerable sum, equivalent to ten times the salary of a respectable middle-class professional like a senior clerk or a civil servant and a hundred times what he paid his cook. It is difficult to translate this into modern money: one complication is that housing costs were a much smaller proportion of total outgoings than they are today, while the cost of labour was lower. Multiplying his income by 50, as is conventional, gives £100,000, which although a large sum is not enough to raise a family in upper middle-class comfort in central London today. If he earned 100 times the wage of a full-time, live-in cook today, that would imply an income of £2–£3 million, which is far too much. The Bank of England's inflation index suggests an income of £183,146 in today's money, which sounds more reasonable.[3] So Charles's gross income was a significant amount by any measure and should have guaranteed a comfortable existence. Surely it was enough to provide for Gertrude and the children?

Charles took her fully into his confidence on his business affairs, and they spent many an evening discussing mortgages, tonnages, rental arrears and the incessant litigation that was the bane of his life. As a professional lawyer, he stood to benefit when his clients became embroiled in the protracted lawsuits that were characteristic of the age of *Bleak House*. However, Charles was himself on the receiving end of litigation every bit as soul-destroying and interminable as *Jarndyce* v. *Jarndyce*, the monumental, multi-generational lawsuit at the heart of Dickens's novel, which impoverishes all who are involved in it, apart from the lawyers. In May 1854, he cut out a leading article from *The Times* which seemed to point to parallels between his own situation and that of the country at large as it became embroiled in the Crimean War. 'I have found myself step by step,' Charles wrote in his diary, 'and in spite of my wishes and my resolutions brought by circumstances into a conflict with powerful enemies and placed in a situation where to advance is dangerous, and to retreat impossible.'

One powerful opponent was Lord Jersey, the Whig grandee who filed suit against Charles and various other members of the Tennant family, including his mother and brother, in October 1852. The dispute related to the forty-seven years that Charles and his father before him had acted as the earl's land agent and legal adviser in Wales. Preserved in the attic is a small mountain of filings and counter-filings, in which with elaborate courtesy and all formality, the earl and his former legal advisor sling verbal mud, vitriol and worse at one another. The earl's main complaint is that he repeatedly asked Charles for a statement of the accounts in relation to the Briton Ferry estate, and when he finally got them (in four bound volumes, in Charles's immaculate copperplate hand), they were a confection designed to cover up the systematic plundering of the earl's estate by the Tennant family. 'Being a recent fabrication of said Charles Tennant,' alleges the earl's writ, 'there is a studied looseness and imperfection in the explanations of most of the charges therein contained, but plaintiff [Lord Jersey] charges that where the items are not altogether fictitious and fraud-ulent they are grossly overcharged and utterly disproportionate with the work done.' The purpose of such accounting skulduggery, the earl contends, was to cover up the large amount of money he believed to be due from the Tennant family to him, namely £18,151 11s. 3d. (or £1.76 million in today's money). Charles, meanwhile, combative as ever, counter-sued and argued that the earl owed him and his family £32,129 17s. 3d. (£3.12 million). Even if repaid, Charles claimed, this would be a 'very inadequate remuneration for the immense quantity of business trans-acted' by the Tennants on behalf of the Jerseys over a period of nearly half a century. Both sides employed forensic accountants to go through the books that Charles had himself compiled from the mountains of unsorted paperwork left behind by his late father.

There had clearly been an irreparable breach of trust between the earl and the Tennant family, who had served him and his forebears since before the beginning of the century. Decades had gone by when George Tennant and thereafter Charles had managed the earl's affairs, sold off peripheral land from the 32,000-acre Briton Ferry estate, and remitted to the family over the period nearly one million pounds, a remarkably large sum given that much of the estate consisted of 'miserable sheepwalks and bogs' when the earl inherited it in 1814. Charles's accountant swore in an affidavit that he 'had not discovered a sixpence which had not been duly paid to Lord Jersey or accounted for to him'. Charles argued that the increase in the value of the earl's estate was in no small measure due to the creation of the canal itself, which his father had financed out of his own pocket. Lord Jersey had originally had no objection when Charles bought out the land to construct the canal; now he had his lawyers take a fine-tooth comb through the conveyancing for every transaction, claiming that the canal had added no value to his coal-mines and was damaging his agricultural interests because so much water was seeping into the fields.

Another enemy was Lady Jersey herself, who disliked Charles as much as she had despised his contumacious father: they fell out after Charles blocked the appointment of her nominee to a partnership of Child's Bank. The imperious Lady Jersey was hereditary senior partner of the bank, while Charles was long-term adviser to the banking house. She ousted him from this position, sued him on a variety of counts, and cast aspersions on his creditworthiness (he owed the bank some £60,000 and struggled to make interest payments). He retaliated by suing her for libel, in his writ gleefully recounting details of the Jersey family's 'pecuniary embarrassment', caused, Charles alleged, by the earl's incessant gambling, Her Ladyship's extreme extravagance, and the improvidence of their children, one of whom was 'driven by exasperated creditors to escape his country, and live and die an outlaw in a foreign land'. (He did not mention the fact that one of Lord Jersey's sons was quite respectable, having married a daughter of Robert Peel, the Tory Prime Minister.) Charles's position was as intractable as the Crymlyn bog through which part of the Tennant Canal had been cut: the dispute with Lady Jersey damaged his standing with the bank, which imperilled the financing of the canal, not to mention his own personal solvency, at a time when he was locked in a desperate existential fight with her husband.

Other opponents came from within the bosom of the family, particularly his two brothers Henry and George. Both were barristers who struggled to make their way in the world and establish an income commensurate with their standing as gentlemen. They mooched around the house at Cadoxton, rough-shooting on the estate and hobnobbing with the local gentry, but neither helped manage the estate and they were regarded as parasites by their brother. Gertrude admitted to herself that she rather liked them, acknowledging that they had noble qualities. Henry, the brother who had tried to oust Charles from Russell Square, had good manners and was 'quite the *grand homme* manqué' – he was older than Charles by a year and saw the estate and the trappings as his birthright. But the fact of the matter was that the three brothers just did not get on: Gertrude fretted that the Tennants 'cannot and will not understand each other!' In Charles's judgement, his brothers were feckless and improvident; worse, their natural predisposition to intrigue against him and each other might actually threaten the well-being of his young family. The birth of baby Alice had concentrated his mind wonderfully on the unresolved question of legal title.

The problem was as follows: Charles had taken responsibility for running the canal and related estates since the early 1830s, and had offered up personal guarantees against the heavy debts taken on to keep the canal solvent. He had also lent significant amounts of money to his mother, paid off part of the mortgage to Child's and expanded the property by buying a farm called Compton Estate. His total investment was in the region of £60,000, a very considerable sum of money for a man earning £2,000 a year. Quite where it came from, is an open question: he may have inherited it from his father (possible, but unlikely); earned it in some unspecified business venture (possibly the financial reconstruction of the Swansea docks in the 1830s, in which he was heavily involved); siphoned it off from Lord Jersey (again, unlikely) or raised it as a mortgage on some part of the property not covered by the mortgage to Child's. But he did not actually own the Tennant Canal and the associated lands in Glamorganshire: all this property belonged to his ageing mother and, when she died, it would pass in trust to her children and grandchildren. His brothers and sisters would thus be co-owners and administrators of the estate, notwithstanding their idleness and incompetence and the fact that he had in effect managed the estate since his father's death. In Charles's mind, this endangered the viability of the estate as a whole and threatened to leave him saddled with enormous debts. In addition to the £60,000 he personally had put into the estate, there was a further £50,000 owing to Child's Bank, secured on different parts of the Welsh property. The sheer scale of the loans explains why Charles, who had a shrewd grasp of money matters, felt the family finances to be precarious despite the scale of his income. If Charles was forced to write off the loans to the estate, or was unable to swap his mortgage for full ownership of the estate, he and his family would be sunk. In short, it seemed to him as if the whole comfortable edifice of upper middle-class life was teetering on insecure foundations. He must have feared the fate of John Sedley in *Vanity Fair*, who is made bankrupt and the contents of *his* house in Russell Square disposed of by public auction.

Whatever you do, he told Gertrude in 1853 when he took the unusual step of making her sole executrix of his will, 'never deliver the [mortgage deeds] out and out to any other member of the family'. The deeds and other papers relating to these transactions were kept in a small iron box, itself locked inside a chest located in his study at Russell Square. None of the original documents should ever leave the chest without a copy being made, he cautioned. He urged her not to trust anyone at all, apart from Mr Jennings, the land agent who handled the day to day running of the estate. As early as February 1848, he had become convinced of the 'necessity of more decided measures on my part for the protection of my family interests'. After months of legal plotting, he went down to Cadoxton in January of the following year and asked his mother to execute a formal deed of receivership, which would clarify the position, making him the legal receiver of all rents and profits deriving from the estate. She signed the document, but the brothers were incensed as this manoeuvre threatened to cut them out of their share of the inheritance. George came to Russell Square to protest, the result being an awkward conversation on money matters that left a 'most painful and ineffaceable impression on

[Gertrude's] mind'. Henry also objected, claiming that the elderly Mrs Tennant was imbecile and therefore not of sound mind when she executed the deed. When their mother eventually died in June 1850, just short of her eightieth birthday, the scene was set for two decades of litigation. 'May God give me patience and temper to bear these trials with Christian fortitude,' Charles wrote in his diary, 'and wisdom to defeat and confound my enemies.' *Tennant* v. *Tennant* was filed in the Chancery division of the High Court in 1859, and this bitter legal dispute that pitted brother against brother was not resolved until shortly before Charles's death in 1872. Truly a *Jarndyce* v. *Jarndyce* of a case, one which ran on for decades without any of the parties being sure what it was all about, with whole families inheriting legendary hatreds with the suit, and which impoverished some if not all of those involved.

Charles, meanwhile, had become so disillusioned with South Wales that he determined not to visit his estate and put its management entirely in the hands of his trusted agent Mr Jennings. His visit to Cadoxton in June 1852 was the last for fifteen years. 'What events in the interval . . .' he wrote in his diary on 1 August 1867, when he finally resolved to return to the estate. 'And how sorrowful all my associations with Glamorganshire!'

* * *

The Tennants followed fashionable practice and left London for the summer, but they visited respectable south coast resorts like Worthing or Brighton, and not the grouse moor. Charles abhorred field sports and abominated country house society. ('A gentleman's park is my aversion,' he used to say, a sentiment shared by his wife.) Four months after his mother died, Charles and Gertrude were on holiday in Wales with the infant Blanche and the two-year-old Elsie. The holiday was going well – Elsie had just taken her first ride on a donkey on the sands of Aberystwyth – when Charles received an urgent communication from Henry Collier containing the 'fatal and unexpected intelligence of the death of Mrs. Collier from Typhus Fever'. Gertrude's mother had died at four o'clock in the morning of Wednesday, 22 October 1850, at home in Upper Grosvenor Street. This descendant of Oliver Cromwell had fallen victim to a disease that killed upper and lower classes alike, transmitted from mice and rats via lice and fleas. Far from returning to London forthwith, Charles and Gertrude continued with their tour, visiting Dolgellau, Beddgellert, Porthmadog and the Llanberis Pass before travelling back to Chester and on to London, a full two weeks after Harriet's death. Perhaps we should not interpret this as a lack of concern or grief on Gertrude's part – we shall never know for sure, as during this phase of her life she kept her diary entries to a minimum – but she was clearly in no hurry to return for the funeral or to offer her condolences to her father and sisters.

Worse than this apparent indifference, from the point of view of her father and sisters, was Charles's conduct as executor of Mrs Collier's will. (He had retained his position as the Collier family solicitor.) Shortly before Christmas, the Admiral, together with Henrietta and Clementina, descended on the house in Russell Square to register their disapproval of the way Charles was handling the distribution of the deceased's assets. They alleged that he was withholding the moneys she had left and diverting the proceeds to his own account. The allegation was reiterated early in the New Year by Dr Verity, the physician who had looked after Henrietta during her mysterious illness and was now sent as an ambassador to treat for a settlement. Charles rebutted the accusations and refused to yield; whatever money the Colliers felt was their due was not paid over. (It seems likely that Charles was waiting to turn Mrs Collier's assets into cash before paying over the money, and thus could claim that he was scrupulously adhering to his obligations to all the Collier children; the Admiral, with a dim grasp of business matters, probably wanted all his share up front. We do not know how much money was at stake, but certainly enough to poison relations with the rest of the Collier family.) The result was that for several years Gertrude was not on speaking terms with her father and siblings. The rift with Henrietta was particularly severe, and they did not see each other at all from 1850 to 1856. Thereafter they had virtually nothing to do with one another for the rest of their long lives.

The estrangement of the sisters helps explain why Gustave Flaubert did not come into contact with Gertrude when he arrived in England in September 1851, together with his ageing mother and his niece Caroline. The purpose of the visit was to find an English nanny to succeed the pock-marked Miss Jane who had served the Flaubert family for many years at Croisset. Miss Jane was now Mrs Farmer and lived near the Holloway Road in north London, where the author stayed during his visit. He found time to visit the Great Exhibition, the Chinese Exhibition in South Kensington, the East India Company museum in Leadenhall Street in the City, and Highgate Cemetery, the Victorian necropolis where Gertrude and her husband would eventually be buried. He also looked up Henrietta, no longer the charming invalid but still unmarried at the age of 28, and as voluptuous as ever. Admiral Collier was wise enough to send a chaperon to accompany his daughter and the Frenchman when, one foggy Sunday afternoon, they went for a walk in Hyde Park.

Flaubert had spent the intervening years in a variety of dissolute pursuits, including a tour of the Middle East with his raffish friend Maxime du Camp and a passionate affair with Louise Colet. He had lost his looks, put on weight and still, at the age of nearly 30, had nothing to show for the many years spent toiling in his study at Croisset. He had, it is true, conceived the tale that would develop into *Madame Bovary*, and began the painstaking process of writing his first masterpiece when he returned to Paris; but the book took four and a half years to complete and would not be published until 1857. The Admiral would have recognised Flaubert as a dangerously charming Frenchman with a small income and no prospects; in short, thoroughly unsuited even for a daughter who was in danger of being left 'on the shelf'. When Gustave arrived back in Paris, he wrote to Henrietta saying that when they parted 'there was more fog in his heart than there was over London', cursing all the while the 'jolly oaf' of a cousin who had dogged their every step through the park and prevented the deepening of their previous intimacy.

The correspondence continued for several years, Flaubert's tender and yet manipulative letters in marked contrast to the bawdy correspondence with his dwindling band of male friends and the erotically charged exchanges with Louise Colet, the minor poetess who was the recipient of regular progress reports on the writing of *Bovary*. He asked Henrietta for a favour: to help find a buyer for an album of autograph manuscripts collected by Louise – not the first time he would seek to take advantage of the Collier sisters' connections in London society. He lays on thick his remembrances of their times together at Trouville and the Rond-Point of the Champs-Elysées. How sad it was that she was no longer there! What a marvellous afternoon they would spend, she lying on the couch, her head propped up by a pink cushion, while he would sit on a chair beside her, reading aloud from the romantic poets! 'If you only knew, my dear Henriette, how so often memories of those days return to me and fill me with a sense of sad tenderness!' If she would only return to France, how he could tell her of his adventures of the previous six years, of the Nile, the sun-drenched Orient, of bedouins, dervishes and caravanserai! He takes both her hands in his and raises them to his lips! He is constantly reminded of her presence. 'I have your eyes right there in front of me, and I am looking you.' He bids her adieu, corrects himself and says that he hopes it will only be *au revoir*, saying that he will resume his English lessons so they can converse more freely next time he is in London.

All this stirring talk of dervishes and bedouins had a predictable effect on the emotions of a headstrong young woman who was bridling at her role as housekeeper to her father. She wrote back, despairing of her lot. Flaubert consoled her by return with lyrical descriptions of the Pyramids; of a giant scarab encountered during a ride through a grove of palms, of the snow-covered mountains near Scutari. 'It's very sad and very beautiful,' he wrote, saying that her state of 'spleen' was not confined to London, it was universal.

In February of the following year, she wrote to him in more detail about her woes; her side of the correspondence has not survived but one imagines she complained about the difficulties of finding a husband; and indeed later in the year her engagement to a Major Frankland was broken off, the second time she had been jilted. (Frankland was probably a distant cousin, but there are no clues as to why Henrietta should have been rejected twice in a row.) 'Be patient, poor Henriette,' Flaubert wrote. 'There is nothing durable in this world, nor pain nor pleasure, and if the humidity of sadness penetrates your soul, rays of sunshine may shine later to warm up your happiness. Read, make music, try not to think. Therein lies the evil: to dream – however, it is so sweet to dream, is it not?' He asked for her portrait, and later in the year she sent him a picture which he hung in pride of place on the wall of his study. 'To the side of the fire-place, above the place where I sit to smoke and to think,' he explained. 'It will be very close to a view of Egypt and not far from the bust of my sister. You are going to become, dear Henriette, one of the guardians of my life of silence. Your face which I loved so much is going to look at me all year round.'[4]

So bad was the rift between the Collier sisters that in one of Henrietta's letters she asked him to be sure not to pass on any details of their correspondence to Gertrude; by return, he reassured her that he had lost touch with her, and in any case he firmly believed that Gertrude had no interest in him, his letters or his visits. In turn, however, he asked Henrietta for news of Gertrude. Presumably she was able to tell him that she was pregnant with her third child (Charles was born in July 1852), but little else, as the sisters were still not on speaking terms. It was not until Christmas 1853, when Henrietta wrote to her sister to apologise for making unfounded allegations against Charles, that they were formally reconciled, and they did not meet again until a family wedding in 1856.

By this time, the correspondence between Henrietta and Flaubert had petered out, but the portrait remained in his study, and he was desolate when he heard, several years later, that Henrietta had at last got married. 'One less sylph in the world,' he complained to a friend. 'The angels of my youth are turning into housewives'.[5] Henrietta married a Scottish baronet called Sir Alexander Campbell of Barcaldine, at St George's, Hanover Square, on 20 August 1855. It was a fashionable Mayfair wedding, and the prelude to a long life of good health and respectability. Unlike her sister, she never saw Gustave Flaubert again, but the memories of Trouville and the Rond-Point must have meant something, as she kept the letters. They were discovered in the early 1950s by a student researching the Campbell family archive in a solicitor's office in Edinburgh, and subsequently auctioned off by Henrietta's descendants.

* * *

Two weeks after Henrietta's wedding, Charles and Gertrude travelled to Weymouth for their annual summer holiday, together with their four children, including Dolly, the latest addition to the family who was just three months old. The family stayed in modest rooms at 3 Johnstone Row, overlooking the seafront. The weather was fine, they all went to the beach, and Gertrude read *Romany Rye* by George Borrow. Charles and Gertrude made day trips to nearby beauty spots. There was no premonition that this happy family holiday was to be blasted by tragedy. On Tuesday, 18 September, Blanche was taken ill. This vivacious girl, who shortly before the holiday had celebrated her fifth birthday with six friends in Russell Square, did not seem to be in danger and Gertrude left her and the other children with the nurse while she and Charles made a day trip to Portland Head. Two days later, however, the child's condition had deteriorated. A doctor was called, and 'congestion of the brain' diagnosed – possibly meningitis? On Wednesday the 26th, Blanche woke after twelve hours sleep and appeared to be out of danger. That night, however, she was seized by another convulsion. In a scene reminiscent of the death of Paul Dombey, the child lay in her bed in the front bedroom overlooking the seafront, drifting in and out of consciousness, watched over by her parents and nurses. Her parents prayed for the girl, using the words of her own special prayer:

> Oh Dear God, who knowest all things, Thou seest me by night as well as by day – I pray Thee, for Christ's sake, forgive me all I have ever done amiss this day, and keep me safe while I am asleep . . . bless my dear Papa, and my dear Mama, my brothers and sisters, help me always to

serve them in love – so that when I have done Thy will here, I may dwell with Thee in Heaven for ever – for the sake of Jesus Christ thy Son.

The vigil was in vain. Perhaps the prayer was not?

'At half past ten this morning, our angel child Blanche was taken from us aged five years, three months and 28 days,' Gertrude wrote in her diary for the fateful day of Thursday, 4 October 1855. Six days later, Blanche was buried in Radipole Church in Weymouth.

'Her father, and myself, alone accompanied her to her grave – in a mourning carriage. Her coffin by our side!'

CHAPTER 15

RITA AND EMMA:
TWO LITERARY HEROINES

If there was one person from outside the immediate family circle whom Gertrude was pleased to see at this time, it was her first cousin Hamilton Aïdé. Aïdé (pronounced 'aye-eee-day'), it will be remembered, was the son of her mother's sister Georgina and uncle George, the cosmopolitan businessman killed in a duel after an altercation at a Parisian ball. Aïdé was six or seven years younger than Gertrude, but they had been close since childhood and would remain intimate friends until he died in 1906.

Aïdé is now completely forgotten, but in his day was known as a versatile man of letters, who produced fifteen popular novels, nearly all light romances 'in the French style'; wrote poems and plays and also achieved prominence as a song-writer, singer, amateur actor and painter. He was the quintessential Victorian dilettante: a rich amateur, a dabbler in many and various arts, whose paintings were said like his writing to have achieved no more than 'the very best amateur standard'.[1] 'He was a man of many accomplishments, dramatic, literary, artistic, and social,' commented his obituary in *The Times*, 'and though he never made a very deep mark in any direction, his versatility and amenity of character had made him something of a personage during two generations.' The novelist Elizabeth Gaskell met him on the continent in 1858 and left a barbed but affectionate pen-portrait:

He acts beautifully in either French or English private theatricals, sings enchantingly – draws passably – and is altogether full of *tastes* – about the *talents* I am not so sure . . . he is very amiable & kind, [and] has lovely eyes, and neat little moustachios . . . altogether graceful and gentlemanly.

'Pray make him sing,' Mrs Gaskell urges in this letter to George Smith, the publisher. 'The passers by, even in Corn Hill would stop to listen, and think it was Wordsworth's sky lark at the corner of Wood St.'[2]

Beyond his multifarious talents, he was (in the words of *The Times* obituarist) 'one of those people who you "met everywhere" – at worldly or literary dinner parties, at great receptions and at first nights'. Throughout the second half of the century, his name regularly appears in society reports of royal levees, garden parties and afternoon Drawing-Rooms, at Sandringham or at Buckingham Palace. But he was equally at home in the bohemian company of the painter James McNeill Whistler or the poet William Allingham. As Henry James described his sometime friend, he was 'a capital country-house man, polished and supple by much living in the world . . . an amiable, very amiable literary bachelor, who has charming rooms, innumerable friends and hospitable habits'.[3] Everyone noted how small, delicate, sensitive and amiable he seemed, although years later James did also make the strange observation that Aïdé was the 'Diane de Poitiers *de nos jours*'. De Poitiers was the beautiful mistress of King Henry II of France in the mid-sixteenth century, generally regarded as the power behind the French throne, and James seems to be making a mischievous comment on Aïdé's influence on London cultural life, on his looks and possibly also on his sexuality: he never married and lived for many years with his mother in the New Forest before he came up to London to embark on his social and literary career.

In the years since the holiday on the sands of Trouville, Aïdé had almost completely disappeared from Gertrude's life. He had joined a crack Guards regiment, appropriate for a young man of wealth and fashion, and could visit his cousin only on the rare occasions that he found himself back in London on leave. They would sit and chat for hours, entertaining each other with their recollections of the people they had known in Paris, and then he would leave to rejoin his regiment, his head full of ideas for books, plays, poems and operas. In truth, he was singularly ill suited to the martial life, even in a gentleman's regiment such as the 85th Dragoon Guards. He eventually got back in touch with his old friend Gustave Flaubert, visiting him at Croisset and sending him some of his poetry. Flaubert was encouraging and his letter of praise (preserved in the Tennant archive) must have been one factor behind Aïdes's decision to buy himself out of his commission and pursue his bent as a man of letters. In 1854, he left the army and resolved to write. A volume of poetry was not well received, but he also set about writing a light novel about the upbringing he shared with his cousin in Paris. The stroke of originality was to write the story as if it were the autobiography of an innocent English girl, brought up amid the temptations and depravity of French high society.

The book, entitled *Rita: An Autobiography*, was published anonymously in 1856 and proved very popular with the mid-Victorian public, running into four editions in nine years and translated into French in 1862. The plot is too melodramatic and full of improbable coincidence for this to be a literal account of Gertrude's early life. But the parallels between Marguerite Perceval, alias Rita, and Gertrude Collier are too numerous for there to be any doubt that Aïdé's novel is a thinly disguised account of Gertrude's youth in Paris. Rita, the heroine of the novel, is born in England (inside the Tower of London); she is the eldest child; the fictional father is a soldier and not a sailor, and the parents do not marry for love: but these are about the only points of dissimilarity between her and Gertrude. The grandmother 'Lady Roxborough' was painted by Sir Joshua Reynolds, which was true of the first Lady Collier, née Gwyn. Rita's mother is the beautiful younger daughter of an aristocratic family, just like Harriet Collier, née Nicholas. Rita's father is described as a very handsome man, who kept his looks marvellously, for years, just like the real Captain Collier. The father-figure in the novel also left England, consumed with money problems. 'After the birth of a second child, he sold out and came abroad, overwhelmed with debt, and chose Paris – of all places – to begin his career of economy.' They live in the Champs-Elysées, where 'the want of money tended to depress the family thermometer . . . and [Rita's mother] struggled to make ends meet'.

The portrait of the fictional parents is unflattering and unlike anything Gertrude ever says directly about her real parents.[4] The Colonel resents the children and there are frequent, tempestuous rows between the parents. Mrs Perceval, left at home to care for the children and to scrape together the household budget, eventually 'lets herself go': she becomes an invalid, spends much of the time lying on her couch, and never goes out into society but will occasionally receive visitors in her sitting-room. She is large and unwieldy as a result of this inactivity, but 'her face remained beautiful to the last'. Colonel Perceval, meanwhile, abandons himself to further dissipation: he takes a mistress, gambles heavily, and is thrown into the debtors' prison.

The main action takes place when Rita is a young woman of marriage-able age. It is a dangerous, exciting world, where one false step can condemn a girl to a lifetime of unhappiness, or worse, the social ostracism that attends upon those fallen women who follow their passions and conduct liaisons outside the confines of marriage. Rita's father, rather than protecting his eldest daughter, is in fact scheming to trade her to the marquis d'Ofort, an ageing French aristocrat, in return for paying off his gambling debts. As it dawns on her what is intended, Rita becomes aware that her childhood has well and truly passed away.[5] Her father, in league with a rich society widow called Lady Greybrook (an echo of Lady Aldborough?) contrives to launch Rita into this marriage market by taking her to her first grown-up ball. She is dressed up in white, as if to emphasise her purity in so corrupt a world, and Lady Greybrook – detecting an unnatural paleness of complexion – daubs the girl's cheeks with rouge. Rita blushes with shame: 'The first thing I can remember when we entered the ball-room . . . was the painful consciousness of being stared at . . . I thought my cheeks were attracting general attention, and that was sufficient, of course, to dye them the deepest crimson.'

As she enters the ballroom, a woman says: 'There goes Lady Greybrook . . . what is it she has got with her?'

'Don't know – something raw – dressed quite *au naturel*, you see,' another replies.

'For shame! The chaperone at least has plenty of *sauce piquante* . . .'

The unmistakable subtext of this passage is the new girl being primped and preened as if for her first night in a brothel, her transparent innocence goading the men to pay the highest price. She attracts two English suitors – one a rakish aristocrat (Lord Rawdon), the other a good-hearted landed gentleman (Hubert Rochford) – as well as the ancient marquis. Rita's father makes it clear to her that her romantic preferences are irrelevant: 'You understand, honourable or not, the first eligible offer you have, by God, you shall accept it'.

Some time later, she is dropped off late at night at the wrong address and deserted by her chaperon. Inadvertently, she enters the salon of a great courtesan:

I stepped into a large and brilliantly-lighted drawing-room, and the doors closed behind me. Never, as long as I live, shall I forget my bewilderment – bewilderment growing into terror every moment, as I stood and looked around me; hesitating whether to advance, and with retreat cut off.

Where was I? Who were all these people lying about on sofas and divans, playing at cards, smoking, laughing loudly, and rattling small boxes on a green-baize table? Men and women, but no face I had ever seen before!

Yes one! That lady in white with camellia in her hair, I knew full well, from seeing her drive daily in the Champs Elysées. I used to recognise the carriage from the camellias in her horses' heads, and I had been told, alas! That she had a melancholy notoriety. She was half-sitting, half-lying on a sofa, upon the back of which a young man leant, and passed his hand familiarly over the smooth bandeaux of her hair . . .[6]

All eyes turn to Rita. She wakes up, as if out of a trance, to the danger of her position and flees the room, pursued by two or three men. As she is running from the high-class bordello, she is rescued by Lord Rawdon, who happens to be riding by. Without asking what she might have been doing there, he fights a duel to defend her honour, which is in danger of being irrevocably besmirched. He is seriously wounded, but her good name is preserved. From this point, the plot charges forward with brio and absurdity, and after a series of improbable adventures, Rita marries Hubert Rochford, the solid Englishman.[7]

In its sensationalist way, Aïdé's novel dramatises the question of a woman's choice: how much right to self-determination does she have in a society driven by material interests? Does she have the right to put her own happiness, her own emotional well-being, before the interests of her family and society at large? The fictional Rita is intelligent, active and strong-minded, and refuses to submit to that which society has in store for her: she is determined to make her own choices on the journey to fulfilment as an adult and a woman. In this, she has much in common with other heroines of other early to mid-Victorian novels, for example Jane Eyre, Esther Summerson in *Bleak House* or Dorothea Brooke in *Middlemarch*. The public loved the work: the Parisian setting was thrillingly exotic; the fast-paced, first person narrative and melodramatic plot were gripping in the French way; the material risqué without being downright immoral. In short, the novel was a titillating read, and it established Aïdé as a best-selling writer. When he finally unveiled himself as the author, many found it difficult to believe that the book had not been written by a woman. He went on to capitalise on its success with a series of autobiographical novels written 'by the author of *Rita*'.

Privately, many readers had reservations. 'Although most of the reviews speak well of it,' Elizabeth Gaskell wrote before reading the novel, 'he has been much blamed for its publication by private friends. He is a nice person, though I suspect I shall agree with the private friends rather than with the public reviews.' Her premonition was correct: she didn't like the book. 'We Manchesterians are too English to have such a French novel in

our circulating libraries,' she concluded on finishing the work. 'It intro-
duces one just exactly into the kind of disrepuble [*sic*] society one keeps
clear of with scrupulous care in real life. I don't think it is "corrupting" but
it is disagreeable, – a sort of dragging one's petticoats through the mud.'[8]

Although Gertrude, at the time an unknown housewife, was too obscure
to be 'outed' as the model for *Rita*, her father and sisters read the book and
were horrified:

> You must by some means get a book called *Rita* (an Autobiography, it is
> Hamilton's, given out as such) [writes Clementine to Henrietta]. Every
> incident in the story and every character you can trace in it all comes
> from Gertrude, beginning in the rue Ponthieu. There is no mistaking . . .
> pray read it. It does not reflect any credit on her; and it is a most heart-
> less and silly thing . . . none but the family of course would understand.
> She herself stands out as the heroine, and the wonder of the house. As
> a novel, I was made the remark by a lady, 'Oh! It's a very bad book but
> very amusing'; when you have read it, you feel a disagreeable sensation,
> and what good to either of them, it's difficult to say, and when one
> reflects how wilful, spoilt she was and everything sacrificed for her; it
> leaves a bitter feeling of disgust, at least that was my feeling when I read
> it, though one would never acknowledge to anyone that she was the
> person, in my own mind there is little doubt about it.[9]

We will never know what Gertrude herself thought, as she kept a dignified
silence and does not mention the book once in her diaries or letters. By
contrast, her views on Flaubert's *Madame Bovary*, published later in the
year, were very forceful.

* * *

If *Rita* is forgotten, *Madame Bovary* is now rated as one of the great works
of nineteenth-century literature. It was first published in instalments in the
Revue de Paris from October to December 1856, and unleashed a storm of
protest for its uncompromising portrayal of a beautiful young woman's
delusions, adulteries and ultimately her sordid suicide. While it proved
immediately popular with women readers, who complimented Flaubert
for his psychologically accurate portrait of Emma's frustrations and
fantasies, the French political establishment was mortified by Flaubert's
merciless debunking of the bourgeois pieties of marriage, religion and
family. Conservative readers were horrified as much by the pitiless

harshness of Flaubert's realist style as by the graphic descriptions of Emma's depravities, particularly the scene in which Emma Bovary and her paramour make love in a closed carriage careering around the streets of Rouen. (This scene was cut slightly for the *Revue*, in deference to the publisher's justified concerns about the likely reaction of the authorities, but the excisions had the effect of making the chapter still more suggestive and salacious.) Flaubert, his publisher and his printer were charged with 'offending public morality, religion and decency'. The resulting court case was a literary *cause célèbre*, a Second Empire equivalent of the trial of D.H. Lawrence's *Lady Chatterley's Lover* in the Great Britain of the 1960s. 'What the author is showing you is the poetry of adultery and I ask you once again if these lascivious pages are not profoundly immoral,' thundered the public prosecutor. 'Voluptuous one day, religious the next, no woman, even in other countries, even beneath the skies of Spain or Italy, would murmur to God the adulterous caresses she has given to her lover.'

Flaubert's defence lawyer delivered an accomplished if disingenuous counter-attack. Flaubert was presented as a man of sterling bourgeois credentials, of 'impeccable moral character and high social position'. The author was not a pornographer, but a satirist of the highest order, motivated to encourage virtue by delineating vice in uncompromising detail. His dispassionate style and his refusal to pass overt judgement on Emma's conduct, far from suggesting a subversive abnegation of authorial responsibility, was in reality evidence of a 'scientific' desire to present 'things as they really were' and therefore to 'arrive at a useful result'. Like the great authors of the past, he mingled the sublime with the profane . . . and so on for four and a half hours. The appeal to his middle-class background, and to his allegedly moralistic desire to reform the character of the age, would have amused Flaubert as yet another example of the absurd ironies of bourgeois society. In truth, *Madame Bovary* was a seditious novel, less because of the sex than because of its pitiless depiction of human weakness and his refusal to offer his readers the consolations of a happy ending. The ending, in fact, is chillingly brutal in its depiction of Emma's agonising death by arsenic poisoning, prompting the contemporary critic Sainte-Beuve to remark that Gustave Flaubert 'the son and brother of eminent doctors . . . wields the pen like a scalpel'. But the argument did the trick, and a week after the trial, Flaubert was acquitted.

Soon afterwards, the novel was brought out in book form and he found himself a celebrity, acknowledged after long years of obscurity as one of the great writers of the age. The hermit of Croisset, suddenly transformed into a literary lion, remembered his friends in England and sent inscribed

1 Menlo Castle, home of the aristocratic Blake family, close to Gertrude's birthplace on Lough Corrib.

2 Admiral Sir George Collier, Gertrude's distinguished grandfather and hero of the American war.

3 The Admiralty in Whitehall — a scene that would have been familiar to Gertrude's father and grandfather and many other heroic naval forebears.

4 Captain, later Admiral, Henry Collier, Gertrude's rakish father who enjoyed an active and adventurous youth but settled down to a life of indolence after he moved to Paris.

5 Harriet Collier, Gertrude's aristocratic and adventurous mother.

6 A drawing of Gertrude as a young girl (aged either 12 or 13) in Paris. In England it would have been unusual for a girl of this age to put her hair up, but manners were more relaxed in Paris.

7 Gertrude (holding the book) together with two of her sisters – Henrietta (her rival for Gustave Flaubert's affections) behind and presumably Adeline – painted in Paris by an unknown artist.

8 and 9 A sketch of Gertrude (left) at the age of 20, pictured reading a letter at her apartment in the Champs Elysees, as imagined by her favourite cousin Hamilton Aïdé (right).

10 The scene outside the Théatre Francais on 25 February 1830 ahead of the first performance of Victor Hugo's Hernani, as witnessed by Gertrude and her father.

11 Prince Charles-Maurice de Talleyrand, the statesman, as an old man. He took a fancy to the young Gertrude when she met him at the duchesse de Dino's salon.

12 Dorothée de Sagan, princesse de Courlande and duchesse de Dino, Parisian salonniére.

13 Denizens of Parisian high-society. The lady to the far right is wearing a bonnet fashioned by the incomparable (and exceedingly expensive) Herbault.

14 Portrait of Gustave Flaubert at the age of 21, by Edouard Edmond de Bergevin.

15 Flaubert at the age of 47 — no longer the god-like figure of his youth, he was by now one of France's literary immortals.

16 Trouville in 2008 — no longer the primitive fishing village where Gertrude met Gustave Flaubert in the summer of 1842, but the author is not forgotten.

17 A poignant letter from Emile Hamard, widower of Flaubert's sister Caroline, describing to Gertrude the circumstances of her death and enclosing a lock of her hair.

18 Cadoxton Lodge, the Tennant family's country home near Neath in South Wales, which Gertrude first visited on her honeymoon.

19 Charles Tennant as a young man. He and Gertrude first met in the summer of 1834, when he was 38 and she 14.

20 Gray's Inn, where Charles Tennant worked as a solicitor and engaged in numerous protracted lawsuits.

21 A view from the gardens of Russell Square in Bloomsbury. 'Not the first chop in fashion,' Charles Tennant conceded, but number 62 was Gertrude's happy family home from 1848 to 1868.

22 Kingston Maurward, the imposing mansion in Dorset belonging to Gertrude's cousin, where she and her husband spent the early part of their honeymoon.

23 Eveleen Tennant, the future Mrs Myers, painted by George Frederic Watts in the summer of 1876. Gertrude did not like this portrait. 'Too dark, too old,' she wrote.

24 Eveleen with a basket of ferns, by John Everett Millais. Gertrude adored the picture and paid £1000 to acquire it.

25 Dorothy Tennant, the future Lady Stanley, and her pet squirrel Toodles, painted by Watts in 1876.

26 Millais's famous 'No!', the portrait of Dolly making up her mind to reject a suitor. This is a print; the original, painted in 1874, was destroyed in the Blitz.

27 Henry Morton Stanley, the great explorer – described by one observer as 'hard as steel' – left the jungle behind to marry Dorothy Tennant and become Gertrude's son-in-law.

28 Richmond Terrace, Gertrude's home from 1868 to her death in 1918.

29 A photograph of Gertrude taken by Eveleen in the 1880s or early 1890s, when she was around 70 years old.

30 Eveleen's photograph of William Ewart Gladstone, pictured around 1890. It was extremely rare to capture him smiling.

31 Eveleen Myers, née Tennant, who photographed not merely her husband and children but also the great men who frequented her mother's salon.

32 Frederick Myers, psychical researcher and Gertrude's son-in-law.

33 Eveleen's picture of the otherwise unknown Adelaide Passingham.

34 An early portrait of Leopold Myers, Eveleen's eldest son. He was a pageboy at the Stanley wedding and grew up to become a novelist.

35 Dolly's 'The Death of Love', painted to commemorate her doomed love affair with Andrew Carnegie.

36 Engraving of Southwark urchins at play on the banks of the Thames, Dolly's favourite subject.

37 Eveleen's picture of Dolly and Henry Morton Stanley on honeymoon at Melchet Court. '[Dolly] insisted on mother and me ... coming with her,' reads the caption.

38 Gertrude in old age, in the morning room at Richmond Terrace.

39 Winifred Coombe-Tennant, Gertrude's daughter-in-law.

copies of the novel to both Hamilton and Henrietta. Aïdé wrote back to thank him, and Flaubert asked for Gertrude's address by return. He sent her a copy of the book bearing the portentous words 'hommage d'un innaltérable affection' – a similar inscription to the one he had made in the copy of Montaigne he had given her when she left Paris. He added in his blotchy and virtually illegible hand: 'en souvenir de la plage de Trouville, et de nos longues lectures au rond-Point des Champs-Elysées . . .' ('in memory of the beach at Trouville and our long readings at the Rond-Point of the Champs-Elysées . . .'

Gertrude was delighted to hear from her old friend, and pleased that he was making his way in the world. However, her reaction to the novel was as outraged as that of any public prosecutor: 'I will not deliver any fancy phrases,' she wrote to Flaubert, in French:

> but I will tell you straight that I am astonished that you, with your imagination, and your admiration for everything that is beautiful, that you have written, that you have been able to take pleasure in writing something so hideous as this book! I find all that so bad! And the talent that you have put into the book doubly detestable! To tell you the truth, I did not read every word, as when I plunged here and there into the book I found myself suffocating.
>
> I don't understand how you could have written all that! – where there is absolutely nothing beautiful, or good! – and the day will come for sure when you will see that I am right! What is the point of making revelations of everything that is mean and miserable: nobody could read the book without feeling more unhappy, and *plus mauvais!*
>
> I don't know what your mother felt about it, but she must experience a *chagrin mortel* to see such a work! . . . Maintenant j'ai fini pour toujours avec votre Madame de Bovary et n'en parlons plus! [Now I've done with your Madame de Bovary for ever and let's not talk about it any more!][10]

The diatribe is sometimes cited by French scholars as an example of English philistinism when confronted with great (French) literature. As one of the first readers of the book in England, Gertrude voiced the conventional expectation that a work of literature should convey a moral. It was, in fact, not untypical of the reaction in Britain when, decades later, *Madame Bovary* was finally translated into English. Thackeray called it ' a heartless, cold-blooded story of the downfall and degradation of a woman'. (The fate of Becky Sharp in *Vanity Fair* was presumably warm-hearted and uplifting by comparison.)

The forceful style of Gertrude's letter anticipates that of the *grande dame* she was on her way to becoming, but it was more than a pious put-down from a middle-aged, (upper) middle-class housewife: it was a deliberate attempt to recreate the no-holds-barred badinage of their youthful exchanges. 'I have read a little of [the book] and that has finally made me decide to tell you what I think . . . *en souvenir de la plage de Trouville*.' She appended some execrable verses from a forgotten poet which she said were 'entirely applicable to you':

> We entreat Thee, that all men whom Thou
> Has *gifted* with *great minds* may love Thee well,
> And praise Thee for their powers, and use them most
> Humbly, and holily, and lever-like,
> *Act but in lifting up the mass of mind,*
> *About them* . . .

Some years later, Gertrude read a book that, like *Bovary*, was meticulous in its descriptions of provincial life, but that managed to be morally wholesome at the same time. She sent Gustave a copy of George Eliot's *Adam Bede*, but her attempt to influence the style of her friend's writing was in vain.[11] His next published work was *Salammbô*, a historical fantasy set in ancient Carthage; far from taking her admonitions to heart, Flaubert in his new book created a gorgeously amoral celebration of sex and violence. What she thought when she received a copy and dipped into its blood-drenched pages is not recorded. (When an English translation was finally published in 1886, the publishers asked Gertrude if she would send on three presentation copies to Queen Victoria: it is unlikely that she obliged.)

For now, far from alienating the newly famous author, Gertrude's forth-right letter revived old affections and they stayed intermittently in contact until Flaubert's death in 1880.

CHAPTER 16

LES MISÉRABLES

That loss is common would not make
My own less bitter, rather more:
Too common! Never morning wore
To evening, but some heart did break.

In Memoriam, 1850, Stanza VI

The death of Blanche was a grievous blow, all too common in mid-Victorian England, where small children died in droves, victims of random accidents and incurable illnesses. The statistics describe what one historian has called a 'massacre of the innocents'[1]: throughout the High Victorian period, around 100,000 children a year died before their first birthday. From 1840 to the end of the century, infant mortality stayed relentlessly high at around 150 per thousand live births, despite the rapid advances in so many other fields of human endeavour. The chief killers in the first year were diarrhoea, pneumonia, bronchitis and convulsions; as they grew older, children were vulnerable to measles, whooping cough and scarlet fever. Cholera, typhoid and typhus also took their toll. Despite the advance of sanitary reform and improved medical practices, it was only in the Edwardian era that the great killers of the nineteenth century were tamed, and by 1916 the mortality rate had fallen to 100 per thousand.

These statistics do not tell the whole, poignant story, as they do not capture the prevalence of child death as opposed to the death of infants. At a time when the rapidly growing population was overwhelmingly young (in mid-century a quarter of the English population was 14 years or younger), 'there was so much more early death than at present, when most people in the industrialised West die at a relatively mature age'. Of course, the poor suffered proportionally more than their social betters, but the middle and upper classes were not exempt from this holocaust. The collective grief unleashed when Dickens killed off his child characters – Little Nell in 1841 and Paul Dombey seven years later – was a public manifestation of the private desolation experienced by thousands of families.[2] In one extreme example from 1856, a future Archbishop of Canterbury, Archibald Campbell Tait, lost five children under the age of ten to scarlet fever within one month. Charles Darwin, Elizabeth Gaskell and William Ewart Gladstone, to name but a few well-known personalities, suffered dreadfully when they lost children. Money and faith or social position offered little protection against communicable diseases that would not be understood and conquered for half a century. Infant mortality was commonplace, but that hardly diminished the pain when the victim was one's own beloved son or daughter. Religion offered consolations – for example the notion of a good death (when a loved one 'crossed the line' from life to death in full and theoretically joyous consciousness of the life to come); but so many children did not die 'good deaths'. They were struck down horribly and inexplicably, as when Gladstone's four-year-old daughter Jessy died of tubercular meningitis. Some parents, such as Archbishop Tait and his wife, could draw strength from their faith, but Charles Darwin could not find a glimmer of religious comfort after his eldest daughter Annie died in 1851, aged 10.[3] His only consolation was that she died without pain.

For decades to come, Gertrude would mark the anniversary of her own 'indestructible sorrow' with a cross in her diary. Without fail, she would remember the child's birthday, noting bitterly just how old Blanche would have been had she been alive. It was only towards the end of the century that Gertrude became at all philosophical about this death, reflecting that it was perhaps as well that the child had been called to heaven rather than suffer her share of the vicissitudes of life.

Shortly after Blanche's death, Gertrude fell pregnant again. It was, to Gertrude's thinking, quite literally the answer to a prayer, God's way of making the loss of one child bearable. She and Charles were overjoyed when Eveleen was born at four o'clock in the morning on 21 November, 1856. 'She was layed on my sofa at the foot of my bed wrapped in nursery flannel,' Gertrude noted in her diary. Scrutinising her by the gas and candle light, she found her 'red round and quite plump . . . how little I could believe that it was allowed. I felt deeply thankful my joy was certainly not equal to my past fears.'

For a time, Gertrude's grief was eclipsed by the joy of bringing a new child into the world, and distracted by the continuing sheer hard work of nursing her brood of small children. Even with the help of a wet-nurse and other servants, it was still tough, physical work being the mother of four small children; by now, Elsie was eight years old, Charles, four, and Dolly, not quite eighteen months. Gertrude was very much a 'hands-on' mother, especially when compared to her own remote and aloof parents. She did not simply delegate their upbringing to the staff, as was still the case in upper-class families and in many middle-class homes, and was more than a once-daily visitor to the nursery. At this point in her life, the delights of sophisticated social life offered no especial charms, when compared to a life of quiet, unexceptional domesticity. She played with her children; she read to them and said their prayers with them; she took them out into the gardens of Russell Square or to a toyshop to buy hoops or a rocking horse.

It was often remarked in later life that she was especially close to her children, to the two middle daughters Dolly and Evie in particular. In part, this reflects the more emotionally expansive nature of the times (as the century went on, Victorians became increasingly sentimental about their children). One can interpret this as a backlash against the neglect she experienced as a child: she clearly set out to give her own children all that she felt herself to have missed out on, from love and affection to (eventually) money and unquestioned material security. But another factor was clearly the timing of the births and deaths in her family. Dolly and Eveleen were born on either side of Blanche's death – Dolly was just four months old when her elder sister died, and Eveleen must have been conceived no more than five months after her death. At this vulnerable time, it is no more than natural that she clove to these two girls, and would do so all the more when, tragically, she lost yet another child.

Gertrude's namesake was born on 21 September, 1859 and for the first ten months of her life was a normal infant 'apparently in joyous health', according to Charles's diary. There was no reason to suspect that the family would once again be plunged into grief at the loss of a child. This time, however, the transition from busy normality to tragedy was even more precipitate than in the case of Blanche, and the consequences for Gertrude still more desolating. On Sunday 29 July, 1860, baby Gertrude was seized with convulsions. A doctor visited Russell Square and delivered the devastating and entirely unexpected news: there was no hope. The infant slept fitfully in the arms of a maid, waking once in mid-afternoon, by which time her condition had deteriorated. Gertrude sent her husband to bed with his clothes on while she and the housemaid stood by the child in the nursery, dropping brandy on the infant's lips with a camel-hair brush, in a vain attempt to revive her. 'Perhaps she knew me for a moment,' wrote Gertrude. The clock struck one o'clock in the morning of Tuesday the 31$^{st.}$ She held her daughter's hand as the baby died, 10 months and 10 days old. Gertrude sat alone with the child until six in the morning, when she rose to tell her husband that the baby was dead. 'Little Gertrude and Little Blanche! – both in heaven,' she lamented. A few days later, the child was buried in the family plot at Highgate Cemetery.

The death of this second child signalled the beginning of the darkest period of Gertrude's life; when her husband died thirteen years later she was inconsolable, but at least then she could busy herself with the practicalities of bringing up her by then teenage brood of children. But now, at the age of 40, Gertrude was plunged into a deep depression, and this time her prayers were not answered, and there was no remedy for her grief. For the next two years, her diaries recount in sad detail how she and Charles tried and failed to conceive another child.

Baby been dead five months only on New Year's Day [she wrote early in 1860]. Felt so weary! 25 trials and failures! Fits of tears! Wish myself dead!

This day last year our dear little Gertrude was here – always well, happy with us! [she wrote on 21 March, 1861]. Now she is taken. Charles, and four dear children, are left me – still I am unhappy shall I ever be happy again! With God all things are possible! I must never cease to ask, never cease to pray – the God of life, of the living.

Great hope that we may be blessed. [4 June, 1861]

This day Blanche would have been eleven years old, how sad I feel. [6 June, 1861]

Low, sorrowful and desperate about everything. [July]

'The eve of my dear child's death,' she wrote on 31 July. 'Charles appeared indifferent and read silently in the evening. Went to bed in an agony of spirit.'

Her husband, normally sensitive to his wife's feelings, was in the middle of a vicious bout of litigation and his mind was elsewhere, and for the first time in nearly fifteen years of marriage they had a ferocious row. 'Could hardly speak to Charles – blinded with crying,' she noted on 4 August. 'Grief almost unbearable.'

'A terrible day – bright beaming floods of sunshine – cold sharp wind, blue sky – death in my mind – death in my heart,' she wrote a few days later. 'Oh my God save me from the death of my soul.'

Amid these thoughts of almost suicidal desolation, Gertrude continued to act out the part of mother and wife. Truly, as Sarah Ellis advised, she felt obliged to 'suffer and be still'; or rather, to suffer and maintain a dignified front. The family took a short autumn holiday at Tunbridge Wells. She took the children for a donkey ride on the common; they had their photographs taken at the Pantiles; she read *Great Expectations* out loud to her husband. But still, at the end of the year she wrote, 'Not passed one single happy hour during the whole of these 365 days – but many heartbroken ones.'

Early in the New Year of 1862 she hosted a dinner party for twelve, acting the part of the gracious hostess. A few days later, she thought she might be pregnant again. 'Prayer, prayer! To what purpose? Desperately hoping for the return of the symptoms.'

But it was not to be. By 7 May she was once again 'savage from despair'. Even her cousin Hamilton, who was a regular visitor, producing drawings during the day and singing at the piano of an evening, could do nothing to cheer her up.

'Read *Les Misérables*,' she noted in early June. 'Felt very miserable myself.'

Gertrude was one of the first readers in England to tackle Victor Hugo's gargantuan masterpiece, which had been published the previous month in umpteen volumes and extended to 3,510 pages. It must have had a special resonance for Gertrude, as the pivotal events of the epic story take place in the Paris of her childhood. Ironically enough, she would shortly be reunited with the author of the novel, and her encounter with Victor Hugo would lead to a revival of her spirits and point the way to her vocation for the second half of her life.

* * *

On 20 August 1862, Gertrude, together with Charles, their four children and a Swiss nurse called Louise, sailed from Southampton to Guernsey for their annual holiday. Then, as now, the island was popular with holiday-makers for its narrow lanes, unspoiled beaches and spectacular sea views. For the more discerning tourist, there was another attraction in the form of Victor Hugo, now a patriarchal 60 years old. The great man of French literature was midway through nearly twenty years of exile on the Channel Islands, having fled France in December 1851 after Louis-Napoleon's *coup d'état*, when his life came under threat. He settled at first on Jersey, but after France and Britain became allies in the war against Russia he was expelled from there too, and moved to the smaller island of Guernsey in 1855.

Now, from the belvedere atop his home in St Peter Port, he would gaze out to the coast of Normandy and denounce the depravities of the Second Empire. (Hugo was preternaturally long-sighted and claimed to be able to see the church spire at Cherbourg, and to hear the church bells ringing across thirty miles of sea; in his youth, it was said, he could stand at the top of Notre Dame and pick out the shapely rump of a chambermaid on the street below.) The first major work he produced from his exile was a polemical attack on Louis-Napoleon entitled *Napoléon le Petit*, a sort of *Animal Farm* for the age, which was a samizdat best-seller in Paris; there-after, he finished off *Les Misérables*, the epic story of crime and human redemption that he had been working on for decades, and a vituperative collection of poems entitled *Les Châtiments*. The peer of France was now the self-appointed spokesman for the mass of unwashed humanity; the former royalist, who in his youth received a pension from King Charles X, now an ardent republican. Notwithstanding these inconsistencies, he became a rallying point for opponents of the lesser Napoleon's regime, and allowed himself to be compared to the first and great Napoleon in exile on St Helena. His political philosophy was vague and utopian, but his followers were not shy to see him as a future head of the French state, a judgement to which he himself did not demur. By this time, the 42-year-old Gertrude had severed her connections with the France of her youth and had no thought of looking up the hero of her girlhood. She was rein-troduced to him as a consequence of advertising in a local newspaper for a tutor to impart the rudiments of the French language to her son Charlie, now ten years old. A gentleman with the splendiferous name of Monsieur le Chevalier Hennet de Kesler responded to the advertisement. He was a French nobleman who had followed Hugo into exile, and now lived close to the master in a state of considerable poverty.

Charles and Gertrude invited Kesler to Old Government House, the imposing residence in St Peter Port where they were spending their holiday. 'Truly he looked like a frog,' wrote Gertrude uncharitably. 'He was ugly, small, spotted and misshapen, but warm-hearted, generous and intelligent.'[4] His peculiar charm was his fanatical love for Victor Hugo, which became evident when Charles and Gertrude sought to engage him in polite conversation. Charles voiced his own admiration for Corneille's *Le Cid*. Kesler was mortified. He bounded up and down the room in angry excitement, declaring contemptuously: 'Oh Corneille! Victor Hugo est bien plus beau que Corneille! Lisez *Hernani*! C'est sublime!'

Gertrude assured Kesler that Hugo was the greatest of all living poets, the indubitable Master after whom the age would be called. 'The name that is above every name in lyric song,' Gertrude reiterated, citing the judgement of Algernon Swinburne, the great English proselytiser for Hugo's verse. Still, Kesler was not satisfied, and he took down a copy of *Hernani* from the shelves and began to declaim the very verses that had entranced Gertrude on the beach at Trouville so many years ago. This time, the reading provoked barely suppressed mirth, rather than reverence, as Kesler acted out the drama, playing the parts of both Hernani and his heroine, working himself to a state of tears as he came to the end of the death scene. Closing the book, Kesler sighed:

> It is not only the poet, but the man who is so great; if you only knew how tender the heart is, how it bleeds for suffering humanity, his intense pity, and love, for the helpless, for the ignorant, the oppressed, his womanly sympathy for the desolate and the broken-hearted, his tender kindness to little children, you would not wonder at my love, and my admiration for him, or at my joy at being permitted to live in the presence of this great man, who feels the world's woes far more than any personal sorrows. I forget I am in exile!

After this outburst, there was silence. Kesler snatched his hat, thrust it deep over his eyes, and left the room.

The next time Kesler visited, Gertrude ventured to ask whether she could renew her girlish acquaintance with the great man. Perhaps she should first call on Madame Hugo? She was known to be in want of visitors as the Hugos' domestic arrangements were scandalously unconventional. Hugo lived in Hauteville House together with his wife and daughter and one of his sons (the other had by now fled the tedium of island life and moved back to Paris). In a cottage down the road he had installed Juliette Drouet, the former actress who had been his mistress since 1833 and would remain so until she died fifty years later, two years before Hugo himself.[5] Meanwhile his son Toto compounded the scandal by consorting openly with his working-class mistress. The entire family was shunned by respectable society on the island.

When Hugo's life came under threat after the *coup d'état* of December 1851, Mme Drouet helped hide him in Paris before they both escaped to Brussels, leaving wife and children behind. Far from feeling betrayed, Mme Hugo was said to revere the mistress all the more as she had in effect saved her husband's life, for the benefit of all humanity – at least, so Kesler rationalised the relationship between these two women. In the spirit of Christian charity, Madame Hugo had received her husband's mistress on one occasion shortly after they arrived on the island, but they were not now on visiting terms. Hugo himself, together with his son Toto and his daughter Adèle, had lunch with Juliette every Thursday. Hugo was unfaithful to both wife and mistress. A man whose indefatigable energies extended beyond his vast political correspondence and the production of poems, plays and novels, he had a string of liaisons with servant girls and others captivated by his charisma. Even if Gertrude was unaware of the master's appetites, it took some courage to volunteer a visit to Hauteville House.

Kesler returned the next morning, with the message that Gertrude would be 'la bien venue' – that she should not bide her time, she should come that very afternoon. The Hugos were poor exiles but would receive her as best they could. 'Vous Madame,' he said, 'comprendrez cela par le coeur qui sait tout déchiffrer.' ('You Madame will understand that through the heart that knows how to decipher everything'). So Gertrude set off through the little lanes of Guernsey, nervous as she remembered her visit to the Hugo residence in the Place Royale with her friend Fraisé, in the first flush of her girlhood. 'Those happy days seemed so far away,' she reflected. 'Forgotten words and faces rushed back in my memory with painful vividness.'

The carriage drew up before a large white house with green shutters, surrounded by a green fence, the garden withered and neglected, the only ornaments a damp mossy stone seat and a fountain spraying a jet of water limply into the air. (Hugo detested well-kept gardens, Kesler told her later, preferring a state of wilderness in nature as in art. He also kept ducks.) The front door was opened by a maid and Gertrude was shown into the vestibule, a room dimly lighted by two narrow windows of stained glass depicting scenes from *Notre Dame de Paris*, Hugo's great Gothic novel published more than thirty years before. She followed the maid deeper into the dark and musty house, noting that the walls, the banisters, the furniture and the very ceilings were draped in tapestries and heavy brocade. No light, no sound was allowed to penetrate, the curtains were drawn against the bright autumn sunshine, and Gertrude felt strangely oppressed as she was left alone in the Salon Rouge. She studied the furnishings: a suit of armour, a gold sword and buckler encrusted with precious stones, a line of life-size Negro statues, each holding a lamp, the pale light from which was dimly reflected in a gallery of mirrors.

A shrill 'Bonjour Madame' announced the presence of Monsieur Kesler, who appeared from nowhere and was all of a sudden dancing about, rubbing his hands in glee, his head bobbing with good-natured delight in having effected an introduction to this Aladdin's Cave of genius. Like an unctuous tour guide, he pointed out the wonders of the room, drawing Gertrude's attention to the four gilt figures supporting the mantelpiece, the Louis XV scene embroidered by Madame de Pompadour, and other treasures that she had unaccountably missed in her first inspection. Kesler informed the guest that she had arrived earlier than expected, and that Madame was still in her bedroom.

In the midst of their conversation, Mme Hugo entered the room, dressed in a white embroidered muslin dress and wearing a small straw bonnet, as if she had just come in from outside. Gertrude noted that she had small hands and was wearing a pair of pale suede gloves pulled high above her wrists. Mme Hugo apologised for her husband's absence: he was out walking, he lived entirely by rule, and no breach with his routine could normally be countenanced. But her husband would make an exception for the Tennant family, and promised to pay them a visit. 'Mon mari desire beaucoup de faire la connaissance de Monsieur Tennant, qui était M. Kesler me dit un ami de Cobden.' ('My husband very much wants to make the acquaintance of Mr Tennant, who Mr Kesler tells me is a friend of Cobden.')

At this, Kesler stepped forward and said in a stage whisper, 'Le grand homme se dérange si rarement – jamais il ne fait de visite!' ('The great man puts himself out so rarely – he never visits anyone.') Gertrude observed that this exquisitely polite Frenchwoman was very reserved towards Kesler, who stood by 'as if in the presence of royalty'. Mme Hugo had a sallow complexion and small, chiselled features, communicating overall an impression of melancholy hauteur. 'I wondered if she had ever laughed in her life,' Gertrude thought. She recalled the first time she had met the Hugos, and could not stop herself asking after Fraisé Davidale. A look of pain crossed Mme Hugo's features as she explained that Gertrude's friend had died in childbirth in 1843. 'Année fatale,' she murmured, a tear coming to her eye. Gertrude remembered that this was the year in which the Hugos had lost their eldest daughter Léopoldine, together with their son-in-law, both drowned in a tragic accident shortly after they married.

There was a pause, and to change the subject, Gertrude expressed her admiration for the exquisite embroidery on Mme Hugo's dress. She explained that this was called 'broderie anglaise', but that the only place you could buy it was Paris. 'Les ouvrages à l'aiguille ne sont pas aussi finement travaillé en Angleterre,' she lamented. 'Rien n'égale à la lingerie Parisienne' ('Needlework is not so finely worked in England . . . nothing can compare to French lingerie'). Gertrude found out afterwards that nothing English was much prized in the Hugo household; indeed, the great man spent nearly twenty years on the Channel Islands without learning to speak a word of English, and refused to let his daughter learn the language either. The talk faltered. Mme Hugo complained that the prevailing easterly winds had a tendency to increase her migraines. Gertrude ventured to suggest iced soda water and milk, combined with fresh air. (Madame Hugo rarely left the house; never went for a walk and certainly never went for a ride in one of the open-topped basket carriages that could have taken her about the island without undue exertion; Hugo, by contrast, together with his mistress, enjoyed pacing about the island in all weathers, taking particular pleasure in studying the sea dashing against rocky headlands during the equinoctial gales.) At this, Mme Hugo almost smiled, commenting that the English seemed to need so much exercise, a result of their unhealthy diet of roast beef and too little soup and salad! Gertrude found herself exempted from this general condemnation of England and the English, cast into a role she had not played since before her marriage, that of honorary Frenchwoman. When Hugo himself launched into a similar excoriation of all things English, he playfully made clear that the general criticism was not directed at her: 'Vous n'êtes pas anglaise!'

Gertrude took her leave, convinced that the encounter had gone badly. Yet within a day or two, Kesler popped up and reassured her that Madame was *enchantée*, and that iced soda water and milk was now the order of the day at Hauteville House, and that before too long Hugo would indeed condescend to pay them a visit in person.

The master paid two visits to the Tennants before he found Gertrude at home. He did not deign to make appointments, but still Kesler was indignant at their being out when the great man came by. The first time, Hugo scribbled his name on a piece of paper and left it wedged in the door;

when Kesler saw this memento lying neglected on the drawing-room table, he was horrified. 'Did we know the value of that signature?' he asked. 'Now – and in ages to come? Impossible, I should have put it by with my most precious documents.' Gertrude said she supposed he had forgotten his visiting cards, at which Kesler was mortified. Did I think so great a man as Victor Hugo had ever had visiting cards printed? The next time Hugo dropped in, it was in the middle of a rainstorm, and Gertrude said afterwards she hoped a servant had offered Hugo an umbrella. 'Comment, Madame, comment !' Kesler expostulated. 'Lui – ce grand homme – se servir de parapluie. Jamais! Jamais!' ('Him – this great man – using an umbrella! Never! Never!' He added 'Could you imagine Julius Caesar under an umbrella?')

The third time Hugo paid a visit, Gertrude was down on her hands and knees in the drawing-room, helping her son arrange the animals in a toy Noah's Ark. Her husband and maid were out and she was all alone with her four children, and at first she was horrified when the great man, having let himself into the house, appeared before her. Yet he swiftly put her at her ease, taking her hand in his, looking into her eyes earnestly and searchingly for a moment before raising her hand briefly to his lips. He sat himself down and shook little Charlie's hand, and Gertrude felt somehow that it was quite natural that this giant of French literature should be sitting in her living-room and introducing himself to her children. They met Hugo's legendarily penetrating gaze with innocent wonder, captivated by his strange appearance: close-cropped grey hair, a massive forehead with the sheen of marble, and a short grey beard and moustache hiding his mouth. When he opened his mouth to speak, his voice was sonorous, as befitted a great poet, and he displayed a perfect set of brilliant white teeth. He had small, dark eyes and no eyelashes. 'These children are old friends of mine,' uttered Hugo, mysteriously. 'We know each other well.'

He noticed their dolls reposing on the sofa cushions, and asked what they were called. Gertrude told him that one was Cosette, the other Fantine, at which Hugo was heartily amused. This was probably the only household in the Channel Islands, or anywhere in the English-speaking world for that matter, where the dolls would have been named after two characters in *Les Misérables*. Cosette, the children's favourite, was decorated with blue beads around her waist, and the poet allowed the children to untie the beads from the doll and wrap them round his wrist, pushing up his shirt-sleeve to help them put the bracelet in place. 'It was impossible not to be struck by the perfection of his hands,' Gertrude recalled; 'their shape and proportion, and the form of the fingers were like a fine antique.'

At this juncture, Louise, the nurse, came to collect the children, and Hugo was captivated by her, subsequently talking to her 'with all the reverence due to a Princess'. (Perhaps this was his usual seduction technique.) Charles then returned home, and Gertrude was delighted at the prospect of the two men making each other's acquaintance, as she knew that they had many political views in common. (Both believed that poverty was a result of social injustice rather than personal misconduct. 'Mendicancy and distress were presumptive proof of misgovernment,' as her husband put it.) Yet she was worried that Hugo would not understand Charles's 'English French', and rightly so, as Hugo had exacting standards for spoken French, maintaining that he himself was the only man alive to speak the language perfectly. However, 'Mr Tennant's earnestness, thorough knowledge of what he was talking about, forgetfulness and indifference as to the imperfections in his language, seemed to interest Victor Hugo and rivet his attention.' Hugo told Gertrude later that there was an originality and power in that English French, which conveyed more to him than many a polished phrase. The author took his leave, saying that the Tennants would be welcome to pay a visit to Hauteville House on Thursday or Sunday evenings, when Hugo held court with Kesler and other members of the French community in exile. As General Slade, the governor of the island, would not know him, on account of his relationship with Mme Drouet, few English people ever attended these soirées, with the exception of newspaper editors who were presumably immune to moral contamination.

In due course, they went to dinner with the great man and his hangers-on, who included the inevitable Kesler, Mme Hugo, his son François and daughter Adèle, a local antiquarian and linguist, a Francophile journalist or two. The meal was served on a bone china service of white and gold, given to him many years ago by King Charles X. On the wall behind them hung the picture that had appalled Gertrude and her friend when they visited his house in the Place Royale, the portrait of Inez de Castro given to Hugo by the duc d'Orléans. Gertrude was placed next to Hugo, who launched into a fantastical account of the Channel Islands in ancient times. He adumbrated images of witches and arch-demons holding their Sabbath around the cromlechs and druidical altars that are a feature of the islands. He talked of vast mysterious forests, now buried under mountains of sand; of burning volcanoes and glittering silver mines. And then a mighty rush of water and the island of Jersey was torn asunder from the mainland! 'He spoke,' Gertrude recalled later, 'as if he had been present at it all.'

'Unfortunately,' Gertrude observed, bringing the conversation abruptly back to the mid-nineteenth century, 'French people now refer to the islands as the "Isles Anglaises".'

'Jamais!' Victor Hugo expostulated. 'Never! They are pieces of France fallen into the sea and picked up by England.'

He explained that they should really be called the Isles Normandes. 'Once upon a time the passage between Jersey and France was so narrow that some faggots of wood were thrown across to enable to the Bishop of Coutances to make the crossing without wetting his feet.' In Jersey, you feel yourself in Normandy, the master asserted. By contrast, Guernsey was not at all Roman.

'What proofs do you have for saying that?' ventured Charles Tennant in his English French.

'Roman coins founds on the island,' replied Hugo. 'The Emperor Claudius named the island Caeseria, which is corrupted into Jersey; the Romans never came to Guernsey, it is quite *celtique*.'

'But Julius Caesar in his commentaries refers to islands off the coast of Normandy, not an island,' insisted Gertrude's husband. Hugo ignored the point, and continued by enumerating all the notable persons who had visited the islands, from Rabelais to Magloire, the hermit of Sark.

'At all times in history, the islands have been a refuge for French victims of persecution and revolutions,' said one of the newspaper editors. 'The Huguenots escaped here at the Revocation of the Edict of Nantes and the nobles came here after the Terror, Chateaubriand amongst them.'

'And the greatest of all the names enumerated this evening,' interjected Kesler, 'is before you, an exile.' He pointed at Hugo. Gertrude and her husband looked on in silence. The master was in no way flustered. 'He took it all as a matter of course,' Gertrude wrote later.

The talk turned to religion: although Hugo rejected the notion of a Christian divinity, Gertrude thought that she had never met a more naturally Christian and charitable Frenchman. ('He declared that the first duty of a state was to protect those who cannot protect themselves . . . it was impossible to be in Victor Hugo's presence and not be struck by his chivalrous gentleness towards the helpless.') Then from God to a subject possibly even more sublime: himself and his work. He told Gertrude that he had based the character of Marius in *Les Misérables* on himself, just as Marius's father M. de Pontmercy was modelled on his own father, a general in the Napoleonic army from whom he was long estranged. His mother, meanwhile, had been a royalist who had hidden and saved seven priests in a barn during the Terror.

Gertrude learned that Toto was devoting his years of exile to translating Shakespeare, prompting her to ask the assembled company who was considered the French Shakespeare. 'It is Corneille, is it not?' At which there was an awkward silence and François and M. de Kesler looked at her in astonishment. 'Mais comment vous ignorez qui est le Shakespeare Français?' Kesler spluttered. 'Mais vous êtes chez lui, c'est Victor Hugo!' ('But how is that you don't know who the French Shakespeare is? But you are his home, it's Victor Hugo of course!') Gertrude bowed her head and was silent, reflecting later that 'an Englishwoman could say nothing, unless she said too much, for politeness'.

The food, prepared by Mme Drouet's cook, was served one dish at a time, and was delicious. Hugo favoured local delicacies such as conger eel soup. There were no vegetables. The evening concluded with a visit to Hugo's study at the top of the house where he spent long hours at the belvedere, staring out at the sea and the clouds and sunsets, committing his visions to paper, or reclining on a silk-covered divan over which dangled a contrivance like a desk which he could reach for from any position and jot down his thoughts without being obliged to move and so disturb his concentration. At this stage in his lengthy career, Hugo was painting as well as writing poetry and plays, and he showed Gertrude and her husband his charcoal and pastel drawings, which modern biographers have likened to the productions of Turner. At the end of the soirée, Hugo took leave of the Tennants with his customary farewell: 'Sans adieu.'

The next morning, Kesler asked whether Gertrude had noticed the superior dignity which the consciousness of his intellectual greatness, and long solitary meditation on sublime subjects, imparted to Victor Hugo's countenance and even his movements. She said she agreed, but suggested that the hauteur of his manner might arise from other causes. What did she mean? harrumphed Kesler.

'The world says, but I do not,' Gertrude replied diplomatically, 'that Victor Hugo has an *orgueil immesurable* – an immeasurable pride.'[6]

Gertrude did not tell Kesler that although she had enjoyed the meal enormously, she was now suffering from an upset stomach.

* * *

An inconsequential holiday encounter with the half-crazed genius of French literature? Or a turning point in Gertrude's life?

By the time she and her family returned to London in early November, having spent many more convivial evenings at the Hugos', the mood of desolation that had hung over her for years had begun to lift. She wrote a long, rambling memoir of Hugo and his bizarre family. She became reconciled to the fact that there would be no more children and began to take an interest in the world beyond the nursery. In the year following the visit to Guernsey there were no further tragedies, although she did twist her ankle badly. She inscribed the following dedication in the flyleaf of her diary for 1864:

Thank God
   (1) My husband is still alive
   (2) My four children are still alive
   (3) I hope to recover the perfect use of my ankle
   (4) I can at last say I am satisfied. 'Thy will be done!' Not mine!

CHAPTER 17

MOVING UP IN THE WORLD

Richmond Terrace, to which the Tennant family moved in late 1868, five uneventful years after the holiday encounter with Hugo, is the direct continuation of Downing Street to the east of Whitehall, a cul-de-sac of eight substantial three-storey houses clad in amber brick and Bath stone. The houses are not as imposing as the great mansions of Belgravia or the terraces built by Nash in Regent's Park at around the same time, but the location is if anything better, lying (according to a contemporary guide-book) 'close to the centre of the metropolis, between the parks and the converging point of the great thoroughfares with ready access to the river . . . [and] nothing but a garden and some gravel walks between [it] and Buckingham Palace'. The house was thus located at the very nerve centre of the British Empire; the governmental equivalent of the Greenwich Meridian, or zero degrees longitude, the reference point for the rest of the world.

Turn left into Whitehall at the end of the terrace, and the Foreign Office,[1] the Treasury, the Houses of Parliament and Westminster Abbey are all within minutes' walk; turn right, and you soon reach Trafalgar Square. Whitehall, still the ceremonial centre of the British state, where the glorious dead of two world wars are lamented, was in the nineteenth century the place where crowds gathered at times of national celebration (like Queen Victoria's successive jubilees) or disasters (such as the death of Robert Peel or the fall of Khartoum). Once, when William Ewart Gladstone was expected to give a major speech in the House of Commons, there were so many people in the street outside that a marooned omnibus driver told Dolly (as she came out to join the crowd) that 'we might really think it was the saviour coming' instead of the Liberal Prime Minister. 'Still he is a wonderful man,' added the driver cheerily, 'and I would be glad to drink his health.'[2] Trafalgar Square, then as now, was the site of spontaneous as well as planned public gatherings, and the occasional riot. Only slightly further afield are Pall Mall, Piccadilly and St James, the heart of London's clubland. Mayfair, Belgravia, Kensington, Knightsbridge and other more conventionally fashionable addresses seemed remote, almost provincial, from so central a vantage point.

There was tranquillity, amid the bustle of crowds and power. At the eastern end of the terrace was a private garden leading to the Thames, where Sir Joseph Bazalgette would shortly begin the construction of the Victoria Embankment. (As Trollope noted in *Can You Forgive Her?* this would reach from Westminster to the remoter desolations of Pimlico.) Opposite, on the site of what is now the Ministry of Defence, was Montagu House, London home of the dukes of Buccleuch, and further to the east Whitehall Gardens and Peel House, the mansion constructed for the former Tory premier. From the terrace, you could hear the tolling of Big Ben, the hooting of horns from the river traffic and the clip-clop of hoofs, but it was otherwise insulated from the hubbub of busy central London. The street is cordoned off today, and easily overlooked, squashed in between the monolithic Ministry of Defence and the Department of Health. While Peel House and Montagu House have long gone, the terrace survived the Blitz and today forms part of the Department of Health. Inside, the fireplaces and chandeliers remain, but otherwise there are few traces of former grandeur. The façade can be viewed from Whitehall. Peeping through the railings, it is possible to see a blue plaque celebrating Stanley's residence, on the house one in from the left-hand end; that is, the river end of the street. It has now been renumbered No. 6 but was then No 2. Where carriages once waited for Gertrude's distinguished guests, policemen now stand guard.

Late in the afternoon on Saturday, 5 June 1869, Gertrude was looking after her eldest daughter Elsie, who had taken ill and was recuperating in her bedroom at the new family home, when a visitor was announced. It was John Bright, the President of the Board of Trade, who had dropped in unexpectedly after a meeting of the Cabinet. 'I did not feel very much up to receiving pleasantly the great politician,' Gertrude confided to her diary. 'However trying "a smiling face to put on", I went into the drawing room and found John Bright earnestly talking to my husband, both my little girls at his side.'

Bright, the prominent Manchester Radical politician (by now an MP for Birmingham) and the first of countless statesmen, writers, artists and celebrities to pay a visit to No. 2 Richmond Terrace over the next forty years, would have approached the double doors of the house up a small flight of stone steps with a fanlight above. The door was opened by a butler, who then showed the visitor from the gaslit vestibule into the ground-floor library or dining-room, or straight upstairs to the first-floor sitting-room, which extended the full length of the house, nearly 50 feet long by 20 feet wide. On the day of John Bright's visit, the 14-year-old Dolly was especially curious to meet the distinguished man.

'Why did you want to come and see me?' John Bright asked the girl.

'My father is always speaking of you with so much admiration,' she replied, 'and Mamma has your photograph, so I myself want to have your Bust.'

'Ah,' said Bright, laughing heartily at this early demonstration of Dolly's artistic inclinations – and her precocious interest in social trophy-hunting. 'My girls are much more interested in me than my boys are. You too, take an interest in what interests your father, so I come in for a share!'

He took his tea without sugar, and devoured four slices of bread and butter, talking all the time of the terrible conditions in the cotton trade and the necessity of a settlement to the Irish Question. The political issues of the day were of limited interest to Gertrude at this time. Her husband chuckled as her eyes glazed over. 'I declare, my wife only cares for what is going on in her own home,' Charles said. 'The Irish Question, and all the Ministers might vanish away together into eternity for all that my wife cares!'

Bright recollected the last time he had visited Richmond Terrace, to visit the Member of Parliament for Stroud who lived in a neighbouring house. It was in the summer of 1858, at the time of the Great Stink, when the river clogged up with untreated sewage. 'I could hardly eat my dinner,' he recalled. 'The waters from the Thames stunk so, the stink was unbearable!'

Gertrude was horrified. 'Would a very polished gentleman have so expressed himself?' she wondered. The word 'stink' was not used in polite society. Bright said he admired a photograph of Gladstone that Gertrude displayed on the mantelpiece – quite the best he had ever seen – and promised to visit again soon.

* * *

Charles had left Russell Square on 23 December of the previous year with mixed feelings – he had lived in 'dear old No. 62' for more than forty years, a time 'varied with much happiness, much anxiety and many afflictions'.

The move, though tinged with regret, was a statement of new-found financial and social self-confidence. Charles took an initial lease of 14½ years at a rental of £390 a year to include the coach-house and stables to the rear; in addition there was a premium of £400 to be paid, plus a further £592 for fixtures and fittings. He knocked this down to £900 11s. (This compared to the annual rent of £140 at Russell Square.) In the eyes of the world, Charles Tennant had long been a wealthy man, and an outlay of nearly £400 a year should have been well within his means. As we have seen, however, the family's prosperity was imperilled by the constant legal challenges from his brother and others who fought for a share of the assets and the income from the canal. Yet by the 1860s, as he himself was approaching his seventieth year, he began, at last, to feel secure in his wealth. Business was booming – traffic on the canal reached its peak in 1866 and the new railway through the Vale of Neath was making slow inroads into the trade. Higher revenues meant he could reduce the debt, which fell from more than £60,000 in the mid-1850s to £42,500 ten years later. By January 1868, shortly before his seventieth birthday, he had paid off all the arrears on the interest due to Child's. Charles calculated that the value of the estate was more than £100,000 before borrowings and rolled-up interest, leaving a very comfortable margin of equity for the family.

One by one, the threats to his family's material well-being had been eliminated. First, *Tennant* v. *Tennant* was dismissed in Charles's favour, then his disputatious elder brother Henry died in 1865 in straitened circumstances, leaving an estate worth less than £100. The conflict with Lord Jersey was settled without ever coming to court: both sides gave ground, presumably because neither wanted the publicity or the expense of a long-drawn-out trial. (Neither side had to pay any money, but there was some exchange of assets and the title to various properties was clarified.) At the time when the family removed to Richmond Terrace, only a niece and her husband were causing trouble. There was a moment of crisis in 1870 when a preliminary judgment went against him in their favour, and it looked as if the property might have to be sold and broken up; but once again Charles outwitted his opponents, and the estate remained securely in his hands.

There was another consideration that may have weighed on the decision to move: in August 1866, Charles's great friend Charles Coombe died at the age of 89. Tennant was sole executor to the estate and there were awkward scenes at the reading of the will when it emerged that Mr Coombe had left the main part of his fortune – a smallholding at

Broomfield, Somerset and a town house in Maddox Street, Mayfair – to Charles's son, rather than any surviving family member (Mr Coombe had no children of his own). The younger Charles inherited this property while still at school, on condition that he took on his benefactor's name – which he duly did, and was henceforth known as Charles Coombe Tennant. This meant that Charles senior could feel reasonably confident that his only son would be provided for in life. Charlie was packed off to boarding-school (Harrow, like his father) and thereafter to Balliol College, Oxford (then in its High Victorian heyday under Benjamin Jowett), and was expected to make his own way in the world. Henceforth, Charles senior reasoned, he need only worry about making provision for Gertrude and their three daughters.

Elsie, it was already clear, would never be able to support herself: for many years, Charles and Gertrude had been worried about the development of this much-loved child. She was slow-witted, capable of making polite conversation but not otherwise thinking for herself, still less looking after a husband and children. She experienced occasional hysterical fits but was able to read, write, attend social functions and take the train on her own. Like her parents and siblings, she kept a diary, in her case an unreflecting account of outings with her parents and encounters with famous people. It is to the Tennant family's credit that they were never ashamed of her and did not try to hide her away: she lived quietly at Richmond Terrace until the late 1890s.

That left Dolly and Evie, who had every prospect of turning out well. Gertrude strove to ensure that they had all that had been denied to her when growing up; all, indeed, that the now plentiful flow of money could buy. Investment in the daughters' education did not extend to sending them to school: as was the custom still for upper middle-class girls, they were educated at home or sent out to have lessons with a series of tutors. They learned to speak French and Italian and were encouraged to develop their artistic inclinations. While Evie took singing lessons, Dolly, who from an early age displayed great promise as a painter, was given a studio, a room of her own located off the dining-room on the ground floor of 2 Richmond Terrace. This was known as the birdcage, where in addition to her paintings and sketches Dolly kept a menagerie of domestic pets, including birds but also a vivarium (with lizards, snakes and toads), a fish tank and a succession of pet squirrels. The girls read history and literature, but like their mother before them, they derived a large part of their education from the remarkable people they met. Gertrude was fundamentally conservative in her expectations and aspirations for her daughters: she wanted them to marry well, and devoted the middle years of her life to enhancing their eligibility in the late Victorian marriage market.

Charles could now have afforded to move to a more conventionally fashionable part of town, but this was still not to his or Gertrude's taste and, besides, he clearly longed to return to the thick of public affairs. Since the late 1850s, Charles had pursued a career as independent commentator and pamphleteer, issuing pronouncements on the big issues of the day. The first of his many publications was a treatise on taxation – an unpromising subject perhaps, but his *People's Blue Book* ran to several editions between its first (anonymous) publication in 1857 and his death in 1873. Without the prolixity that marred his youthful travel writing or the tendentiousness of his epic poem, this is a punchy tract which aims to elucidate the principles of taxation so that 'every man and woman in the kingdom may have, in their own hands, the means of knowing, what they *are paying* to the Government for the protection of their persons and property, and what they *ought to pay*.' Tax policy was contentious as the nation struggled to find the funds to pay for the Crimean War and Charles came up with the simple proposal that all income tax should be abolished, and replaced with a property tax. (This, he argued, would benefit the working man at the expense of the property owner.) It was Charles's practice to dispatch his new publications to Gladstone, Disraeli, Cobden, Bright and scores of those, distinguished or otherwise, who might have an interest in the subject. He sent 250 copies to Australia and 25 to Mudie's, the circulating library. According to Charles's diary, Victor Hugo himself was an eager recipient of the taxation treatise, as was Edmund Beatty, the night-watchman on Richmond Terrace, an Irishman who had served as a sergeant in the British Army and fought at Waterloo. There is no independent verification of their enthusiasm for Charles's work, but *The Times* did bracket Charles Tennant with Cobden and Bright as a prominent expert on the subject; and for a time John Bright took up Charles's ideas and they briefly gained what the historian G.R. Searle calls 'considerable political significance'.[3] In the end, they were abandoned as being too utopian for practical politics, but it is no wonder that his central proposition, that income tax should be done away with, remained enduringly popular.

Over the course of the next decade, as British politics moved towards the second Reform Bill of 1867, there were eight or nine publications in a similar vein, dealing with subjects as various as the American Civil War, Railway Reform (where his views were far from impartial) Utilitarianism and the Irish Question. His *magnum opus* was a 990-page history of the Bank of England, publication of which was timely due to the collapse of

Overend, Gurney & Co., an event that shook public faith in the financial system and the central bank just as in the case of Lehman Brothers in 2008. (Charles delivered the enlarged second edition of this in April 1866, days before the bank failed, and the book was reissued shortly afterwards.) After 1865, when he retired from his legal practice, he wrote numerous letters to the newspapers on subjects ranging from the construction of the Victoria Embankment (which he regarded with suspicion lest the engineers trespass on his garden) to the war between France and Prussia. No fewer than six of his letters on the 1870 Budget were published in *The Times*. All these contributions are now completely forgotten, but in his day Tennant was well respected as a controversialist of deep learning and an independent streak of mind, whose opinion was taken seriously by John Bright and others of his standing.

By virtue of his deafness, which had failed to respond to any number of cures, he went out rarely and reluctantly. When he attended a dinner he would impress his interlocutors as much with his bluntness as with the eclectic range of his learning. One evening in 1866, for example, Charles met Robert Browning and could not resist telling the poet how he had never been able to understand one word of his verse. Many, faced with the legendary impenetrability of poems like *Sordello*, felt the same way, but few would have had the nerve to confess this to the author himself. Charles explained how, wishing to discover whose fault this was, he had put some of the poetry into prose, and found that it still made no sense at all. Browning laughed and took the remarks in good spirit, saying he was preparing a new work for the press, which would be thoroughly comprehensible to any mind. He hoped Charles would read it.

* * *

Forty-nine years old at the time of the move to Richmond Terrace, Gertrude had given no thought to going out into society, still less to turning her home into a fully fledged salon. As late as 1863, after hearing Fanny Kemble read aloud from *Romeo and Juliet* at her cousin Hamilton's club, Gertrude maintained to herself that 'scenes of the *grand monde* sadden me – I feel no part really with any of them'.[4] But the mistress of a prominent house in the centre of town could not remain obscure for long. She found that she was called on by all manner of people – and was expected to go out calling. Elaborate conventions governed this form of social exchange:

It is usual on a first visit merely to leave cards without inquiring if the mistress of the house is at home. Thus Mrs A leaves her own card and two of her husband's cards upon Mrs B. Within a week, if possible, certainly within ten days, Mrs B should return the visit and leave cards upon Mrs A. Should Mrs A, however, have called upon Mrs B, and the latter returned it merely by leaving cards this would be taken as a sign that the latter did not desire the acquaintance to ripen into friendship. Strict etiquette demands that a call should be returned by a call and a card by a card.[5]

There were rules on who should make the first call, on the size of the visiting cards, on where they should be put (on the hall table or in a special card basket) and how long one's visit should last (no more than half an hour). Gertrude kept careful notes of those who came to visit her; often she had 30 to 40 calls on a Saturday afternoon, and would be disappointed if numbers were a dozen or less.

Hamilton, now living in Queen Anne's Gate off St James's Park (perhaps ten minutes' walk from Richmond Terrace), helped her get out and about. He took her along to the publisher George Smith's famous 'at homes' at Oak Hill Lodge in Hampstead, where up to forty guests sat down to dinner.[6] On one occasion there she met Charles Dickens's daughter ('a conceited, stuck-up would be beauty, [dressed] in an affectation of mourning' – for her recently deceased father), and George du Maurier, the artist and writer who later in the century was suspected of satirising Gertrude in the pages of *Punch*. She enjoyed the chance encounters with the great or merely fascinating, as when Hamilton introduced her to Anthony Trollope. Here is how Gertrude describes the novelist in July 1869:

A large, burly, bald-headed man, with a thick grizzly beard, and a strange expression about his mouth, as if continually puffing out smoke – there is something vigorous and sensual in his appearance – his hands are thick at the fingers and his clothes badly made – his eyes are fine, his manner pleasant and easy, but not refined.

Trollope had recently had a medallion of Thackeray erected in Westminster Abbey, and spoke of his unbounded admiration for the author, declaring that the novel *Henry Esmond* was the finest thing in the English language.

'At 21, Thackeray possessed £30,000 and he lost it all at gambling, and was penniless at 22,' Trollope said. 'When he died he was where he had started in life, the possessor of £30,000.' All this money was left to his two daughters, Trollope remarked.

'Women have a very fair share of liberty,' he said. 'But I hope men will always be masters in their own homes – so that indeed the person that holds the money-bags must necessarily always be the master.'

Talk turned to the growing craze for velocipedes, an early form of bicycle. 'Women cannot ride on them!' Trollope exclaimed.

Gertrude assured him they could.

'For my part, I would prefer a balloon, I dislike responsibility,' he said. 'If you were destroyed, it was not by your own fault. In a velocipede, all depends on your own skill.'

'A woman's fate is to be in a continual balloon,' Gertrude responded tartly, 'floating about at the will and pleasure of others, the men guiding it.'

This Trollope denied, with a laugh.

To her own surprise, Gertrude found that she rather enjoyed bringing people together. 'I wish him to like her, and her to like him,' she said of her purpose in introducing Hamilton to a lady novelist called Miss Edwards, and this became her creed for the remaining decades of her life. It gave Gertrude special pleasure to combine people from different walks of life when she could see the potential for mutual interest and entertainment. A pivotal moment came in June 1871, when the Dorsetshire poet William Barnes came to stay at Richmond Terrace for a week. Barnes was a retiring parson whose dialect poetry had a big influence on Tennyson. He and Charles had corresponded for years, but this was the first time they had met in the flesh. To secure such a literary celebrity, albeit a minor one, as a guest, and to introduce him to London society, was a coup. Gertrude asked 'all we know most distinguished to meet them'. The guests included Lord Houghton, the statesman and scholar,[7] and Eugène Vivier, 'quite the first horn player of his day . . . and the spoiled child of nearly every court in Europe'.[8] Gertrude went so far as to organise the private printing of a pamphlet of his poems to accompany the reading. A foretaste of many illustrious gatherings around the Richmond Terrace dining table, the party was a great success. If she could make the most of her new social network to introduce Dolly and Evie to the great persons of the day, so much the better – it would replicate the spirit of the life she had enjoyed in Paris as a young woman.

* * *

In the summer of 1871 Charles received an invitation to visit the recently exiled Emperor of the French. The ex-Emperor Napoleon III, captured on the battlefield of Sedan on 1 September 1870, had precipitated the war with Prussia which led to national humiliation for France. The man denounced by Victor Hugo as Napoleon le Petit had exchanged the Tuileries Palace (burnt down by the mob in the aftermath of the war) for Camden Place, a villa in Chislehurst, thirty-five minutes by commuter train from Charing Cross. 'Nobody would know what I would have done for France, had I been permitted, and not over-ruled,' the ex-Emperor lamented, impressing Charles as a shambling grey-headed, short-legged man in grey trousers, of no great intellectual powers but mild-mannered and kindly. He spoke of 'the difficulty of his position' and the violent opposition to free trade in the country that he had formerly ruled. At the end of the interview, Charles had the presence of mind to suggest that his wife and two younger daughters would be greatly honoured to pay a visit to ex-Empress Eugénie. 'Oh, certainly, bring them tomorrow,' Napoleon responded. That being Sunday, Charles demurred. 'Then bring them on Monday,' the ex-Emperor urged. Charles said this would not be convenient. The audience was arranged for one o'clock on the following Tuesday afternoon. Gertrude looked forward to the interview with some trepidation: this was the man whose repressive regime had brought Flaubert to trial and forced Hugo into exile. Her husband assured her that Napoleon III was nowhere near the ferocious figure depicted by his enemies. Dolly and Evie had different concerns: they had a hazy idea of the importance of an ex-emperor and felt that the visit was on a par with an appointment with the dentist.

Gertrude, Charles and the two girls took the train to Chislehurst. They walked up the hill to Camden Place, the Emperor's residence (now a golf clubhouse), and rang the doorbell. A woman came to the gate to ask them what they wanted; they told her they had an appointment with the ex-Empress and were shown along an avenue of trees into the house. After a moment's wait, the Emperor himself came forward to greet them. Gertrude felt rather awkward as he took her hand in both of his – just like Victor Hugo. He placed himself behind a table and leaned forward, resting on both arms and bidding the girls to approach. Dolly and Evie were overwhelmed and said nothing, simply staring at this short, unimpressive man in grey trousers, who used to be an emperor. 'They greatly desire, Emperor, to look at you,' said Gertrude, in French, apologetically. 'Forgive their staring so.' He smiled and instructed a servant to bring in the ex-Empress.[9]

The Empress Eugénie had an aristocratic nose, Gertrude noted when she entered a few moments later, but artificially dyed eyelashes, no ear-rings or rings on her fingers, and a tooth missing on the back left-hand side of her mouth, as became apparent when she laughed. This happened infrequently; most of the time she seemed close to tears, as they discussed the state of the country they had been forced to flee.

'If the rulers ruined France by unwise measures, they would look once more to the Emperor,' said Gertrude, diplomatically.

'Yes,' the ex-Empress replied. 'But France will be utterly ruined and destroyed as a nation, before a reaction will set in.'

'I hear the working man in the Faubourg Saint-Antoine talked of emigration to the United States, and that there are still numerous commu-nists among them,' ventured Gertrude. 'They must be in a helpless state to think of emigrating.'

The ex-Emperor was pleased at this idea.

The conversation turned to the Queen of England, still in mourning after the death of Prince Albert in 1861. ('The Queen is becoming very unpopular,' Gertrude reflected in her diary. 'They now call her The Woman in Black.')

'You seem to think she ought to act the part of a Maîtresse de Maison, and do all the honours of her house,' said the ex-Empress. 'Recollect the Queen is an idea – her presence is not really necessary, and you reproach her for not spending money, not encouraging luxury, and [yet] your news-papers found fault with me, for receiving continually and encouraging dress, and luxury and expenditure! So how can Royalty please?'

'I hope your Majesty will forgive me,' replied Gertrude. 'But everybody knows in their inward conscience whether they are doing their duty or not, and there seems to be a *"juste milieu"* – something between the two.'

The ex-Emperor laughed outright at this. The phrase was politically charged: he and Louis-Philippe before him had tried in vain to steer a course between the extremities of French politics. 'It's certainly true that there is a happy medium!' he agreed.

'Alors,' interjected the Empress. 'Je l'ai donc manqué!' ('In that case then . . . I missed it!')

She seemed interested in hearing more about the popular feeling towards monarchy. When Gertrude said that the English people only wanted the Queen to show herself, to come amongst the people, to drive in the park, the ex-Empress exclaimed: 'Oh happy Queen, that they only reproach her for that. I myself, I'd go ten times, twenty times a day to show myself in the park if that's all the people asked for.' She laughed and shook her head. 'Yes, twenty times a day.'

'I received often,' she said. 'Continually, but oh, the weariness of it! I spent money freely, I feared they would say I had put money by in foreign hands, that I was hoarding! So you see how difficult it is.'

The ex-Emperor was surprised at how much poverty there was in London. 'I believe there was much less abject poverty in France in my reign, than here in England,' he said.

Gertrude told the story of a woman in the Westminster parish who had died a few days earlier of starvation and who had lived just a few streets from her own house. This was normal for London, where the extremely poor lived cheek by jowl with the super-rich. Gertrude explained that she visited the poorhouse in Westminster and read aloud to the inmates: they seemed to particularly enjoy hearing Tennyson, and Dickens's *Pickwick Papers*.

'The Emperor seemed to have read *Pickwick*, and was mightily amused at the paupers of Westminster having this read to them,' Gertrude later recalled.

Gertrude mentioned that she was descended from Oliver Cromwell, and what did His Majesty think of the plans to erect a statue of the Lord Protector outside Parliament among the kings?

'It would hardly do to have Oliver Cromwell figuring by the side of Charles 1,' Louis-Napoleon laughed. 'No, no, it would not do.'

The ex-Emperor lived for less than two years at Chislehurst. On the last morning of his life (Thursday 9 January 1873), his surgeon Sir William Gull found him in a semi-conscious state.

'Ah,' said the dying man, 'Vous revenez de Sedan.'

'Non, sire, je viens de Londres,' the physician replied.

According to Hamilton, who had it directly from Sir William, the Emperor then shook his head. 'Non, vous venez de Sedan,' he insisted.

These were the last words he uttered.

* * *

The year 1872 did not start well: on Wednesday, 3 January 1872, thieves broke into the house while Charles and Gertrude were out to dinner. They were disturbed rifling through Gertrude's bedroom on the second floor and escaped by climbing down a rope on to the drawing-room balcony, whence they climbed over to the portico of the next-door house and down to the street. Evie's cash box was found wrenched open; four sovereigns had been stolen – the only items of value that they managed to get away with.

A few days later, Charles was taken ill. As he lay feverish and in pain in a bed made up near the window in the morning room, Gertrude gave thought to the years ahead. She knew that – despite the depredations of the burglars – the material circumstances of her life had never been so secure. In her fifty-third year, she found stimulation in her burgeoning social life and happiness in her family. Elsie would never be able to pursue an independent life, but all the other children were 'turning out well'. The only cloud on the horizon was her husband's mortality. But for his deafness, he had long been in remarkably good health for a septuagenarian, bounding up the hill to see the ex-Emperor and taking the family on robust autumn holidays (they visited Scotland in 1870 and Ireland in 1871). Now she was forced to dwell on the inevitable. She flicked through the pages of her diary to the month of September. 'If my dear husband is spared to see this day,' she wrote in the space for 11 September, 'we should have been married for twenty-five years.'

Charles found the strength to climb upstairs to his bedroom, where he stayed, bedridden, for weeks. He came down to breakfast on 18 March, the first time since the end of January. Over the next six months, eight medical men came to visit and examine him. There was no consensus as to what was wrong with him: perhaps it was ulceration of the bowels, perhaps cancer. He was prescribed morphine and opium to dull the incessant pain in his stomach, together with strychnine and bromide of potassium in a vain attempt to reverse the progress of the disease. On 1 July 1872, he celebrated his 76th birthday, lying in bed. He was too ill, and Gertrude too distracted, to follow the furore unleashed by a report in the *New York Herald* of the following day, when an unknown journalist by the name of Henry Morton Stanley broke the story that he had 'discovered' the long-lost missionary explorer David Livingstone, in the village of Ujiji on the shores of Lake Tanganyika, some 600 miles inland from the Pacific coast of Africa. Within days, English newspapers picked up Stanley's highly coloured account of how he doffed his helmet and uttered the immortal words 'Dr Livingstone, I presume.' There was of course no reason to suspect that the author of the greatest newspaper scoop of the nineteenth century would himself be fated to live, and die, in the house where Charles Tennant was eking out the last days of his life.

An indication of the gravity of Charles's illness came when Gertrude received a letter from an estranged niece, suing for reconciliation after a lifetime of conflict and animosity. The niece expressed sorrow for the past and a great desire to see Charles once more.

'It is too late,' said Charles after Gertrude read him the letter. 'She has embittered my existence, as much as she could.'

He paused again, looking lovingly at his wife. 'I forgive her, I forgive them and wish them every success in life. I have no ill will towards them, and never had. I am sorry for them, very very sorry.' With a look of extreme earnestness, he added: 'But don't let her come near me.'

On 2 August, he felt the end was coming and called Gertrude to the bedroom.

'You will employ Mr. Martin of Southampton Row, Russell Square, to make arrangements for my funeral,' Charles directed. 'Have it as plain as possible and [go to] no expense whatever. Have only one mourning coach, and our own carriage[s] to return in. Let no-one attend my funeral but you and Charlie and my sister Margaret – it will be too much for the girls.

'You will have great worldly trials,' he cautioned. 'You will not be able to continue in this house when the lease is expired it will be too expensive for you.

'I give no direction about Charlie's future career, it must depend on circumstances, he will have enough to do looking after his own affairs. If you do not [long] survive me, Charlie must take care of his sisters, and give up his Oxford career.

'Be prudent and economical and don't get into debt, you have not a friend in the world who can help you if you do.'

He went on to give a few instructions as to legacies – £20 to her sister when she leaves after the funeral ('she will be at expense, and it will be useful to her'), and a similar bequest to a poor woman called Mrs Graham 'if she wants it'. He said he would now write to Child's to put the money he owned in the funds and his Turkish bonds into her name. 'Or after my death you would find yourself penniless 'til my will was proved. You are my sole executrix.

'I wish my death to be inserted in *The Times* newspaper only – and put thus – Died on [blank] at Richmond Terrace, Whitehall, Charles Tennant Esq. of Cadoxton Lodge, Neath, Glamorganshire, aged [blank].' He said his age was of no interest to anybody, and she could insert it, or not, just as she pleased. On another subject, he was more emphatic:

'I hope you will never change your name.'

The girls were brought to take leave of their father, but he lingered on. He had time to instruct Gertrude on important business matters. He took her through the various securities that would provide her with an income after he died: Turkish bonds producing £750 a year, railway debentures producing a more modest £10 a year. There were £6,000 of shares in the Neath and Brecon Railway Company – Charles's hedge against the decline of the canal: apply to the Secretary at the company's offices, No. 17, Tokenhouse Yard in the City . . . and so on, as he enumerated the family's assets and liabilities. He told her to do everything she could to evade Probate Duty (a scandalous tax, in the opinion of this expert).

'Should the estates not be sold' – he thought it unlikely they could be kept together after he died – 'all the title deeds must be restored to [you] – and all put by in the iron chest [in the muniment room]. Family title deeds ought not to be in the hands of strangers.' Also in the iron chest, Charles told her, was a smaller tin box containing the title deed to the plot of ground in which he wished to be buried.

'I leave my watch to dear Dolly,' Charles said on 15 August.

'Make your will and leave each of the girls £500 a year to be theirs on attaining 21,' he instructed a few days later. 'Let Charles be his sisters' sole trustee. If the property is saved let him increase the £500 a year to £1000. The £500 a year is to go to the survivors of the girls and finally to go back to their brother, should they die unmarried.'

'Never sacrifice [our] children's interest to that of my nephews or nieces,' he continued. 'Do not let the things be sold up and divided.' You can trust Mr Jennings (his agent in Wales), he said, 'but do not let him encroach on his position. Be the high-born dame.'

A few days later, he continued in this vein: 'Do not take upon yourself any generosities. Do not lead anybody to expect anything of you. Do not live beyond your means or put your trust in fashionable friends.'

* * *

In taking stock of her future financial position, Gertrude knew that she could count on a legacy of £4–£5,000 from her father. In the event, this would come to her rather sooner than expected. Less than a mile away from Whitehall, at 25 Ryder Street in the heart of fashionable St James, another deathbed scene was taking place. It was a short distance in terms of geography, but in other ways an immense journey for Gertrude: into the past to pay her last respects to the father she had had so little to do with in almost a quarter-century of married life. She was shocked to see his condition and sent him some oysters to aid his recovery. However, he deteriorated rapidly and three days later she made the journey once more and took her final leave before he lost consciousness. He died at 6.30 p.m., at sunset, on Tuesday, 10 September. Gertrude's sister Henrietta was in attendance, as was her brother-in-law, Sir Alexander Campbell. 'He died without a struggle, he had suffered much before,' Gertrude noted in her diary. George Collier, Gertrude's elder brother whom she had not met more than a handful of times in recent decades, arrived too late to see their father alive.

Gertrude did not attend the funeral, which took place at Brompton Cemetery a few days later, sending her carriage instead. Her aunt Georgina paid a visit. It was an unhappy call, as Gertrude's suspicions as to her father's integrity were confirmed. The conversation yielded 'sad revelations regarding my father's worldly position and conduct'. Quite what this entailed, Gertrude's diaries do not relate. It is telling, however, that the Admiral had remarried late in his life, taking as his bride a woman many years younger than his daughters.[10] This suggests that he preserved his power of attraction, and his love of pleasure, until late in his life. One imagines that like Colonel Perceval, the debauched character modelled on the Admiral in Hamilton Aïdé's *Rita*, Gertrude's ageing father sought to satisfy the same appetites as in his youth and middle age, 'but with enfeebled powers'.

There was no time, however, to dwell on the past. Her husband, so close to her father in age, so different in outlook and moral standing, was still desperately ill. 'Dr Dickenson saw Charles,' Gertrude noted two days after her father's death. 'Does not think him worse, but can hold out no hopes of recovery . . . I am getting stunned, almost hardened,' she wrote. 'I have suffered too much, to have much power left to suffer in me.'

Against all expectations, Charles did stage a partial recovery, and on 23 November came downstairs from his bedroom to join the family for lunch for the first time since June. Three days later, he and Gertrude even went out for a drive in their carriage. But this was to be the last time he left the house. He was bedridden again in the early New Year. 'I am so ready to go,' he said to Gertrude in one of their last conversations. 'Do not give way to sorrow . . . I just want rest, rest.'

Gertrude offered consolation with the thought that 'a part of ourselves is in eternity in the presence of God – Blanche and [baby] Gertrude.'

'Yes,' Charles replied. 'I am thinking of it – and of our meeting.'

Bleeding and in intense pain, taking opium pills every four hours, he lasted until Monday, 10 March 1873. 'Gone,' was the stark entry in Gertrude's diary for that day.

A post-mortem revealed a tumour the size of an orange, located in the region of his left kidney, which had burst and given rise to a fatal haemorrhage.

'First day of a long – an everlasting agony,' she wrote the next day.

Charles was buried on Thursday in the family plot in Highgate Cemetery. As he had intended, it was a quiet affair. Alone of the family, Gertrude, Charlie and Dolly witnessed the burial.

CHAPTER 18

GERTRUDE'S DARK NIGHT
OF THE SOUL

A month after Charles's death, Gertrude began a diary written in the
form of letters to her deceased husband. On 11 April, 1873, she resolved
to write to:

> Him who is only 'Gone before', who for a little time must be absent from
> me, to whom I shall speak again, see again, and be with again for ever in
> the Holy presence of My God, and my Saviour. I mean to speak to Him
> – my own dear Charles, my Husband and My Friend, as if he was only
> gone on a voyage to some distant part, where I must prepare hourly soon
> to join him. I am now 53 years of age. I think I shall now live about
> sixteen years longer – in those sixteen years I have a great deal to do for
> my surviving children, and also for the sanctification and purification of
> my own soul.

She kept up the diary for a little over a year, recording her visits to church
and to Charles's grave in Highgate Cemetery, as well as her prayers for
herself and for her children. At times, Gertrude seems almost suicidal, but
she draws consolation from the conviction that she will sooner rather than
later be reunited with Charles and her two dead children. 'I have been
dear Charles to the Temple with our four dear children,' she wrote on
Easter Sunday

> and I heard Dr Vaughan preach, on those words from the III Chapter of
> Coloss. 'If ye then be risen with Christ, seek those things which are
> above, where Christ sitteth on the right hand of God.' I thought of you,

and only of you, and that you were there, with Christ! And then your words: Parting! Parting! rushed back into my agonized, bewildered heart, and a terror came to me! An agony of Despair that I must wait till I see him again. If you could only speak one word to me . . . if I could be where you are. I humbly pray to God Almighty and all merciful not to spare me, to send down upon me every personal affliction which may best fit me for that blessed change, when I shall be taken from this world to my true Home, and that is where you are, you and my two little darlings, my eyes so long to behold! If you could see these words, see my broken heart, see how I yearn, even in my sleep, for the comfort of your dear presence, I would tell you how I wish I had been less worldly . . . how valueless everything has become but the hope that I may one day be with you and my six children – and that the four now here may join us – spotless, forgiven – and fit to be in the presence of their God.

At times, she is overwhelmed by a desire for self-annihilation.

Since the 10th of March things I could not the least comprehend, have burnt upon me – and – a something that was me, no longer exists – am I myself? Where is my former wilful, fearless, world-loving self? Am I, too, dead? Most certainly I am, and when I think that in 16 years I shall be 70, very near being released, can I not bear it bravely, nobly, patiently? That thought gives me such strength, something like joy.

'At times, I feel a heavy despair,' she writes on 20 April, 'so that I do not know how to bear myself, but I pass through such an infinite variety of feelings, in one day, even in one hour, that I positively fear my poor self . . . My God, is it only 41 days since I heard your voice? If 41 days have been such an eternity, how shall I live 16 years? Which I must live if I am to reach 70? Dear Charles, for Christ's sake, Go – Go – and ask him to help me!'

Balancing the desire for an early death is a powerful sense of worldly responsibility to her four living children, particularly her three daughters:

I may be kept here for long years and years [how right she was – she would be a widow for more than forty years]! God's will be done! May my children find worldly protectors and friends, that is now my most intense desire. I should so thank God if he would take them from me, and [deliver] them to those, Good and Worthy, who could throw strong arms around them, watch over them, steer them, and fit them for English homes. [13 July]

Amid sombre predictions about the future, there is a hint of the physical passion that Charles must have expressed towards her: 'I intend on Thursday the 10ᵗʰ of March 1874, the first anniversary of your no longer being here with us, to go with your three girls Elsie Dolly and Evie to your grave in Highgate Cemetery, where please God I shall be permitted to rest by your side, at least this poor old body, *you once so much admired* [author's italics], and will be placed side by with yours . . .'
She bemoans her lot as a widow:

Oh, why is life so unutterably sorrowful? And who would think it, to look at me? I wear no widow's cap! (How you hated those caps!) How I hate the word widow! It sounds so helpless, so poor, so abandoned, so godforsaken, and that alas, is what I feel!

I am not always what is called unhappy, but I think even in my sleep I am uneasy [she writes just before Christmas]. I have no longer anyone on whom I can cast my many cares! I pray to God ! sometimes – but I can never pray truly without agonies of tears, which undo me for hours, unfit one for work, for duties, for seeing after the home he left me!

The last of these poignant letters is written in May of the following year. By now, strong practical concerns are uppermost in Gertrude's mind:

Oh! That I could see my way clearly before me. I am not satisfied with the atmosphere that my dear girls are in. I am trying to get them homes of their own! But I see nobody I or you would think worthy companions for them! I pray you who loved them so, to be near them, in all dangers to their souls and bodies . . . guard over them and make them fit for our meeting . . .

She concludes by telling her husband that she is still thinking of him daily and hourly.

It seems so wonderful to think that you have only been away to my earthly eyes one year and three months. It seems truly years and years and years ago! Oh dear Charles, where are you? I pray, I more than pray, I implore you to be near me. If I am ugly to your sight, please take pity on me! When alive, you once said, that if I committed crimes, you must love me all the same! Oh say so now, and love me still, till we meet.

For all the private sense of desolation expressed in these poignant letters, the practical side of her nature recognised that she had a job to do – to get the girls off her hands. Convinced, quite incorrectly, that she would not live much longer, she believed she needed to strain every sinew to ensure that the girls married suitably and happily; and to get the job done as quickly as possible.

CHAPTER 19

Re-entering the Marriage Market

Just three weeks before Charles died, Dolly attended her first ball, at the home of Mr George Smith, the publisher. The vivacious red-headed girl danced every dance and was very happy. Gertrude must have been reminded of her gregarious younger self, 'hoofing it' until the early hours with the young princes at the Tuileries Palace, but she would not allow the comparison with her own youth to be taken any further. Her parents had left her to her own devices at this critical point of her life and she had been obliged to take matters into her own hands. Thirty or so years later, Gertrude was determined that Dolly and Eveleen (17 and 16 years old when their father died) should not suffer a similar fate.

Gertrude's campaign to marry off her daughters began in earnest on 5 May 1874, just over a year after she was widowed. (It was conventional to spend a year in full mourning.) On this day, she took Dolly and Eveleen to be presented at court, signalling the official 'coming out' of these two eligible young women. The ritual presentation of upper-class girls to the monarch continued until well after the Second World War; it was the starting gun for the London season, a frenetic round of social events at the end of which it was just possible that one's daughter had met an appropriate mate; if not, the whole procedure would have to be repeated the following year. Gertrude's younger brother Clarence, now a colonel in a Guards regiment and the only one of her siblings whom she saw at all regularly, stood in at the ceremony for her deceased husband. The presentation was followed a week later by the first of Gertrude's parties, to which she invited 150 guests, of whom 134 came. This was 'said to have gone off well', Gertrude wrote in her diary, while acknowledging that many things had been mismanaged and would be put right next time she entertained in her splendid first-floor drawing-rooms.

In these early days of Gertrude's social career, long before her home can properly be called a salon, Hamilton Aïdé, by now well established in his career as artistic dilettante and man about town, was a constant presence. The actor Henry Irving became a family friend by virtue of his close connection with Aïdé: the actor produced and starred in Aïdé's romantic drama *Philip*, which opened at the Lyceum Theatre on 7 February 1874. Other frequent visitors were Millais, the painter whom Gertrude had befriended early in his career, and Thomas Huxley, the scientist and social reformer known as Darwin's Bulldog for the vehemence with which he championed Darwin's evolutionary theories.[1] Although these three men were among the greatest living Victorians, it is too early to see the guest list as the fruit of a sustained effort on Gertrude's part to attract celebrities into her home. Like Gertrude, Millais and Huxley both had a superabundance of unmarried daughters (seven between them) of a similar age to Dolly and Evie. They visited with their wives and children and the talk was less likely to touch on natural selection than the choice of a husband. (Huxley said he never went out to dine unless he made an exception, 'and Mrs Tennant has always been an exception'.)[2]

Gertrude, Dolly and Evie went to Oxford for May Week, a frolicsome week of sporting contests and parties that takes place in June, where it seemed that Gertrude's match-making might bear rapid fruit. There were garden parties and a picnic at Blenheim Palace up the road in Woodstock; boat-racing on the Thames and summer balls in the medieval college buildings. Gertrude herself seems to have attended at least some of these events. 'Danced one dance, walked about the old quad by moonlight, walked home,' she wrote after one evening's entertainment. 'Very tired, too tired to enjoy my joy!' In the exquisitely romantic environment of an Oxford quadrangle on an early summer's evening, Dolly had met and danced with a college friend of her brother's called Andrew Mulholland, the eldest son and heir of a wealthy Belfast linen magnate. 'Great expectations,' Gertrude wrote a few days later, after the girls ran into this young man again at the Henley rowing regatta (his brother was in the Eton eight, which conferred glamour by association). He agreed to come to lunch with the family at Richmond Terrace. 'Thirty people called,' Gertrude noted the following Saturday. 'Feel happier than I have done for some time. God grant we may be protected – and my greatest wish be accomplished before I am taken.'

The fledgling romance, which one senses flourished as much in Gertrude's imagination as in fact, continued over the next weeks when Gertrude and her children joined Millais and his family for their summer holiday in Scotland. The artist was in the habit of spending the summer months at Birnham, near Dunkeld in Perthshire, painting and enjoying country pursuits such as stalking and shooting. Within days of their arrival, he asked Gertrude if he might paint the girls' pictures. Dolly's first sitting took place on 17 August, the very day that Mulholland and his family appeared at the hotel. There was a party that night, when seventeen people sat down to dinner, followed by reeling and singing. Gertrude put aside her normal objections to such boisterous festivities by noting the glow on her elder daughter's face. 'No sleep last night,' she wrote the next morning. 'Excited by thoughts of future possibilities and impossibilities.'

In the finished picture, Dolly is holding a letter (evidently a proposal of marriage). The pose was supposedly modelled on a scene from a novel, but it had a peculiar pertinence in the circumstances. Her red hair is swept back in ringlets and there is a look of intense concentration on her creamy-white face (which is otherwise, according to a newspaper report, 'charmingly expressive and *spirituelle*').[3] The brightness of her face and hair stand out against the grey background of the room and a dark grey silk dress adorned with lace sleeves and collar. In her right hand she holds a pen and she seems poised to put it to paper to communicate a momentous decision. The slightly stern expression on her face suggests that she has made up her mind to reject her suitor, and the painting (the image of which circulated around the world when she did at last say 'yes') was entitled 'No!' The picture conveys a proud assertiveness, suggesting that a young woman has the right to say 'no' not only to a man she does not love, but perhaps to marriage altogether, to a life of tedious domesticity. In that, it was of its time: the young women of the 1870s and 1880s enjoyed more freedom than their mothers had done at the same age, and many 'New Women' of the last decades of the nineteenth century decided not to get married at all. Given the iconic status of this image and the many years Dolly spent as a single woman, it is somewhat ironic that she might well have said 'yes' to Andrew Mulholland on the day she first sat to Millais. The conflict between the desire for happy domesticity and her vocation as a painter had not yet emerged.

During the sitting, she carefully observed Millais's technique: as an artist herself, Dolly was interested in the way he used very small brushes to apply layer and layer of paint, without applying varnish. She and her mother enjoyed his chit-chat about Frederick Leighton, a fellow Royal Academician whom Millais said had no feeling for the beautiful. Over succeeding days, Millais embarked on the companion piece to the portrait of Dolly, an image of Evie in the open air with a basket of ferns over her arm. She has a mass of long dark hair and a long face with high cheekbones; she wears a dark red dress, black Van Dyke hat tilted across her head at a rakish angle, a severe choker about her neck, and strings of turquoise beads. She holds the viewer with a frank, innocent gaze, and long before Millais had painted in the background, Gertrude decided she must own the picture. Declaring herself delighted with the face and expression, she arranged to buy the portrait there and then. (There was a misunderstanding about the price: Millais said he would let her have the picture for half his normal fee, namely £1,000. When the bill did come, Gertrude was horrified to find that it was for £1,000, not £500, as Millais's usual fee was £2,000; this led to anguish and strict economies, as the purchase absorbed about half the household income for that year.)

A few days later, Mulholland took his leave, thanking Gertrude for her kindness. This seemed a suggestive remark. 'I am sure I feel kindly towards him,' Gertrude thought. However, the days went by and a letter of proposal did not come, and so Dolly did not get the opportunity to say 'no'. A wealthy, charming Old Etonian, close to Dolly in age, he was the only conventional young man that she ever fell for and, to Gertrude's lasting chagrin, Dolly's romantic entanglements became steadily more complicated as she grew older. (In due course, Andrew Mulholland married someone else, and died of typhoid on his honeymoon.) For now, she and her mother were left with one consolation for the fizzling out of the romance: the two portraits were very well received when they were exhibited at the Royal Academy. 'Great day, great success,' Gertrude noted jubilantly in her diary on Friday, 30 April 1875. 'To the opening of the Royal Academy!!!! NO and Eveleen's portrait great great great success [*sic*] . . . Deeply thankful and pleased.'

Two years later still, another portrait of Dolly was exhibited at the Royal Academy, this time painted by George Frederic Watts, the leading portrait painter in England. Watts met the girls in the autumn of 1876, when they were on holiday with their mother at Freshwater on the Isle of Wight, where the distinguished painter had a home known as the Briary. At a time when he was painting some of the most prominent women in Victorian society, including Blanche, Lady Lindsay, the Hon. Mrs Percy Wyndham and Lillie Langtry, he was taken by the beauty of the still rela-tively obscure Tennant sisters and asked Gertrude for permission to paint them. Gertrude soon became nervous at the amount of time the girls spent with Watts up at the Briary: they went there for hours every day. Watts started with his picture of Evie: Dolly records how she stood in the middle of a large, bare, whitewashed room with an umbrella in her hand, tilted so that it made a background to the face.[4] He set down a yellow base and painted in watercolour before outlining the contours of the face and head with light brush-strokes of raw umber earth; two dabs for the eyes, another for the mouth. Then the painting began in earnest: rose white, yellow and light red, colours arrayed not on a palette but in big white china dishes. He talked as he worked, explaining how he used benzoline to moisten the colours, as he preferred the human texture this gave the flesh rather than the artificial shine of oil. He said of Millais that his preference for a pure white background to his portraits was holding him back. 'No artist is happy,' Watts told Dolly as he was painting, 'unless it is Millais, who is constitutionally happy.' (Indeed, increasingly sleek and rich, Millais had turned his back on the bohemianism of his Pre-Raphaelite phase, living proof that artists did not necessarily starve in a garret.) Dolly listened and watched, fascinated, as Watts talked of Titian and called forth 'the most subtle, most tender, undiscoverable I was going to say unpaintable greys', the soft shadows of the human face and throat, touched with pinks, purples, browns and a hint of ultramarine. This portrait took at least six sittings of three and half hours each (and even then it was not complete; it had to be finished off in London.) In the final portrait, Evie is also dressed in period costume and is posed rather formally, standing up and looking away from the artist. She holds a parasol which fills the dark, glowering sky, giving the whole picture a sombre effect. 'Do not like it,' Gertrude confided to her diary when she was shown the work-in-progress on 12 September 1876. 'Too dark, too old . . . As it is not mine could not make disparaging remarks. Mouth too small,' she added.

Watts might well have been the most distinguished living painter, but Gertrude knew from her own experience of Pradier's *louche* studio that the bohemian society of artists could be corrupting. 'Girls up again at the Briary,' she noted on 19 September. 'Told them I did not think it suitable.' These maternal warnings were not heeded. Dolly began sitting to Watts ten days later. 'Am not pleased with the intimacy at the Briary,' Gertrude grumbled again. 'It is too excessive.' For all the risk of moral contamination, she was pleased with the portrait of Dolly. She was also more successful in her negotiation over the price. At first Watts refused to take a fee, so Gertrude suggested that he paint Charles, and they agreed a price of £300. In the end, Watts decided that he was too busy to paint Charles, so Gertrude acquired a masterpiece for nothing.

In this picture, Dolly is lost in thought, dreamy rather than stern and decisive as in the Millais image. She is wearing an antique dress ('suggesting seventeenth century Van Dyckian costume in the lace trim of the neckline')[5] and holds a squirrel in her left hand. Art historians have conjectured that this was a reference to Holbein's *Lady with ta Squirrel and a Starling*, but in fact it was a picture from life of Dolly's pet squirrel Toodles. Painted from the side, Dolly's elaborately twisted auburn hair is lifted and swept back to expose an expanse of neck and the creamy complexion of her face. The picture revels in her beauty and is an altogether more feminine image than the Millais portrait. When it was finally exhibited, it bore a portentous title: *Miss Dorothy Tennant, second daughter of the late Charles Tennant, Esq., of Cadoxton Lodge, Neath, Glamorganshire*. One suspects that Gertrude encouraged the hint of landed status in order to enhance her daughter's eligibility. A generation earlier, she had been exiled in Paris; now Gertrude's daughters were painted by the greatest artists of the day, their pictures exhibited in the galleries of the Royal Academy and reproduced in the pages of *The Times* and the *Illustrated London News*. They were recognised when they went out into society. 'In fact we are novelties and sights, we are introduced as the Misses Tennant painted by Millais,' Dolly chuckled. She herself was introduced as 'No.' The girls found this all very amusing.

After Gertrude acquired Watts's portrait of Dolly and Millais's of her sister, she displayed them prominently at Richmond Terrace. A guest would mount the stairs and walk into the first of the two drawing rooms to be confronted with the pictures of these 'singularly lovely young women' hung on a backcloth of brilliant turquoise wallpaper.[6] When Gladstone saw Watts's portrait of Dolly for the first time, he said it was equal to any other portrait he had seen by that painter, and whilst he affirmed his conviction that Watts was the greatest painter of the nineteenth century, he expressed reservations about his own most recent portrait by the master. It took at least forty sittings, he complained, involving a considerable expenditure of time, and the result was a rare failure, especially when compared to Watts's highly successful portrait of Cardinal Manning.[7]

* * *

From the mid-1870s, there is a contradiction between Gertrude's private protestations of world-weariness and the increasing vigour of the life that she actually led. Gertrude's diaries expressed her conviction that her life was entering its last phase, but in reality just the opposite was true: far from hiding away like Queen Victoria after she was widowed, Gertrude was making the most of her new independence. She had loved her husband deeply, and continued to miss him intensely and to look forward to their reunion in the afterlife. She certainly abided by his wish never to change her name, though as a handsome and wealthy widow she could have remarried had she so wished. For the first time in her life, however, she was well off, independent, and sovereign in her own splendid home, and she liked the fact that her interactions with other people were now largely on her own terms – so different from her experience as a young woman and even as a wife in a very loving marriage. She would not be the first middle-aged woman to find a degree of contentment in widowhood, notwithstanding the agonising over her daughters' future. The need to propel the girls into the marriage market provided the perfect psychological cover for pursuing the kind of social life that she relished (and that had been denied to her for twenty-five years, due to her late husband's deafness). Without the legitimising purpose of getting the girls out and about, she might not have been able to justify enjoying herself so much.

In the summer of 1875, Gertrude went to garden parties and dinner parties with Hamilton and the girls. There she met the Queen of the Netherlands; Robert Browning; Herbert Spencer, the stern philosopher and Matthew Arnold the poet, to name but a few of the distinguished persons she encountered in this very sociable season. She gave a dinner party for Lord Houghton, Matthew Arnold and Millais. Later she was responsible for introducing Houghton to Flaubert, which led in turn to the latter's meeting with Henry James. She herself met James in May 1877, when she sat next to him at a dinner party given by Hamilton. The novelist described her as 'very handsome and agreeable . . . an old friend and flame of Gustave Flaubert'.[8] She remained friends with James until the end of the century, although as we will see he had mixed feelings about other members of Gertrude's family.

Perhaps the highlight was a visit with the girls to George Eliot and her consort George Henry Lewes at the Priory, their home far away in north London. Lewes, Dolly reported, had a red nose, long, frizzed grey hair, and a spark of real intelligence in his eye. Eliot herself looked older and uglier than they expected. 'Her face is long, and appears to be more so, because of the way she wears her brown hair closely over her eyes, narrowing her forehead with an acute angle. Her eyes are small and blinking; she has a long man's nose, a mouth ugly certainly, and looks long certainly owing to her long teeth.' Her charm was in her manner, rather than her appearance. She listened carefully to what was said to her, bringing her face close before uttering 'low and slowly some beautifully put harmonious sentence'. She talked at first to Gertrude about domestic matters, asking what it was like raising a family on her own, what she did of an evening. Nothing gave her so much joy as domestic affection, the writer said, nothing struck her as so fine as home love. 'I can't imagine anything happier than loving many people, not only one's nearest and dearest, but to love people about one.' Then she turned to the girls, saying she recognised them from the pictures in the Academy. When Dolly told her she wanted to be a painter, the novelist said 'how fine it was for a woman to have a career', and how women were not supposed to aim at excellence, but that Dolly should try to. She told them that she was never satisfied with her writing, and each new book should be an advance on the last. 'I must not write trash,' she said. 'If what I have written is good what I write must be equal or better.'[9]

In August and September of this year, Gertrude and her daughters went to the Isle of Wight, where they were reacquainted with Andrew Mulholland and his family. (The young man's father was a noted yachtsman, owner of the 77-foot schooner *Egeria* which dominated its racing class for decades.) During Cowes week they attended a ball at Lord Harrington's, where another guest was the Prince of Wales; Gertrude was thrilled when the young Lord Londonderry danced with Evie three times during the course of the evening. She and the girls took a steamer across the channel to Le Havre, and then went on to Trouville, scene of Gertrude's encounter with Flaubert: she found that the place had changed immeasurably. They waited for the racing yachts to arrive from Cowes, and attended a ball at Deauville, a town that had barely existed the last time she was here; once again the Prince of Wales was a fellow guest. When Dolly and Evie went to the Portsmouth Ball with the four sons and two daughters of a brandy merchant, Gertrude was rather disappointed. Returning to the Isle of Wight a year later, she and her daughters went to the ball once again. It was not a success. Two men were very drunk. 'Felt low at the company one is thrown in with,' she lamented, 'and at the Ball all together. Poor UN-married girls!'

Despite the increasing vigour and indeed glamour of her social life, the year 1876 ended on a disconsolate note: the girls were still without husbands, and she had to put up with a tedious visit from a pair of unwanted artistic visitors. 'Had to labour to amuse Mr Burne-Jones and Mr Oscar Wilde,' she wrote dismissively on 27 December. 'Oh how bored! Vexed.' (One would very much like Gertrude to have written more expansively about this and other visits from the great men of the day, but her diary entries for this period are tantalisingly brief.) Gertrude's mood improved on New Years' Day 1877, when Burne-Jones returned with his son Philip and a young nephew. The nephew, who was fascinated by the animals and reptiles collected in Dolly's birdcage, carried a notebook around with him in which he wrote down wildly fanciful stories about his two pet dormice. This bright, quaint boy was the eleven-year-old Rudyard Kipling. A few days later, Gertrude cheered up still further when she received a poignant letter from Flaubert, with whom she had recently been reunited after thirty years. The great novelist had been thinking tenderly of Gertrude over the Christmas holiday.

CHAPTER 20

REUNITED WITH AN OLD FLAME

Early in 1876, Gertrude decided to take her daughters to see Paris, the city where she had grown up and which she had not visited in more than thirty years. She and the girls, together with the omnipresent Hamilton Aïdé, left Richmond Terrace for Victoria station on the morning of Tuesday, 25 April, from where they took the 7.30 boat train via Calais to the French capital. They required two carriages for the short journey to the station, so they must have taken a quantity of luggage, not the least of which was Dolly's adored pet horned toad which had been brought back from America by a friend and rejoiced in the name of Angeles, after the city from whence it came. Gertrude left no account of the journey: the train would have rattled through the grimy suburbs of London, and on through the orchards of Kent, before delivering them to the steamer which would have conveyed them rapidly across the Channel. Before long, in the words of Mona Caird, a near-contemporary novelist describing another middle-aged lady's journey to Paris:

The coast of France [became] clear . . . they were making the passage very quickly to-day. Presently, the boat had arrived in the bright old town, and every detail of outline and colour was standing forth brilliantly, as if the whole scene had been just washed over with clear water and all the tints were wet . . . The first impression was keen. The innumerable differences from English forms and English tones sprang to the eye. A whiff of foreign smell and a sound of foreign speech reached the passengers at about the same moment. The very houses looked unfamiliarly built, and even the letters of printed names of hotels and shops had a frivolous, spindly appearance – elegant but frail. The air was different from English air.

Finally, they arrived in Paris, after a mere six-hour train journey compared to the all-day nightmare of the coach journey Gertrude had made as a child. Coming blearily out of the station they would find that 'The great Boulevard was ablaze and swarming with life. The *cafés* were full; the gilt and mirrors and the crowds of *consommateurs* within, all visible as one passed along the street, while, under the awning outside, crowds were sitting smoking, drinking, reading the papers.'

Gertrude's motives for this expedition were mixed: she wanted her daughters to become acquainted with the city where she had spent her youth, to pick up the language and to absorb something of French culture. She wanted to see for herself the vast changes in the physical fabric of the city in the decades since she had lived there: how the Tuileries Palace and the *hôtel de ville* and many other buildings had vanished, destroyed during the suppression of the commune in 1871, and the medieval heart of the city had been opened up and penetrated by Baron Haussmann's boule-vards. But just as for the heroine of Mona Caird's *Daughters of Danaus*, there was something profoundly liberating about a visit to Paris. Gertrude would be freed, for a month or two, from the *convenances* of English society, and rediscover some of the gaiety of youth. Thus it was that on the first Friday of their visit, after they had installed themselves in the luxurious Hôtel Meurice, Gertrude and her daughters went to pay an unannounced visit on her old friend, Gustave Flaubert.

Gustave and Gertrude had been in intermittent contact over the years – he sent her a copy of *Salammbô* and she received a letter from him when on holiday in Guernsey in 1862 – but they had not actually seen each other since the year before Gertrude had married. She was now 56, he 54. It was a gulf of more than half a lifetime, in which the dreamy law student had become one of France's literary immortals (even if the public did not always buy or indeed appreciate his work). However edifying for Dolly and Evie to meet him, this reunion could hardly be approached with insouciance. She and Gustave had been young together, they had flirted, kissed at the opera, she had even fallen in love, and he was the probable cause of her permanent estrangement from her sister. This would be an encounter with an old flame, with all the attendant risk of emotional turbulence or outright disappointment should he turn out to be different from the way she remembered. She told the girls that in his youth he had been very slight in figure, with small feet and beautifully shaped hands; the young man who had been a bosom friend of the Collier family and spent evening after evening reading aloud to the sisters had had an exquisite complexion, dark hair and wonderful eyes. To look at now, Gertrude would find, Flaubert was not the god-like figure of his youth, but was fat and jowly, a mountain of a man, with unhealthy mottled skin, bulging eyes, full cheeks and a rough, drooping mouth. He was bald on top of his head with grey hair and a grey moustache. Youthful exuberance had given way to intermittent depression as his friends died off one after another and he found himself enmeshed in intractable money worries. The stress of losing his cherished financial and artistic independence led to a recurrence of his epilepsy. Self-assured *grande dame* though Gertrude now was, with almost thirty years as a respectable English wife and widow behind her, she would be hardly human if she did not suffer a tremor of trepidation as she got back in touch with Gustave. Who knows how he would respond to her approach? Had he forgiven her for her caustic remarks about *Madame Bovary?*

Flaubert was not at home when they first made the arduous journey up what felt like innumerable flights of stairs to his apartment at 240, rue du Faubourg Saint-Honoré. Gertrude made an appointment to see him the following day at two o'clock, but refused to leave her name. With the vestigial coquettishness of youth, she wanted to take him by surprise. 'You may imagine our feelings as we climbed up the many flights of stairs,' Dolly wrote of the next afternoon's visit; 'mine reflective, mother's expectant, I having a kind of imaginary picture in my mind, mother a picture of the past.' They rang on a sort of electric bell, the door was opened by the *bonne*, and they were ushered into a room where a man was sitting with his back to the door. Before he could turn round, Gertrude went up to him, put her hand on his shoulder and said: 'Gustave'. The great author started up in astonishment and seized her hand. 'Madame Tennant . . . Gertrude. Gertrude!!!!' he said. He was stout, strangely dressed in a chocolate-coloured coat hanging down to his knees, a white frilled shirt, a large loose scarf of red silk tied around the waist of his chocolate-coloured pantaloons. He appeared stupefied by this apparition from half a lifetime ago, and sat in silence before he took proper note of her. 'He was so unfeignedly delighted at seeing my mother,' wrote Dolly that evening, that he eventually cried out: ' "oh mais vous me faites de bien, mais de bien!!!" ' ('How it does me good to see you, how it does me good!!!')

After overcoming the mutual shock, Gertrude explained her presence in Paris, and they talked of Victor Hugo, who had returned in triumph to France after the fall of Louis-Napoleon. Having lived through the humiliations of the Franco-Prussian War and the horrors of the Commune (when due to his stature Hugo avoided the diet of rats and dogs endured by his fellow Parisians and was given the choicest animals from the zoo), the great author was now occupied in ineffectual Third Republic intrigues. Gustave said Hugo was as lively as ever, still clambering to the top of omnibuses and inclined to pour a carafe of cold water down his neck if he found himself dull in company. Another name came into the conversation, that of Ivan Turgenev, the great Russian novelist who was living in Paris at the time and had become one of Flaubert's closest friends. At this, Dolly cried out: 'Oh, what I would not give to see the man.' That could easily be arranged, Flaubert replied: he was coming to visit the very next day, would Gertrude and her daughters care to join the party? The next day at 3 p.m., Gertrude, Dolly and Evie returned to Flaubert's apartment. Turgenev talked to Gertrude in his fluent but heavily accented French about his admiration of Swinburne and Tennyson's poetry, 'quietly interested in all around him, very calm and unexcitable' and then Evie sang half a dozen songs, concluding with a rendition of Shakespeare's 'She never told her love' (presumably Haydn's setting of Viola's lines from Act 2 of *Twelfth Night*). Flaubert declared himself ravished by the song, but (still) not knowing English he wanted to know what the words meant. Turgenev was able to provide an instant, word-perfect translation. Having learned that Evie wanted to take singing lessons while in Paris, Flaubert offered to arrange a *cours* with his friend Mme Viardot. ('Don't mention money,' he told her, 'everything is arranged. It's an *affaire d'amitié*.')[1]

Against the odds, perhaps, the reunion proved a tremendous success. Writing later in the year, Flaubert pleaded with Gertrude to come back and rent an apartment in Paris for the entire winter season. 'How is it possible for me to tell you how much pleasure you visit gave me?' he wrote from Croisset on 19 October. 'It seemed to me that the intervening years had disappeared and that I was embracing my youth. It's the only happy event that has happened to me in a very long time. May God bless you . . .' On Christmas Day, he continued in a similar vein:

In the long years since I have lived without knowing what had come of you, there is perhaps not a single day that has gone by without my thinking of you. That's the way it is! Blessed be the inspiration that pushed you to come over here to find me again! Now there is no way I will leave you ever again. We must write to each other and see each other again . . .[2]

They met frequently during Gertrude's month-long visit. On Thursday, 11 May, Flaubert was a fellow guest at Victor Hugo's for dinner. The conversation on this occasion appears to have been moderately disappointing, as before the meal, sitting on a sofa between Flaubert and Gertrude, Hugo talked incessantly about republican politics and how his doctor had prescribed damp sheets as a cure for shingles. Matters improved when he said he knew Millais and was particularly delighted by his picture of a beautiful young girl walking through a wood carrying a basket: he was greatly astonished when Gertrude told him that this was the portrait of Eveleen. He then took Gertrude's arm and led her down to dinner.

A hitherto unpublished (and undated) note from Flaubert to Gertrude gives further clues. He asks Gertrude alone to attend a reading. 'My dear Gertrude,' he writes. 'Today at four o'clock precisely I must read *mon Julien* before a small group of *intimes* [intimate friends who formed his *cénâcle* or literary circle].' ('My Julien' is the story that would be known as 'La Légende de St Julien Hospitalier,' the first of the *Trois Contes* to be finished, in February 1876.) Come along if you can, he says, but don't be late, as his door will be locked from four to six. After six would also be possible. 'Let me know what suits you,' he concludes, signing off as 'your old friend' Gustave Flaubert. Then, at the bottom of this brisk and businesslike note, he adds:

> Je suis triste en songeant que bientot vous partez! Quand nous reverrons-nous? (I am sad to think that you will soon be leaving! When will we see each other again?)

Flaubert came to visit Gertrude and the girls at their hotel on the last Saturday of their stay, when he read aloud from the works of his friend Louis Bouilhet. 'He read as I never heard poetry before,' Dolly confided to her diary, 'quite forgetful of self and audience, no showing off of feeling, but [with] real inward earnestness.' Flaubert took Gertrude to meet his close friend and protégé Guy de Maupassant, whom she found 'heavy, silent, self-absorbed and sullen in manner': she begged him never to ask her to meet the short story writer again.[3] Then, on Sunday, 27 May, Gertrude and the girls went to pay a farewell visit to Flaubert at his apartment, and on this occasion they also met Caroline Commanville – the only daughter of Flaubert's beloved sister; she had been brought up at Croisset by her grandmother, and by Flaubert himself, who doted on her when a child and sought to impart his insights into literature and history as she was growing up. In 1864 she married Ernest Commanville, a feck-less entrepreneur who had more recently managed to embroil Gustave in some dubious business ventures which would eventually be the ruin of Flaubert's finances. Caroline would have been very interested in Gertrude's recollections of the mother she never knew and indeed many years later, when gathering material for the first collection of her uncle's letters, she was moved to tears when she read Gertrude's written account of that long-ago Trouville holiday. Flaubert insisted on coming one last time to Gertrude's hotel, at five o'clock on the very last day of their visit, to say a final farewell.

From Gertrude's point of view, any unease about the wisdom of the encounter would have been dispelled by Gustave's immense and genuine pleasure at being reconnected with these reminders of his youth. Gertrude and Hamilton were as good as the only living survivors of the long summer at Trouville. As Flaubert wrote on Christmas Day:

The best part of my youth took place there. Since we were together on the beach, how much water has flowed under the bridge. No storm, my dear Gertrude, has effaced those memories. Does the perspective of the past embellish things? Was it really so good, so beautiful? What a pleasant corner of the earth that was you, your sisters, mine! O abyss! Abyss! If you were an old bachelor like me, you would understand better. But now, you understand me, I can feel it . . .

Dolly and Evie were not merely pretty (they visited Paris just months before their youthful beauty was captured by Watts), they reminded him of the young Collier sisters with whom he had argued and flirted so many decades before. When, some years later, he received from Gertrude a copy of Dolly's portrait by Millais, he made this explicit: 'Je contemple la fille en songeant à la mere' ['As I look at the daughter I think of the mother'], he wrote on 3 May, 1878,[4] and pressed her to come and see him in France. In his letters, Gustave asked after Dolly's menagerie (had the horned toad been replaced?) and Evie's larynx. 'How are you and your superb daugh-ters?' he wrote. In 1879, amused by a letter from Dolly in which she made the bizarre claim to have known him in a previous life, he told his niece that she was slightly mad and full of charm. ('Quelle drôle de *young lady*,' he wrote. 'C'est fou et plein de charme.'[5])

The reunion came at a time when Flaubert was engaged in an intense imaginative recreation of the past. The previous month, he had returned from a four-week field trip to Pont L'Eveque and Honfleur, the purpose of which was to gather material for the new story he was working on – the famous 'Un Coeur simple', in which a peasant servant woman called Félicité leads a life of selfless piety and dies after confusing her stuffed parrot with a vision of God almighty. Flaubert was adamant that the story was not meant at all ironically, and the tale, when it finally appeared in 1877, delighted the most critical readers; in time, even Gertrude wrote to say how much she liked it. Set in the Normandy of an earlier age, it seemed a return to the style and content of *Madame Bovary*, but without the cynicism. As he explained to another correspondent:

> The *Story of a Simple Heart* is quite simply the tale of the obscure life of a poor country girl, devout but not given to mysticism, devoted in a quiet sober way and soft as newly baked bread. One after the other she loves a man, her mistress's children, an old man she nurses, then her parrot; when the parrot dies she has it stuffed, and when she is on her deathbed she takes the parrot for the Holy Ghost. It is in no way ironic (though you might suppose it to be so) but on the contrary very serious and very sad. I want to move my readers to pity, I want to make sensitive souls weep, being one myself.[6]

The tale was inspired by George Sand, the novelist who had criticised *L'Education sentimentale* for its lack of humanity, and by Julie, the Flaubert family maid for fifty years. From the timing of their meeting, Gertrude must also have had an influence on this masterpiece: her reappearance quickened the workings of his imagination and helped put him in the right frame of mind to finish off a work that was inspired by tender memories of the past. After Gertrude and her family returned to London, Flaubert went back to Croisset and completed the story later that summer.

Gertrude and Gustave stayed in contact and letters went backwards and forwards from Croisset to Richmond Terrace until the last months of the author's life. Only one of Gertrude's letters has survived, in which she thanks Gustave for a copy of *Trois Contes* which arrived on Saturday, 28 April, 1877, just as she was sitting having lunch with her daughters. 'Cher Gustave,' she writes in her not quite perfect French,

> Mon volume est là, sur ma table – il est arrivé pendant que nous déjeunions. J'ai dit à mes enfans [*sic*]: 'Nous allons passer de bonnes soirées, je vais vous lire çela tout haut, puis écrire à Gustave pour le remercier'; 'pas du tout,' me dit Dolly, 'écrivez de suite à Gustave, voyez ce qu'il a écrit sur la première feuille 'affection inaltérable et profonde'.

[Dear Gustave, my copy is right here on the table before me, it arrived as we were having lunch. I said to my children, we are going to spend many happy evenings, I am going to read you the whole thing out loud and then write to Gustave to thank him. 'Certainly not,' said Dolly. 'Write immediately to Gustave, you see that he has written on the first page 'deep and unchanging affection']⁷

Noticing that Dolly was right – the book did contain the dedication that he had written on the copy of Montaigne and *Bovary* and *Salammbô* – she dashed off this letter of thanks, and urged him to send a copy to her friend Lord Houghton.

Some twenty-three of Flaubert's letters to Gertrude have been preserved in the Tennant papers. Of these, fourteen were published in the earliest editions of his correspondence, collated by Caroline in the 1880s, but the originals were thought to have been lost until they were rediscovered as part of Gertrude's archive; taken as a whole, the correspondence demonstrates that the friendship between Flaubert and Gertrude was deeper and more enduring than the novelist's biographers have hitherto suspected. If not an affair, in the modern, crudely sexual sense of the word, it was what the French call an *amitié amoureuse*, a passionate friendship, where emotions were deeply engaged on both sides. The later letters show that Flaubert continued to think fondly of his old flame, even as his own health and finances deteriorated in his last years. The Christmas Day missive, from which excerpts are quoted above, seeks to build common ground between the ageing author and the respectable English widow: 'On this day, the English are *en fête!*' Flaubert wrote. 'And I imagine you, as best I can, at home, surrounded by your beautiful children, with the Thames at your feet, [while] I myself am completely alone . . .'

Flaubert explains to Gertrude that he needs to closet himself in Croisset in order to meet the deadline for the publication of the new work. He is making good progress with the book, he tells her, and *dying* to read the three stories to her, but this does not stop him feeling acutely lonely. 'When are you next going to come and see me?' he pleads. Flaubert juxtaposes his monastic loneliness with what he believes to be the fullness of her existence; his faithlessness against her religious certainties; her charming children against the books that he produced instead. The rhetoric is in part flirtatious, reminiscent of Flaubert's surely disingenuous and manipulative letters to Henrietta so many years before. (Had he really thought about Gertrude every day? That sounds like Flaubertian hyperbole. He is hinting, playfully, that if fate had ever ordained him to settle down it would have been with Gertrude, or perhaps Henrietta, the only woman he ever considered marrying, thus reviving the old tensions between the sisters.) Yet, Flaubert implies, there is no need to play games now, they are just two old survivors with a shared past. Flaubert conjures up all that they have in common, despite the profound differences of circumstance and the separation of thirty years. He imagines her to be looking out of the windows of her home over the River Thames, just as he looks out over the Seine through the tall windows of his study. He insists that the shared memory of the past brings them together. He concludes with a blessing:

> At this time of the year one wishes a heap of things. What can one wish you? It seems to me that you have everything. I regret not being a believer so that I could pray to heaven for your happiness.

The appeal to shared intimacies continues in subsequent letters, as in March 1877 when he writes to tell her about the impending publication of *Trois Contes*: 'How I want to see you, how I would have things to say to you, one to one by the fireside! Do you know what I call you, deep down inside of me, when I think of you (which often happens)? I call you: "my youth".'[8]

He keeps her informed of his various projects – after the *Contes* were out of the way he proceeds with his chronicle of human stupidity, *Bouvard et Pécuchet*, which remained unfinished on his death – and there is occasionally an element of business, as in 1877 when he asks Gertrude to see if she can enlist the support of Lord Houghton to join a committee to erect a public memorial to George Sand (President: Victor Hugo. The other distinguished English member of the committee: Georges Elliot [sic].) Through Gertrude's good offices, Houghton did indeed meet Flaubert on a subsequent visit to Paris in April 1878, bringing with him the gift from Gertrude, a copy of the portrait, '*No!*', which Flaubert greatly relished; Houghton joined the committee and in due course introduced Henry James to Flaubert – a good example of the power of Gertrude's networking. In June 1877, Flaubert even sought to enlist Gertrude's support in rebuilding his family finances.

Flaubert ought, by rights, to have been a rich man: not so much from the proceeds of his works, but because his mother had left him a substantial property in Deauville; the farm, acquired earlier in the century, was an extremely valuable piece of real estate, estimated to be worth 260,000 francs in 1872 and as much as ten times more than that by the turn of the century. He did not inherit the house at Croisset, which was left in trust to Caroline with the understanding that Flaubert could live there to the end of his days. In 1875, however, he sold the farm for a knock-down 200,000 francs into order to bail out his niece's husband Ernest Commanville, who was teetering on the verge of bankruptcy after his speculations involving Scandinavian timber and a sawmill at Dieppe had gone spectacularly wrong. According to Frederick Brown, Flaubert's most recent biographer, the decision to advance the money to Commanville was a 'suicidal act of avuncular devotion' and he eventually lost the lot, leaving him impoverished and reduced to cadging a state pension.[9] Here is how Gustave explained it in this hitherto unpublished letter to Gertrude, from 18 June 1877:

> You know, don't you, that my nephew Commanville, has completely ruined himself and *par contre-coup*, ruined me as well, as the money I advanced him has been lost – and in order to prevent his bankruptcy, a serious matter in France, I handed over everything that remained to me.

He then goes on to say that Commanville was seeking to re-establish himself and needed only another 400,000 francs to capitalise his new joint stock company (the sawmill and its fixtures and fittings, allegedly worth 600,000 francs). Further details are to be found in a prospectus, which he has enclosed. He explains that investors have put up a little of the money, but are proving to be quite timid. Typical of the French to be so cautious, he says. 'I've heard that they are braver in England. Is that right?'

> The business I am talking to you about is *excellent*. Would you like to take it up? Do you know any industrialists who might be willing to invest? That's the entire question.
>
> NB, [he adds] I don't need to tell you that this is for me a question of the highest importance and it is even a <u>*question vitale*</u> [a <u>matter of life and death</u>] Show the [prospectus] to those friends of yours who are up to understanding it and doing something about it. You have numerous relatives and perhaps you'll find the money we need.

Flaubert was a literary genius, but as a securities salesman he was truly hopeless. To start the pitch by explaining how he has been ruined, and then to commend a wonderful scheme devised by the architect of his ruin and to make it clear that sensible investors are steering clear of this fool-proof opportunity, smacked of desperation. The emotional appeal to avert his own imminent downfall was the only powerful part of the argument, and the one to which Gertrude (and indeed other friends in France to whom Flaubert was writing in a similar vein, for example Mme Pelouze, the proprietor of the château of Chenonceau), did respond. Gertrude did not invest, but she must have passed the prospectus on to friends, for on 27 June Flaubert wrote back from Croisset to thank her for acting so promptly and putting the idea to a certain Mr Rolt. ('The enterprise is excellent,' he insists, unconvincingly. 'I recommend that you activate his zeal. Use your good friendship and [our shared memory] of [Gertrude's brother] Clarence.')

Nothing came of the scheme, and, despite Flaubert's pleas, Gustave and Gertrude would never meet again, even though both had the opportunity to do so. Gertrude was in France with Dolly in the autumn of 1878, but they missed each other. Still, they continued to write: Gustave kept her informed about the progress of *Bouvard et Pécuchet*, while Gertrude shared her domestic news – the death of a nephew, drowned in the Thames while a student at Oxford, and the more pleasing news that at last one of her daughters was engaged to be married.

Things went from bad to worse for Flaubert. In January 1879, he fell on the ice at Croisset and broke his leg. The following month, his financial ruination was confirmed after Ernest Commanville's business finally failed and the assets were sold off, without a sou of the enormous loan being repaid to Flaubert. Bedridden and broke, he continued to work on *Bouvard et Pécuchet*. He died suddenly on Saturday, 8 May, 1880, at the age of 59, of a heart attack brought on by years of unhealthy living, a few days after hosting at Croisset a last raucous dinner party for his old friends: Zola, Daudet, de Maupassant, the publisher Charpentier and Edmond de Goncourt. Three months later, Caroline sold Croisset, and later in the year the house was torn down and a distillery built on its site.

The English newspapers carried the news of Flaubert's death on the following Monday. 'Dear Gustave,' wrote Dolly that evening, 'I shall not see you again. Mother whose happiest part of girlhood was spent with the Flauberts, who was so loved and admired and appreciated by Gustave, that even up to these last days his letters to us full of warm loving tenderheartedness were unequalled . . . It is true we saw him very seldom and unfortunately missed him on our last visit to Paris. But we felt that he was there, and we could hear from him when we could, and we always knew we might go to Paris and find him. Now all is passed, this dear old link with mother's girlhood broken away. One who loved and understood her, one of the very few to whom she could write what she really felt is taken away by a sudden merciful death.'

Later in the year, Gertrude set down the following in her own diary:

> Took the sacrament . . . with Dolly and Elsie . . . I am glad I did so and feel it was right to do so. The person administering the sacrament is lost to me in the solemnity of the act, and I feel myself then and there at the altar, specially in the presence of <u>My Dead</u> – Charles, Blanche, My Baby, My Mother, Gustave Flaubert . . . and many who I know loved me . . .[10]

'My Dead' is an expression that conveys the utmost intimacy. More than just a friend, Gustave was a loved one, one of those whom she most cherished.

CHAPTER 21

AN ELIGIBLE MATCH

The very last letter Gustave Flaubert wrote to Gertrude was to console her on the news of the impending marriage of Eveleen, now aged 23, to Frederic Myers. He tells her not to be sad at the loss of a daughter and to think of all the others who are likely to come to depend on her as a result of the match, a reference to the *épicier* consolations of grandchildren:

> I wish Eveline [*sic*] all the happiness that her lovely character and her extraordinary beauty deserve. A poet for a husband! *Diable*, a bourgeoise would not have done that and I love you only the more for it, if that is possible. To be young, a poet, rich and to marry the one that one loves! There is nothing that tops that! How I envy your son-in-law, when I think back to my arid and solitary existence.[1]

Flaubert's tongue-in-cheek amazement was well founded: it is not often that poets are rich. Frederic Myers was very wealthy, but of course the money did not come from the poetry. Born and brought up for the first thirteen years of his life in the Lake District, where his father was perpetual curate of St John's, Keswick, he inherited a fortune from his maternal grandfather, a Leeds mill-owner. As a boy, he was marked out by a mystical disposition and precocious intelligence. By the time he left school, he had learned the whole of Virgil by heart and won prizes for his poems, in both English and Latin. After he went up to Trinity College, Cambridge in 1860 he achieved high academic honours and became a fellow of the college. He owed his fame as a poet to 'St Paul' (1867), a sentimental statement of religious faith that was popular as a counterweight to the gloomier meditations of Matthew Arnold and others who wrote about the tide of religion withdrawing from the world. It was written when Myers was fired up with evangelical rapture, but by the time he and Evie first met in Paris in 1879 he had long since abandoned Christianity and had made a name for himself as an essayist, brilliant classical scholar and unconventional Cambridge intellectual.

Once, walking around the Fellows' Garden at Trinity with George Eliot, Myers had been on the receiving end of the novelist's lapidary utterance on the nature of morality in a godless world. 'Of God, Immortality, Duty, the "inspiriting trumpet-calls of men"', she had said to him: 'how inconceivable is the *first*, how unbelievable the *second*, and yet how peremptory and absolute the *third*.'[2] For all his loss of faith, Myers believed, with every yearning fibre of his poetic being, that there was more to the mystery of life than Eliot's bleak materialism. Long before he met Evie, overwhelmed by the tremendous idea of immortality, he had become intensely interested in the study of the paranormal, with a particular emphasis on the search for proof of 'survival of bodily death'. It is to him that we owe the word *telepathy*, the concept of thought transference (between the living and the dead as well as between the very much alive) that he spent much of his life investigating. In 1874, he had resigned his fellowship of Trinity and taken up a post as Inspector of Schools in Cambridge, freeing up time for his experiments into the paranormal: investigations of mediums, clairvoyance, mesmerism, extra-sensory perception, automatic writing and ghosts and other *phantasmogenetic* apparitions. He saw himself as the pioneer of a new science, comparing himself with all due modesty to Magellan and Columbus, 'ploughing through some strange ocean where beds of entangling seaweed cumber the trackless way'.[3]

Myers's ideas put him well outside the intellectual mainstream, but were not considered quite as crackpot in the late nineteenth century as they might be today. Established religion was in retreat and science was making great advances, not least in the fledgling discipline of psychology, which at the time was viewed with almost as much scepticism as Myers's ghost-hunting. Intelligent men and women yearned for an alternative to the ebbing certitudes of conventional faith, while some open-minded Christians were willing to use science as a way to validate their beliefs. In 1882 Myers established the Society for Psychical Research (SPR), a body which aimed to investigate psychical phenomena 'without prejudice or prepossession of any kind', and in the same scientific spirit that would help solve so many other imponderable questions, from the speed of light (first measured in 1879) to the development of the internal combustion engine (patented by Gottlieb Daimler in 1883) and the discovery of radio waves (first produced by Heinrich Hertz in 1887). Despite the scepticism and ridicule that inevitably attended the project, the SPR attracted to its membership some of the most distinguished Victorians, including a brace of bishops; the prime ministers William Gladstone and Arthur Balfour; the poet Alfred Tennyson and the critic John Ruskin; the philosopher Henry Sidgwick; and scientists of the calibre of Oliver Lodge, the pioneer of radio transmission and inventor of the vacuum tube and spark plug, and Lord Rayleigh, the Nobel-prize winning physicist. Much later, the poet William Butler Yeats, who found automatic writing a useful source of esoteric metaphors, would join the Society, and Sigmund Freud became a corresponding member and contributed to its journal. William James, brother of the novelist Henry and one of the greatest thinkers of the late nineteenth century, was a close friend of Myers's and in time became President of the SPR. 'To brand as dupes and enthusiasts a set of gentlemen as careful as these English investigators have proved to be, seems to be singularly unjust,' he wrote, a trifle defensively.[4]

Myers was at the forefront of a late Victorian backlash against materialism. But there was also a purely personal dimension to his preoccupation with the afterlife. Some years before he met Evie, he had fallen in love with a turquoise-eyed cousin by the name of Annie Marshall, who was already married. Unstable and unhappy, the beautiful Annie jumped into Lake Ullswater, close to Myers's birthplace in the north of England, and drowned herself. For several years thereafter, Myers had been obsessed with finding proof of Annie's survival after death. Meeting Evie dispelled, for the moment, this morbid fixation with the afterlife, and Myers found himself entranced by a flesh and blood society beauty. Evie, the less cerebral of the two eligible Tennant daughters, loved Myers for his mind, but may also have been partial to his looks: he was tall with intense grey eyes, a mane of hair and clipped grey beard, a striking figure of a man who looked a lot younger than his 37 years. 'With you,' Evie told Myers, 'I can be my wild natural self.'[5]

Myers and Evie's rapid courtship took place during Gertrude's second winter in Paris, which commenced in early December 1879. As we will see in the next chapter, the principal reason for the visit was to establish Dolly in her painting career, and her sister's engagement was a wholly unexpected and unintended consequence of the visit. They had already been installed at the Hotel France et Bath in the rue du Faubourg Saint-Honoré for a fortnight when they learned that Myers was in Paris. (It is not clear where Evie had met him – perhaps at the Oxford Ball a few seasons before.) He called on the Sunday before Christmas, and there were no suspicions that this distinguished acquaintance harboured any romantic designs on Gertrude's youngest daughter. On the Monday, they all went to the theatre; on Wednesday, Myers accompanied Gertrude and the girls to a lecture. A day or two later, Gertrude was taken ill and suggested that Myers should accompany the two girls on a visit to the Louvre while she stayed at home in bed. He walked with the girls into the Palais de Justice. Sitting them down on a bench, he produced two letters, one for each of the sisters. They were acrostic poems (where the first letter of each line spells out a message, perhaps the girls' names), in which he expressed his admiration for the sisters, but still neither Gertrude nor Dolly suspected that anything momentous was afoot.

That evening, the three of them went to the Théâtre Français to see the great comic actor Benoît-Constant Coquelin perform,[6] while Gertrude stayed at home, composing a letter inviting the novelist Alphonse Daudet to lunch (having had a warm letter of introduction from Flaubert, who was not in Paris at the time). On Christmas Day, Myers came to visit once again and asked if he could read some of his poems. Gertrude consented, thinking him 'a strange and original young man'. She deemed him melancholy, suspecting (correctly) that he might have loved and lost. Taking pity on him, she encouraged him to come and take solace with her family, and he stayed to read to her until eleven o'clock that night. On Boxing Day, Myers once again accompanied the girls to the Louvre. Somehow, during this outing he found an opportunity to declare his love, for Evie returned to the hotel looking pale and distracted, and remained silent that afternoon when Caroline Commanville came for tea. Only after Flaubert's niece had left did Evie produce a second letter from Fred, evidently handed over earlier that day, in which he declared his love.

Gertrude was flabbergasted: everything seemed disconnected and incoherent. But then later that day Myers came in person to plead his cause, saying over and over again that he felt he ought to be a duke, that he had nothing worthy to offer Evie but his unbounded pure love, a stainless name – and a soul struggling towards God. (The last protestation suggests that the immensity of his love for Evie caused him to rediscover his faith.) 'His love for Evie is too deep for words,' noted Dolly, amazed, 'it approaches worship – perhaps his poet nature gives his love something of a spiritual character.'[7] The intensity of his passion for her was equalled by her love for him. 'It bathes her soul in life-giving floods,' Dolly wrote in her diary. Gertrude was touched by the evident sincerity of their love, and rapidly gave her consent to the marriage. She might also have been impressed by Fred's private income of £3,000 a year. By the end of the following day, it was all settled, down to when the marriage would take place (as quickly as possible) and where they would live immediately after the wedding (in Bolton Street, Mayfair, for three months, before moving to Cambridge).

The ceremony took place in Westminster Abbey on Monday, 15 March 1880, less than three months after his proposal. There was little of the pomp or society glamour of her sister's wedding in the same location ten years later, if only because the ceremony took place in the Lady Chapel of Henry VII, a side chapel which (according to Francis Bacon in his History of Henry VII) housed 'one of the stateliest and daintiest monuments in all Europe,' thus limiting the number of guests to exactly 100, rather than the 2,000 or more who can fit into the transepts, choir and nave of the Abbey proper. But it was still a considerable privilege: there were just two weddings there in 1880s, and those getting married usually had a close connection with the Abbey or Westminster School. The fact that the bride lived close by, and that her father had been an MP, may have swayed the judgement of the Dean, and certainly Gertrude was able to pull some strings. The sun streamed in as the couple took their vows, and it was said that Myers looked pale, and was inaudible as he murmured a vow that he cannot have made with any great conviction: 'till death do us part'. Then they and their guests left by the west door and returned to No. 2 Richmond Terrace for a tea party. It was a subdued affair by Gertrude's usual standards and by 5.30 only Hamilton Aïdé and Uncle Clarence remained. The most distinguished guest was to have been Prince Leopold, Queen Victoria's youngest son, who was a great friend of Myers's. He had to cry off because he had sprained his knee,[8] but Gertrude could not fail to have been impressed when the Prince came round to take tea and plum cake a month before the wedding. He told Gertrude that he greatly admired her home, which she felt should be taken as a real compliment, given that he had been brought up in the finest palaces in the land.

Gertrude, together with Dolly and Charlie, went out that evening to a party. On her return, she found a letter from Fred pinned to her pillow.

'Dear mother of my beloved one,' Myers's letter read, 'I want to tell you how deep and unique a debt I feel that I owe to you, in that you gave birth to my darling, that you have raised her so tenderly and loved her so well . . . my love for her has grown with every word [we have spoken] and she seems already one of the shining ones. Nothing, not even death itself, shall part us, nor dissever the most intimate and loving union that is permitted to heart and soul.'[9]

After a honeymoon abroad, the newly married couple eventually went to live at Leckhampton House, a mansion set in four acres of grounds they had constructed for themselves on the outskirts of Cambridge. (Their former home is now part of Corpus Christi College.) For the best part of two years, Fred put his psychical studies to one side, temporarily preoccupied with the here and now rather than the hereafter. *The Renewal of Youth* was the title of the book of poetry that he published in 1882, testament to the invigorating influence of his marriage. ('It might be called the renewal of hopes of immortality,' Gertrude commented after Myers read the title poem to her. 'Very fine!') Leopold Hamilton, the first child (named in honour of Fred's friend the Prince), was born in 1881, followed by Silvia Constance in 1883 and Harold in 1886.

Gertrude had spent much of her widowhood creating the conditions for her daughters to find appropriate husbands, and yet the moment one of them made a match, she was disconsolate. In truth, she found it wrenchingly difficult to part with Evie and could not easily accommodate the notion that this was the natural order of things. 'Eveleen called, said she could not stay one minute,' she lamented after the new Mrs Myers popped in for a fleeting visit in the summer of 1880. 'Gave her my mind on the subject of these visits – felt sorry for her and for myself.' The dressing-down cannot have made Evie any more willing to spend long visits with her mother. She complained later to her husband that staying at Richmond Terrace without him there was oppressive: 'to you I can rush & talk loud & say all the things that come into my head & hug my baby & and be my natural wild self'. With Evie out of the picture, and Elsie incapacitated, the sole remaining marriageable daughter at home was Dolly, who at the time of her sister's wedding was 25 years old. She was a complex and accomplished young woman, who had no intention of following in her sister's footsteps to the altar, despite being surrounded by distinguished admirers.

CHAPTER 22

THE DELICIOUS DOLLY

When Henry James met Dolly for the first time in May 1879 at a party given by her mother at Richmond Terrace, he sat alone with her in the drawing-room while the other guests were at dinner. 'The Delicious Dolly,' he wrote to his sister, 'is one of the finest creatures I have met here – as free and natural as an American girl, as handsome as the youthful Juno, and with the dimpled English temperament *en plus*.'[1] He was not alone in being captivated by her. Edwin Arnold, the influential poet and editor of the *Daily Telegraph*, said of her that she was 'tall and statuesque, handsome in face and figure. She moved like the Goddess of old story.' Jules Bastien-Lepage, the French painter, visited her at home in the summer of 1881 and painted a number of pictures of the Thames and St Paul's Cathedral in the birdcage, dedicating these works to her. Many others, from the novelist Alphonse Daudet, to the risqué journalist Frank Harris, to the grand old man of English painting G.F. Watts and even the sculptor Auguste Rodin were charmed by her.

As Gustave Flaubert had noted, Dolly's charm was accentuated by the hint of barminess that went hand in hand with her beauty and intelligence. Her practice of keeping a detailed diary written in the form of letters to her long-deceased father, is one clear example of eccentricity. While Gertrude abandoned her therapeutic journal-writing after a year, Dolly kept it up, day in, day out, for the twenty-eight years between her father's death and her wedding, and at intervals afterwards. The result, is without exaggeration, millions of words of confessional prose set down in a series of thick black-cardboard bound diaries that start not with the beginning of the calendar year, but with the anniversary of her father's demise.[2] She addressed him almost daily as 'Dear Father' or on occasions 'My Own Darling', and signed off: 'Goodnight Dearest' or 'Good night my beloved father'. Dolly's belief that she would one day be reunited with her loved ones in heaven was consistent not merely with her religion, but also with her brother-in-law's belief in the psychical afterlife. One could say that corresponding with the dead ran in the family.[3]

Another element of her oddness was her unhealthily close relationship with her mother. 'There is no companion no friend no love equal or comparable to you,' Dolly wrote to her mother in June 1874, when she was 19 and Gertrude 54 years old, a gushing tone that she kept up in her letters to her mother until well after her wedding sixteen years later. 'She is so much my companion, so dear to me, I sleep with her, I consult her, I love her,' Dolly wrote of Gertrude in a typical diary entry. On occasions, as this suggests, Gertrude and her daughter slept in the same bedroom or even the same bed, not abnormal in the nineteenth century, but still peculiar. (While Queen Victoria put a stop to this practice immediately after taking the throne, Dolly seems to have kept at it, on and off, until her marriage in her mid-thirties.) They also entertained together, read aloud to one another and travelled together and wrote each other lengthy letters if they chanced to be apart. This mutual dependency originated in their shared grief in losing Charles as husband and father, and deepened during the long years of Gertrude's widowhood. The private history of Gertrude in the remaining decades of her life is thus very much the story of her relationship with Dolly, which remained on an excellent, if overripe footing until Gertrude was approaching her ninetieth year, when there was at last a rupture. One senses that from the 1880s onwards Gertrude lived both *for* her daughter, by bestowing on her the material advantages that she could now afford to provide, and *through* her, enjoying vicariously the freedoms that were open to her daughter's generation of women and sharing in the drama of her personal and professional life.

Dolly was highly intelligent, inquisitive and interested in all that the great men of the world had to say and do, and had the opportunity to meet them at her mother's dining table. She developed her own strong opinions on the political and artistic questions of the day and was unusually assertive, for a young woman of the 1880s, in expressing them. As she grew older, and remained unmarried, this assertiveness could be interpreted as unfeminine stridency, but in her early womanhood the great men of the world were delighted to meet her and enter into correspondence with her.[4] They found her flattering, interested and informed, and if she had an object in view, men twice her age found it difficult to stand in her way. As we will see, she talked Henry Morton Stanley into letting her paint his portrait, and then eventually into marrying her and entering Parliament, the latter at least against his better judgement. But, for now, Dolly was preoccupied with making her own way as an artist. Here she showed a single-mindedness and seriousness of purpose that is at odds with the image of a flippertigibbet socialite that tends to be promoted in hostile biographies of her future husband. She was encouraged in her ambitions not merely by her mother, who went to great lengths to advance Dolly's career, but also by some of the most exalted personalities of the day.

One Sunday morning in December 1879, for example (shortly before the fateful Paris trip which led to Evie's engagement), the Richmond Terrace household was sent into a panic after a note arrived from Oscar Wilde saying that John Ruskin, the greatest critic of the age, had heard about Dolly's pictures of children and they were planning to visit that very lunchtime. Gertrude sent a servant across the river to find a chicken for lunch, while she and Dolly hurriedly tidied up the house, taking down the dirty muslin that hung inside the velvet curtains of the living-room and cleaning the smut-begrimed windows. They were worried that the Duke of Buccleuch might look across from his own residence and see them carrying out these servants' tasks; but the risk of mild social embarrassment was eclipsed by the fear that the house would be a mess when the guests arrived. All was presentable when Wilde and Ruskin arrived and were shown upstairs. Ruskin took a seat in a large armchair, looking thin, hungry, small and aged, his grey hair swept back over his forehead and his hands (Dolly noted) like the claws of a little bird, thick at the joints and the fingers square at the tips. He wore a bright blue necktie, a grey waistcoat and a thick overcoat which came high up over his shoulders.[5]

While Gertrude made polite conversation with Oscar Wilde (which to the best of this author's knowledge was not incorporated into the dramatist's subsequent portrayals of *grandes dames* in his plays), Dolly sat beside Ruskin and showed him her drawings. The great critic laughed a delighted 'ho-ho' at the images, telling her to be silent as she sought to pass on other pictures, putting his hand on her arm and telling her he wanted to look more closely. 'Oh, this is beautiful, this is joy,' he cried at one picture of a ragged boy. Of another picture of children playing in the street on a Bank Holiday, he said: 'I don't like it, [but] I admire it.' Of a bully boy in Seven Dials, he said: 'wonderful, what power, what genius'. His verdict: 'You will paint, dear, you will succeed,' and he told Wilde later that she would become great if she worked. After Dolly had displayed her drawings, Evie sang, which Ruskin said was better than any opera. They went down to lunch where, despite the preparations and Ruskin's hungry look, he would take no more than a glass of sherry and a biscuit. He left, after paying profuse compliments to Gertrude ('why did you not write to me, why did you never ask me to come and see you, that I should have lost so many years before making your acquaintance') and cancelled his planned afternoon visit to Lillie Langtry, the society beauty. 'I have given my heart to those two dear girls,' he said.

'Your work has all the delicacy and the directness that faery tales require,' Wilde wrote to her later, 'and has the rare quality of giving pleasure to children by its fancy and its truth.' (Dolly had illustrated Mrs W.K. Clifford's popular *Anyhow Stories, Moral and Otherwise*; nothing came of plans to do the same for Wilde's children's tales.) Other admirers included Watts himself, who having painted her then let her paint alongside him, and Millais. 'Dear Dolly,' the latter wrote in a letter transcribed into her diary on 15 January, 1875, 'I congratulate you sincerely on your series, they really are admirable, full of originality . . . you may reach fruit far beyond the ordinary female [artist] . . . you have worked hard at these drawings and they show signs of an ability to do much better still.' 'Sincere gratitude for the delightful sea-baby picture,' wrote Robert Browning on 25 May, 1888, on receiving a copy of a drawing, 'as charming as it is pathetic.'

Ever since she was a child, Dolly had displayed genuine talent as an artist: the sketches preserved in the margins of her schoolbooks show that she had an acute eye and a vivid imagination. Although she painted portraits in oils, she also had a special interest in drawing street urchins, ragamuffins of both sexes whom she picked up on the streets of Lambeth across the river from Whitehall. On occasions, she would bring the children back to her mother's house, where they were invited into her studio or encouraged to thump away on her piano while she sketched. These visits could lead to misunderstandings, as when Gertrude's butler, a flunkey in full livery (consisting of a cutaway coat, yellow vest, knee-breeches, pink stockings and powdered hair), opened the door on a party of guests from the slums. Awestruck, a ragged crossing-sweeper once asked Dolly: 'Why does your brother dress in that rummy way?' Later, replete with cakes and pies, the same boy observed in all innocence: 'My eye, but yer mother can cook.' Another time, a sweep became bored with posing for Dolly, entered the dining-room fireplace and disappeared up the chimney. Gertrude was prepared to tolerate the little urchins in her home, indulging both Dolly and her conscience, but Evie was not enthusiastic. After she had children of her own, she wrote imploring Dolly to make sure there were no ragamuffins on hand when Leo, Harold and Silvia were brought up to town – she really didn't want them to catch scarlet fever or influenza.

Dolly's drawings of street children are Hogarthian, original and fluent, funny but often sentimental, as although the rags are depicted in lurid detail, the children always seem to be happy and well fed, and are depicted cart-wheeling or vaulting over one another and generally having a splendid time, as well they might have been after being given a treat by the auburn-haired gentlewoman from across the Thames. 'Most of the pictures I had seen of ragged life appeared to me false and made up,' Dolly wrote, explaining the genesis of these images. 'They were all so deplorably hideous – pale whining children with sunken eyes, holding up bunches of violets to heedless passers-by; dying match girls, sorrowful water-cress girls, emaciated mothers clasping weeping babes. How was it, I asked myself, that the other side is so seldom represented? The merry, reckless, happy-go-lucky urchin; the tom-boy girl; the plump, untidy mother dancing and tossing her ragged baby . . . who had given this side of London life?'[6] She had a point: numerous writers, from Charles Dickens to W.T. Stead, the campaigning journalist, and Andrew Mearns (author of *The Bitter Cry of Outcast London: An Inquiry into the Condition of the Abject Poor*, a pamphlet which caused a sensation when published in 1883), tended to dwell on the awfulness of the physical and moral degradation of the London underclass. It would not be until the end of the decade that Charles Booth published the first results of his quasi-scientific investigations into the London poor, seeking to replace prurient fascination with statistical analysis.

During the 1870s it had become apparent that Dolly's painting was more than a girlish pastime, and Gertrude went to great lengths to promote her daughter's talent. In January 1879 she had her enrolled at the Slade School of Art, the fine arts school founded in 1871 as part of University College, London, and Dolly thus became one of the first women to take advantage of the Slade's enlightened programme to bring young ladies into the hallowed halls of academic art education.[7] Thereafter, Dolly spent three winters in Paris as a pupil of Jean-Jacques Henner, a celebrated painter who had overcome humble origins to become one of the most prominent establishment artists of the Third Republic. His studio was on Place Pigalle, adjacent to the Café de la Nouvelle Athènes, where the new generation of poets and painters gathered to drink absinthe and talk art: but while Degas, van Gogh, Henri de

Toulouse-Lautrec, Sisley and Cézanne painted the bohemian world they could see around them, Henner specialised in portraits of classical scenes, often naked adolescents frolicking around waterfalls or by the side of streams. These stylised genre pictures were complemented by formal portraits of Third Republic statesmen and plutocrats. His conservatism did not affect his success at the time, indeed may have helped him curry favour with the authorities: he was heaped with medals and all the honours that the state could bestow upon an artist, and there are hundreds of his pictures in museums around France. But his reputation today is negligible compared to those of the great Impressionists who drank and painted within sight of his atelier.

Henner walked with Dolly and Gertrude around the galleries of the Louvre, and he singled Dolly out for special attention in his classes for women, both at Place Pigalle and at the quai Voltaire. Dolly's own oil paintings were created very much in the image of the master. They include *The Death of Love*, which shows a naked girl and boy, the boy lying dead on the ground, the girl kneeling to his side, hands clasped to her face, weeping.[8] Others are *A Water-Lily*, which shows a naked young woman dipping her toe into a pond, against a dark backdrop of trees, and *Sweet Echo! Sweetest Nymph that Liv'st Unseen*, which depicts a naked nymph sitting on the edge of a cliff and calling out across the sea. In a different genre, *For Dear Life* showed a street urchin running, pursued by a London bobby and a crowd, a loaf of bread stuck under his arm. Her genre pictures tended to be small, perhaps 18 inches by 12, and set into deeply recessed gold frames. This framing device was modelled on Henner's practice. 'I like to compel all eyes that gaze upon these pictured nymphs to climb golden steps before they may feel themselves worthy to worship at the Shrine of Grace,' Dolly explained to a friend. From 1880 to 1888, eighteen of her pictures were exhibited at the Grosvenor Gallery, the neo-classical gallery established by Sir Coutts Lindsay and his wife in 1877 as an alternative to the Royal Academy.[9] She was also proud to earn more than £100 a month from selling her work – not because she needed the money, but as proof that she was in earnest as a professional artist.

After Evie's engagement, Dolly threw herself into her painting with redoubled energy. 'This past week,' she wrote in her diary, 'I have frequently gone into my room, flung myself to my knees and prayed to almighty God, the God of Raffael [*sic*], the God of Holbein, the God of Correggio, the God of Rembrandt, or rather I should say the creator of these painters, I have prayed to him, supplicated to him to bless my painting, to grant my prayer that I might become a great painter. He will hear my prayer, and grant it in his good time – of this I feel something like certainty.'[10]

Gertrude watched and encouraged the development of Dolly's career with mixed emotions. She desperately wanted Dolly to be happy, and was enlightened enough to understand that her daughter sought this happiness and fulfilment through her work. But at heart, she was conservative in her aspirations for this remaining, eligible daughter. She wanted Dolly to get married. But there was a further confusion, which prevented her pushing all out to find Dolly an appropriate husband, in that she did not want to lose her as she had lost Evie. The result was uncharacteristic passivity: she did not try to interfere with her daughter's personal life, and increasingly adopted an exasperated, 'hands-off' approach as Dolly took advantage of the freedom which her mother had granted her. She expressed this ambivalence in a diary entry for 18 June 1884 when she watched Dolly go off to Gladstone's party, with her brother Charles as chaperon. Dolly looked charming, Gertrude noted in her diary. 'I hardly know what to think – hope or fear,' she sighed. 'Must try and ask fervently that our father in heaven will give us what is best for us.'

Mother and daughter were drawn together in their love of company. Just as Dolly re-dedicated herself to her vocation after Evie left home, it was at this time that Gertrude truly discovered her own *métier* as a society hostess. Three or four times a month, she would host a lavish dinner party for between fourteen and twenty-five guests. She took great care to prepare the house, ensuring that the drawing-rooms and dining-room were bedecked with flowers, and supervised elaborate menus. One lavish Saturday night, for example, dinner for twenty-one consisted of: turtle soup from Fortnum and Mason; turbot smelts; venison cutlets; sweet-breads; bacon; *filet du boeuf chèvre*; roast chicken; sea kale; tongue; partridges; caviare; *meringue militaire*; chocolate gateau and coffee – all served by Gertrude's staff of powdered and liveried servants. The food was served on a 101-piece dinner service of Limoges porcelain. Her guests drank an indeterminate number of bottles of champagne, hock, claret, best sherry, common sherry and St Emilion. Typically, but not always, her dinners took place on a Saturday night from 9 p.m. and lasted until well after midnight; sometimes they were earlier, enabling the guests to go off together to the theatre; often the dinner was followed by an informal 'at home' when scores of guests turned up for late night drinks and conversation. As the century progressed, her Sunday afternoon gatherings became quite as legendary as her dinner parties. Gertrude was operating a salon at the heart of Whitehall.

CHAPTER 23

A SALON IN WHITEHALL

Some time before Gertrude's social career thus began in earnest, the now forgotten man of letters Abraham Hayward sought to analyse whether the essentially French institution of the salon could be transplanted to British soil. He was pessimistic: England had produced its fair share of great society hostesses, and givers of parties, 'who have done good service in blending, harmonizing and elevating society . . . in facilitating, refining and enhancing the pleasures of intellectual intimacy'. Among these historical figures, he numbered Georgiana, Duchess of Devonshire, Lady Palmerston, the wife of the famous Foreign Secretary, and Countess Blessington, who had held court at Kensington Gore with comte d'Orsay in mid-century. 'But not one of them has set about her appointed task in the manner of a Frenchwoman,' he concluded, 'not one of them has successfully attempted the institution of the salon.' Gertrude, who would in due course befriend the author, had of course grown up in France and preserved a proper understanding of the French, and of French hospitality. She herself never used the word, but if Hayward had written his article in the mid-1880s, he would surely have singled out Gertrude Tennant as a true *salonnière*.[1]

To qualify as such, Hayward argued, the hostess would have to promote a milieu wholly distinct from 'those numerous fetes where we crowd people together . . . who do not converse, and who are only there to dance, to hear music or to display dresses more or less sumptuous'. There were parties like this in London every night during the season, when bejewelled fashionable women in low-cut dresses were crammed together with men in full evening attire, so many choked into one place that movement, let alone conversation, was virtually impossible. One evening, for example, Gertrude and Dolly set out to the home of Sir Stafford Northcote, the Tory Chancellor of the Exchequer who lived in Downing Street. Usually this would be a journey of perhaps two minutes on foot from Richmond Terrace, or a matter of seconds in a carriage. But the throng of guests was so great that the carriage had to go to the back of a queue which snaked all the way up Whitehall to Trafalgar Square, and then back again to Downing Street. When they finally arrived, they had to fight their way into the house, and after a long hour of being hustled and trodden on, without being able to progress further than the stairs, they turned round and began the long journey home. It was estimated that 1,500 guests were there that evening. This form of entertainment was called a *crush*. Sometimes, London would get so crowded that guests would set out from one end of Mayfair and never reach the other, so great was the throng of carriages. Even when distinguished musicians were hired to give a recital, it was usual for the boorish British to come and go and chatter throughout. Gertrude was bored by this conventional social life. 'To Lady Lubbock's with Dear Dolly,' she lamented early in 1885. 'Deadly dull and disappointing like most parties.'

A salon, as distinct from a mere party, had to have an essential serious-ness of purpose. This was true of Gertrude's 'at homes', as if she took quite literally Thomas Carlyle's pronouncement that 'great men, taken up in any way, are profitable company'. Interpreted in this light, Gertrude's preoccupation with celebrity was the social equivalent of the work done by Watts to capture the essence of Victorian greatness in his sequence of portraits of distinguished persons of the age, or indeed of the photo-graphs taken by Julia Margaret Cameron, which hauntingly depict the blurred majesty of Tennyson, Gladstone and other monumental figures. The *Dictionary of National Biography*, an epic project sponsored by Gertrude's acquaintance George Smith and first edited by her friend Leslie Stephen, was another late Victorian attempt to document the spirit and actions of great men (and some women). According to the ethic of the time, a sanc-tity adhered to these personages. Their doings and sayings were worthy of recording and transmitting for the edification of society as a whole, and their images conveyed profound truths. Rather than write about them or paint and photograph them, however, Gertrude liked to attract such people to her drawing-room. She revered achievement, greatness and talent in all their forms, and sought to create a *frisson* by bringing diverse, fascinating and successful people together around the dinner table. Dolly felt it too: she confided to her diary that 'gifted, remarkable, original people' intoxicated her. 'I feel a kind of exaltation in their company, and I feel compelled to expand and glow and roar like a furnace when the blast is applied'.[2] Such language lends itself to Freudian deconstruction, and Dolly's giddy pursuit of celebrity may be interpreted as displacement activity for her apparent lack of interest in men of her own age. We will return to Dolly's amatory adventures.

According to Hayward, a salon needs to promote a common purpose and sensibility, brokered by the exquisite tact of the hostess, an urbanity 'which quickly allows relations [and] allows talking with everybody without being acquainted'. This explains Gertrude's un-English habit of inviting complete strangers into her home: one did not necessarily have to know one's fellow guests, but one could safely assume that the mere fact of them being there meant that one had a great deal of exquisitely good things in common. 'One day I received a note by hand, headed No 2 Richmond Terrace, Whitehall, signed Gertrude . . . Tennant,' recollected Marie Belloc Lowndes, sister of Hilaire and a successful novelist in her own right, who was delighted to receive this invitation out of the blue. 'It . . . stated that Mrs Tennant was always at home on Sunday afternoons, and that she hoped Mademoiselle Belloc would give her the pleasure of coming the following Sunday, at any time between four and seven o'clock.'[3] Another who accepted such an out of the blue summons was Prince Kropotkin, the Russian anarchist who advocated peaceful revolution, an end to property rights and a general levelling of hierarchical society so that the working man could enjoy the fruits of his labour. Gertrude saw in the newspaper that he had moved to Harrow Hill for the sake of his health and dropped him a note, and when he accepted, gathered a modest ten people to meet him over dinner on Saturday, 3 April 1886. 'No revolution caused desolation equal to the desolation of wars,' he told the assembled company. 'There is wealth enough and food enough for all, but it is all held back by the rich. They have got hold of the land which should be enjoyed by all.'[4] Dolly confided to her diary she rather liked a man who – having escaped from prison in St Petersburg – exuded a whiff of romance and adventure, as well as strong smell of tobacco. Another guest, the jurist and writer Frederic Harrison, thought Kropotkin a 'most misguided man', while Gladstone conceded that 'however wrong he is, he is intensely sincere, with a frenzied indignation at the hidden injustices of the world'.

Not all of Gertrude's would-be guests appreciated her forwardness. 'I have been for some time past in one of my states of nervous relapse and have been obliged to be very particular in respect of social engagements,' wrote Herbert Spencer on 5 March 1877. 'Indeed during the first month of this year I declined all invitations and since then have excused myself from many sometimes having to send a messenger to beg off at the last minute. I shall be for some time to come obliged to be thus careful and I must on that account ask you to excuse me.' 'Please excuse me from joining in your festivities on the 13th,' he wrote three years later, after receiving another unsolicited invitation. 'I have done so on but three occasions in my life, and those exceptional occasions were in the cases of extremely intimate friends. I am obliged to restrict my social excitements within narrow limits.' He preferred to spend his evenings snoozing in the companionable fug of the Athenaeum Club. For the open-minded, however, the freedom to talk openly with other guests signalled an atmosphere of total trust, as well as talent and good breeding. As Hayward explained, it demonstrated proof of 'familiarity with circles to which none were admitted otherwise than on the supposition of their being able to mix with the greatest and the best'.

Thus the ideal of the Enlightenment salon: it is doubtful whether the reality of the Parisian salons in the days of Mme de Staël matched up to this, let alone Gertrude's soirées of the 1880s and 1890s. And in the foggy air of London, as opposed to the vast bright Babylon of Paris (as Henry James called the city), such professed seriousness of purpose, allied to something as ephemeral as an evening party, could prompt a streak of *rosbif* scepticism and satire. From Charles Dickens to George du Maurier, the social-climbing lion huntress was routinely a figure of fun. 'I want to introduce two very clever people to each other,' cries out Mrs Leo Hunter in *Pickwick Papers*. 'Mr Pickwick, I have great pleasure in introducing you to Count Smorltork.' Smorltork, the foreign aristocrat whose real-life successors may well have attended Gertrude's 'at homes', was gathering materials for his great work on the English nation. Mrs Leo Hunter, meanwhile, was the proud authoress of her far-famed 'Ode to an Expiring Frog'. There was a suspicion, no more than a rumour reported by Mrs Belloc Lowndes, that Gertrude was the model for George du Maurier's depiction of Mrs Lyon Hunter in *Punch* – although the dates make this very unlikely and Gertrude never a wrote anything akin to the ode to a dying frog.

* * *

'Here one meets every one worth knowing, unless society be limited to mere fashionable commonplace people,' wrote a breathless American reporter at the time of Dolly's wedding. 'Gladstone is a frequenter of the

Richmond Terrace salon, and with him come the very choicest of the parliamentary and diplomatic fraternity. This house is what Holland House was in the day of Macaulay . . .'[5] The comparison with Holland House, a Jacobean mansion in Kensington which for centuries had been the home of successive generations of the immensely grand Fox family, was an exaggeration, as Gertrude would have recognised. In its heyday, Mme de Staël had dined there, as well as Talleyrand and King Louis-Philippe himself, while English guests had included Byron, Scott, Disraeli and Dickens.[6] Although Gertrude would have been delighted to entertain such celebrities, had they been alive in her time, she did not belong to the Whiggish world of Lord and Lady Holland and their acolytes, and she never sought out aristocratic company for its own sake. As Mrs Belloc Lowndes recalled, Gertrude was quite democratic by the standards of Victorian society hostesses, entertaining men of every type and with a decided preference for the workers of the world, rather than aristocratic drones. Gertrude's establishment did, however, have a more direct connection with Little Holland House, the confusingly named dower house to the main Holland family residence. This was a more bohemian social centre than its aristocratic neighbour. Occupied from the mid-century by Henry Thoby Prinsep, an Indian civil servant, and his wife Sara, Little Holland House attracted artists and writers including Thomas Carlyle, Robert Browning, Dante Gabriel Rossetti, Edward Burne-Jones, Millais and Watts, of whom it was said that he came to visit one day and stayed for the best part of thirty years, living and working in the house. The photographer Julia Margaret Cameron, Sara Prinsep's elder sister, was also a regular visitor.[7]

Number 2 Richmond Terrace picked up some of the clientele of Little Holland House after it was demolished in 1875, but Gertrude had no intention of recreating this purely artistic milieu. She liked individual artists such as John Millais, but she was not keen on them *en masse*, noting that 'artistic society [was] too much concentrated in one single direction'. Nor, despite living opposite Downing Street, was she especially enthusiastic about politicians, declaring (after a dinner party on 12 July 1885) that her frequent guest William Ewart Gladstone was 'the very dullest man I ever met' while Austen Chamberlain, the future Tory statesman, was 'very, very tiresome'. She revised her opinion of Gladstone later that summer after his administration fell and he became her next-door neighbour and family friend. Over a cup of tea, he explained to her how he had lost his finger in a shooting accident (it had been peculiarly painless, he told her), and expressed great interest in her descent from Oliver Cromwell. Gertrude told him how as a child she had been obliged to pray for the soul of King Charles I, and had been told by her nurse that no good came from being descended from a regicide. Gladstone reassured her that there was no taint of sin associated with the crime of regicide, given the seven generations separating Gertrude from Cromwell, and thereafter they got on famously. Gladstone told Dolly how much he enjoyed reading Robert Louis Stevenson's recently published *Treasure Island*, and helped select her pictures for exhibition at the Royal Academy and the Grosvenor Gallery.

Many distinguished Liberal politicians, including Joseph Chamberlain (father of Austen and Neville), John Morley, Sir William Vernon Harcourt and Sir George Trevelyan, regularly attended her evening parties, and there was much plotting and harrumphing around the dinner table as Gladstone's immense career stuttered towards an end over the divisive issue of Home Rule for Ireland. Gertrude's dinner table was a convenient and congenial place to visit on the way back from the House of Commons, but she was by no means a political hostess like Lady Stanhope (at whose house all the leading Conservatives would gather) or Lady Hayter (who gave big dinner parties every Saturday night during the season for the leading lights of the Liberal Party). Arthur James Balfour's frequent presence at her dinner table can be explained by a family connec-tion rather than party affiliation: the future Conservative Prime Minister's sister was married to the Cambridge philosopher Henry Sidgwick, Frederick Myers's greatest friend and fellow psychical researcher. In any case, at Richmond Terrace, as at grander houses in London at this time, sworn political enemies would gather on terms of perfect civility. The English did not carry politics into private life as they did in France. 'Men of opposite sides lavish abuse on each other in the House,' noted one diarist, 'but there it ends, and they meet at dinner and chaff each other, and their wives are perfectly intimate.' In the Paris of the Third Republic, by contrast, just as during the war of the salons in the 1830s, there was a profound gulf between the parties, and it was not unusual 'to see people in society turn their backs upon some perfectly distinguished gentleman because he had not the same opinion as themselves in politics.'[8]

Nor again was Gertrude a predominantly literary hostess, although there were writers, notably Henry James, an inveterate party-goer and diner-out in the London of the 1880s, who came looking for material for his stories. 'I heard the other day at Mrs Tennant's of a situation which struck me as a dramatic and pretty subject,' he wrote in his notebook on 29 January 1884.[9] Nothing came of this particular anecdote, but he remained a regular visitor throughout the 1880s and 1890s. Bundled to this day in the attic are around twenty letters from James to Gertrude and

Dolly, many of which do little more than convey his delight in being able to accept an invitation to dine. He typically writes to Gertrude in French, in one letter comparing the drudgery of London life with the joys of Paris, which he describes as a vast *bonbonnerie* of delights. Equally expressive are the letters in which he is compelled to decline Gertrude's hospitality: 'a word to say I am in *despair* at the prospect of not being able to come to our friend's reading this afternoon,' he pleads in April 1888. 'Please tell him my extreme and inconsolable regret I *must* go this afternoon to Matthew Arnold's funeral.' Robert Browning, too, was an occasional guest in the last years of his life, and again this writer's letters of refusal are more eloquent than his acceptances. 'I am sure it is with no light heart that I throw myself on your good nature in this instance,' he writes on 3 January 1889, 'but greatly as I should enjoy your company on the 10th I dare not promise myself this enjoyment. Three consecutive months of wonderful weather in Venice, broken by but two rainy days, have been a bad preparation for this London fog, and I have been forced already to refuse not a few kind invitations from friends . . . I count upon your goodness to understand the sacrifice I make, and to sympathise accordingly.'

To add further spice to the social mix, there were Henry Irving and Benoît-Constant Coquelin, the leading actors of their generation on both sides of the English Channel. Coquelin visited so frequently in the late 1870s and early 1880s that he became a close family friend and even a potential suitor for Dolly. Gertrude arranged readings for him and facilitated introductions with eminent men of the stage, for example Herbert Beerbohm Tree, the great theatre director, who showed him round the Haymarket Theatre. Frederic Myers would come to dinner whenever he and Evie were in London, bringing his literally esoteric contribution to the conversation. Edwin Arnold, who referred to Gertrude teasingly as 'the powerful ambassadress', came every fortnight throughout the 1880s. As an editor and contributor to the *Daily Telegraph* for some forty years, Arnold was one of the most powerful figures of an age when the mass media was in its ascendancy. He found Richmond Terrace a useful source of political gossip and insight and would scurry home towards midnight to write leaders based on what he gleaned from Mrs Tennant's dinner table, as he did a few days before Gladstone's long-awaited marathon speech unveiling his Irish policy. He was prized by Gertrude as a man with a harmonious temperament, able to build conversational bridges between the incongruous elements gathered around the dinner table. Indeed, as an eminent orientalist and a popular poet, Arnold could more than hold his own on literary subjects as well as current affairs. When, in the mid-eighties, he left

London for Asia he thanked Gertrude for her 'endless kindness [that] gilds this by-gone year with a "light" which I shall not find in "Asia" . . . To thank you adequately for all your grace and kindness to me is quite impossible, but like an indulged debtor I pay by constant instalments of attachment and gratitude.' (*The Light of Asia* was his immensely popular poem about Buddhism.)

Finally, we should not forget Hamilton Aïdé, who attended most of Gertrude's dinners and parties and could be relied upon to entrance his fellow guests with his account of a recent visit to the continent, or his polished anecdotes of long-dead celebrities. He was the first to hear of the impending scandal of Sir Charles Dilke's divorce case, or to pick up the last words of the ex-Emperor Louis Napoleon or gossip from his widow the Empress Eugénie, whom he visited regularly in her retirement in Farnborough, Hampshire. '*Un très vieux* gentleman,' is how one French visitor described Aïdé working his way round an evening party late in the century. 'A very old gentleman . . . You'd imagine he was a hundred and fifty years old, and one is assured that there is not a single British celebrity since the times of the Georges that he hasn't spoken to. He passed stealthily from one group to another, listened for a moment, and then moved on nodding his head.'[10]

Gertrude's tastes were eclectic, bringing together men and women from all walks of life. The resulting *mélange* was a pot-pourri of late Victorian society, a mixing of artistic figures such as Oscar Wilde with intellectuals (such as Beatrice Potter, the future socialist Mrs Sidney Webb) and down-to-earth men of business and politics, and a flavouring of ambassadors and sophisticated European and American expatriates.[11] Gertrude's skill as a hostess came in blending these disparate elements. 'Mother wins everyone she comes across,' Dolly noted. 'There is an intelligent sympathy, a quite rare understanding of what is best in everyone. She comes across as a power of drawing out that best, which attracts everyone to her, as the amber gently rubbed draws towards itself.'

* * *

Gertrude kept a careful log of her social life, evaluating the mix of guests, the success or otherwise of the menu and the quality of the service and conversation. She considered that her best dinner party, in point of company, took place on Wednesday, 24 July 1885, when in addition to Hamilton and a High Court judge, her guests included William Ewart Gladstone, who less than a month before had resigned as Prime Minister, and who now counted more as a neighbour. Gladstone, though somewhat down-hearted after being ousted from office, was on lively form, legendary for being able to hold a disquisition on any subject, from Greek poetics to theology and the finer points of constitutional reform for Ireland. 'He has a fine voice, bright, keen, dark eyes, and apparently knows everything about everything,' a fellow guest that night noted after an earlier meeting with the Grand Old Man of English politics. Dolly, by contrast, was struck by how shabbily he dressed: ill-cut-trousers, worn buttonholes on his waistcoat, and a loose grey tie slung in a bow around his neck.

Another former Prime Minister, this time of France, was also in attendance, namely William Henry Waddington, now serving as French ambassador to the Court of St James. Although born in France, Waddington, as his surname suggests, had English ancestry and most unusually for a Frenchman had had a classic English gentleman's education: public school (in his case Rugby) and then Cambridge, where in 1849 he rowed for the University in the first boat race and earned the gratitude of Queen Victoria by, like Sir Walter Raleigh for Elizabeth I, gallantly throwing his academic gown into a puddle so she could dismount from her carriage without getting her feet wet. He returned to France and had enjoyed an improbably successful political career, culminating in his tenure as Minister for Foreign Affairs in 1877 and Prime Minister in 1879. He was exactly the sort of sophisticated Anglo-French man of the world whom Gertrude delighted in entertaining. His wife Mary King Waddington was American-born and together they had recently returned from attending the coronation of Tsar Alexander III in Moscow, where Waddington had been ambassador extraordinary. Her vivid letters describing diplomatic life were published early in the twentieth century.

On this occasion the fame of these statesmen and the charm of their wives was eclipsed, if that were at all possible, by the man Gertrude described perfunctorily in her diary as 'Stanley, Congo', the explorer who had been invited at Dolly's behest. Hearing that Stanley had returned to London after his third great African expedition, Dolly had asked Edwin Arnold to bring him along to her mother's dinner party. The editor had another engagement on this fateful evening and so, to make up the numbers, Gertrude invited Gladstone in his stead. Thus it was that Stanley came unaccompanied, and Dolly sat between two of her heroes.

CHAPTER 24

BULA MATARI IN THE DRAWING-ROOM

Gertrude's *placement* or seating plan was not well judged, for, although Dolly revered both Gladstone and Stanley, they did not like each other at all. Their mutual antipathy was not surprising, in that they represented very different types of Victorian greatness. Gladstone was pious, learned to a fault, an Old Etonian constitutionalist, the embodiment of establishment values. He was genial, otherworldly, most at home in the Oxbridge senior common room or the protocol-bound House of Commons, and his manner that of a donnish clergyman rather than a great parliamentarian. Stanley, by contrast, had exceedingly humble origins, and had clawed his way to international celebrity by virtue of his ruthlessly successful African exploits and a talent for self-publicity. Workhouse-raised, illegitimate, shifty about his origins and his nationality (he was an American citizen at this point), the explorer was never going to hit it off with the Eton- and Christ-Church-educated son of a millionaire who had been groomed for high office from his schooldays. There is a malicious passage in Chapter XIX of Stanley's *Autobiography* in which he describes a later meeting with Gladstone at Richmond Terrace, capturing nicely the difference in their temperaments:

'Excuse me one minute,' said [Gladstone, pointing to a map showing two mountains in the Ruwenzori, discovered and named by Stanley]; 'what are those two mountains called?'

'Those, sir,' [Stanley answered], 'are the Gordon Bennett and the Mackinnon peaks.'

'Who called them by those absurd names?' he asked, with the corrugation of a frown on his brow.

'I called them, sir.'

'By what right?' he asked.

'By the right of first discovery, and those two gentlemen were the patrons of the expedition.'

'How can you say that, when Herodotus spoke of them twenty-six hundred years ago, and called them Crophi and Mophi? It is intolerable that classic names like those should be displaced by modern names and . . .'

'I humbly beg your pardon, Mr Gladstone, but Crophi and Mophi, if they ever existed at all, were situated over a thousand miles to the northward. Herodotus simply wrote from hearsay, and . . .'

'Oh, I can't stand that.'

'Well, Mr Gladstone,' said I, 'will you assist me in this project of a railway to Uganda, for the suppression of the slave-trade, if I can arrange that Crophi and Mophi shall be substituted in place of Gordon Bennett and Mackinnon?'

'Oh, that will not do. That is flat bribery and corruption'; and, smiling, he rose to his feet, buttoning his coat lest his virtue might yield to the temptation.[1]

Stanley's was a modern kind of fame, owing much to his sure touch with the mass media and an easy accommodation with the forces of emergent imperialism, the factors that Gladstone had been slow to understand during the crisis in the Sudan that came to a grisly conclusion earlier in the year with the murder of General Gordon in Khartoum. Gladstone viewed Gordon as an insubordinate fool, and a drunken and self-regarding one at that, ignoring the fact that the popular press had turned the General into a national hero. In the increasingly jingoistic environment of the 1880s, this was a gross miscalculation – especially with an ever-expanding electorate in the wake of his Reform Act of 1884. 'One of Gladstone's most dangerous blind spots was that he could not comprehend the force of Gordon's appeal to the British public and hence his capacity to damage the government,' notes Roy Jenkins.[2] His inept handling of this situation was one reason for the fall of his second administration.

'What a charming lady Miss Dorothy is!' Stanley wrote to Arnold the day after the dinner party. Dolly was also impressed, and lost no time in following up. She sent a cajoling note to the explorer, asking him whether she could paint him. 'I would let you be very comfortable, you shall smoke, and feel just as though you are in your own tent . . .'[3] Stanley accepted the invitation and returned a few days later to sit to Dolly; over the coming months he became a regular feature at Gertrude's lunches and dinners – so much so that Gertrude was reduced to registering in her diary that Stanley came for lunch 'as usual'. His personal history, which would become intertwined with that of Dolly and Gertrude for the remainder of his life, was one of the more remarkable of the age.

* * *

Stanley was born John Rowlands in Denbigh in 1841, the illegitimate son of a barmaid, and at the age of six was abandoned by his family at the workhouse at St Asaph. According to his autobiography, edited and bowdlerised by Dolly after he died, he escaped after clobbering the principal of the workhouse for one insult too many, jumping over a wall and eventually shipping to New Orleans, where he claimed to have been adopted by a prosperous trader called Henry Hope Stanley, whose surname he took as his own. Tim Jeal, the author of the most recent biography, has shown that both the dramatic escape and the adoption were largely make-believe. His upbringing, amid poverty, disgrace, rejection by his mother and most probably what we would call abuse in the workhouse, was too traumatic to be owned up to, and needed to be covered up at any price. After a series of adventures, in which he served on both sides in the American Civil War and narrowly avoided being raped on a botched expedition to Turkey (a companion was not so lucky), he found his vocation as a newspaper reporter. He covered the frontier wars in the Wild West of the 1860s before signing on with the *New York Herald* as a war correspondent. His first big story was an exclusive report of the fall of Magdala, the culmination of the British campaign in Abyssinia, followed by dispatches from the front line in Spain.

In 1869, the *Herald*'s proprietor James Gordon Bennett sent him to Africa with the order to 'find Livingstone'. Relayed back to the *Herald*, his account of the meeting was one of the great newspaper scoops of the nineteenth century (although it seems likely that Stanley cooked up the famous greeting in order to create a good headline). He was a compulsive embellisher of the truth, a talented writer of fast-paced adventurous travel books, which were churned out in marathon 18-hour-a-day feats of composition. They remain thrilling to read, interlarded with graphic descriptions of arduous marches, perfidious coolies, terrible swamps and canoe-swallowing cataracts, evil Arab slave traders, mysterious diseases, attacks by crocodiles and man-eating natives – plus tips on how to survive all these hazards – and have influenced generations of travel writers and adventure novelists, from Rider Haggard to Bruce Chatwin. His powerful rhetoric conveyed the notion of a spiritual journey and of bringing light to darkness, a trope picked up by writers from Charles Booth to Joseph Conrad.

As much as the mass public thrilled to his exploits and his sensational account of them (in *How I Found Livingstone*) the British establishment was sceptical. They detested the fact that he was an American adventurer, not a respectable explorer, and they were sniffy about his origins. 'It must rather have been Livingstone who discovered Stanley,' quipped the President of the Royal Geographical Society; Florence Nightingale dismissed his account of the expedition as 'the very worst book on the very best subject I ever saw in my life', and whilst Queen Victoria gave him an audience and a snuffbox, she was not impressed, describing him as 'a determined ugly man, with a strong American twang'. As he wrote much later in his autobiography: 'all the actions, and all my thoughts, since 1872, have been strongly coloured by the storm of abuse and the wholly unjustifiable reports circulated about me then. So numerous were my enemies that my friends remained dumb.'[4] Underneath the explorer's carapace of invulnerability, he remained sensitive and easily slighted throughout his life.

In the years between discovering Livingstone and his invitation to Richmond Terrace he completed two further expeditions to Africa. The first (1874–77) was an epic journey that took him from the Indian to the Atlantic Ocean. He circumnavigated two of the three Great Lakes for the first time in history and disentangled the source of the Congo from the Nile, thus answering the last great question of African geography. He saw this expedition as completing the work of Livingstone, who after parting from Stanley had headed off west from Lake Tanganyika into the unknown.[5] Having secured a commission from the *Daily Telegraph*, and another from his previous employer the *Herald*, Stanley picked up the journey where Livingstone had left off. The missionary-explorer had died before he could advance very far westwards, but he did make some crucial headway, becoming the first white man to lay eyes on a great river located hundreds of miles to the west of Lake Tanganyika. At the point where he discovered the Lualaba, as the natives called it, the river flows northwards and thus not in the direction of the Atlantic, and Livingstone made the reasonable assumption that it was another tributary to the Nile. But it took Stanley to establish that the Lualaba in fact forms the upper reaches of the

Congo itself, the great crescent-shaped watercourse that drains an area the size of Europe and which runs for just under 3,000 miles from its source to the Atlantic, a serpent uncoiling right across Africa (as Joseph Conrad described it). The river is so vast that it takes six months for water to flow from its source (in what is now Zambia) to the Atlantic and, unlike the Nile or the Amazon, it flows at a terrific pace all year round: because it arches from south of the equator to the north and back again, there is always one part of the river in a rainy season.

'The secret of the centuries has been solved!' noted an article in the *Cornhill Magazine*. 'The Dark Continent is, geographically at least, dark no longer!'[6] Stanley's account of the stupendous journey (*Through the Dark Continent*, 1878) was a best-seller, but his fame was achieved at the price of considerable notoriety – this time, less for the *Boy's Own Paper* hyperbole of his account than for the violence with which he achieved his goals. His three young British associates died on the expedition, as did hundreds of native porters, testament to the single-minded brutality of his leadership. One incident attracted especial condemnation: in August 1875, Stanley and his men opened fire on the natives of Bumbiri Island on Lake Victoria, killing more than thirty from a distance of fifty yards. Tim Jeal argues that Stanley acted more in self-defence than with vengeful sadism, and that the explorer's own luridly detailed account of an early skirmish was exaggerated to demonstrate his manful lack of pity in quashing the native threat. His critics were not easily appeased. 'He has no concern with justice, no right to administer it,' commented the *Saturday Review* on his return. 'He comes with no sanction, no authority, no jurisdiction – nothing but explosive bullets and a copy of the *Daily Telegraph*.' 'Exploration under these conditions is, in fact, exploration plus buccaneering,' adjudged the *Pall Mall Gazette*. 'Although the map may be improved and enlarged by the process, the cause of civilisation is not a gainer thereby, but a loser.' In the spring of 2007, following the publication of Jeal's sympathetic biography, there was angry correspondence on the subject of the Bumbiri incident in the pages of the *London Review of Books*: evidence of Stanley's ability to stir up hostile passions more than a century after his death.

The subsequent expedition, from which he returned the year before he was first a guest at Richmond Terrace, was at the behest of Leopold II, King of the Belgians. The King was a cousin of Queen Victoria and the man whose ambition to create a personal empire in the Congo would later in the century contribute to immeasurable human suffering. But the rapine was some way in the future when Stanley came into Leopold's employment. As Europe's great powers jostled for position ahead of what would become the fully fledged scramble for Africa, the King followed newspaper accounts of Stanley's African adventures with great interest. He had always been depressed at the prospect of ruling over a country as insignificant as Belgium, and he dreamed of a more substantial empire.[7] When Stanley returned to Europe, his contracts with the *Daily Telegraph* and the *New York Herald* at an end, the King lost no time in summoning the explorer to Brussels, coaxing him into undertaking a mission to the Congo on behalf of the newly established Comité d'Etudes du Haut-Congo, an innocuous-sounding front for Leopold's imperialistic ambitions. It had the stated objective of establishing 'stations for scientific, philanthropic and commercial purposes' on the Congo and was backed by, among others, the wealthy Baroness Burdett-Coutts and Stanley's friend William Mackinnon, a Scottish shipping magnate. In fact, Stanley was mandated to broker treaties with local chiefs, in which territory was ceded to the King on favourable terms, thus (his critics have argued) providing the spurious legal basis of what would become Leopold's immense personal fiefdom.

Stanley signed up for five years, returning in August 1879 to the mouth of the Congo, from where he pushed laboriously upstream to a great lake-like widening of the river which he had reached from the other direction on his earlier journey. Here, on the Stanley Pool, he established a trading station which he named Leopoldville (the modern Kinshasa) before pressing further into the interior as far as Stanley Falls, a 60-mile stretch of impassable rapids that lie a full 1,000 miles from the Atlantic coast. His indefatigable energy, his iron discipline, and his seeming immunity to the diseases that felled other Europeans, earned him the sobriquet Bula Matari, or breaker of rocks, a nickname bestowed on him in a light-hearted way by an admiring African chieftain. Axe or pick in hand, he was a literal rock-smasher as he opened up the road from the coast into the heart of the continent, but in the eyes of his many detractors the name came to connote the brutality with which he treated his fellow human beings, Europeans as well as Africans. Stanley saw himself as a missionary for peace, Christianity and commerce, a true successor to Livingstone, but his combination of military efficiency, ruthlessness and professed high moral purpose differed from the comparatively quixotic efforts of earlier explorers.[8]

* * *

One day, as Stanley was sitting to Dolly as she worked on his portrait, Gertrude popped her head into the birdcage and observed how strange it was that Gordon of Khartoum had never married. 'I am sure he must have been jilted by some girl in the past of whom no-one has heard yet,' Gertrude said. She saw Dolly and Stanley looking at each other significantly: the breaker of rocks had just been telling Dolly about his own ill fortune in love. He had been engaged to a woman named Alice Pike when he set off on his first Congo expedition, and had written to her throughout the voyage and even named his collapsible boat after her. The boat was true to him, and trustily helped him negotiate the perilous river, but the woman was not so reliable: when he arrived home, he found that she had married someone else two years previously. He had a similar experience when he returned to the Congo. Unsympathetic modern biographers have developed all sorts of theories to explain his lack of success with women, from repressed homosexuality to sadomasochism, which is said to have found an outlet in the extreme conditions of central Africa. Perhaps, for all the romance attaching to him and his adventures, it was simply that he was short and far from conventionally good-looking? Mrs Waddington thought Stanley looked 'as hard as steel,' adding that he had to be, to have done what he had done.[9] But he was not without charisma, as Dolly noted after the sitting:

> His chin is very square and would be a beautiful chin but for a slight thickening under the chin, not of superfluous fat, but of rather the muscular throat of a man prematurely aged . . . his face is somewhat marked by exposure to sun, by fever, by responsibility, by anxiety.[10]

During the numerous, extended sittings for the portrait, Stanley spoke 'frankly . . . so confidingly . . . about himself, his hopes, his ambitions, his struggles'. It became clear that he was once again in search of a wife, but he was awkward with women and did not rate his chances with Dolly. 'Further than Platonism I doubt my affair will go,' he told a friend a month after he first met Dolly. 'It is so very innocent . . . I am so easily rebuffed & very sensitive. If she proposed to me, it might be very different, but if I have to propose to her, do you know I rather think I will not have the courage.'

Stanley foresaw yet another obstacle to the furtherance of his suit. Somewhat improbably, the man who had completed the greatest feats of African exploration in modern history, who could shrug off the perils of jungles, cannibals and crocodiles, affected to be terrified of Gertrude herself. 'There is a mother in the case,' Stanley explained, 'and I am rather afraid of her.' Gertrude's self-assurance and the evident prosperity of Richmond Terrace intimidated him. 'I think it would be a boon to shy people like myself, if there were no such people as mothers. I find them sadly in the way. Having brought eligible people up – they insist on interfering at the wrong time. My bachelorhood is solely due to these mothers.'[11]

In fact, if Gertrude did not actively encourage Stanley's suit, she did not stand in the way: she gave her tacit blessing to their friendship by joining Dolly on a visit to Stanley's bachelor rooms in New Bond Street, and making both the explorer and his friend Mackinnon a fixture at her lunch and dinner parties. It would be helpful to have the benefit of Gertrude's perspective on Stanley at this time, but, frustratingly for the modern reader, she made no more than the most perfunctory observations on him in her diary. She did not look upon Stanley as a future son-in-law, but as a diverting semi-permanent house-guest who added to the diversity of the Richmond Terrace milieu. It cannot have escaped her attention that Stanley was pursuing Dolly, but she knew that Dolly was not taking him seriously as a suitor. Dolly's heart was elsewhere.

CHAPTER 25

DOLLY'S CHOICES

Oscar Wilde had summed up Dolly's dilemma long ago, on the day of the visit with Ruskin, telling her he did not know anyone great and good enough for her to marry.

Surrounded by the great men of the world, Dolly was utterly uninspired by the younger, marriageable men she met, one of whom had underwhelmed her by stating that he wanted to be her pet, like an animal or bird in her studio. How could the gaucherie of such a boy compete with the thrill of conversing with Gladstone or Henry James? It was, Dolly told her father, a case of 'aut Caesar, aut nullus', either the Emperor, or no one at all.[1] Whether she told her living mother quite as much is not clear, but Gertrude was agonisingly aware of Dolly's infatuations and desolations.

On Tuesday, 28 July 1885, Gertrude invited Stanley and Hamilton to lunch. After the lunch, she noted, Dolly took the carriage to a nearby flower shop. As Gertrude wrote cryptically in her diary: 'D saw AC pass by – rushed out – spoke – and arranged to spend the day [with him].' Gertrude felt dazed by this development, but 'comparatively willing to accept whatever joys or trials are appointed for me'. She passed a sleepless night. The next day, Dolly was up early, dressed in her finest, looking radiant. 'That's the supreme thorn in my crown of thorns,' Gertrude lamented. 'To see her disappointed.' The radiance, and the potential disappointment, had nothing to do with the next scheduled visit from Henry Morton Stanley; rather, it was the sudden reappearance of the mysterious 'AC'. As Gertrude was only too well aware, this was Andrew Carnegie (1835–1919), the Scottish-American industrialist who was one of the richest men in the world and who qualified in Dolly's estimation as a veritable Caesar among men. Now 50 years old to Dolly's 30, Carnegie had come to London briefly in the summer of 1883, and in passing produced a *coup de foudre* in Dolly's heart. They met at a party given by Gladstone, but quite what passed between the steel magnate and Dolly thereafter, we will never know, as Gertrude could not bring herself to write about the liaison, and Dolly ripped out the relevant pages of her diary and inked out all but a few subsequent references to him. In the one mention of the affair which has not been deleted, Dolly said she had foolishly believed in him. 'Then came the bewildering trial, its volcanic eruptions of folly . . .'[2] She vowed to tell any future husband everything apart from the identity of 'AC'. The language suggests a degree of passion beyond mere infatuation: maybe she even slept with him, and this was the truth that she would have to tell a future husband?

In meeting Stanley for the first time, both Gertrude and Dolly were primarily impressed by his similarity to Carnegie – in looks, temperament, and indeed background. 'Mr Stanley very much reminds me of Andrew,' wrote Dolly in a diary entry that is otherwise heavily crossed out.[3] And then again, when he returned for tea and a portrait sitting: 'he is a very short exact, determined man though one could not call him a little man,' she writes. 'I felt what seized me when I first saw him is his powerfulness, you could use such word, his physical and moral [power] . . . and his resemblance to Carnegie.' (The last few words are crossed out but, for once, they are legible.) 'Mother also felt it,' she adds.[4]

The revival of the relationship in July 1885 proved short-lived. 'End of all things!' wrote Gertrude when her daughter returned that evening after spending the day with Carnegie in Putney. 'What a termination to a romance of two long years duration.' Gertrude felt stupefied and weary. Stanley reappeared on Friday, 31 July for his next portrait sitting, but while Dolly painted and Gertrude presented him with a small copy of Newman's *Dream of Gerontius*, neither mother nor daughter saw the explorer as more than a welcome distraction after the emotional upheaval of the previous week. 'Nothing pleasant to look forward to or hope for,' Gertrude noted after Stanley's visit. 'Future seems a blank.'

Gertrude was aware of Dolly's feelings for Carnegie, but how much did she know about her daughter's more dangerous attachment to a married cabinet minister? If she could have read Dolly's diaries for 1885–86, she would have been horrified at the extent of her daughter's infatuation with George Otto Trevelyan (1838–1928). Trevelyan was neither as rich as Carnegie, nor as famous as Stanley, but still he was a cabinet minister, a nephew of Lord Macaulay (whose biography he wrote), and in due course he would inherit a title and an estate in Northumberland. He was cultivated, accomplished, and well and truly married. (Carnegie, at least, had no wife when they met.) Trevelyan was a regular visitor to Richmond Terrace in 1885 and 1886 and would often take tea with Dolly and Gertrude, talking over the latest political intrigues as Gladstone's second government tottered towards collapse, mired in disputes over Ireland, Egypt and the Sudan. On 11 May 1885, however, politics was not on the agenda. Gertrude was out when Trevelyan called. Dolly invited him in and after a cup of tea they went to the birdcage. 'Trevelyan stood very close to me,' Dolly wrote in her diary that night. 'I did not mind feeling his hand over mine and his breath warming me.'

Trevelyan told Dolly how first he had admired her and now he loved her. 'This feeling should give way to friendship,' he said, without any great conviction.

And then they kissed each other.

'I cannot say who began – our lips met together,' Dolly confessed. 'He knows it may never be again. I know this love is guilty, but I feel no remorse as yet, like someone shot but doesn't feel the pain yet. I was entirely frank with him in manner as in words. I did not shrink or draw back because I felt joy at being near him.'

'No-one ever filled me with the spirit of glowing exultation as he does,' she wrote a few days later. 'No-one gives me the longing for self-immolation.'

'This feeling must be destroyed,' she added.

Gertrude knew enough to be extremely concerned: of course, married men had affairs in late Victorian times as they do now, but the consequences for both parties were inconceivably graver then than they are today. Sir Charles Dilke, a family friend, would soon be ruined when details of an alleged affair were made public; later in the decade, Charles Stuart Parnell's parliamentary career would come to an end as details of his affair with Mrs Kitty O'Shea were unscrupulously exploited by political opponents. Were the liaison to develop, and the gossipy world of Westminster to get hold of the story, Trevelyan's downfall would be assured, and Dolly and her mother would be ostracised. While Dolly struggled to curb her feelings for Trevelyan, Gertrude strove to remove her daughter from harm's way, taking her on a late summer holiday to Hunstanton in Norfolk and packing her off on various country house expeditions with Hamilton. For six months or so, while Dolly was deepening her friendship with Stanley, she did not see Trevelyan at all, but this enforced separation did nothing to dampen her passion. 'I sometimes think that a husband and children would satisfy my soul,' Dolly wrote later. 'But no-one I could marry could give me any happiness. I could not endure to marry anyone I knew or ever knew excepting him to whom I can never be anything. I pray for deliverance but when his name appears in the papers I feel the magic numbs my conscience.'[5]

There was increasing reason to see Trevelyan's name in the papers. Lord Salisbury's short-lived government was on the ropes and in February Gladstone returned to power, and with him Dolly's admirer, who was appointed Secretary of State for Scotland. Before long, Trevelyan was again visiting Richmond Terrace, but this time Gertrude insisted on being present when he and Dolly took tea in the birdcage. There were momentous political issues to be discussed – Gladstone was preparing his Irish Home Rule Bill and Trevelyan was among those who thought the premier was misguided in his strategy. Joseph Chamberlain was more intemperate. 'What can be done when we have a madman for a leader!' he told Gertrude. 'Gladstone will break up the country and then we shall step in to find it in fragments.'[6] As the details of Gladstone's Home Rule plans emerged, Trevelyan's exasperation gave way to rebellion, and on 27 March, he and Chamberlain dramatically resigned from the Cabinet, walking out in mid-meeting. The Home Rule Bill was eventually voted down, and in July Gladstone called another election – in which Trevelyan lost his seat. The Sunday before the resignation, Trevelyan came for tea at Richmond Terrace.

'I felt the old, indefinable joy, the immense joy of being near him,' wrote Dolly. 'He left at 4 and the light went out.'[7]

A few months later, Dolly was still under Trevelyan's spell when at last Stanley overcame his shyness and plucked up the courage to ask for her hand in marriage. In August 1886, Stanley and Dolly, together with Gertrude and around seventy others, were guests on board Sir William Mackinnon's luxury yacht *Jumna* on a week-long cruise of the western isles of Scotland. The explorer penned a tentative, ponderous proposal. 'HM Stanley wrote to Dolly,' Gertrude noted tersely in her diary for Tuesday, 16 August. '[She] answered NO.'

Splenetic with rage, the jilted Stanley felt that he had been led a merry dance by the flirtatious Dolly. 'I have been living [for the past year] in a fool's paradise,' he told Mackinnon. 'That woman entrapped me with her gush & fulsome adulations . . . her sweet scented notes written with a certain literary touch . . .'[8] Soon afterwards, he returned to Africa for the consolations of the jungle, on what would prove the last, and most controversial of his expeditions. Gertrude sent Dolly off to stay with their rich and glamorous namesakes, the Tennants of the Glen, with whom there was no blood relationship, but a degree of family friendship.[9] Gertrude stayed at home, brooding on her darling Dolly's continuing inability to find a husband.

* * *

Dolly still had not found her Caesar, but at least she had her painting. In mid-1886, Millais visited and encouraged her with what she called his exuberant frankness and charm, his joyous, exhilarating consciousness of work – and what we might deem a patronising manner. 'Well Dolly, you astonish me,' Millais told her as he examined her picture *The Death of Love* (painted as a memorial for the dalliance with Carnegie). 'You have done nothing to equal this. I think this very remarkable, far beyond anything I have ever seen of yours. Frankly, I never thought you would make progress, but now you ought to become a great artist. Your work is singularly, exceptionally unequal, but it is work of the highest promise. Your progress I repeat very much astonishes me.' He offered to let her come and watch him paint a baby. 'I don't think there is anyone living who can paint children as I can,' he said, with the immodesty of talent and success. 'Dear Watts says the same.'[10] Keep at it, was the message, and so she did, taking note of pictures sold or exhibited by the Royal Academy, and illustrations published in magazines such as the *Weekly Echo* and the *Penny Popular*. When Stanley's friend Mackinnon turned out to have paid £45 for a picture of an Arab Dame, which was on display at the RA, she hoped that he had bought it for his collection and not just to make her feel better.

'Dear father there are days when I long to paint wonderfully, when I desire to make a name,' she wrote, 'and then this subsides and I feel a longing just to be nothing, just to be taken care of and not to have to struggle or aim at success.'[11] This conflict between happy domesticity and fulfilment in her chosen career is perhaps banal in modern terms, when all have to juggle the demands of family life and professional life, but it was a new phenomenon at the time, expressive of a dilemma faced by many young women of the 1880s and 1890s. A profound social and demographic transformation was under way. Women had been admitted to London University from 1878; even if they could not graduate from the ancient universities of Oxford and Cambridge, the women of Girton and Somerville could take the same exams as the men, and regularly outscored them, even in supposedly masculine subjects such as mathematics; they were beginning to make headway in the professions; they could own their own property at last, and they were increasingly represented in local government and policy-making Royal Commissions. They did not win the vote until 1918, but they came frustratingly close as early as 1897, when the Parliamentary Franchise (Extension to Women) Act had the support of all parties and passed its second reading by 71 votes. (The legislation fell victim to a filibuster by reactionary MPs and fell by the wayside.) All in all, there were more women, and more of them were single and educated, and they in turn found their way into the upper echelons of the workforce. 'There must be a new type of woman,' declares a character in *The Odd Women* (1893) by George Gissing, 'a new worker out in the world, a new ruler in the home.' Such women were lampooned by unsubtle bastions of male chauvinism such as *Punch*, which portrayed them as mannish, unattractive, disobedient, denatured by their apparent determination to put career ahead of children.

Dolly's sister Eveleen was proof that young women of the 1880s could enjoy a fulfilling family life as well as pursue a vocation, in her case as a photographer. Her album of more than 500 family photographs captures the happy intimacies of prosperous upper middle-class domestic life in the 1880s. Her strikingly handsome husband stares out of these images, willingly distracted from his studies of the supernatural to cavort with his sons or play games with his daughter in the carefully tended walkways of the enormous garden at Leckhampton House. In the way of Victorian subjects, the children stare soulfully at the lens as they interrupt their frolics to pose for their mother's pictures (less because they were intrinsically mournful, and more because of the length of time they were obliged to hold themselves still for the exposure). There are also more formal genre pictures in which family and friends dress up as angels or characters in the Bible or Shakespeare plays. The pictures of Leo in sailor suit or wearing an angel's wings follow the model established by Julia Margaret Cameron, and are affecting to this day. There is also a frankly erotic picture of the beautiful Adelaide Passingham, an otherwise unknown model, her eyes averted and her hair cascading down over a revealing nightgown. They are among the more poignant amateur photographs of the late Victorian period, and the picture of the farouche Miss Passingham appeared on the cover of a 1994 exhibition catalogue from the National Portrait Gallery.[12]

Dolly could have settled down to a life with husband and children, relegating her painting to a hobby if she had wanted to. But her actions in the 1880s suggest that somewhere beyond the level of conscious choice she did not want to marry at all. Unlike many New Women, it was not fear of sex that drove her into relationships that were never going to lead to marriage – her passionate nature is proof of that – but rather, one suspects, fear of losing everything she had as a consequence of remaining single: her independence, her career as a painter, her exhilarating social life, her relationship with her mother and her magnificent home at Richmond Terrace. The Millais portrait thus captured an essential truth of her nature: it was easier, more congenial, somehow inevitable for Dolly to say 'NO!' to proposals of marriage. Even where her heart might have compelled her to say 'yes', she contrived to fall in love only with men who were unobtainable, by virtue of the immense gulf of wealth (in the case of Carnegie) or simply the fact that they were married.

By 1888, Trevelyan had been supplanted in Dolly's affections by Sir Alfred Comyn Lyall (1835–1911), a charming and learned Old Etonian who had recently returned to England after fifteen distinguished years as a colonial administrator in India. Gertrude liked him more than Dolly's other admirers, noting that he had 'all the charm of a philosopher joined to being the perfection of a perfect English gentleman . . . he is to me the Grand Seigneur, and so manly'. He was clubbable, intelligent, witty, and twenty years older than Dolly – all the qualities she appreciated in a man. Predictably, he too was married. Gertrude turned a blind eye as he and Dolly met for lunch; they wandered surreptitiously through empty college quadrangles on a visit to Evie in Cambridge; they exchanged presents – she sent him her drawings, he gave her a necklace made of ancient coins (which she would eventually wear on her wedding day). He visited her at Richmond Terrace on Christmas Day, 1889, and the following spring even went to stay with Gertrude and Dolly at Cadoxton, the Welsh country house which Gertrude now made a habit of visiting once or twice a year. Lyall was infatuated with Dolly, but had the good sense to see that the relationship could lead nowhere. 'He strongly advised me to marry,' Dolly recorded. 'I shouldn't have any illusions about love but he advised me to marry a man who might be good and honourable without expecting more.'[13]

Gertrude played no part in the resulting campaign to woo Stanley. The explorer returned to Britain in April 1890, amid huge fanfare, the newspapers full of accounts of his triumph in finding and rescuing Emin Pasha, the governor of equatorial Sudan. It mattered little at this stage that when Stanley had found the Pasha (in fact a German adventurer by the name of Eduard Schnitzer), after another formidably arduous journey across Africa, he had shown little inclination to be relieved. (When he fell off a balcony, it was assumed that he had jumped, so great was his desire to avoid being rescued.) The full nastiness of the expedition had yet to be made public. There had been a heroic march through the Ituri rain forest, but Stanley's expedition had become divided and a dreadful fate befell those left behind. The so-called Rear Column had suffered a moral and physical collapse worthy of the bleakest pages of Joseph Conrad's *Heart of Darkness*: hundreds of Africans had died, as well as most of the European officers, one of whom had gone so far as to pay a tribesman to demonstrate an act of cannibalism so that he could make a drawing. The man had obliged and there and then a little slave-girl was taken and chopped up in front of the officer's eyes, quite literally butchered for a feast. There had been whippings, executions, even sex slaves. Truly, this was 'The horror! The horror'! but of this nothing was suspected as yet. All the public had to go on was Stanley's typically racy account of the journey, the evocatively titled *In Darkest Africa*, which he had tossed off in two frenetic months before returning to England, and which rapidly became an immense best-seller.

Despite the dubious politics of the venture (was intended to further the interests of King Leopold as well as the fledgling Imperial British East Africa Company), Stanley on his return was more than just the Lion of the Season: his success reassured those fearing the decline of British influence, so vividly illustrated by the failure of the relief of Gordon in Khartoum, which Stanley's expedition consciously sought to redress. For a brief while, there was Stanley-mania, and his rhetoric and achievements helped define an agenda for domestic social reform as well as imperialist foreign policy. Before the year was out, General William Booth (founder of the Salvation Army) answered Stanley's book with a polemic *In Darkest England and the Way Out*, which sought to draw public attention to the squalor and backwardness of Britain's impoverished classes and to shed a civilising light on places no more remote than Lambeth, just across the river from Gertrude's home. Stanley was awarded honorary degrees by the Universities of Oxford, Cambridge, Durham and Edinburgh, while the Royal Geographical Society gave a reception in his honour at the Royal Albert Hall, attended by 10,000 people. The Queen received him at Windsor Castle and this time he made a favourable impression on the monarch who had previously been so dismissive.

At the time of the wedding, it was put about in the press that he and Dolly had been secretly engaged throughout the expedition, while Gladstone and other friends were told that Dolly had seen the error of her ways in initially rejecting him and had fallen in love during his long absence. This was romantic propaganda, as in May 1889 she had made it clear to Mackinnon that while she admired Stanley's achievements, she had no residual tenderness for him. Now she and Lyall calculated that Stanley would make a good husband after all. But after jilting him so unceremoniously, how could she possibly win him back? On Wednesday, 16 April, Lyall came to tea with Dolly, and again on the Friday. A plot was hatched.

On Saturday, Gertrude noted that Dolly was in high spirits. 'D full of her own thoughts and views,' she wrote in her diary. 'Do not see the possibility of her carrying out [her wishes].' At around this date, as her mother was beginning to suspect, Dolly wrote the first of a sequence of letters designed to make Stanley her husband.[14] 'Feel doubtful if the desire on one side will be responded to on the other side,' Gertrude wrote in her diary a week later. 'What the result?' Gertrude's instincts were correct: Stanley wrote back, a cold little formal note signalling his intention to break off all future contact with Dolly. There was a further exchange of letters, and the minx-like Dolly pursued her cause with single-mindedness and a complete lack of candour. She contrived to bump into Stanley at parties, whispering to him how she would have him as her husband, and on 6 May wrote a long, passionate and entirely disingenuous note:

> Before saying goodbye, let me tell you this . . . suppose a wild, uncultivated tract of land, and suppose that one day this land is ploughed up and sown with corn, if the field could speak it might say: 'I have never borne corn, I do not bear corn, I never shall bear corn.' And yet all the while the wheat lies hidden in its bosom . . . when you were gone, when you were out of reach, I slowly realised what you had become to me, and then a great anguish filled me. I then made to myself a vow that . . . when you came back I would see you, and tell you all quite simply, and say: 'truly I have never cared for anyone but you . . ..'

The days went by; there was no response. 'To clench a thing that is impossible: how to set to work?' Gertrude noted. 'Heard of a letter sent. Am unutterably vexed. Learn to suffer in silence all indignities.' Gertrude still adhered to the moral code of an earlier generation of Victorian women, while Dolly was determined not to suffer or to be silent but to get her chosen man, on her own terms, in her own way.

Gertrude's peace of mind was further disturbed at this time when her son Charles rushed into her bedroom to tell her he was engaged to be married to a Miss Edith Benyon, whom he had met a few evenings before at a ball. 'Got through this day somehow,' she wrote in her diary that night. 'I thought at seventy years and six months some great culmination of joy would surely be mine.' For unexplained reasons, Gertrude disapproved of her son's choice of fiancée. Charles was no milksop, and by this time was administering the Welsh estate, but he lived in awe of his mother and the metaphorical raising of her eyebrow was enough to terrify the young man into breaking off the engagement. (Gertrude and her only son maintained affectionate and cordial relations, but there was none of the extravagant emotional interdependence that bound Gertrude and Dolly to each other.) Charles eventually married Winifred Pearce-Serocold, a second cousin of Elizabeth Bowes-Lyon, the future Queen, in 1895. She was twenty-two years Charles's junior, a curious echo of his parents' experience, and she was another strong-minded woman who would prove to have much in common with Gertrude.

On Saturday, 10 May, there was at last a reply from Stanley. 'I have nothing more I can say or do,' wrote Gertrude. 'So let it go. His letter is affectionately kind but perhaps it is like the man in Tolstoy's lovely story "It is dead," though he does not say so. He has given up everything except his taste for duty etc etc so let it go.' Dolly, meanwhile, contrived to meet Stanley at another party, and asked him to marry her. '[I] told him quietly that that I would be his wife if he still loved me.' He said no, but still Dolly pressed on, writing yet another letter in which she protested (once again, disingenuously) that she had been praying night and day for three years that he might love her. 'My love is a flame, never to be extinguished . . . I am yours, whether you will or no, till I die . . . Goodbye my beloved. I am yours for ever and ever.'

This letter at last did the trick, and on Tuesday, 13 May, Stanley wrote back, saying he consented to see Dolly on her own, at his rooms in De Vere Gardens, Kensington. While Gertrude stayed at home and completed some correspondence relating to the canal, Dolly took the brougham out for her audience with Bula Matari. Alone with Dolly, the explorer did not stand a chance. 'We had a short talk and we were engaged,' Dolly noted prosaically in her diary, not before she had tipped off the editor of *The Times*.

In the following weeks, when the explorer was busy with dinners, addresses and awards ceremonies, he wrote a series of sober and somewhat bemused letters to his bride-to-be (now preserved in a bundle in the attic). 'Is this love?' he asks her on the 21st. 'Well you know I used to think of Africa but your image has quite put out every other and follows me about and thrusts itself before me . . . If this is not love, it must be something like it. It is getting to be a passion.' His trepidation with regard to his future mother-in-law at last overcome, he sends his 'reverential regards' to Gertrude. Just two months after Dolly talked Stanley into saying 'yes', they were married in Westminster Abbey, in the presence of more than 2,000 guests. Among those present at the signing of the register were Gertrude, Gladstone, Millais, Sir Frederick Leighton – and Sir Alfred Lyall, so recently displaced as the object of Dolly's affections. Gertrude gave the party of a lifetime, and went to bed that night thanking God that, at last, '*all* is safe for Dolly'.

CHAPTER 26

QUEL BEL AVENIR?

A journalist jokingly suggested that when Stanley asked Gertrude's permission for the match, she replied: 'She is yours, and so am I!'[1] Following the honeymoon, the Stanleys moved into Richmond Terrace with Gertrude, and there they all lived, in a more or less harmonious *ménage* (together with half a dozen servants and ultimately an adopted baby) for nine years, until at last the Stanleys got a place of their own, a mock-Tudor mansion at Furze Hill, near Pirbright in Surrey. Much against the odds, the *grande dame* and the man of action got along famously, and well into her seventies Gertrude travelled with him and Dolly on Stanley's lecture tours in Australasia and North America, and gamely joined them on less strenuous expeditions to France, Spain and Italy. It must have helped that Stanley had recently discovered Flaubert's writings, and was a great fan of *Salammbô* in particular, which he held to be a masterpiece. When obliged to lighten his luggage, it was the last work before the Bible and Shakespeare that he would throw away.

The day after the wedding, Gertrude took the train down to join Mr and Mrs Stanley at Melchet Court, the mansion loaned to them for the first stage of their honeymoon. Just as she had found a note on her pillow on the night of Evie's wedding, she would find billets-doux waiting for her now, but not this time from her new son-in-law. Dolly, writing to her mother conspiratorially in French, told her that the marriage did not mean that she loved her any the less.

'Dors bien,' she wrote to her mother on Sunday, 13 July. 'Je t'adore, toi et lui, et Eveline, toi premièrement.' ('Sleep well. I adore you, you and him, and Eveleen, but you first of all').

'Il faut être heureuse car le Bonheur est beau chez nous,' she wrote the next day. ('You must be happy because happiness has made its home with us.') On the 15th: 'Ne sois pas triste, car nous voilà deux que j'adore, au lieu d'une seule' ('Don't be sad, as now I adore two people, instead of one alone'). Two days later, she was still more emphatic. 'Je pense tout à toi,' she wrote. 'Si tu savais combien je t'adore – avant tout – et lui aussi . . .' ('I'm thinking only of you. If you only knew how much I adore you – above all – and him also . . .') And then: 'Comme nous allons être heureuses – quel bel avenir – tu seras oh si heureuse. Dors bien mon ange.' ('How we are going to be happy – what a bright future we have ahead of us – you will be oh so happy. Sleep well my angel . . .')

On their return to Richmond Terrace, there were minor domestic adjustments. Whether these extended to moving Gertrude's bedroom, we don't know: she probably kept hers on the second floor, while Dolly and Stanley had the whole of the third floor (with separate bedrooms). But Elsie, the forgotten elder sister, a silent and uncomprehending witness to the drama of the previous decade, was eventually encouraged to move out, and would find a degree of independence living in a care home in Richmond. Over time, the look of the house changed. Still the portraits of Dolly and Evie hung upon the wall, but they were joined by the booty of Stanley's African career: shields, assegais, stuffed animals, elephant tusks, a necklace of lion claws, a quiver of antelope skin containing eight poisoned arrows, a famous elongated elephant gun and Winchester rifles. In addition to these reminders of more primitive societies, the household embraced the trappings of modernity. It was during the 1890s that guests would come to Gertrude's dining-room to watch the first rudimentary motion pictures, and to listen to 'the queer sounds produced by an experimental phonograph'.[2]

In October 1890 Gertrude joined Stanley and Dolly on a journey possibly as arduous as her childhood voyage to the Cape Colony and back. It took seven stormy days to cross the Atlantic on the SS *Teutonic*, but this was only the beginning of a punishing expedition that must have been wearying for Stanley, let alone his 71-year-old mother-in-law. Stanley had been hired to give a lecture tour, and from November to April he gave 110 talks from one end of the continent to the other, earning the monumental sum of £12,000. It is difficult to discern Gertrude, or her cousin Hamilton who was also invited on this jaunt, in the pictures of Stanley and his retinue standing at the back of his personalised Pullman car, the Henry M. Stanley, which was used to convey the party from New York to Toronto, Chicago, Washington, New Orleans, Cincinnati, St Louis, Omaha, Des

Moines and scores of other cities. Gertrude was impressed by the harmonious singing of a choir of deaf children in Omaha, and was rather taken by a young American girl who told her that she had been expelled from school for playing whist and smoking cigarettes. 'Why did you do such a thing?' asked Gertrude. 'Oh!' exclaimed the girl, 'if you had been three years at school, you would be glad enough to smoke a cigarette, it would make you think there was a man about the place.' The highlight was lunch at the White House on Saturday, 6 December, when she sat to the left of President Benjamin Harrison, and Dolly in the place of honour to the right. They returned to England in April of the following year. Less than six months later, Gertrude set off once again as part of the Stanley entourage, this time to Australia and New Zealand. They spent the best part of six months away. Gertrude was intrigued to see kangaroos and cockatoos, but detested the outback. On 18 November 1891, she concluded that 'decidedly this country is far less interesting than America'. She spent a 'terrible, unforgettable' Christmas Day 1891 at sea on the stormy voyage to Auckland, and was glad at last to return to civilisation.

In London, Gertrude's salon continued to operate, but the dynamics as well as the clientele inevitably changed to reflect the new balance of domestic power. Whereas in the past Dolly had played a secondary role, she now had a claim to be an equal partner in the Richmond Terrace establishment, reflecting her status as wife of the great explorer. Her husband was never clubbable, and whilst he enjoyed the company of fellow explorers, geographers, soldiers like Generals Wolseley and Kitchener and other men of action who came to visit him at his new home, he lacked the appetite to mingle with the politicians and artists so beloved by Dolly. As Stanley himself remained a controversial figure, Richmond Terrace inevitably lost something of its inclusive social cachet. 'Mr and Mrs Stanley have returned to London, but . . . the boom is over,' reported a snide correspondent in the *Gentlewoman* magazine as early as October 1890. 'Mrs Stanley has always certain artistic circles open to her, but socially the Stanleys are done for. They are no longer the craze, except perhaps at Clapham, and Camberwell, and Peckham. They are no longer sought after by the rich and great in the west. Mr Stanley's overbearing and objectionable manner are largely responsible for this result.'

The first detailed reports of the fate of the infamous Rear Column had started to emerge as the Stanley party set off for America, and from then on the press gleefully reported every lurid revelation. On arrival in New York, and at every speaking engagement on the North American tour, Stanley was dogged with controversy. His admirers compared him to

Alexander the Great and Christopher Columbus, 'crowned with laurels as the greatest hero among travellers and the most illustrious of living men', as *The Times* reported on 6 November 1890. His enemies portrayed him as little short of a murderer. The most damaging blows came in the form of the posthumous diaries of Major Edmund Musgrave Barttelot, one of the officers left in charge of the ill-fated Rear Column, which chronicled Stanley's alleged brutalities. Stanley went on the counter-attack, explaining how Barttelot and his fellow officer Jameson had conspired to procure the little slave girl for a display of cannibalism. Dolly and Stanley's new brother-in-law Frederic Myers lent their weight to a press campaign which sought, with considerable success, to discredit his critics.

To the mass of the population, Stanley remained a hero whose exploits demonstrated an exemplary robustness, a manly, no-nonsense riposte to the degeneration and effeminacy that conservative observers saw in aspects of modern society as well as foreign policy. At home, this was the decade not merely of the New Woman, but of Oscar Wilde's theatrical triumphs and subsequent humiliation, and of Aubrey Beardsley and the decadent publication, *The Yellow Book*. (A few years later, fears about the robustness of the British Empire were borne out in the ignominy of the Boer War, in which those regarded by the British as little more than peasant farmers came close to administering a drubbing to the most powerful empire the world had ever seen.) To his critics, Stanley was a brute, midwife to the despoliation of the Congo, the promoter of what Gertrude's friend Sir William Harcourt called 'filibustering expeditions in the mixed guise of commerce, religion, geography and imperialism, under which any and every guise of atrocity is regarded as permissible'. Frank Harris, editor of the *Fortnightly Review* and friend of Oscar Wilde, thought Dolly very charming, but spoke for many critics when he described her husband as a 'force without a conscience'.[3] The Tory government would eventually honour Stanley with a knighthood,[4] but the establishment delivered a posthumous snub by refusing to allow his burial next to Livingstone in Westminster Abbey. As Gertrude accurately observed shortly before the publication of his *Autobiography* in 1909: 'the people will love it, but the upper will sneer and throw it aside.'

To visualise the Richmond Terrace salon in the 1890s, we are fortunate in having dozens of photographic portraits taken by Eveleen, many posed in the Richmond Terrace drawing-room. Gladstone, as dishevelled as ever, looks out from one picture, avuncular and kindly, as if taking leave from this world and meditating on the next. His visits would become less frequent, given his and Stanley's mutual antagonism. Balfour, Lord

Salisbury's nephew, looks at the camera with chilly hauteur; Joseph Chamberlain, by contrast, with barely suppressed frustration at the direction of British politics and his role in it: Evie managed to cajole him into having the photograph taken wearing his spectacles. There are pictures of Edmund Gosse, the critic and biographer, and of John Addington Symonds, the valetudinarian aesthete who in his Swiss mountain exile helped invent winter sports and wrote an impassioned defence of homosexuality – but otherwise the artists and writers are absent. There is no image of Oscar Wilde in the days before his downfall, nor of Henry James (who missed the wedding and on returning from his Italian holiday declared himself astonished to learn that the flirtatious Miss Dolly had been transformed into Mrs Stanley). There are Henry Irving; Sir Frances Galton, founder of the dubious science of eugenics; Lord Rayleigh, the patrician physicist; Cyril Flower, Lord Battersea, the politician said before his ennoblement to be the most handsome man in the House of Commons. There are many images of Stanley looking dapper and determined, his hair and moustache now completely white. In a photograph widely circulated at the time of the marriage, Dolly herself looks stately, severe, even matronly, the early bloom of youthful beauty supplanted by an impression of self-importance. Evie also took photographs of Eusapia Palladino and Leonora Piper, two notorious mediums who were the subject of extensive psychical research. Eusapia was an illiterate Italian peasant who had the gift of making heavy furniture move or creating storm-blasts of air half-way across the room, all while she was tethered to a chair. These pictures were not taken in Richmond Terrace, but Gertrude did allow her house to be used for occasional meetings of the Society of Psychical Research.

There is one picture of Gertrude from this time, which Gertrude detested. 'It is too too hideous for words,' she told Dolly after seeing the image. 'I did not know I was so hideous . . . [I look] . . . so so vulgar and so ill-tempered, and so wrinkled and with a would-be-young done-up look . . . if I saw that photo anywhere I should have no desire to know that person or ever to meet her.' Gertrude was right: it was not a flattering image, as she looks old and stern. No other photographs were taken of her until she was well into her nineties.

Henry James continued to come to dinner parties at Richmond Terrace throughout the 1890s, and there is something Jamesian about the milieu documented in Evie's portfolio. Like the characters in his novels, those who attended Gertrude and Dolly's salon were super-refined and profoundly cultivated, international in outlook, typically rich but by now a generation or two removed from the rude energy of the early Victorian entrepreneurs who created the foundations of late nineteenth-century prosperity. Just as Chad Newsome, the heir to an industrial fortune at the centre of *The Ambassadors*, never discloses the product which is the source of his wealth (nobody even mentions it), it is unlikely that Gertrude ever talked about the family canal or that Fred Myers alluded to his grandfather's mills and factories, or Hamilton Aïdé to the distant Anatolian origins of his own fortune. James told his brother that there was something *queer* about the Tennant milieu, which I take to mean that he sensed a hint of *fin de siècle* decadence in Gertrude's (and by now Dolly's) elaborate striving to be civilised.[5] The French word to describe the salon in the 1890s would be *faisandé*, which means gamey, like a pheasant on the turn from exquisite to unpalatable. At around this time, it should be noted, James fell out with Hamilton, ostensibly because of Hamilton's presumption in inviting himself to dine with William James on his visit to America with the Stanleys in 1890. (Hearing of this impertinence, Henry described Aïdé to his brother as a 'foolish, faded, fribble'.)[6] Envy of his former friend's continuing success on the London stage may also have been a factor in their estrangement. In the mid-1890s, Aïdé achieved a surprise transatlantic hit with *Dr Bill*, a comedy in three acts about a physician to the ladies of the theatre. ('It was only an adaptation,' noted *The Times*, 'but it gave scope for Aïdé's happy turns of phrase, his sense of fun, and his lightness of touch.')[7] Henry James, meanwhile, was humiliated when his own play *Guy Domville* failed dismally. The decade saw a deepening division between high and popular culture, and while Aïdé had little problem catering to the tastes of the masses, James's work grew increasingly obscure and elitist.

Gertrude would occasionally organise a set-piece soirée for a visitor who was distinguished enough to dissolve the conflicts stirred up by her son-in-law. She held a reception for Mark Twain, a friend and admirer of Stanley. 'Stanley is magnificently housed in London,' wrote the author of *The Adventures of Tom Sawyer*. 'He had an extraordinary assemblage of brains and fame there to meet me – thirty or forty (both sexes) at dinner, and more than a hundred came in after dinner. Kept it up until midnight. There were cabinet ministers, ambassadors, admirals, generals, canons, Oxford professors, novelists, playwrights, poets and a number of people equipped with rank and brains.'[8] Speaking in a southern drawl, Twain entertained this audience by telling ghost stories. In 1895, there was an 'at home' for Alphonse Daudet, the French novelist who (Henry James noted with some surprise) knew no one in London apart from James himself,

Gertrude and Dolly. In a different vein, Lord Kitchener's first social engagement after returning from the Egyptian campaign in 1898 was tea with Gertrude at No. 2 Richmond Terrace.

Dolly continued to paint throughout the 1890s; indeed she took advantage of her new-found celebrity to publish a compilation of her ragamuffin drawings immediately after her wedding (for which she was teased in the pages of *Punch*).[9] She would continue to exhibit and in 1896 one of her urchin paintings was acquired by Sir Henry Tate, a considerable accolade at the time: *His First Offence* is kept in his gallery to this day. She eventually painted a poster used in the recruiting effort for the First World War (a picture of a young woman with a babe in arms. The caption was: 'The call of the women – save us from the Hun!') But she gave up her ambitions to be a great artist, and instead devoted herself to furthering the career she thought her husband should have.

Stanley was minded to return to Africa, perhaps in some kind of sub-Cecil Rhodes role as governor of his friend Mackinnon's putative colony in East Africa. Dolly persuaded her husband to give up this ambition, in part by the ingenious tactic of tripping over him during a holiday romp in an Alpine meadow, breaking his leg and rendering him unfit for any further strenuous expeditions. Thereafter, she harangued him into standing for Parliament. Stanley, who would have been happy to pursue his lucrative journalism and lecturing assignments, was unenthusiastic from the first. In 1892, he stood as Liberal Unionist candidate for the conveniently located constituency of North Lambeth. There was formidable barracking at the hustings, and while Dolly initially elicited sympathy for her husband by bursting into tears, she undid it moments later when she told the crowd: 'When all of you are dead, the name of Stanley will live.' Derisive laughter ensued. The humorist Thomas Anstey Guthrie, a friend of Stanley's, described the conclusion to the campaign:

At his meetings [Stanley] was a forcible but by no means an ingratiating speaker, and I had an impression that he was intensely bored by the whole business, and cared very little whether he won or lost the election. But I heard him give a vivid and picturesque account of life in the African forests once when addressing the workmen at Price's Candle Factory, and they listened with evident interest. Other meetings were less orderly, for reports had been circulated by the opposition suggesting – of course quite untruly – that Stanley's expeditions had been characterized by cruelty. This, of course, had its effect on many of his hearers, but a great deal of the hostility was carefully organized; after one meeting the

Stanleys and I made a rush for their Brougham between a lane of hired prize fighters, who kept off the crowd until we were safely inside, when we drove off, minus one of the carriage doors. I was one of the tellers in the counting of votes, and for some time I thought we were doing very well. Then an enthusiastic supporter of Stanley's – a pompous person with a high sandy crest, who struck me as the living image of Mr. Pumblechook – leaned over my shoulder and whispered, 'Prepare your mind for a defeat.' And a defeat it was –Coldwell, the Radical candidate, being returned by a considerable majority. I drove back to Richmond Terrace with Stanley, and if he made any allusion to the election at all, I have forgotten what it was. But I remember that Hawke, his man, opened the front door, and that Stanley's remark to him was: 'Hawke, you're beaten.' Which I thought an oddly detached way of announcing his defeat.[10]

Dolly had her way at the next election, and Stanley was returned in 1895 with a majority of 405 votes. On his arrival at the House, the doorman greeted him with the words: 'Mr Stanley, I presume.' Gentle ridicule and indifference attended the entirety of his undistinguished political career.

For Stanley, the tedium of parliamentary life was relieved in 1896 when he and Dolly adopted a child. It has been variously speculated that the marriage was unconsummated; that Stanley, the ruthless conqueror of the African wilderness, was impotent in the bedroom; or that Dolly was herself barren. Whatever the reasons, they could not have children of their own and they adopted a six-month-old child whom they named Denzil, after Denzil Holles, friend of Oliver Cromwell. (He was brought down from Wales, said to be the son of one of Stanley's relatives.) Stanley doted on the infant, of whom Gertrude also became very fond. As Denzil grew up, Gertrude took pleasure in taking the child to his lessons or to have his hair cut. It was for him and for her other grandchildren that Gertrude wrote down her vivid memories of her childhood in France. Three years later, when she was 79, the Stanleys bought their country home at Furze Hill, in Surrey. Increasingly detached from his parliamentary duties, Stanley spent his last years playing with his adoptive son and landscaping his garden, naming the pine woods Ituri Forest and the pond Stanley Pool in homage to his African expeditions. A harmless Home Counties stream was dubbed the Congo. (It is a wonder that he did not call the house Dun Explorin'.) Gertrude, left alone at Richmond Terrace with half a dozen servants, was a frequent visitor, driven up and down to Surrey in Dolly's motor car. (There, she read Tolstoy's *Guerre et paix*, and in a lighter vein, Du Maurier's *Trilby*, and she met Mrs and Mrs Bernard Shaw, an encounter that passed without Gertrude making more than a perfunctory note in her diary.) They would take the train to Cadoxton where the former workhouse boy from another part of Wales, now rich and freighted with honours from all round the world, would sit on the lawns of this country house and consider how far he had travelled. Growing on the wall of the house was the largest magnolia tree in Wales, petals from which would be collected and placed in a bowl of water on the dining-room table. This perfumed, manorial existence was as remote from the circumstances of his upbringing as it was possible to be. It would be absurd to make too direct a comparison between Gertrude's origins and those of her son-in-law, but as she was being pulled along the lanes in a pony trap for her morning outing, she may well have reflected that it was also a long and improbable journey from genteel poverty in France three-quarters of a century ago to her position as *de facto* owner of an estate in Wales, the big house in London and octogenarian *mère de famille* with four grandchildren and two distinguished sons-in-law.

It was her fate to outlive both Frederic Myers and Stanley. Myers died in Rome in January 1901, his friend William James lurking outside the sick-room, waiting for Myers to 'reach through the drawn curtains of death' and send a signal from the 'other side'. James recorded that Myers was fairly panting with enthusiasm to die so that he could explore the afterlife (the cause of death was pneumonia, for which he had been treated by a serum developed from goats' testicles). 'His eagerness to go . . . his extraordinary intellectual vitality up to the very time that the death agony began, were a superb spectacle,' James noted, admiringly. Influenced by his medicine, perhaps, he had promised to come back as a 'cross between an old goat and a guardian angel'. Though various mediums would claim to pick up communications from Myers, only the credulous believe that he successfully 'ran the blockade' from the spirit world to our own.[11] A few days later, Queen Victoria died, at the age of 81 (prompting acidulous remarks from William James, who predicted that Fred would be delighted to be reacquainted with his sovereign).

Stanley, meanwhile, by now retired from politics, managed to attend the coronation of Edward VII in the summer of the following year, but suffered increasingly from a variety of debilitating ailments, crippled by the legacy of his African adventures. He was subjected to unpleasant treatments such as castor oil enemas and was obliged to inject himself with morphia. In 1903, he had a stroke ('there was a sudden twist of his mouth, and an affliction of his left eye,' Gertrude noted), and in April of the following year was brought to Richmond Terrace in an ambulance. 'Every function in his body is disordered,' Gertrude recorded on 1 May. 'Stanley dying!' she wrote four days later. 'Nothing to be done! Waiting, waiting, waiting, he sleeps the best part of the day and night.' And eventually on Tuesday, 10 May 1904: 'At 6am on this day Stanley departed this sorrowful life.'

CHAPTER 27

'WHOM SHALL I MEET IN HEAVEN?'

Within two years of Stanley's death, Dolly wrote to her mother in considerable distress: she said she wanted desperately to marry Henry Curtis, Stanley's doctor, and that if she could not marry him, she would kill herself. The terrible, incoherent letter reflects the extremity of Dolly's nervous state; she had been driven to the verge of breakdown by the strain of caring for Stanley in his last years: 'Dearest mother, I will write down for your quiet consideration a few facts,' she wrote in a letter simply dated 1906:

I cannot trust myself to speak them, so I write them down as they arise in my mind. I have for a long time deeply and intensely cared for H.J [Curtis] . . . it grew and grew . . . his divine kindness all those terrible years sustained me in a way, you of course *cannot* understand, his weekly letter kept me afloat . . . I asked him to marry me and he refused. And yet though he refused to marry me I knew he cared for me . . . with this decision I *must* be content and manage to go on, but think of what this decision means to me. It means living on without the best hope in life . . . by his will I am deprived of the companionship which would have made life Divine. When you are gone I have the sole prospect of Elsie as my lifelong companion . . . I smile at your talk of 'not understanding what I can see in him, your not caring for him'; dear mother what has your opinion got to do with it! What does it signify what you think about him? . . . [had he married me] life would have revived in me. No long dark dreary days – but hope, pride in his work, working myself, painting even, not minding the horrors of visiting or dining out . . . so long as I see him frequently . . . I can bear life . . . and not otherwise . . . if this were taken from me I would make the plunge . . . I would give up life . . . sulphate of morphia of which I have a very ample supply would give me the rest I want.

Later, the doctor relented, and in 1907 they married and lived together at Furze Hill and in Whitehall Court, around the corner from Richmond Terrace. For reasons that are not clear, Gertrude detested the arrangement and swore never to spend any time under her favourite daughter's roof. ('I hold to my determination not to have either her [Dolly] or you, as inmates in my house,' she wrote to Mr Curtis in 1906. 'I am sure that neither of you would wish it otherwise.') Dolly's second marriage spelt a decisive break with her mother, precisely at the time when old age was at last beginning to take its toll on Gertrude's health and independence (she was now 86 years old). She may well have assumed Dolly would have simply moved back into Richmond Terrace and they would have lived on as two widows together; instead Dolly rushed into a marriage with the family doctor. Gertrude might also have been uncomfortable at the thought that Curtis was her own doctor, as well as Stanley and Dolly's, and perhaps there was a snobbish concern that Curtis was a mere physician, rather than a great man like Dolly's first husband and so many of her early admirers. It seems that with this second marriage Dolly achieved a belated growing up, freeing herself from her morbidly close relationship with her mother and forging a union without regard to her husband's worldly fame. No correspondence or diaries survive to shed light on this second marriage. Mother and daughter were eventually reconciled, but they never restored their previous intimacy.

'How all the people I once knew are dropping off,' Gertrude had noted in October 1905, shortly before her 86th birthday. 'Feel like I am getting old,' she observed a year later, 'find small talk fatiguing.' 'I hope this painful and miserable year will be the last,' she wrote as she turned 88. In early December 1906 she gave a dinner party for ten, but was alarmed to receive a note from her almost equally ancient cousin Hamilton, asking to be excused. 'My dear Gert,' he wrote from his new apartment in 28½ Half Moon Street, telling how the night before he had taken the actress Ellen Terry to the theatre to see Shaw's new play *The Doctor's Dilemma*. 'The first Act . . . is much too long, it goes on for over an hour,' Aïdé wrote. 'It has some brilliant things. The fourth Act is abominable in all respects. When the heroine says: 'I am married,' Ellen Terry who sat on one side of me and a man on the other simultaneously turned to me and said: "who to?"' He continued in a more sombre tone. 'I arrived [home] this morning . . . [suffering from] a constant cough and vomiting and great trembling in my legs. I am unhappy at missing your delightful party, but what can I do?' This was Hamilton's last letter; two days later Gertrude visited him for the last time. He died close to midnight, his last words: 'No pain.'

In September 1909, she heard that her younger sister Henrietta, the last survivor of the youthful holiday in Trouville, had died in Putney. They had not seen each other for half a century and Gertrude did not attend the funeral.

Year in, year out, Gertrude expressed private amazement that she lived on and a willingness to join the increasing numbers of friends and family who had left this world, but this private melancholy did not stop her pursuing a valiant and energetic social life. On 28 February 1909, she had sixteen to dinner. 'Perhaps my last dinner party,' she wrote, inaccurately. 'Went off brilliantly.' The same number came again in March of the following year. She was still able to regulate her household, as when she came downstairs one day to find the cook and a maid called Clara in a 'most improper condition': she told the cook to leave. She saw Dolly and Evie regularly, and their children were welcome visitors as long as they did not treat her home as a hotel. In June 1911, in her 92nd year, she got up at six o'clock and walked the few hundred yards down Whitehall and Parliament Street to the stand erected outside the Houses of Parliament, where she witnessed the coronation of King George V. 'A fine sight,' she recorded. 'Glad I saw it. Thank God for the energy and the courage'. Later that summer she was shocked to read a 'hideous article in the *Figaro* about the love letters of Gustave Flaubert and a certain vulgar Frenchwoman called Mme Colet. Felt unutterably disgusted.' She wrote immediately to Caroline Commanville to express her dismay at these lubricious revelations. In 1912, she read and was horrified at accounts of the sinking of the *Titanic*. We have a portrait of her from April of this year:

To Furze Hill to stay with Lady Stanley [wrote Mrs Belloc Lowndes]. I had an interesting talk with her mother, Mrs Coombe Tennant [*sic*], who though ninety-one was perfectly clear-headed, remembering everything and everybody, and able to read the *Times* without glasses. She had known Flaubert intimately from childhood . . .[1]

Elsewhere, the novelist described Gertrude thus:

> She had been startlingly beautiful, and in old age she was still an impressive, even a splendid-looking, figure. Her white hair was massed in curls around her face; her cheeks were rouged; and her large grey eyes had kept something of their fire. She always wore a black satin gown, and a fine piece of old lace was loosely arranged about her head and neck.[2]

As another friend noted: 'she was essentially one of those people who do not date . . . age had done little to rob her of the beauty of feature and colouring for which she had been famous; she seemed gifted with perennial youth.'[3]

Inevitably, there were setbacks as Gertrude entered extreme old age. She fell repeatedly; on one occasion she broke her arm and then followed a restorative exercise regime prescribed by Eugen Sandow, the Prussian strongman turned Professor of Physical Culture to King George V, acquiring a pair of his patented dumb-bells. A granddaughter died in childhood, and she who had lost six uncles in the Napoleonic Wars now lost a grandson in the carnage of the First World War. Charles's son, the gifted and much-loved Christopher Coombe-Tennant was killed in action in September 1917 at the age of 19 years and 10 months, shortly after completing his officer's training at Sandhurst. He had been a prize pupil at Winchester College and gave up his place at Cambridge to enlist with the Welsh Guards. He crossed to France on 9 August, 1917, and was killed by shell fire less than a month later, at dawn on 3 September, in the trenches at Langemarck in west Flanders. A further nineteen of his contemporaries from Kingsgate House at Winchester laid down their lives in the service of their country, while nearly 500,000 Allied troops died over a period of three months in this, the Third Battle of Ypres.

Gertrude kept her Christian faith to the end and fully expected to be reunited with Christopher, and with her husband and her two dead children, together with Flaubert, her parents and sisters and the hundreds of friends she had outlived when she finally crossed to the other side. She read a book about Dean Stanley, the distinguished theologian and Dean of Westminster (no relation of the explorer), and concluded that she would very much like to have been part of his circle. 'Whom shall I meet in heaven?' she wondered. 'What I hope for in the next world,' she wrote, 'is an increase of knowledge, an enlargement of my sphere of action and multiplication of my affections.'

She died in London on 27 April 1918, some seven months after her grandson, the woman who had outlived so many others falling victim to the influenza that raged through Europe in the closing months of the Great War. She was buried in the family plot at Highgate Cemetery, reunited at last with her husband Charles and her baby Gertrude.

EPILOGUE

In 1927, Virginia Woolf published an article in an American newspaper in which she sought to draw a line between Victorian life-writing and what she called the New Biography.

'The Victorian biographer was dominated by the idea of goodness,' she wrote. 'Noble, upright, chaste, severe: it is thus that Victorian worthies are presented to us.'[1] This moral worthiness was conveyed by an exhaustive accumulation of factual, preferably documentary evidence. The result was to fossilise the subject of the biography, rather than bring him (and more rarely her) alive, presenting a carapace of externalities rather than the person within. Skilful biographers of the modern era, she exhorted, needed to harmonise the 'granite' (i.e. the factual and the objectively verifiable) with the 'rainbow' (the transient and the purely personal).

The confrontation between the old and the new biography was acute and personal as regards Woolf's own father and Gertrude Tennant's friend, Sir Leslie Stephen, whom the novelist vilified in the barely fictionalised form of Mr Ramsay in *To the Lighthouse* (1927). In this novel, Mr Ramsay is a lachrymose old patriarch, morbidly obsessed with his own literary reputation; obtuse and selfish; and desperately manipulates others, particularly his wife and children, in order to satisfy his craving for praise and affection. In his attempt to measure his own contribution to human and literary greatness on the scale of A to Z, and reaching the conclusion that he had managed to get only as far as R, Woolf is not so gently parodying her father's work on the *Dictionary of National Biography*, which he edited from its inception in 1882 until he was forced to quit midway through the project due to ill health (he literally did not quite reach R). Meditating on his personal insignificance in the face of eternity, he imagines himself as the leader of a party of mountaineers 'climb[ing] high enough to see the waste of the years and the perishing of the stars' – a jibe at Leslie Stephen's passion for mountain climbing. Ramsay/Stephen is further lampooned as the type of the discredited Victorian Sage: as he self-absorbedly recites 'The Charge of the Light Brigade', we see that Woolf's satirical target is not merely her father but the patriarchal and imperialist ethic of the Victorian age in general.

The point of this digression is that there is inevitably more of the rainbow than the granite in a life of Gertrude Barbara Rich Tennant, someone who on the Ramsay/Stephen scale of conventional achievement would not reach the letter R. She did not write enduring novels, climb mountains, draft legislation or explore undiscovered continents. Nor did she build a canal or accumulate a fortune through commerce. But she came into contact with many of the men who did, and of course her relationships with Flaubert and Stanley in particular, and the countless other great men whom she knew well or merely tangentially, make her more fascinating than otherwise. Her life story, from youth to marriage to motherhood, widowhood, independence and old age, demonstrates how one remarkable woman overcame the constraints imposed on her and millions of others by their gender. Like so many women in the nineteenth century, she had to struggle with the consequences of poor education and of a limited, that is to say an almost exclusively domestic sphere of action.

Perhaps – as, when a small child, she went too close to the parrot and was rewarded with a scratch on the face – she paid a price for her obsession with fame. The happiest phase of her life was indeed when she was most obscure, and it is an irony that the most enduringly famous person she knew (Gustave Flaubert) was someone she befriended long before there was any hint that he would attain celebrity. Much of the rationale for her salon, in which she brought together famous people for the edification and amusement of her daughters, was to make sure that her daughters found eligible husbands. This was understandable – no one had taken care of her at that vulnerable stage in her life, as dramatised in her cousin's scandalous French novel *Rita* – but limited, in that it implied there was no avenue to fulfilment open to her talented daughters other than marriage and children. In the end, for all their abilities, both Dolly and Evie lived in the shadow of their celebrated husbands, and it is poignant that both, when widowed, should devote themselves to the difficult task of burnishing their husbands' posthumous reputations. Like so many widows of distinguished Victorian men, they took it upon themselves to prepare their deceased husbands' biographies. Evie, in the end, could not bring herself to publish more than a fragment of Fred's life, as she discovered that so much of his psychical energies had been dedicated to reuniting himself with another love, his cousin Annie who had drowned herself in Ullswater. Dolly, meanwhile, ignored Virginia Woolf's precepts for a new kind of biography and struggled to fit the facts of Stanley's life into a narrative designed to demonstrate his moral worthiness. She styled herself Lady Stanley for the rest of her life, even when in reality she had become plain Mrs Curtis. Stanley's reputation, though now in the process of rehabilitation, has never been as sturdy as the lump of granite that Dolly had erected over his grave in the churchyard at Pirbright, bearing the words Bula Matari. His *Autobiography*, which she stitched together from his papers, is a readable farrago of invention and omission.

The family standard-bearer for women's rights would turn out to be Gertrude's daughter-in-law, Winifred Coombe-Tennant, wife of her son Charles. This distant cousin of the future Queen Elizabeth did not lack social or intellectual self-assurance. Nor did she acknowledge constraints on her scope of action, simply by virtue of her gender. In fact, after she gave birth to her fourth child in the build-up to the war, she reached the position that women were inherently superior to the men blundering towards carnage:

> Three days in [her son's] company, looking into his starry eyes, make me feel the appalling European war – Servia running in blood, innumerable atrocities to the whole Armenian race, massacre of mothers and children, Belgium, everywhere slaughter and destruction – and my work in life giving life and the human body – maternity – and then the contrast of this frenzy of bloodshed, cruelty and hate. Say what you will, that is a man's world and maternity is a woman's. These horrors could not be in a world where women were equal in stature and power to men and the unit was the human being, regardless of sex. Women must enter into public life and wrestle there with male blindness.[2]

The contrast with her sister-in-law Dolly is telling: while Dolly pursued a career in public life vicariously, through her reluctant first husband, Winifred just got on with the job. It was one way of coping with the grief of losing her eldest son in the trenches. So while Charles managed the declining canal (commercial traffic finally coming to an end in 1934) Winifred became by turns President of the Neath Woman's Suffrage Society; a JP, and unsuccessful Liberal candidate for the Forest of Dean constituency in the 1922 election. In the same year, she was sent by the Liberal Government to the third assembly of the League of Nations, the first British woman delegate to this institution. She was also a prominent Welsh Nationalist and chair of the Arts and Crafts Committee of the National Eisteddfod. The Archdruid honoured her with the sobriquet Mam o Nedd ('Mother from Neath') for her role as a member of the circle of bards. She was a patron of Welsh art and artists, accumulating a fine collection of paintings that lay hidden for decades, until they were unearthed and exhibited in Wales early in 2008. With David Lloyd-George a regular visitor, Cadoxton was the South Wales equivalent of her mother-in-law's salon. 'I have lived many years and travelled much in many quarters of the globe,' Stanley once told her, 'and I have come to the conclusion that there is not more than five per cent efficiency among human beings . . . I should put you in that five per cent.'[3]

After she died in 1956 it was revealed that there was another, esoteric aspect to Winifred's character. For many decades, she was a prominent trance medium; well known, at least, to those who carried the torch for the study of psychical phenomena into the mid-twentieth century. The rest of the family had no idea of this. She had made a pact with her son Christopher that he would try to contact her should he fall in the trenches. When, with gruesome inevitability, he was killed, she came to believe that he fulfilled his part of the bargain. Assuming the identity Mrs Willett, she was in dialogue with the dead for many decades, and for those who are prepared to put their scepticism to one side, the transcripts of the messages she received from the other world are considered among the most significant in the annals of the Society for Psychical Research.[4]

Winifred thus united the social, political and mystical aspects of the Tennant family inheritance. Her younger surviving son, Augustus Henry Coombe-Tennant, was a hero of the Second World War and ended his days as a Benedictine monk at Downside; his brother Alexander was a distinguished City stockbroker. The wealthy, dilettante dimension to the Tennant milieu, exemplified by Hamilton Aïdé in the nineteenth century, was carried forward into the next generation by Gertrude's nephew Leopold Myers, the subject of his mother Evie's exquisite angel photographs who as a child was pageboy at the Stanley wedding. He wrote a number of esoteric novels that were celebrated in their time but are not nowadays much read. He associated with various figures on the fringes of the Bloomsbury Group, and was a benefactor to his fellow Old Etonian George Orwell. Myers eventually killed himself in 1944, having destroyed what would have been a fascinating memoir, a man who failed to come to terms with the modern world.

Winifred said of Gertrude: 'to the last . . . [she] retained a warm admiration for French ways of life and thought, the experiences of her early days having, indeed, stamped her whole personality with something of the charm and distinction of the great ladies of the ancien regime'.[5] This was also the tenor of the obituaries of Gertrude that appeared not merely in *The Times* and *Telegraph*, but in the *Western Mail*, the *Yorkshire Post*, *Daily Mail*, *Glasgow Herald* and the *Lady*. 'A notable survivor of the Grandes Dames of the nineteenth century,' is how *The Times* described her. The *Telegraph* emphasised Gertrude's role as a 'startling illustration of the links that bind us to the past'. The brief, hurried catalogue of artists, writers and politicians she had known, carried in all the obituaries, was testament to her power of making connections, of bringing people together. She stood for a form of civilisation which put human relationships above all else. 'Personal relations are the important thing for ever and ever,' E.M. Forster had written in *Howards End* (1910), 'and not this outer life of telegrams and anger.' The epigraph to that novel could well have been her credo, too: Only Connect.

It is to be hoped that Gertrude was too old to be fully alert to the tragedy of her grandson's death in the trenches. As millions of shells exploded in a strategically pointless wasteland, Christopher Coombe-Tennant, and hundreds of thousands of other young men, were pulverised until their bodies were indistinguishable from the Flanders mud. The Third Battle of Ypres was the ultimate rebuke to the values Gertrude stood for: the triumph of industrialised killing over life and human interconnectedness.

There is one story that encapsulates Gertrude's spirit and values. In June 1913, she and Dolly paid a visit to the theatre with some overseas visitors. The guests, who had never seen a play before, were the 19-year-old King of Uganda and four of his gentlemen in waiting. The 93-year-old Gertrude and the young monarch got on famously. In Gertrude's words, at the end of the evening 'the King and I vowed eternal friendship.'

NOTE ON PRIMARY SOURCES

As described in the opening chapter, the attic chests yielded a tombola of treasures: diaries, sketches, reminiscences, even an attempt at light fiction and a 200-page handwritten draft of an unpublished biography of Victor Hugo. The earliest papers are located in a black tin box, 20 inches by 12 across and 8 inches deep, buried deep in the left-hand corner of the larger of the two chests. It contains at least a thousand family letters from the early nineteenth century. There are also bundles of letters to Gertrude from Lady Aldborough and the comte de Rambuteau, as well as a separate collection of papers relating to Gustave Flaubert: four letters from Gustave's sister Caroline to Gertrude and or her sister Henrietta (in which she recounts how she and her brother are amusing themselves by translating Byron's poetry into French); three from Maxime du Camp, Emile Hamard and a friend called Fauvel, which contain accounts of Caroline's death as well as a lock of her hair. There are two, hitherto unknown letters from Gustave himself, dating from around this time, together with the letter from early November 1846 ('Est-ce que je ne vous reverrai plus?. . .') in which he sends his best wishes on her marriage. There are scores of love letters written by Charles Tennant in the year leading up to their marriage.

Elsewhere in the chest is a locked diary, which Gertrude began on her wedding day, 11 September 1847, and put aside only on the death of her husband in 1873. This is a handsome maroon-leather bound book, probably a wedding present, the lock hardly sturdy enough to deter anyone who really wanted to peep inside, but enough to put off a casual reader – a servant, perhaps, her husband or a child. The entries are not sequential, but rather a series of reflections on the things that matter to Gertrude: marriage, her early life, the birth of her children, deaths, money, family relationships. This I used as a key to the main events of Gertrude's life. To complement these private thoughts, there is a series of A5 legal diaries dating with barely a break from around 1850 to 1917, in which she records the externalities of her life – social engagements, visits to shops, doctors' appointments, details of her children's ailments, notes of expenditure and so forth. One or two volumes are missing, others have disintegrated with age and mould. Later volumes of this diary have found their way into the comprehensive Tennant family archive held at the West Glamorgan Archives Service in Swansea, and in the pages of one of these I found the last two letters from Hamilton Aïdé – as well as a comprehensive account of Gertrude's dealings in stocks and shares, which continued well into her nineties. Appropriately, given the nature of her late husband's business, she had an attachment to canal stocks (owning a number of shares in the Suez Canal) and must have been a capable investor: when she died, her portfolio of more than eighty investments was worth £63,345 11s. 10d.

After she was widowed, Gertrude had more time to write, and there are further special diaries, including a journal kept in the form of letters to her recently deceased husband and a more cheerful summary of her early encounters with remarkable men. There are two, long memoirs of her upbringing in France (one entitled 'Recollection of Bye-gone Times for my Grand-children') and a 40-page account of her friendship with the youthful Flaubert prepared in 1886 for Caroline Commanville, the novelist's niece. ('Chère madame et amie,' Caroline wrote on reading this for the first time, 'remplie de choses charmantes, je l'ai lu avec une emotion profonde. La manière dont vous parlez de ma famille est si tendre et si gracieuse.' ('Dear Madame and friend, [the memoir] is full of charming things, I read it with profound emotion. The way in which you speak of my family is so tender and so gracious'). The passages about her mother moved her to tears, she writes, saying she disagrees with Gertrude on one point only: although Gustave was not a practising Christian, he did have a sense of the infinite which might be equivalent to a religious sentiment. 'But perhaps at the age of twenty he hadn't started having visions of eternity,' Caroline wrote in her letter dated 14 January 1887. An extract from Gertrude's memoir was translated into French and appeared in the first collection of Flaubert's letters in 1887. The Tennant family papers contain a total of twenty letters from Flaubert dating from 1876 to 1880, of which eight were hitherto unknown and unpublished. Gertrude must have made many of these available to Caroline Commanville when she was putting together her uncle's correspondence. Like many recipients of Flaubert's letters, Gertrude held back what she considered the more intimate correspondence (the very early letters) and perhaps the later ones asking for money as well (although it is possible these were censored by Mme Commanville). There are many letters from Mme Commanville preserved both in the attic and between the pages of Gertrude's later diaries in Swansea.

As explained in Chapter 10 (and in more detail in note 8), the chest also contains a black-covered notebook containing 'Written by Request', a memoir in the style of a romantic novel, which deals with the love of a young English girl for a French artist called César – a barely disguised Gustave Flaubert. There is also a letter which must date from the early 1850s in which Flaubert congratulates Hamilton Aïdé on his first attempts at poetry and urges him to pursue his vocation as a writer; and there are the presentation copies of three of Flaubert's major works – *Madame Bovary*, *Salammbô* and *Trois Contes*. Some of the early Flaubert papers, including 'Written by Request' but none of the letters from Gustave, were reviewed by the late Dr Philip Spencer of Clare College, Cambridge, for his article 'New Light on Flaubert's Youth', published in the journal *French Studies* in April 1954. Spencer however made the error of confusing Gertrude and her sister Henrietta with the two English girls described in Flaubert's *Mémoires d'un fou*, a work of juvenilia completed in 1838, which is also set in Trouville. The two English girls in this story are staying in a pension in Trouville and are quite hard up; Flaubert dallied with both of them and one went so far as to invite him into her bedroom. Since Caroline Flaubert's letter to her brother of 14 July 1842 proves without a shadow of doubt that Flaubert first met Gertrude and Henrietta four summers later, the flirtatious English girls described in Chapter XV of the *Mémoires* could not have been the Collier sisters. This mistake was occasionally made after Gertrude's death and suggested that her relationship with Gustave was racier than it actually was: they kissed at the opera, but there was no invitation to her bedroom.

The later writings are designed to be read and appreciated within the family circle or by friends. 'Dear Children,' she writes at the beginning of one of the memoirs. 'I was looking over old journals, letters and papers and thought it might some day amuse you, if I told you about the people, I once knew, a long time ago in my childhood and youth. You must not expect from me anything learned, or particularly edifying. These stories snatched from the past, are only to amuse you. And to amuse myself . . .' One can imagine that they formed a kind of oral history, told and retold over the years, and that at some point she was encouraged to commit them to paper before they were forgotten. (In one fragment, she states that she is 92 years of age at the time of writing.) They are not polished narratives – they are repetitive and there are errors and omissions – and, with the possible exception of the Hugo memoir, they do not seem to have been intended for publication. But as biographical material, the memoirs are rich and fascinating: she has a gift for the vivid anecdote, and tremendous recall for domestic detail, for what people wore and how they furnished their rooms, and in particular what they said. All the dialogue in this book is drawn verbatim from Gertrude's papers. In contrast to Dolly's papers however, Gertrude's memoirs, letters and diaries are jumbled, unpaginated and often undated. As a result it is not practical to reference every quotation, although where possible I have sought to provide guidance as to the sources in the text or the notes.

If Gertrude was a scribbler and a hoarder, the same was true of her husband and her children. The chests contain thousands of documents relating to her husband's business affairs and legal disputes in the 1850s and 1860s. For the 1880s and 1890s, there are hundreds of letters from Dolly and Eveleen, her two grown-up daughters, as well as many more from family and friends, including the bundles which have been tied up and labelled as *Correspondence from Distinguished Persons* and carry the exhortation *Do Not Throw Away*, as described on page 4.

The two distinguished Tennant sons-in-law both have extensive archives preserved outside the attic: an entire pavilion is dedicated to Stanley's papers at the Musée Royale de L'Afrique Centrale at Tervuren, near Brussels, while many of F. H. Myers's papers are preserved at Trinity College, Cambridge. Hundreds of Dolly's later letters are spread between London institutions such as the British Library, the Wellcome Library and the Royal Geographical Society, but for the later chapters of this book I drew most heavily on her diaries, which are stored at Tervuren amid the relicts of Stanley's African career. This is an anomaly in that they have little to do with Stanley himself and it is to be hoped that an enterprising publisher will before too long bring out an edited version of these fascinating writings.

ACKNOWLEDGEMENTS

This book would not have been possible without the encouragement of Jenifer Coombe-Tennant, who let me loose in her attic and left me to rummage, or the support of Mark Coombe-Tennant, who has generously allowed me to quote freely from the family papers. I would like to thank my wife Jane for her support and for her tolerance, as for several years she had to accept that there was another woman in my life, albeit one who died in 1918 at the age of 98. Others who shared my conviction that the forgotten Gertrude was worth writing about, and have helped turn a private obsession into this handsome book, include chiefly Heather McCallum of Yale University Press, who has been an enthusiastic editor from the outset; Bill Hamilton, my agent; Edgar and Primrose Feuchtwanger, who read an early draft with great attention to detail and immediate sympathy for the subject-matter. Thanks also to Duncan Campbell-Smith, for his acute commentary and constant encouragement; Dr Andrew Cull, for his views on Henrietta's illness; Debbie Harrison, for her reading of early chapters; the late Prof. Sally Ledger, formerly of Birkbeck College, for inspiring me with a love of the Victorian period; Munro Price, for giving me the benefit of his deep insight into the July Monarchy; Jonathan Peacock QC for his opinion on Charles Tennant's legal disputes; the ever-helpful members of VICTORIA, the online discussion group for Victorian Studies, for their inexhaustible knowledge and their generosity in sharing it; Angela Thirlwell, for encouraging me to keep at it, and her son Adam for his insights into Gustave Flaubert's literary genius; Pieter Van der Merwe of the National Maritime Museum, for commenting on Admiral Collier's early career; Mathilde Leduc-Grimaldi for welcoming me to the Stanley

Pavilion at Tervuren and helping me navigate Dolly's diaries; Patrizia di Bello of Birkbeck for putting Eveleen's career as a photographer into context; Clare Freestone, Assistant Curator of Photographs at the National Portrait Gallery, for showing me Evie's albums; Andrew Dulley, Assistant County Archivist and his team at the West Glamorgan Archives Service in Swansea, who look after the public Tennant archive; the staff of the London Library and the British Library; Diana Neill at the British Embassy in Paris, who searched Foreign Office records in vain for evidence that Captain Collier might have been gainfully employed at the embassy or elsewhere in the diplomatic service. Others who have provided practical assistance or encouragement include Kate Faire; James Fairweather; Giles Foden; Prof. Hilary Fraser; Fenella Gentleman; Elaine Haslam, Buildings Manager at Richmond Terrace; Rosalie Hoffmann; Beth Humphries; James McCabe; Mark McCallum; Hazel Mills; Robert and Susanna Morgan-Williams; Martin Pick; Jim Ring; Paul Seaward, Director, History of Parliament; Ian Singleton; Hilary Wilce; Michaela Wrong. It goes without saying that despite generous help received from the above, all omissions and errors of fact or judgement are entirely my responsibility. Finally I would like to note the heroic patience of my children Max, Pippa and Munro, who have seen rather less of me than they might otherwise over recent years. The final word goes to Max, now aged 10, who has seen his father preoccupied with this project for more than a third of his lifetime. When he learned that Dolly had written letters to her deceased father for the best part of thirty years, he asked the very sensible question: 'Did she ever get a reply?'

London, February 2009

NOTES

1 How I Found Gertrude Tennant

1. John Guille Millais, *The Life and Letters of Sir John Everett Millais*, President of the Royal Academy (London, 1899), Vol. 2, p. 69.
2. Gertrude's admonition to newspaper editors was published in the *Illustrated American* of 28 June 1890. The build-up to the wedding and the ceremony itself were covered extensively. The *Pall Mall Gazette* and the *St James's Gazette* managed to produce full accounts of the wedding late on Saturday, 12 July, the day of the event itself, while North American publications such as the *New York Herald* got the full story into their Sunday editions. In the week of Monday 14 July, *The Times* and the *Daily Telegraph* both published not merely details of the wedding, but a full list of wedding guests and their presents.

2 Born into a Long Line of Heroes

1. This description, and the dialogue in this chapter are taken primarily from Harriet Collier's letter to Charles Tennant, dated 23 December 1847, in which she explains the circumstances of Gertrude's birth and of her first meeting with Lieutenant Collier and their courtship.
2. A heroic but futile encounter between the English and the French that took place on 13–14 April 1814, when French troops fought their way out of the citadel city of Bayonne on the River Adour. Napoleon had already surrendered, and the Bourbon monarchy had been restored at the beginning of the month; but neither side knew it until too late. Lieutenant Collier lies buried in the cemetery in the nearby village of Beaucoup.
3. 'Five thousand loads of fine seasoned oak-knees for ship-building, an infinite quantity of plank, masts, cordage and numbers of beautiful ships of war on the stocks, were at one time in blaze,' he wrote later, not without regret at seeing so much fine-quality *matériel* go up in flames. Source: Admiral Sir George Collier's *A detail of some particular services performed in America, during the years 1776, 1777, 1778 and 1779*, cited in the *Oxford Dictionary of National Biography*.
4. In Parliament the Admiral continued to do himself no favours by the independence of his views, telling the government that the war was being carried on 'with a total want of

humanity and consistency'. His lack of political judgement was exposed still further when he backed the losing side in the dispute between the Prince of Wales and the King over establishing the Regency. He left Parliament after many reversals and went back to sea in 1790. Quick to take umbrage, he felt that his contribution to the American War had never been properly recognised, and on one occasion launched a formal protest to the Admiralty after he was ordered to fly a flag that (he believed) demeaned his status as an independent commander. There were undoubtedly sound professional reasons for this prickliness, but perhaps there were more deep-seated, personal grounds for his sensitivity to a snub? His first marriage, to a famous beauty by the name of Christiana Gwyn (her portrait was painted by Sir Joshua Reynolds), foundered in the most humiliating fashion. She ran off with Collier's First Lieutenant, an Irishman by the name of Malloy, giving the Admiral grounds for divorce. (Malloy was later 'broken' and thrown out of the Navy for disobeying orders, while the first Lady Collier ended her life in ignominious exile in Belgium, having converted to Catholicism.)

5. *France on the Eve of the Great Revolution: France, Holland, and the Netherlands, a Century Ago.* Edited by *Mrs Charles Tennant* (London, 1865). The book was reviewed favourably in *The Times* on 26 December 1865. Gertrude's preface to this book contains the story of Nelson's taking a fancy to the young Frank Collier.

6. The second husband of Cromwell's daughter Frances was Sir John Russell (4th Baronet) of Chippenham in Cambridgeshire; their daughter married Sir Thomas Frankland (2nd Baronet) of Thirkelby in Yorkshire; their grandson was Admiral Sir Thomas Frankland (5th Baronet), whose daughter Charlotte married Robert Nicholas and produced Harriet and three other children. The fifth baronet was a hero of the Seven Years War and ended his career as Admiral of the Fleet. Through these connections, Gertrude's mother had three uncles and several cousins who were admirals.

7. Like Jane Austen herself, Gertrude grew up with 'a perpetual awareness of a *cousinage* extending over many counties and even beyond England' (Claire Tomalin, *Jane Austen: A Life*, London, 1997, p. 11). To suggest just how complex the combinatorial possibilities for such families might be, Gertrude's maternal grandmother was one of eleven children and her mother herself had ten siblings. By 1867, when Gertrude sat down to work out her family tree, her father's bloodline alone had produced sixteen grandsons and eleven granddaughters – and so many cousins that she didn't try to count them. The *cousinage* formed a root system of kinship under the surface of nineteenth-century society.

3   Early Adventures

1. By 10 p.m., when the French flagship *L'Orient* exploded (with 'flaming wreckage soaring to vast heights in all directions . . . [and] then burning spars and timbers and red hot embers' raining down), the Battle of the Nile was won, and Nelson had destroyed the French fleet and halted once and for all Napoleon's ambitions to take possession of India. It would be wrong to suggest that Frank's subsequent rise was effortless, as it was not achieved without the intercession of his mother. As a recent biographer of Nelson has noted, Lady Collier wrote 'an extraordinary number of letters' on Frank's behalf, to Nelson and others. In 1800, for example, she wrote a wheedling epistle to Nelson: '[Frank] has had the good fortune . . . to have stood near you in the ever memorable and never to be forgotten Victory of the Nile.' (See Roger Knight, *The Pursuit of Victory: The Life and Achievement of Horatio Nelson*, London, 2005, p. 629.)

2. 'The pirates' chief fortress, Ras al-Khaimah, was captured, their fortifications all round the coast were blown up, and their shipping was destroyed' – a result his father would have been proud of. Frank was knighted in 1830 and after a spell as superintendent of Woolwich Dockyard, went on to take command of the China station, fighting off

pirates from his base in Hong Kong. See the entry by J.K. Laughton on Sir Frank Collier in the *Oxford Dictionary of National Biography*.
3. *London Gazette*, 15 February 1823.

4 Arrival in Paris

1. Captain Rees Howell Gronow, *Captain Gronow: Reminiscences of Regency and Victorian Life 1810–60*, ed. Christopher Hibbert, London, 1991, p. 128. Gronow's diaries were first published in four volumes in 1862.
2. In *The Paris Sketch-Book* (1840). See the first sketch: *An Invasion of France*.
3. *Lady Morgan in France*, ed. Elizabeth Suddaby and P. J. Yarrow, (London, 1971), pp. 201–202.
4. Charles, Baron Stuart de Rothesay (1779–1849), was ambassador to France from 1815 to 1824 and again from 1828 to 1831. It was an open secret that he kept an actress as a mistress.
5. Fashionable English ladies visiting Paris tended to express wonder at Herbault's ravishing creations, and horror at his prices. 'His chapeaux look as if made by fairy fingers, so fresh, so light, do they appear; and his caps seem as if the gentlest sigh of a summer's zephyr would bear them from sight, so aerial is their texture, and so delicate are the flowers that adorn them,' wrote Lady Blessington. 'Three hundred and twenty francs for a crepe hat and feathers, two hundred for a chapeau a fleurs, one hundred for a chapeau neglige de matin, and eighty-five francs for an evening cap composed of tulle trimmed with blonde and flowers, are among the prices asked, and to my shame be it said, given' (Countess of Blessington, *The Idler in France*, Paris, 1841, Chapter V).
6. This policy of 'Throne and Altar' offended the more liberal elements of public opinion and was abolished, along with religious processions, after Louis-Philippe took the throne in 1830.
7. In 1789, Lally-Tollendal spoke up for a revolution by compromise, modelled on England's Glorious Revolution of 1688. He was a passionate supporter of the monarchy and offered to return from exile to defend the King. He was heaped with honours when the Bourbons were restored to the throne.
8. Sir James was a passionate gambler, known for losing a massive bet that a Captain Barclay, a noted pedestrian, could not walk 1,000 miles in 1,000 hours (which he did on Newmarket Heath, in 1809); his wife was rumoured to have been the lover of both Lord Byron and the Duke of Wellington. The marquis was godfather to one of their children.
9. The abbé (1749–1836) returned to Paris from exile in 1830 after the July Revolution, when Gertrude was 10. He was notorious for saying at the King's trial: 'La mort, sans phrase' – 'Death, without rhetoric'. He admitted voting for the King's death, but always denied saying 'sans phrase'.
10. John Simpson, *Paris after Waterloo: Notes Taken at the Time and Hitherto Unpublished*, (London and Edinburgh, 1853), p. 131.
11. 'At my ball,' wrote Harriet, Lady Granville, a later chatelaine of the British Embassy, 'I heard that when French people came up a quadrille they turned from it in disgust if there were any English. "Ah mon Dieu il y a des Anglais." The fact is that the butter is spread upon a *fonds* of hatred and jealousy towards nos autres . . .' (Betty Askwith, *Piety and Wit: A Biography of Harriet, Countess Granville 1785–1862*, London, 1982), p. 149).
12. Princess Catherine Skavronska de Bagration (1783–1857) was widowed when her husband Prince Peter was killed at Borodino; she held a salon and was said to love 'noise, commotions and newcomers' (Steven Kale, *French Salons: High Society and Political Sociability from the Old Regime to the Revolution of 1848*, Baltimore, 2004, p. 6).
13. Simpson, *Paris after Waterloo*, p. 106.

14. *Galignani's Messenger* was set up in 1814 by Giovanni Antonio Galignani, an Italian who had lived in London and spotted the opportunity to cater for the information needs of the English expatriate community. His publishing venture was very successful and the newspaper carried on until 1884. There exists, to this day, an English bookshop on the rue de Rivoli called Galignani's, which is owned by his descendants.
15. Simpson, *Paris after Waterloo*, pp. 112–113.
16. It seems that from a very early age George Collier was brought up by relatives in England, not an uncommon practice at the time. Gertrude never lived with him and, astonishing though this is to modern sensibilities, she met him only a few times during her long life.

5   Unsentimental Education

1. *The Diverting History of John Gilpin*, by William Cowper, was a popular ballad of 1782 chronicling the exploits of a linen draper on a runaway horse.
2. Admiral Lord Cochrane (1775–1860), tenth earl of Dundonald, was a great character. After the fall of Napoleon, he commanded the fleets of Chile, Brazil and Greece, and was regularly in disgrace with his superiors for his outspoken views. His adventurous life inspired the novels of Frederick Marryat and Patrick O'Brian; his wife lived in Paris while he was travelling the world and is reputed to have taken Lord Auckland as a lover. Gertrude's father was a pall-bearer at his funeral. See David Cordingly, *Cochrane the Dauntless* (London, 2007).
3. Lytton Strachey, *Landmarks in French Literature* (London, 1923), p. 195.
4. Balzac, essay in *Feuilletons de journaux politiques*.
5. A word coined to describe those who committed a form of idolatry in their reverence for Hugo.
6. Hugo sought to break 'the stranglehold of classical conventions and open [. . .] up the possibility of Romantic forms of theatre which highlighted passion and social movements' (Colin Jones, *Paris: Biography of a City*, London, 2004, p. 322)

6   Gertrude Meets Her Future Husband

1. 'Spent a happy summer,' Gertrude wrote of this holiday in her 'locked diary', many years later. 'Felt how dear Charles was to me – and felt very sad the morning the Tennants embarked for England.' 'She is a very remarkable girl, and always struck me so, even when she was a little girl,' Charles wrote to his sister Margaret on 24 July 1846, when he and Gertrude were engaged.
2. Charles Dickens worked as a lowly office lad in Gray's Inn from 1827 to 1828.
3. From the preface to Charles Tennant's *The People's Blue Book: Taxation as it is, and as it ought to be* (London, 1857), p. v.
4. *The State of Man*, 2nd edn 1852 pp. 54–55.
5. Works like Isaac Taylor's *Physical Theory of Another Life* (1836) or John Pye Smith's *Relation between the Holy Scriptures and Some Parts of Geological Science* (1839) also attempted to reconcile traditional religious beliefs with the discoveries of scientists such as Charles Lyell, whose *Principles of Geology* was first published in 1830–33 and grew in notoriety during the course of the decade.
6. Published in full in Keith Tucker, *A Scratch in Glamorganshire: George Tennant, 1765–1832*. (Neath, 1998). See p.142. This is an excellent source for the early history of the Tennant family and the construction of the canal.
7. The volume of goods carried along the canal rose from 85,000 tons in the year of his death to a peak of 225,000 tons in 1866. The Vale of Neath Railway Act passed in 1846, despite Charles's strenuous opposition, and the line was opened in 1851. It had little impact on the canal's traffic until the 1860s.

8. Sir Oliver Lodge, *Christopher: A Study in Human Personality* (London, 1918), p. 80.
9. It is conventional to multiply by 80 to arrive at a value in today's money, which would give a total of £5 million – which is on the low side for the financing of a major infrastructure project.
10. Lady Jersey (1785–1867) was sole heir to the Child's Bank fortune; a considerable society figure, one of the termagant aristocratic patronesses whose whim determined who was smart enough to enter Almack's, a ballroom-cum-club in King Street, St James's, that was so exclusive that even the Duke of Wellington was (on one occasion) refused admittance. As gatekeeper to this 'seventh heaven of the fashionable world', Lady Jersey was imperious, beautiful, as rich as Croesus and profoundly unpleasant. 'Inconceivably rude, and in her manner often ill-bred,' was the judgement of Captain Gronow; 'a disagreeable foolish tiresome woman', concurred Lady Granville, a daughter of the Duke of Devonshire and thus Lady Jersey's superior in breeding if not in wealth. She was nicknamed 'Silence', because she chattered incessant nonsense, which by virtue of her money few had the courage to interrupt.

7 Gertrude Enters Society

1. The duc de Bordeaux was a grandson of Charles X, nominated by the latter as his successor after he abdicated in July 1830. However the Chamber of Deputies proclaimed his cousin the duc d'Orléans, the head of the cadet branch of the Royal family, as the next king; on ascension to the throne, he became Louis-Philippe, King of the French.
2. There were several de Praslin sisters, daughters of the duc de Praslin, who were brought to the school by their governess, Mme Déluzy. In 1847, the duke murdered his wife, an event that was said to highlight the decadence of the aristocracy in the dying stages of the Orléanist regime. It was rumoured that the duke was driven to the crime by his passion for the governess; he killed himself shortly afterwards. See Stanley Loomis, *A Crime of Passion* (London, 1967).
3. *Les Misérables* would not be published for thirty years, but the climax of the book is based on the bloody uprisings of 1834, to which Hugo was an eyewitness. He drew on the massacre of the rue Transnonain, which took place on 12 April 1834, when troops butchered twelve innocent men, women and children as part of a brutal crackdown on a workers' insurrection; Gustave Flaubert also used this for a scene in *L'Education sentimentale*. Much of Hugo's novel is set in or indeed underneath the labyrinthine medieval streets of old Paris.
4. This story is not as tall as it sounds. The head was in the possession of Gertrude's friends the St-Aubyn family, who had it from the executioner, and it was subsequently acquired by Prince Roland Bonaparte, a great-nephew of Napoleon, who allowed it to be exhibited at the Second International Congress of International Criminology in Paris in 1889. There it was examined by Cesare Lombroso, founder of the pseudo-science of phrenology, and by other craniologists. A fierce debate ensued over whether the skull (by now stripped of all vestiges of flesh) demonstrated Corday's heroism or criminal degeneracy. See Frederick Howard Wines, *Punishment and Reformation: A Study of the Penitentiary System* (London, 1895), p. 239.
5. The aristocrat in question is the comte de Rambuteau, of whom more in later chapters. See his *Memoirs* (London and New York, 1908), p. 21.
6. See Kale, *French Salons*, pp. 170–171.
7. The Faubourg Saint-Germain on the Rive Gauche to the south of the Seine was the home of the most ancient aristocracy, who were typically legitimists and fervent opponents of the Orléanist regime. In the Faubourg Saint-Honoré, they were also aristocratic, but not quite so grand, and they were more tolerant of the new regime. The new money was to be found in the Chaussée d'Antin, in the 9th *arrondissement*, where

the Rothschilds and Lafites resided. They tended to be enthusiastic supporters of the July Monarchy. See Letter XII in Frances Trollope, *Paris and the Parisians in 1835* (London, 1836).

8. Kale, *French salons*, p. 37.
9. The article is quoted in Kathryn Hughes, *George Eliot: The Last Victorian* (London, 1998), p. 225.
10. Henry James to his sister Alice, 2 March 1877, in *Letters*, ed. Leon Edel (London, 1978) Vol. 2, pp. 103–104.
11. Mary Clarke (1793–1883) made a great impression on the young Florence Nightingale, who attended her salon at 120 rue du Bac in 1838. She later married the orientalist Julius Mohl and as Mme Mohl continued, into her seventies, to entertain the flower of French literary society, together with visiting English writers such as George Eliot and Elizabeth Gaskell.
12. Henrietta Elizabeth (Harriet) Leveson-Gower, Countess Granville, née Lady Henrietta Elizabeth Cavendish (1785–1862), was the younger daughter of William Cavendish, the fifth duke of Devonshire, and his first wife, Georgina Cavendish. She spent a blissfully happy childhood at Chatsworth, but suffered after her mother died and her father married his mistress. In 1809, she married Lord Granville Leveson-Gower, who became the first Earl Granville. Despite the complication that he was her aunt's long-term lover, it proved a long and very happy union.
13. Askwith, *Piety and Wit*, p. 144.
14. 'Today is Lady G's regular reception,' wrote one English guest. 'Always the pleasantest thing in Paris. There are never more than 300 people, with four rooms open, beautifully furnished and lighted, and opening into a conservatory which goes all round the inside of the garden front, also lighted and carpeted. It is lovely and the French are in fits of delight and admiration about it.' See Caroline Grosvenor and Lord Wortley, *The First Lady Wharncliffe and her Family*, (London, 1927), Vol. 2, p. i.

8   The Marriage Market

1. The 'contemporary novel' is Hamilton Aïdé's *Rita: An Autobiography* (London, 1856). See Chapter 15 below for further details.
2. Born in 1810, Julia Augusta was Gertrude's first cousin, one of the three daughters from the Admiral's first marriage. In 1845, she and her husband would move to Dorset where, as we shall see, Julia Augusta befriended the young Thomas Hardy.
3. Gronow, *Captain Gronow*, pp. 167–168.
4. Greville, *The Greville Memoirs* (London, 1874), Vol. 2, p. 38. The entry is for 29 August 1830.
5. Lady Aldborough wrote to Gertrude almost daily when she was in Paris or on holiday in Boulogne, over a period of three years.

9   Phantoms of Trouville

1. Benjamin J. Bart, *Flaubert* (New York, 1967), pp. 64–65.
2. Gustave Flaubert, *Correspondance*, ed. Jean Bruneau, 4 vols (Paris 1973–1997). Vol. 5, ed. Yves Leclerc (2007). This letter is in the Pléiade edition of the *Correspondance*, Vol. 1, pp. 114–115, 14 July 1842. Unless indicated otherwise, the translation into English is the author's.

3. *Madame Bovary*, for example, would be a quest for style:

> How many times have I fallen flat on my face, just when I thought I had it [style] in my grasp, he wrote later amid the composition of his first great novel. Still, I feel that I mustn't die without making sure that the style I can hear inside my head comes roaring out and drowns the cries of parrots and cicadas . . . (Letter to Louise Colet, 19 April 1852)

He writes elsewhere of the the heroic impersonality of the style he seeks to attain:

> Style is achieved only by dint of atrocious labour, fanatical and unremitting stubbornness . . . [but] the artist must no more appear in his work than God does in nature. Man is nothing, the work of art everything . . . (Cited in Julian Barnes, *Flaubert's Parrot* (1985), London, 1995, pp. xi and 95)

And:

> What I should like to write is a book about nothing, a book dependent on nothing external, which would be held together by the internal strength of its style, just as the earth, suspended in the void, depends on nothing external for its support. (ibid., p. xii)

4. Geoffrey Wall, *Flaubert: A Life* (London, 2001), p. 66.
5. Bart, *Flaubert*, p. 70.
6. This story is entitled 'Written by Request'. See Chapter 10 and note 8, below for further details.
7. In the Flaubert correspondence, Henrietta is often referred to as Henriette, the French version of the name, while the Tennant family papers call her Harriet, like her mother. This is very confusing and I refer to her as Henrietta throughout. See Bart, *Flaubert*, p. 68, for further details of the letter.

10   At Home with the Flauberts

1. *Correspondance*, Vol.1, p. 24, 24 June 1837.
2. C.B. West, 'Gustave Flaubert et Harriet Collier: Premier rencontre à Trouville,' *Revue d'Histoire Littéraire de la France*, 57(1), January–March 1957, pp. 1–9.
3. *Correspondance*, Vol. 1, pp. 127–128, 16 November 1842.
4. This crucial letter from Le Poittevin to Flaubert is quoted in Bart, *Flaubert*, p. 81.
5. *Correspondance*, Vol 1. pp. 137–139, 21 December 1842.
6. This is the novella in which Nellie Neville alias Gertrude Tennant befriends a beautiful young Frenchwoman (Marguerite Hébert, alias Caroline Flaubert) and falls in love with her brother, a student she names César Hébert, alias Gustave Flaubert. In the story, Nellie/Gertrude will not marry César/Gustave because of his contempt for established religion and his French nationality. In the end, Nellie inherits a title and marries a respectable Englishman. The conclusion to the story is pure make-believe, but there is enough in it for it to be taken seriously as a commentary on the intensity of her early feelings for Gustave Flaubert. 'If we compare the points where it touches her other reminiscences, the variations are slight and defensible,' argued the late Philip Spencer in 'New Light on Flaubert's Youth,' *French Studies* 8, April 1954, p. 102. 'The value of *Written by Request* lies in its frankness; it shows what Gertrude really felt. Here, as in her other writings, she displays a remarkable visual memory; she seems one of the very few reliable witnesses of Flaubert's youth.' Judging by the handwriting, the story was written late in Gertrude's life, in the 1880s or even the 1890s. It is not clear who made the request: perhaps Gertrude's daughters, eager to see their mother set down a romantic story from her youth, or Hamilton Aïdé, her cousin who, we will see, was to fashion aspects of Gertrude's life into a successful novel. Flaubert aficionados will note

that Gertrude gives the Flauberts the name of their long-standing domestic servant, Caroline Hébert (always known as Julie), who should not be confused with Juliet Herbert, the English governess at Croisset who produced the first (and lost) English-language translation of *Madame Bovary* and was Flaubert's long-term lover. See also note 2, above to Flaubert's letter to Emmanuel Vasse, 17 November 1842, Vol. 1, p. 130.

7. Ibid., pp. 147–148, 15 March 1843.
8. Ibid., pp. 149–150, 25 March 1843.
9. Gertrude's flirtatious letters are transcribed in Jean Bruneau, 'La Famille Collier et Gustave Flaubert (Lettres inédites 1842–1879),' *Nineteenth-Century French Studies*, Fall–Winter, 1988–89 pp. 70–88.
10. Vol. 1, p. 166, 25 May 1843.
11. Gertrude's enthusiasm for the man and his works was distinctly risqué as Pradier specialised in sculpting beautiful naked women, portrayed as nymphs and goddesses, and as a result his studio 'breathed an atmosphere of infinite sexual opportunity', comments Geoffrey Wall (*Flaubert*, p. 74). No wonder that Flaubert felt at home there. See *Correspondance*, Vol. 1, pp. 194–196, 3 December 1843.
12. Flaubert, *Voyages* (Paris: Société des Belles Lettres, 1948), Vol. 1, p. 155. Quoted by Spencer in 'New Light on Flaubert's Youth', p. 105.
13. Letter to Louise Colet, *Correspondance*, Vol. 1, pp. 359–360, 22 September 1846. This translation is from Francis Steegmuller's edition of Flaubert's letters (London, 2001), pp. 115–116.
14. He refers fondly to his visits to Gertrude at that time in his letter of early November 1846. Vol. 1, pp. 402–403.
15. *Correspondance*, Vol. 1, p. 257, 15 March 1846.

11 An Improbable Romance

1. *Correspondance*, Vol. 1, pp. 402–403, early November 1846. This letter was published by Caroline Commanville and thought lost; the original is one of the twenty or so preserved as part of the Tennant family papers.
2. Leonore Davidoff and Catherine Hall, *Family Fortunes: Men and Women of the English Middle Class 1780–1850* (London, 1987), p. 334.

12 Portrait of a Marriage

1. Hardy's parents were tenants on the estate and the kind-hearted and childless Mrs Martin took a deep personal interest in the boy. She would establish a school in Lower Bockhampton, but young Thomas was too frail to attend and for two years she gave him lessons at her home, in the study. Hardy was smitten by this glamorous older woman and built her and the house into several of his novels and stories, including his first, unpublished novel, suggestively titled *The Poor Man and the Lady*. When Hardy was a little older he was sent to school at Dorchester; on one occasion he ran away so that he could catch a glimpse of Gertrude's cousin at a barn dance. At the time of the honeymoon, the future novelist was just six years old.
2. 'May God forgive this woman and enable me to forget all the incomparable mischief of her duplicity and falsehood,' Charles Tennant wrote of his sister-in-law (4 March 1845).
3. Probably Sir John Guest and his wife Charlotte, Lady Guest. The Dowlais Iron Company was the largest ironworks in the world and Lady Guest became a society hostess in her own right.

4. Charlotte Brontë's *Jane Eyre* was published earlier in 1847, and *Wuthering Heights* by her sister Emily in the December that Gertrude spent at Cadoxton.
5. 'No, indeed – *we* are not at all in a bad air,' argues the heroine's sister in Chapter XII of *Emma.* 'Our part of London is very superior to most others! – You must not confound us with London in general, my dear sir. The neighbourhood of Brunswick Square [also in Bloomsbury] is very different from almost all the rest. We are so very airy! I should be unwilling, I own, to live in any other part of the town; – there is hardly any other that I could be satisfied to have my children in: but *we* are so remarkably airy!'
6. Roy Porter, *London: A Social History* (London, 1994), p. 36.
7. The Imperial Hotel was built in 1969 and described by Sir John Betjeman as 'three dimensional chartered accountancy'.
8. The 1848 revolution was witnessed by Gustave Flaubert, who was on a rare visit to Paris and later fashioned his haphazard experiences of the rioting into the backdrop for *L'Education sentimentale.*
9. Sarah Stickney Ellis, *The Wives of England* (London, 1843), p. 31.
10. Matthew Arnold, letter to Arthur Clough, 23 September 1849.
11. 'The validity of my title,' wrote W.L. Burn in his book of this name, 'remains to be proved but what I sought was a generation in which the old and the new, the elements of growth, survival and decay, achieved a balance which most contemporaries regarded as satisfactory.' (*The Age of Equipoise: A Study of the mid-Victorian Generation,* London, 1964, p. 17).

13 Charles's Angel in the House?

1. 'This was a ruthless, grabbing, competitive, male-dominated society, stamping on its victims and discarding its weaker members with all the devastating relentlessness of mutant species in Darwin's vision of Nature itself' (A.N. Wilson, *The Victorians,* London, 2002, p. 120).
2. 'And wherever a true wife comes, this home is always around her,' Ruskin continued. 'The stars only may be over her head; the glow-worm in the night-cold grass may be the only fire at her foot: but home is yet wherever she is; and for a noble woman it stretches far round her, better than ceiled with cedar, or painted with vermilion, shedding its quiet light far, for those who else were homeless.'
3. Judith Flanders, *The Victorian House: Domestic Life from Childbirth to Deathbed* (London, 2003), p. xxii.
4. Virginia Woolf explained how she had had to kill the Angel in the House in an address to the National Society for Women's Service on 21 January 1931. A shortened version of the speech became the essay 'Professions for Women', which was published posthumously in *The Death of the Moth, and other Essays* (London, 1942).
5. Helena Michie, 'Under Victorian Skins: The Bodies Beneath', in *A Companion to Victorian Literature and Culture,* ed. Herbert F. Tucker (Oxford, 1999), p. 420.
6. Caroline Norton was well-born and attractive, one of three beautiful but impecunious sisters who entranced London society when they first 'came out' in 1826. She married, in the following year, George Norton, who had first been captivated by Caroline's charms when she was a schoolgirl. 'The marriage was a disaster from the outset,' comments K.D. Reynolds in the *Oxford Dictionary of National Biography.* 'Two less compatible individuals would have been harder to find. Norton was slow, rather dull, jealous and obstinate; Caroline was quick-witted, vivacious, flirtatious, and egotistical'. He was an uncouth loafer, albeit a Member of Parliament and a lawyer, while she was soon able to make a good living from her pen. Frustrated at his wife's growing prominence, George became violent, beating and abusing her and the three children who

arrived in the early years of the marriage. In 1835 they separated, and he took the boys (they were then six, four and two years old) and hid them away on an estate in Yorkshire. As a lawyer, he knew full well that he was entitled to deny his wife access to their children and that they were, in effect, his property. Mrs Norton, with society connections, wit, beauty and talent on her side, waged for years a fruitless campaign to have the boys returned to her. It was only after one of the boys fell off a horse and died an agonising death, aged eight, that her husband was shamed into returning the two others to their mother for six months of the year. Despite her husband's cruelty, Caroline herself was shunned by society for having the temerity to speak up.

7. Sarah Ellis, *The Wives of England* (London and Paris, 1843), p. 65.
8. M. Jeanne Peterson, *Family, Love, and Work in the Lives of Victorian Gentlewomen* (Bloomington, 1989), p. 84.
9. 'The multi-volume biographies in which so many eminent [male] Victorians were embalmed are full of letters between husbands and wives,' observes Theodore Hoppen, 'letters brimming with confidence, sharing, reflection and mutual trust. Surely too it is the nineteenth, rather than either the eighteenth or twentieth centuries, which can most accurately be described as the great era of companionate marriages.' *The Mid Victorian Generation* (Oxford, 1998), p. 324. See also John Stuart Mill, *The Subjection of Women* (1869; edn, 2006, p. 237).

14   Births and Deaths

1. Sarah Ellis, *The Wives of England* (London and Paris, 1843).
2. Frederick Denison Maurice (1805–72), Royal Chaplain at Lincoln's Inn from 1846 to 1860, was one of the pioneers of the Christian Socialist movement. His forgiving, all-inclusive form of Christianity appealed to Charles and Gertrude, but alienated him from the more pharisaic elements of English society, including the council of King's College, who sacked him from his post as Professor of English Literature and History for questioning the doctrine of everlasting damnation.
3. http://www.bankofengland.co.uk/education/inflation/calculator/flash/index.htm
4. See Flaubert's letters in Vol. 2, pp. 19–21, 8 December, 1851; pp. 47–48, 24 February 1852 and pp. 73–74, 18 April 1852.
5. Ibid., pp. 590–591. Letter to Louis Bouilhet, 13 September 1855.

15   Rita and Emma: Two Literary Heroines

1. See Hamilton Aïdé's obituary in *The Times*, 17 December 1906.
2. Letter 407 to George Smith, 1858, in *The Letters of Elizabeth Cleghorn Gaskell*, ed. J.A.V. Chapple and Arthur Pollard (Manchester, 1996), p. 522.
3. In his letters to Alice James on New Year's Eve 1878 and to Grace Norton on 4 January, 1879 (see *Letters* Vol. 2, pp. 199 and 209).
4. Of the father, Rita writes:

> He had been brought up in the ways of his fathers, and was no more vicious, I suppose, than most of the young men of the Regent period. He was by nature *debonnaire* – what is called 'good-natured' by the world, where he was certainly a popular man on the whole. But he was selfish and sensual . . . [and] incapable of a strong and deep affection . . .

Colonel Perceval cannot resist the temptations of Parisian night-life:

> My father was . . . immersed in the dissipations of Paris [writes Rita]. Often have I heard him come home at four or five in the morning: the heavy step, the click of

the latch-key in the door, the stumbling through the rooms in the dim light of a perishing lamp, and the curse if it suddenly went out. With years, indeed, and the life he led, together with the harass of his accumulated debts, he became irritable, even violent at times. We children seldom saw him; he was very little at home.

5. 'I must be got rid of – no matter how, or where – at any price – no I am wrong – to the highest bidder, and on the best terms the market could afford . . . Is it for this that I was brought into the world? Am I a thing, then, of so little value to those who gave me birth, that their only anxiety is to sell me, like a slave in their own market?'

6. Aïdé may have had in mind Violetta from Verdi's *La Traviata*, first performed in 1853, or the novel on which the opera is based, Alexandre Dumas's *La Dame aux camélias*, first published in 1848.

7. She has to flee Paris or else she will be forced into marriage with the marquis – and does so with the assistance of Lord Rawdon, who has recovered from his injuries to find that he is so in love with Rita that he abandons his dissolute lifestyle on her account. But Rita decides that, much as she is indebted to Rawdon, she does not love him – and flees a second time, just as she is about to be married. She ends up recuperating in rural England, where by improbable coincidence she finds herself living in the same village as her true love Hubert Rochford, who is of course engaged to be married to someone else, a minor obstacle that does not stand in the way of their eventual conjugal felicity. Her father is exposed as the parent of the poor seamstresses' love-child, and ends his days bent with age, with the same appetites as in his youth and middle-age, 'but with enfeebled powers'.

8. Letters 410 and 412 to George Smith, 4 February 1859 and 10 February *Letters*, pp. 526 and 528.

9. Cited in Enid Starkie, *Flaubert: The Making of the Master* (London, 1967), p. 80. The original was in the Tennant family papers but is now lost.

10. The original of Gertrude's letter is transcribed in Jean Bruneau's article 'La Famille Collier et Gustave Flaubert', pp. 78–80.

11. The book is in Flaubert's library at the Mairie de Canteleu-Croisset, with the following dedication: 'For her friend Gustave Flaubert from his sincere friend and well-wisher, Gertrude Tennant, January 1860, London.' It was the seventh edition in two volumes, published by Blackwood.

16 *Les Misérables*

1. Gerhard Joseph and Herbert F. Tucker 'Passing on: Death', in *Companion to Victorian Literature & Culture* (Oxford, 1999), p. 115. See also Pat Jalland, *Death in the Victorian Family* (Oxford, 1996), p. 120.

2. 'Nobody shall miss her like I shall, it is such a very painful thing to me, that I really cannot express my sorrow,' Charles Dickens wrote to his friend John Foster as he was composing the tragic last chapters of *The Old Curiosity Shop* in December 1840. Many readers pleaded with the author to keep her alive.

3. Darwin's friend Joseph Hooker the botanist also lost his daughter, the six-year-old Maria Elizabeth, in 1863. He wrote to Darwin: 'it will be long before I cease to hear her voice in my ears – or feel her little hand stealing into mine, by the fire side & in the garden. – wherever I go, she is there.' Darwin, who saw the death of Annie and two other children as evidence of the pitiless forces of natural selection, replied: 'I understand well your words: "wherever I go, she is there."' 'She did not suffer much,' he reflected. 'This was to us with poor Annie the one great comfort.' Correspondence cited in the *Times Literary Supplement*, 16 March 2007.

4. All the references in this chapter come from the long unpublished memoir of Victor Hugo located among Gertrude's papers in the attic.

5. Juliette Drouet was a famous beauty and actress of limited talents when Hugo met and first fell for her charms. She had been mistress to Louis Pradier, the sculptor, bearing him a daughter who died at the age of 17. Drouet was the model for Pradier's statue of *The City of Strasbourg* in the Place de la Concorde.

6. English readers of Victor Hugo were polarised into those who revered him, like Algernon Swinburne, and those who found him and his verse pompous and grandiloquent, for example Gertrude's future son-in-law Frederic Myers. See Algernon Swinburne, *A Study of Victor Hugo* (London, 1886) for the former perspective and Myers's essay on Hugo in his *Essays: Modern* (London, 1885) for the more sceptical viewpoint.

17   Moving Up in the World

1. Construction of Sir George Gilbert Scott's Italianate Government Offices started in the year the Tennant family moved to the area.
2. Dolly's Diary (DD), 8 April 1886.
3. G.R. Searle, *Entrepreneurial Politics in mid-Victorian Britain* (Oxford, 1993), pp. 141–143.
4. Gertrude's Diary (GD), 20 June 1863.
5. From an article in *The Lady*, cited in Andrew St George, *The Descent of Manners: Etiquette, Rules and the Victorians* (London, 1993), p. 114.
6. George Smith (1824–1901) was a very considerable figure, the publisher of Charlotte Brontë's *Jane Eyre*, John Ruskin's *Stones of Venice* and George Eliot's *Romola*, among many of the great works of nineteenth-century English literature. He went on to establish the *Cornhill* magazine, the *Pall Mall Gazette*, and to publish the *Dictionary of National Biography*.
7. Richard Monckton Milnes, the first Baron Houghton (1809–85), was a noted man of letters, politician, champion of the poetry of Algernon Swinburne and sometime suitor of Florence Nightingale. He also collected erotic books.
8. *Musical Times*, 1 February 1895.
9. The first and last Empress of the French, Eugénie de Montijo was born in Granada in 1826 and died in Madrid in 1920. She was highly intelligent, conservative in outlook and a staunch Catholic. She and the Emperor had one child, Louis Napoléon, who was tragically killed in Zululand in 1879 when serving with the British Army.
10. The 1871 Census return shows him living at Ryder Street with a second wife called Stepney aged 25, and their four-year-daughter. He was 79 years old at the time.

19   Re-entering the Marriage Market

1. Famously, during a public debate with Bishop Wilberforce which took place in Oxford in 1860, Huxley was asked whether he descended from an ape on his grandmother's side or his grandfather's. To which he is said to have rejoined: 'I would rather be the offspring of two apes than be a man and afraid to tell the truth.' (The debate is legendary, but there is no transcript of what was actually said.)
2. DD, 1 November 1875.
3. *Daily News*, 31 March 1875.
4. DD, 10 September 1876.
5. Barbara Bryant, *G.F. Watts Portraits: Fame and Beauty in Victorian Society* (London, 2004), p. 258.
6. Marie Belloc Lowndes, *The Merry Wives of Westminster* (London, 1946), pp. 121–122.
7. DD, 25 May 1885.
8. Henry James, *Letters* ed. Leon Edel (London, 1978), Vol. 2, p. 114, 20 May 1877.
9. DD, 12 December 1875.

20   Reunited with an Old Flame

1. The reunion and the meeting with Turgenev is described in DD, 30 April 1876.
2. *Correspondance*, Vol. 5, pp. 124–125 and 154–156.
3. As recounted by Mrs Belloc Lowndes in *Diaries and Letters 1911–1947*, ed. Susan Lowndes (London, 1971), 20 April 1912.
4. *Correspondance*, Vol. 5, pp. 381–382.
5. Ibid., pp. 803–804.
6. Ibid., pp. 55–58.
7. Cited in Bruneau, 'La Famille Collier et Gustave Flaubert, p. 81.
8. *Correspondance*, Vol. 5, pp. 194–195.
9. Frederick Brown *Flaubert: A Life* (New York, 2006), p. 505.
10. Entry in Gertrude's diary for 5 September 1880.

21   An Eligible Match

1. *Correspondance*, Vol. V, pp. 786–787.
2. In Frederic Myers's essay on George Eliot, in *Essays: Modern* p. 269.
3. Cited in Deborah Blum, *Ghost Hunters: William James and the Search for Scientific Proof of Life after Death* (London, 2007), p. 121.
4. Cited ibid., p. 83.
5. Cited ibid., p. 71.
6. Coquelin (1841–1909) made his name playing Molière at the Théâtre Français, but he is most celebrated for his more than 400 performances in the title role of *Cyrano de Bergerac* (1897), by Edmond Rostand. He toured North America in this role. Dolly painted his portrait, the original of which is owned by the author.
7. DD, 8 May 1880.
8. No trivial matter for a haemophiliac like the Prince. He died in Cannes in March 1883, just short of his 31st birthday, after once again injuring his knee.
9. The letter is transcribed in DD, 8 May 1880.

22   The Delicious Dolly

1. Henry to Alice James, *Letters*, Vol. 2, p. 235, 19 May 1879. Edwin Arnold's reverence for Dolly is reported by his son Julian Arnold, in *Giants in Dressing Gowns* (London, 1945), p. 79.
2. 'This is the third volume of the book in which I write everything I feel and do,' she wrote for example on 20 March 1875, shortly after the second anniversary of his death, 'solely for my own dear father who is gone to heaven. We are parted from one another temporarily only, so I keep as close to him as I can, I on earth, he in heaven, by writing to him at the end of each day. I cannot write all I feel, all I dare think, all my longing for him. Almighty God, bring me some day to him, surely and safely to him, and help me to act all through my life as I know he would wish me to act.'
3. There is, to the best of this author's knowledge, nothing directly comparable to this marathon confessional work, although Sir Leslie Stephen's *Mausoleum Book*, written for his children to commemorate the death of his second wife Julia in 1895, has a similar emotional intimacy. The result is a remarkable social document, in which Dolly vividly chronicles her thoughts and feelings as well as her observations on the events of the day. She had been very attached to her father, who was 58 years old when she was born, and grew up with a quite rational fear that this elderly man whom she loved so much would die suddenly and leave her in the lurch. He lived on until just short of her eighteenth birthday, and she was desolate when he died.

4. An example of Dolly's forceful charm comes from an exchange of letters with Watts in early 1879. She has been to see Watts with a French friend, and she describes to Signor, as the painter was known to his friends, how the Frenchman looked at his pictures. 'He thinks that you should stand before a picture, and that it should tell you the clearest, simplest story, and that it should appeal to you by its style and execution – by its being masterly.' Watts writes back, saying that he is disappointed but not surprised to hear that the French see art as mere 'embroidery on the intellectual needs and yearnings of our nature'. Of course, he goes on to argue, it should be pleasing to look at, but a 'great picture should be a thing to live with, to respond to varying moods, and especially should have the power to awaken the highest of our subtle mental and intellectual sensibilities'. Dolly urges him to set down these ideas in writing and at greater length, and persuades the editor of the august *Nineteenth Century* magazine to give him a platform should the master be coaxed into writing. The result was the manifesto 'The Present Conditions of Art', seen as the definitive statement of Watts's artistic credo, which appeared in that journal in February 1880. 'I do so much want to see you again, I have so much to talk to you about,' cooed Dolly after the article had appeared. 'I always felt certain that if you took to writing you would do much good, and surprise the public who think that a painter cannot be anything but a painter. Your article . . . has created a great sensation . . .' She goes on to encourage him to write another piece, about his theory of curves. The article on curves was never written. An account of the correspondence is given in Mary S. Watts, *George Frederic Watts: The Annals of an Artist's Life* (London, 1912), Vol. 1, pp. 314–316.
5. The episode is described in DD, 1 December 1879.
6. Dolly's artistic credo is spelt out in the introduction to *London Street Arabs* (London, 1890), a collection of her ragamuffin pictures she published (under the name Mrs H.M. Stanley) shortly after her wedding in the summer of 1890.
7. The mainstay of formal art education was painting from life, and of course it was deemed entirely unsuitable for women to see men or indeed women with no clothes on. This was frustrating for the many gifted amateur artists who happened to be women, and the Slade hit upon a compromise. Women would not be admitted into the same life classes as the men, but would be given access to their own classes, where they would draw from a partially draped nude. They were then encouraged to complete their studies in Paris, where the same restrictions did not apply. There was a strong connection between the Slade and French artistic circles, as the first professor of the school was Sir Edward Poynter, who had studied in Paris, and his successor from 1876 to 1892 was Alphonse Legros, a friend of Courbet and James McNeill Whistler, who was at the forefront of bringing the ideas of the new school of Impressionism into the country. Legros became a friend and frequent visitor to Richmond Terrace, on one occasion helping Dolly to boil some toffee for a party of visiting street urchins.
8. 'The pale prostrate body of Love [is] shockingly illuminated against a dark background and set off by sanguine wings,' notes Alison Smith in *Exposed*, the catalogue to the 2001 Exhibition of the Victorian Nude at the Tate Gallery, in which the picture was exhibited. Another modern critic deemed the picture 'oddly poignant and direct' (Andrew Lambirth in the *Spectator*, 17 November 2001). It was painted to commemorate a failed love affair, of which more in due course. The background is a rural scene, showing a river and mountains that would not be out of place in South Wales.
9. As Christopher Woods explains:

> The gallery was situated in a grandiose Italianate building in Bond Street, richly decorated and furnished. In deliberate contrast to the Royal Academy method, the pictures were widely spaced apart, with groups of one artist's work placed together. This enabled the spectator to form an overall impression of an artist's style, and was widely welcomed by the artists themselves. The Grosvenor was also the first gallery to be lit by electric light . . . The opening was a highly fashionable event,

attended by the Prince and Princess of Wales, and before long the Grosvenor was well established as a serious rival to the Academy . . . The tendency at the Grosvenor was to paint decorative, vaguely allegorical figure subjects, usually in classical robes, and usually with a suitable classical title of a nymph or goddess. (Christopher Wood, *Olympian Dreamers: Victorian Classical Painters, 1860–1914*, London, 1983, pp. 155–156).

The new gallery gave rise to the celebrated contretemps between Whistler and John Ruskin, when the latter accused Whistler of throwing a 'pot of paint in the public's face' with his picture of fireworks going off above the Thames at Chelsea. *Nocturne in Black and Gold: The Falling Rocket* was first exhibited at the Grosvenor in 1877. Whistler retaliated by suing Ruskin and won the case, but was awarded a nugatory farthing in damages, and was declared bankrupt shortly afterwards. Watts and Burne-Jones both exhibited at the Grosvenor in preference to the Royal Academy, and the Grosvenor Gallery became an important centre of the Aesthetic Movement in British art, as well as a target for merciless lampooning from the more philistine elements of English society, including George du Maurier's *Punch* and Gilbert and Sullivan, who satirised the gallery as the 'greenery-yallery' in *Patience* (1881).

Dolly's own pictures were not always well received: critics complained that they were derivative (too like those of Henner) and that she hadn't learned enough about painting the nude. (How could she have done, given that women had only just been permitted to study from semi-nude life?) But thanks to her hard work and her mother's encouragement, her efforts place her among a group of far-sighted and talented late Victorian female artists who were making inroads into a profession previously reserved to men. Her peers included Annie Louisa Swynnerton and Louise Jopling (both of whom, like Dolly, were trained in Paris) and Helen Allingham, whose watercolours of Surrey country cottages are now much-prized. The Victorian view was that women could not paint and it was not until the 1920s that they were admitted as full Associates of the Royal Academy.

10. DD, 19 January 1880.

23   A Salon in Whitehall

1. Hayward's article 'Salons' was first published in *Fraser's Magazine*, May 1866, and reprinted in his *Biographical and Critical Essays* (2 vols, London, 1873), Vol. 1, pp. 350–383.
2. DD, 23 November 1885.
3. Belloc Lowndes, *Merry Wives*, p. 120.
4. DD, 29 March 1886.
5. *Illustrated American*, 28 June 1890.
6. Holland House remained a glittering social centre for many generations. King George VI and Queen Elizabeth attended the last ball to be held there, just before the outbreak of the Second World War; the house was largely destroyed in an air raid in September 1940. Nowadays, there is a café in what is left of the old ballroom and a youth hostel in the east wing. Holland Park is the much-shrunken residue of the estate.
7. From this list of names it is evident there was considerable overlap between the *habitués* of Little Holland House and the denizens of Gertrude's salon, and a degree of family friendship, as Gertrude and the girls had befriended Mrs Cameron during their holidays on the Isle of Wight. Dolly and Evie had spent time there sitting to Watts while their portraits were being completed. Another connection was Sir Leslie Stephen (1832–1904), a celebrated man of letters and first editor of the *Dictionary of National Biography*, not to mention a great mountaineer, who became an occasional guest at Richmond Terrace in the 1880s: his second wife was Sara Prinsep's niece. Stephen is best known today as the father of Virginia Woolf and Vanessa Bell, and thus there is

a direct link from Little Holland House to the salon-like culture of the early twentieth century Bloomsbury Group.

8. Mary King Waddington, *Letters of a Diplomat's Wife 1883–1900* (New York, 1903), p. 183.

9. 'The story was told of young Lord Stafford, son of the Duke of Sutherland,' he noted on January 29 1884. 'It appears that he has for years been in love with Lady Grosvenor whom he knew before her marriage to Lord G. He had no expectation of being able to marry her, however, her husband being a young, robust man of his own age, etc. Yielding to family pressure on the subject of taking a wife, he offered his hand to a young, charming, innocent girl, the daughter of Lord Rosslyn. He was gratefully accepted, and the engagement was announced. Suddenly, a very short time after this, and without anyone expecting it, Lord Grosvenor dies and his wife becomes free. The question came up "what was Lord S to do?" – to stick to the girl – or to get rid of her in the best way that he could and – after a decent interval – present himself to Lady G? . . .' James went on to speculate that the situation might make a 'story, capable of different turns, according to the character of the actors'. *The Complete Notebooks of Henry James*, ed. Leon Edel and Lyall H. Powers (New York and Oxford, 1987), p. 23, 2 January 1884.

10. Léon Daudet, *Quand vivait mon père: souvenirs inédits sur Alphonse Daudet* (Paris, 1940), p. 273.

11. 'It is strange no account has ever been written of [Gertrude] and the noted people, not only English and American, but Russian, Spanish, above all French men and women, who came to the Sunday gatherings where each visitor was made to feel individually welcome,' wrote Mrs Belloc Lowndes (*Merry Wives*, p. 120).

24   Bula Matari in the Drawing-Room

1. Henry Morton Stanley, *The Autobiography of Sir Henry Morton Stanley: The Making of a 19th-Century Explorer* (California, The Narrative Press, 2001), pp. 442–444.

2. Roy Jenkins, *Gladstone* (London: 1995), p. 512 of the Penguin paperback edition.

3. Cited in Tim Jeal, *Stanley: The Impossible Life of Africa's Greatest Explorer* (London, 2007), p. 300.

4. See Felix Driver's entry on Stanley in the *Oxford Dictionary of National Biography* and *Autobiography*.

5. 'Could you, and would you, complete [Livingstone's journey]?' Edwin Arnold had asked him, after Stanley pitched up at the *Daily Telegraph*'s office in Fleet Street, looking for sponsorship.

> 'And what is there to do?'
> 'The western half of the African continent is still a white blank. Do you think you can settle this if we commission you?'
> 'While I live, there will be something done,' Stanley replied. 'If I survive the time required to perform all the work, all shall be done.'

The story is related in Tim Butcher's *Blood River: A Journey to Africa's Heart* (London, 2007), p. 46.

6. *Cornhill Magazine*, July 1904, reprinted in Chapter 18 of *Stanley's Autobiography*.

7. King Leopold (1835–1909) was a cunning and exceedingly intelligent man who sensed the opportunity for self-enrichment that would flow from the opening up of central Africa to Western markets – although at this stage even he could not have conceived of the immense profits to be derived from exports of rubber, which grew in wild super-abundance in the jungles of central Africa. The rubber boom began in earnest only after 1890, fed by demand for products such as bicycle tyres, hosing and insulation for telegraph cables.

8. Like most of his contemporaries, Stanley seems to have been deluded about the scope of Leopold's true ambitions. One of the few to see through the King's designs was Bismarck, the Prussian Chancellor, who hosted the Congress of Berlin at which the great powers carved up Africa. In the margin of a document in which the King professed his intention to eradicate the slave trade in central and eastern Africa, Bismarck scrawled: 'Schwindel'. 'His Majesty displays the pretensions and naïve self-ishness of an Italian who considers that his charm and good looks will enable him to get away with anything,' the Chancellor observed (cited in Adam Hochschild *King Leopold's Ghost: A Story of Greed, Terror and Heroism in Colonial Africa* (London, 1999), p. 83). Stanley, by contrast, has been characterised (chiefly by Frank McLynn in his biography of that name) as the sorcerer's apprentice, beguiled and manipulated by the wily Leopold. Stanley's relations with his patron, though outwardly friendly for many years to come, grew increasingly testy, and his expectations that he would return to Africa as governor of the new 800,000 square mile territory were destined to be disappointed. He attended the Berlin conference (1884–85), not as part of King Leopold's delegation but as adviser to the Americans. He was soon telling Dolly about his frustration with the King, who seemed to be going back on his word. 'The Belgians murmur at an American, or rather an Englishman, becoming the head of the Congo,' he told her (DD, 20 July 1885).
9. Mrs Waddington, *Letters*, p. 355.
10. See DD, 18 July 1885. He had most impressive eyes, which Dolly found extremely difficult to paint:

> The eyes are mysterious, his look most expressive and searching. His look has something intense and penetrating. The upper lid . . . tilts over the eye, giving a sort of earnest grandeur to his expression. The white of his eye is troubled and murky, slightly bloodshot, and yet the eye shines out clear, with the observancy of some keen-sighted bird who is watching you, listening to you rather with the eye than with the ear.

The resulting portrait of Stanley was exhibited at the Royal Academy in 1893. The explorer never liked it.
11. Cited in Frank McLynn, *Stanley: Dark Genius of African Exploration* (London, 2004), p. 126.

25 Dolly's Choices

1. DD, 6 June 1879.
2. Unaccountably, however, Dolly did not destroy the draft of a letter she wrote two years after the passionate encounter, meaning to send it with some of her pictures of London ragamuffins. 'Dear Andrew Carnegie,' the unsent letter reads, 'I dedicate [the enclosed collection] to you, as I shall henceforth, in my heart, dedicate to you everything I may do of any worth, you were the first who told me, who showed me that trying to be something for oneself was far from a selfish aim – I was selfish, I wanted to be first clever and great, I wanted to keep away from and beyond others . . . when your wild fancy died out, when you came to regret your foolish part in all this, comforting yourself with the thought that my pain would be very transient, you left me bewildered . . . So you see it is goodbye dear Andrew. Believe me I loved you more than anyone else in the world, foolishly impulsively childishly but for all that passionately and powerfully. I shall tell the man I shall possibly marry all the truth, all excepting your name, and if he cares for me notwithstanding, he shall have his way. If not, I am indifferent.' She mentions the 'volcanic eruptions of folly' in DD, 6 June 1886.
3. DD, 25 May 1885.

4. If you look at pictures of the two men, they are indeed uncannily alike, with the same resolute features, piercing eyes and silver hair, but the similarity goes beyond the lineaments of gratified mastery. They count as two of the more formidable self-made men of the nineteenth century. Hailing from the social and geographic margins of the British Isles, both escaped to the US to make their name and fortune. Born in Dunfermline, Fife, Carnegie was the son of a linen weaver who had been forced by poverty to emigrate. (Unlike Stanley, however, Carnegie never tried to hide his origins.) He made his first fortune in the railroads before moving into iron and steel. He and Stanley were both ruthless, even violent in pursuit of their objectives: Stanley in Africa, Carnegie in the US, where he extirpated unionised labour and forced through a brutal consolidation of the steel industry which led to the creation of the United States Steel Corporation, the world's first billion-dollar company. (It was only in retirement that Carnegie would become celebrated for his milder qualities, giving away one of the biggest fortunes ever accumulated by a man.)
5. DD, 15 January 1887.
6. DD, 26 May 1886.
7. DD, 21 March 1886.
8. Quoted in Jeal, *Stanley*, p. 312.
9. Sir Charles Tennant of the Glen (1823–1906) was proprietor of the St Rollox chemical works and father of the future Margot Asquith, Laura Lyttelton and the first Baron Glenconner. The two Charleses had been acquainted and were sometimes mistaken for one another, a source of amusement to the two families.
10. DD, 29 April 1886.
11. DD, 30 April 1886.
12. Evie first became intrigued by photography when as a child she posed for Mrs Cameron on holiday on the Isle of Wight. She had had to dress up in a blanket and holding a lily, and Evie fell in love there and then with the rigmarole of dressing up and posing, and she even liked the smell of chemicals. Once her children were no longer babies, she equipped a darkroom in the gardens of her Cambridge home. 'I simply bought a camera, and went to work,' she told Mrs Belloc Lowndes in an interview published long afterwards (in the *Cambridge Graphic* of 3 November 1890). 'I had no intention of doing more than providing myself with a pleasant pastime, which would have the further advantage of enabling me to retain, in a permanent form, fleeting impressions of my little children as they appeared to me at different ages.' Then she started to take posed 'subject' pictures before moving on to portraits of her mother's distinguished friends, where she was successful in making great men relax and look informal. She caught an unprecedented image of Gladstone smiling and another of Joseph Chamberlain wearing his glasses.
13. DD, 28 July 1889.
14. 'I shall be so deeply glad to see you again, not because you have done great things, but because you have come back safe, because I feared I might never see your face again. Bula Matari, do not be too proud to come, since I am not too proud to tell you how greatly I desire it' (Dolly to Stanley, 26 April 1890). For a full account of Dolly's campaign to woo her explorer, see Jeal, *Stanley*, pp. 391–395.

26 *Quel bel avenir?*

1. Cited in Jeal, *Stanley*, p. 415.
2. Belloc Lowndes, *Merry Wives*, p. 121.
3. Frank Harris, *My Life and Loves* (London, 1964), p. 61.
4. 'Hamilton advised his being called Sir Moreton [*sic*] Stanley,' noted Gertrude in her diary of 1 June 1899. 'He said Henry was too common.'

5. *The Correspondence of William James*, ed. Ignas K. Skrupskelis and Elizabeth M. Berkeley, 3 vols (Charlottesville and London, 1994),Vol. 3, p. 100.
6. Ibid., Vol. 2, p. 60.
7. *The Times*, 17 December 1906.
8. Cited in McLynn, *Stanley*, p. 378.
9. *London Street Arabs* (Cassell) sold 4,196 copies by Christmas.
10. See Chapter VIII of F. Anstey (Thomas Anstey Guthrie), *A Long Retrospect (Reminiscences)* (Oxford, 1936), for this and other anecdotes of the Tennant circle at this time.
11. William James blamed Fred's inability to fulfil his side of the bargain on Evie, whom he described in unflattering terms during a shared holiday in France in 1901. Evie, he wrote bizarrely to his brother, was 'perfect "white trash" but with a certain foundation of animal good humour that makes one not take her too seriously' (*Correspondence of William James*, Vol. 3, p. 103). He also despised the Myers children, whom he compared to Miles and Flora, the children in his brother's chilling story *The Turn of the Screw*. Their worldly bustle evidently interfered with whatever signals Fred was supposed to be sending from the spirit world. The deathbed scene is described in Alan Gauld, *The Founders of Psychical Research* (London, 1968), pp. 333–334 and Blum, *Ghost Hunters*, p. 251. Various trance mediums did however claim to pick up messages from Myers and the other pioneers of psychical research in the so-called cross-correspondences: transcript from various unconnected mediums in which a pattern of messages from the dead is supposed to be identifiable. Myers's story thus continues well beyond the grave, and is taken up in Archie Roy's 2008 book *The Eager Dead: A Study in Haunting* (Brighton, 2008). His own *magnum opus* was *Human Personality and its Survival of Bodily Death*, published posthumously in 1903. This study made a major contribution to the science of psychology, but its central attempt to demonstrate the immortality of the spirit was not convincing. 'Mere assertion, fantastic and absurd,' is how Frank Harris described the book (*My Life and Loves*, pp. 898–899).

27 'Whom Shall I Meet in Heaven?'

1. Belloc Lowndes *Diaries and Letters*, p. 32, 20 April 1912.
2. Belloc Lowndes, *Merry Wives*, p. 121.
3. Sir Oliver Lodge, *Christopher: A Study in Human Personality* (London, 1918), p. 94.

Epilogue

1. Virginia Woolf, 'The New Biography,' in Vol. 4 of *Collected Essays* (London, 1967), pp. 221–235.
2. Letter dated 29 November 1915, cited in Peter Lord, *Winifred Coombe Tennant: A Life through Art.* (Aberystwyth, 2007), pp. 26–27.
3. Cadoxton Lodge was knocked down in the 1950s and is now the site of Stanley Close, a housing estate.
4. Her automatic writing and trance-utterances form a part of the so-called Cross Correspondences (see note 11 to Chapter 26). She also played a central role in the so-called Palm Sunday case, in which she supposedly picked up messages from a former love of Arthur Balfour, the conservative Prime Minister. See *Proceedings of the Society for Psychical Research*, 52, 1960, part 189. Her friend, the physicist and psychical pioneer Oliver Lodge, wrote a book about Christopher Coombe-Tennant: *Christopher, A Study of Human Personality*. The title pays homage to Myers's great work.
5. Cited in Lord, *Winifred Coombe Tennant*, p. 15.

SELECT BIBLIOGRAPHY

Aïdé, Hamilton. *Rita: An Autobiography*. London, 1856.

Allingham, H. and Radford, D., eds. *William Allingham: A Diary*. London: 1907.

Anstey, F. (Thomas Anstey Guthrie). *A Long Retrospect (Reminiscences)*. Oxford: Oxford University Press, 1936.

Arnold, Julian. *Giants in Dressing Gowns*. London: Macdonald, 1945.

Askwith, Betty. *Piety and Wit: A Biography of Harriet, Countess Granville 1785–1862*. London: Collins, 1982.

Banks, J.A. *Prosperity and Parenthood: A Study of Family Planning among the Victorian Middle Classes*. London: Routledge & Kegan Paul, 1954.

Barnes, Julian. *Flaubert's Parrot*. London: Jonathan Cape, 1985.

Bart, Benjamin J. *Flaubert*. New York: Syracuse University Press, 1967.

Belloc Lowndes, Marie. *The Merry Wives of Westminster*. London: Macmillan, 1946.

———. *Diaries and Letters, 1911–1947*, ed. Susan Lowndes. London: Chatto & Windus, 1971.

Benson, Arthur Christopher. *The Leaves of the Tree: Studies in Biography*. London: John Murray, 1912.

Best, Geoffrey. *Mid-Victorian Britain, 1851–1875*. London: Weidenfeld & Nicolson, 1971.

Blessington, the Countess of, *The Idler in France*. Paris: Baudry's European Library, 1841.

Blum, Deborah. *Ghost Hunters: William James and the Search for Scientific Proof of Life after Death*. London: Century, 2007.

Branca, Patricia. *Silent Sisterhood: Middle-Class Women in the Victorian Home*. London: Croom Helm, 1975.

Brown, Frederick. *Flaubert: A Life*. New York: Little, Brown, 2006.

Bruneau, Jean. 'Mme Bovary jugée par un fantôme de Trouville', *Revue de Littérature Comparée* April–June 1957, pp. 277–279.

———. 'La Famille Collier et Gustave Flaubert (Lettres inédites 1842–1879)', *Nineteenth-Century French Studies*, Fall–Winter 1988–89 (1–2), pp. 70–88.

Bryant, Barbara. *G.F. Watts Portraits: Fame and Beauty in Victorian Society*. London: National Portrait Gallery, 2004.

Burn, William Lawrence. *The Age of Equipoise: A Study of the mid-Victorian Generation*. London: Allen & Unwin, 1964.

Butcher, Tim. *Blood River: A Journey to Africa's Heart*. London: Chatto & Windus, 2007.

Caine, Barbara. *English Feminism 1780–1980*. Oxford: Oxford University Press, 1997.

Chancellor, E. Beresford. *Life in Regency and Early Victorian Times: An Account of the Days of Brummell and D'Orsay.* London: B.T. Batsford, 1927.

Chevalley-Sabatier, Lucie. *Gustave Flaubert et sa soeur Caroline d'après leur correspondance inédite (1839–1846), La Revue Hebdomadaire* 12 December 1936, pp. 166–201.

Collier, Sir George, ed. Mrs Charles Tennant. *France on the Eve of the Great Revolution: France, Holland, and the Netherlands, a Century Ago.* London: Richard Bentley, 1865.

——. 'A detail of some particular services performed in America during the years 1776, 1777, 1778, and 1779' (Unpublished manuscript, held in the British Library).

Cordingly, David. *Cochrane the Dauntless: The Life and Adventures of Thomas Cochrane.* London: Bloomsbury, 2007.

Craven, Mrs Augustus, trans. Henry James Coleridge. *The Life of Lady Georgiana Fullerton.* London: Richard Bentley, 1888.

Daudet, Léon. *Quand vivait mon père: souvenirs inédits sur Alphonse Daudet.* Paris: Bernard Grasset, 1940.

Davidoff, Leonore and Hall, Catherine. *Family Fortunes: Men and Women of the English Middle Class 1780–1850.* London: Routledge, 1987.

Denlinger, Elizabeth Campbell. *Before Victoria: Extraordinary Women of the British Romantic Era.* New York: The New York Public Library/Columbia University Press, 2005.

Denney, Colleen. *At the Temple of Art: The Grosvenor Gallery 1877–1890.* Fairleigh: Fairleigh Dickinson University Press, 2000.

Ellis, Sarah Stickney. *The Women of England, their Social Duties and Domestic Habits.* London and Paris: Fisher, Son & Co, 1839.

——. *The Wives of England, their Relative Duties Domestic Influence and Social Obligations,* London and Paris: Fisher, Son & Co, 1843.

——. *The Daughters of England,* London and Paris: Fisher, Son & Co, 1845.

Ffrench, Yvonne. *The Great Exhibition: 1851.* London: The Harvill Press, 1950.

Official Catalogue of the Great Exhibition of the Works of Industry of all Nations, 1851. London: Spicer Brothers, 1851.

Flanders, Judith. *A Circle of Sisters: Alice Kipling, Georgina Burne-Jones, Agnes Poynter and Louisa Baldwin.* London: Viking, 2001.

——. *The Victorian House: Domestic Life from Childbirth to Deathbed.* London: HarperCollins, 2003.

Flaubert, Gustave. *Novembre,* first published posthumously in *Oeuvres de jeunesse,* 1910, but completed in 1842; trans. by Andrew Brown, London: Hesperus Press, 2005.

——. *Madame Bovary,* first published in *Revue de Paris* in 1856; trans. Geoffrey Wall, Harmondsworth: Penguin Books, 1992.

——. *Trois Contes.* First published 1877; trans. Roger Whitehouse, Harmondsworth: Penguin Classics, 2005.

——. *Correspondance, première série 1830–1855,* vol. 1, ed. Caroline Commanville. Paris: G. Charpentier & Cie, 1887. This contains Caroline's *Souvenirs intimes,* a memoir of her uncle, which includes a passage from Gertrude's memoir.

——. *Correspondance,* ed. by Jean Bruneau, 4 vols. Paris: Gallimard (Pléiade), 1973–1997. Vol. 5, ed. by Yves Leclerc, published in 2007.

——. *The Letters of Gustave Flaubert: Volumes I & II, 1830–1880,* ed. and trans. by Francis Steegmuller. London: Picador, 2001.

Ford, Colin. *Julia Margaret Cameron: Nineteenth-Century Photographer of Genius.* London: National Portrait Gallery, 2003.

Forster, Margaret. *Significant Sisters: The Grassroots of Active Feminism, 1839–1939.* London: Vintage 2004 (first published Secker & Warburg, 1984).

Garnett, Henrietta. *Anny: A Life of Anne Isabella Thackeray Ritchie.* London: Chatto & Windus, 2004.

Gaskell, Elizabeth Cleghorn. *The Letters of Elizabeth Cleghorn Gaskell,* ed. J.A.V. Chapple and Arthur Pollard. Manchester: Manchester University Press, 1996.

Gauld, Alan. *The Founders of Psychical Research.* London: Routledge & Kegan Paul, 1968.

Goodman, Dena. 'Enlightenment Salons: The Convergence of Female and Philosophic Ambitions, *Eighteenth-Century Studies*, 22 (1989), pp. 329–350.

——. *The Republic of Letters: A Cultural History of the French Enlightenment.* Ithaca, New York: Cornell University Press, 1994.

Greville, Charles. *The Greville Memoirs in Three Volumes: Journal of the Reigns of King George IV and King William IV*, ed. Henry Reeve. London: Longmans, Green & Co, 1874.

Gronow, Captain Rees Howell. *Captain Gronow: Reminiscences of Regency and Victorian Life 1810–60*, ed. Christopher Hibbert. London: Kyle Cathie, 1991. First published in four volumes in 1862.

Grosvenor, Caroline and Lord Wortley. *The First Lady Wharncliffe and her Family*, 2 vols. London: William Heinemann, 1927.

Harris, Frank. *My Life and Loves.* London, W.H. Allen, 1964. (These saucy memoirs were first published privately in Paris in the 1930s.)

Hayward, Abraham. *Biographical and Critical Essays*, 2 vols. London: Longmans, Green, 1873.

Hilton, Boyd. *A Mad, Bad, and Dangerous People: England 1783–1846.* Oxford: Oxford University Press, 2006.

Hochschild, Adam. *King Leopold's Ghost: A Story of Greed, Terror and Heroism in Colonial Africa.* London: Macmillan, 1999.

Hoppen, K. Theodore. *The Mid Victorian Generation.* Oxford: Oxford University Press, 1998.

Hore, Captain Peter. *The Habit of Victory: The Story of the Royal Navy 1545–1945.* London: Sidgwick & Jackson, 2005.

Horne, Alistair. *The Fall of Paris: The Siege and the Commune 1870–1871.* London: Macmillan, 1965.

Hughes, Kathryn. *George Eliot: The Last Victorian.* London: Fourth Estate, 1998.

——. *The Short Life and Long Times of Mrs Beeton.* London: Fourth Estate, 2005.

Hurd, Douglas. *Robert Peel.* London: Weidenfeld & Nicolson, 2007.

Jalland, Pat. *Death in the Victorian Family.* Oxford: Oxford University Press, 1996.

James, Henry. *Letters*, 2 vols, ed. Leon Edel. London: Macmillan, 1978

——. *Letters*, vol 2: *1875–1883*, ed. Leon Edel. London: Macmillan, 1978.

James, William. *The Correspondence of William James*, 4 vols, ed. Ignas K. Skrupskelis and Elizabeth M. Berkeley, 3 vols. Charlottesville and London: University Press of Virginia, 1994.

Jeal, Tim. *Stanley: The Impossible Life of Africa's Greatest Explorer.* London: Faber & Faber, 2007.

Jenkins, Roy. *Gladstone.* London: Macmillan, 1995.

Jones, Colin. *Paris: Biography of a City.* London: Allen Lane, 2004.

Kale, Steven. *French Salons: High Society and Political Sociability from the Old Regime to the Revolution of 1848.* Baltimore: Johns Hopkins University Press, 2004.

Kelly, Ian. *Cooking for Kings: The Life of Antonin Carême, the First Celebrity Chef.* London: Short Books, 2003.

——. *Beau Brummell: The Ultimate Dandy.* London: Hodder & Stoughton, 2005.

Knight, Roger. *The Pursuit of Victory: The Life and Achievement of Horatio Nelson.* London: Allen Lane, 2005.

Ledger, Sally. *The New Woman: Fiction and Feminism at the Fin de Siècle.* Manchester: Manchester University Press, 1997.

Leduc-Grimaldi, Mathilde. 'Une Artiste et son premier ministre: entretiens familiers avec W.E. Gladstone (1884–1890), *Histoire de l'Art*, 55, October 2004, pp. 85–96.

Lewis, Michael. *England's Sea-Officers: The Story of the Naval Profession.* London: George Allen & Unwin, 1939.

Lodge, Sir Oliver. *Christopher: A Study in Human Personality.* London: Cassell, 1918.

Loomis, Stanley. *A Crime of Passion.* London: Hodder & Stoughton, 1967.

Lord, Peter. *Winifred Coombe Tennant: A Life through Art.* Aberystwyth: The National Library of Wales, 2007.

McLynn, Frank. *Stanley: Dark Genius of African Exploration*. London: Pimlico, 2004.

Mill, John Stuart. *The Subjecton of Women*. London: Penguin, 2006.

Millais, John Guille. *The Life and Letters of Sir John Everett Millais, President of the Royal Academy*, 2 vols. London: Methuen, 1899.

Minchinton, Walter, ed. *Industrial South Wales 1750–1914: Essays in Welsh Economic History.* London: Frank Cass, 1969.

Myers, F.W.H. *Essays: Modern*. London: Macmillan, 1885.

——. *Human Personality and its Survival of Bodily Death*, 2 vols. London: Longmans, Green, 1903.

——. *Fragments of Prose and Poetry: Edited by his Wife Eveleen Myers*. London, Longmans, 1904.

Neville-Sington, Pamela. *Fanny Trollope: The Life and Adventures of a Clever Woman*. London: Viking, 1997.

Oliver, Hermia. *Flaubert and an English Governess: The Quest for Juliet Herbert*. Oxford: Clarendon Press, 1980.

Padfield, Peter. *Maritime Power and the Struggle for Freedom: Naval Campaigns that Shaped the Modern World 1788–1851*. London: John Murray, 2003.

Perkin, Joan. *Victorian Women*. London: John Murray, 1993.

Peterson, M. Jeanne. *Family, Love, and Work in the Lives of Victorian Gentlewomen*. Bloomington: Indiana University Press, 1989.

Picard, Liza. *Victorian London: The Life of a City 1840–1870*. London: Weidenfeld & Nicolson, 2005.

Porter, Roy. *London: A Social History*. London: Hamish Hamilton, 1994.

Prettejohn, Elizabeth. *After the Pre-Raphaelites: Art and Aestheticism in Victorian England*. Manchester: Manchester University Press, 1999.

Price, Munro. *The Perilous Crown: France between Revolutions, 1814–1848*. London: Macmillan, 2007.

Rabetti, Rodolphe, and others. *Face à L'Impressionisme: Jean-Jacques Henner, le dernier des Romantiques*. Paris : Musée des Beaux-Arts de la Ville de Paris, 2007–2008.

Rambuteau, comte de, *Memoirs of the comte de Rambuteau* [1781–1869], trans. by J.C. Brogan. London and New York: J.M. Dent, 1908.

Richardson, Angelique and Willis, Chris, eds. *The New Woman in Fiction and in Fact: Fin-de-Siècle Feminisms*. Basingstoke: Palgrave Macmillan, 2001, 2002.

Robb, Graham. *Balzac: A Biography*. London: Picador, 1994.

——. *Victor Hugo*. London: Picador, 1997.

Roy, Archie E. *The Eager Dead: A Study in Haunting*. Brighton: Book Guild, 2008.

St George, Andrew. *The Descent of Manners: Etiquette, Rules and the Victorians*. London: Chatto & Windus, 1993.

Searle, G.R. *Entrepreneurial Politics in mid-Victorian Britain*. Oxford: Oxford University Press, 1993.

Showalter, Elaine. *Sexual Anarchy: Gender and Culture at the Fin de Siècle*. London: Bloomsbury, 1991.

Simpson, John. *Paris after Waterloo: Notes Taken at the Time and Hitherto Unpublished*. London and Edinburgh: William Blackwood and Sons, 1853.

Spaull, Hebe. *Women Peace-Makers*. London: George Harrap, 1924.

Spencer, Philip. *Flaubert: A Biography*. London: Faber & Faber, 1952.

——. 'New Light on Flaubert's Youth', *French Studies*, 8, April 1954, pp. 97–108.

Stanley, Mrs H.M. (née Dorothy Tennant) *London Street Arabs*. London, Cassell, 1890.

Starkie, Enid. *Flaubert: The Making of the Master*. London: Weidenfeld & Nicolson, 1967.

——. *Flaubert the Master: A Critical and Biographical Study (1856–1880)*. London: Weidenfeld & Nicolson, 1971.

Stokes, John. *In the Nineties*. Hemel Hempstead: Harvester Wheatsheaf, 1989.

Strachey, Lytton. *Landmarks in French literature*. London: Williams & Norgate, 1923.

Suddaby, Elizabeth and P.J. Yarrow, eds. *Lady Morgan in France*. London: Oriel Press, 1971.

Surtees, Virginia, ed., *A Second Self: The Letters of Harriet Granville*. London: Michael Russell, 1970.

Swinburne, Algernon. *A Study of Victor Hugo*. London: Chatto & Windus, 1886.

Taylor, D.J. *Thackeray*. London: Chatto & Windus, 1999.

Tennant, Charles. *A Tour through parts of the Netherlands, Holland, Germany, Switzerland, Savoy, and France, in the years 1821–22, containing in an appendix fac-simile copies of eight letters in the hand-writing of Napoleon Bonaparte to his wife Josephine*, 2 vols. London, 1824.

——. *The State of Man: A Poem in Four Books*. London, 1834.

——. *The People's Blue Book: Taxation as it is, and as it ought to be*. London: Routledge, 1857.

Thackeray, William Makepeace. *The Paris Sketch Book, and Art Criticisms*. London: 1837–45.

Thirlwell, Adam. *Miss Herbert*. London: Jonathan Cape, 2007.

Tomalin, Claire. *Jane Austen: A Life*. London: Viking, 1997.

——. *Thomas Hardy: The Time-Torn Man*. London: Viking, 2006.

Tombs, Robert. *France: 1814–1914*. London: Longman, 1996.

Tombs, Robert and Tombs, Isabelle. *That Sweet Enemy: The French and the British from the Sun King to the Present*. London: William Heinemann, 2006.

Trollope, Frances (Fanny). *Paris and the Parisians in 1835*, 2 vols. London: Richard Bentley, 1836.

Tucker, Herbert F. ed., *A Companion to Victorian Literature and Culture*. Oxford: Blackwell, 1999.

Tucker, Keith. *A Scratch in Glamorganshire: George Tennant, 1765–1832*. Neath, Historical Projects, 1998.

Vicinus, Martha, ed. *Suffer and Be Still: Women in the Victorian Age*. Bloomington and London: Indiana University Press, 1972.

Waddington, Mary King. *Letters of a Diplomat's Wife, 1883–1900*. New York: Charles Scribner's Sons, 1903.

——. *My First Years as a Frenchwoman, 1876–1879*. London: Smith, Elder, 1914.

Wall, Geoffrey. *Flaubert: A Life*. London: Faber & Faber, 2001.

Watts, Mary S. *George Frederic Watts: The Annals of an Artist's Life*, 3 vols. London, 1912.

West, C.B. 'Gustave Flaubert et Harriet Collier: première rencontre à Trouville', *Revue d'Histoire Littéraire de la France*, 57(1), January–March, 1957, pp. 1–9.

Wilson, A.N. *The Victorians*. London: Hutchinson, 2002.

Wines, Frederick Howard, *Punishment and Reformation: A Study of the Penitentiary System*. London: Swann Sonnenschein, 1895.

Woolf, Virginia. *The Death of the Moth, and other Essays*. London: Hogarth Press, 1942.

——. 'The New Biography,' in *Collected Essays*, vol. 4. London: The Hogarth Press, 1967.

INDEX